·············· Silver, Trade, and War

Stanley J. Stein & Barbara H. Stein

Silver, Trade, and War

Spain and America in the
Making of Early Modern Europe

The Johns Hopkins University Press   •   Baltimore and London

© 2000 The Johns Hopkins University Press
All rights reserved. Published 2000
Printed in the United States of America on acid-free paper
9 8 7 6 5 4 3 2 1

The Johns Hopkins University Press
2715 North Charles Street, Baltimore, Maryland 21218-4363
www.press.jhu.edu

Library of Congress Cataloging-in-Publication Data will be
found at the end of this book.
A catalog record for this book is available from the British Library.

ISBN 0-8018-6135-7

This book was brought to publication with the generous
assistance of the Program for Cultural Cooperation
between Spain's Ministry of Education and Culture
and United States' Universities.

Contents

Preface

· ·

Historians of the trajectory of modern Europe over the past four centuries are prone to hear in the drama and disarray of recent decades echoes of conflicts long dampened by war, diplomacy, revolution, and counterrevolution, by hegemony and domination. Current challenges to the principle of religious toleration established in the mid-seventeenth century, to the role of the state, and to accepted ethical standards have put in question assumptions that emerged in Europe's early modern epoch and that are associated with the nineteenth-century concept of progress within the liberal model of civil society.

Some now perceive a new age of deep ideological cleavage and intransigent behavior by individuals and societies alike—a new profound crisis of modernity comparable to the turmoil accompanying the onset of the modern age. Others see the end of an era whose modernism has been a flawed construct from its beginning. Whatever the cause—whether temporary malaise, despair, or even anomie, or the proposition that our era and its ideologies of nationalism and individualism are questionable—historians are revisiting the roots of western Renaissance, Reformation, and Counterreformation and the wars and political and economic transformation that vertebrated the sixteenth and seventeenth centuries. It is no exaggeration to propose that current anxieties are comparable to those attendant upon Europe's unplanned expansion into the western Atlantic, to Africa, and then to Asia.

This study seeks to reconstruct and reevaluate the interaction of America, Spain, and Europe between 1500 and 1750, focusing on Spain's pivotal role in Europe's expansion across the Atlantic. We describe how American silver galvanized Europe and set in motion the development of the market economy and the nation-state.

The first part of this book offers a synthesis of the fundaments of Spain's Hapsburg heritage of patrimonialism and dynasticism. We pursue core themes: the structures of late medieval Spain that proved adaptable to the enterprise of overseas conquest; the silver mining complexes of Spain's major colonies of New Spain and Peru; the exchange of silver and goods in Spain's managed transatlantic navigation and trade. We also look at the basic incompatibility between the needs of Spain as a colonial power and its association with the Holy Roman Empire of the Hapsburgs. In this connection we examine the conciliar or polysynodal institutions of governance and how they shaped a patrimonial polity and Spain's "absolutism."

A colonial rather than a metropolitan or peninsular prism informs our interpretation of these themes. There was a two-way exchange. As west European institutions and practices with an Iberian cast were adapted pragmatically to advanced indigenous societies of Central Mexico and the Central Andes, the silver of New Spain and Peru spread through and shaped the colonial world, the Spanish metropole, Europe, and Asia. Mining, processing, minting, and distributing silver permitted Spaniards to refashion the economies of the principal native American peoples, monetizing and commodifying them—in short, bringing to them a Spanish, peripheral variant of early commercial capitalism. At the same time the abundance of silver and new markets in the colonies stimulated the export sectors of Italy, the Netherlands, France, England, and Germany. In its idiosyncratic way, Spanish colonialism was the cutting edge of the early global economy. However, there soon appeared a downside. While Spain's silver-based transatlantic system at first proved a primary source of Hapsburg preeminence, it was also a basic structure of Spain's relative political, social, and economic backwardness as the metropole grew dependent on its colonial world.

These are the themes of the Hapsburg centuries. The second part of the book explores efforts under the eighteenth-century Spanish Bourbons to catch up with Europe's modernizing states. Spanish *proyectistas,* comparing their society with that of England and France, searched for models of development whose elements, judiciously adapted to the circumstances of the metropole and its empire, might reduce backwardness and cultural lag without risking institutional change. By the late 1750s, however, members of the political class were concluding that their Hapsburg legacy continued to permeate Spanish society, that the lag between the economic growth of the Spanish empire and that of England and France had widened dangerously. Great expectations now hung upon the hope that Charles III and his collaborators might realize long postponed adjustments in colonial and metropolitan institutions.

This is a study of men and markets, national rivalries, diplomacy and war, and states advancing or stagnating. It is about backwardness and development, about change and, above all, continuity.

Acknowledgments

· ·

A book is the work of many hands. A Guggenheim fellowship (1958–59) and a summer grant from the American Philosophical Society (1961) helped finance field research in Mexico and Spain. We are especially indebted to the personnel of many research institutions who patiently assisted us: at Princeton University's Firestone Library, Peter Johnson, bibliographer for Latin American and Iberian Acquisitions, and the staffs of Rare Books and Special Collections and Inter-Library Services; at Mexico City, the Archivo General de la Nación and Biblioteca Nacional; at Sevilla, the Archivo General de Indias; and at Madrid, the Archivo Histórico Nacional, Real Academia de la História, Biblioteca del Real Palacio, and Museo Naval; and at Paris the Archives Nationales, Bibliothèque Nationale, and Quai d'Orsay. Our copy editor, Kennie Lyman, has meticulously reviewed our manuscript with critical, always helpful suggestions, striving to turn turgidity into lucidity. Carol Zimmerman, senior production editor, has reviewed the final manuscript with great care and patience.

Finally, we wish to express our gratitude to colleagues Jeremy Adelman, Michael Mahoney, Arno Mayer, and Robert Tignor, invariably generous with encouragement, advice, criticism, and when they were most needed. They have been truly intellectual comrades, *vrais compagnons de route*.

Part One

········· The Legacy

1. Spain, Europe, and the Atlantic System, 1500–1700

· · · · · · · · · · · · · · · · · · · ·

It was not just the king of Spain who was interested in the precious metals, but all the merchants of Sevilla, all the agents of foreign merchants at Sevilla, and all the merchants of Antwerp, Augsburg, Genoa and Rouen, who hastened to garner the profits on what they had exported. Once the returning flota hove into view . . . couriers carried the good or bad news to the four corners of the world.   Michel Morineau, *Incroyables gazettes et fabuleux métaux*

[The marquis de Feuquières, ambassador] should be aware that trade with Spain is all the more vital since it supplies money distributed among all other European states. The more we provide goods to the Spaniards, the more we carry away in bullion and pesos coming from the Indies.   Instructions au marquis de Feuquières

At the end of the seventeenth century, after two hundred years of imperialism, in nominal control of the human and natural resources of dominions in America and the western Pacific, Spain, like its imperial neighbor Portugal, was an underdeveloped, stagnant area of western Europe. In the timespan of four generations of royalty, from the accession of the founder of the Hapsburg dynasty, Charles V, in 1519 to the burial of Philip IV in 1665, the Spanish monarchy projected itself into the Mediterranean, central and northwestern Europe, the western Atlantic and the western Pacific. The shadow that imperial and counterrevolutionary Spain cast over Europe in those four generations was made possible by the silver and gold mines of the distant American colonies of Peru and Mexico.

By the fifth generation of the Hapsburg dynasty, in the closing decades of the seventeenth century under Charles II, the American and Pacific colonies still remained possessions of Spain, but the shadow of Spain in western Europe had contracted virtually to the country's borders. The metropole lacked a developed artisan industry, its agricultural and pastoral sectors were marked by low productivity, and principal exports—aside from reexport of silver—were raw materials and some processed food. Internal communications were rudimentary, domestic demand was limited, and the Spanish merchant marine and navy were insignificant. The anomaly was that, although it administered a vast colonial establishment, Spain was hardly a nation. Even the Spanish colonies in America were more vital to the west European than to the Spanish economy, and stagnant yet imperial Spain was about to become the scene of the worst type of conflict, combined international and civil war.

Structural weaknesses in the economy had long been aired, detailed, analyzed, and lamented, by the Spanish governing elite and the major interest groups with which the high bureaucracy interlocked. Prescriptions for improvement had been suggested. In the seventeenth century the analysts focused upon state finance. Spain's transformation in the sixteenth century from a frontier area of western Europe to a country of international prominence had demanded expenditures for expeditionary forces and mercenaries. Despite the metropole's large receipts of Peruvian and Mexican silver, the state constantly faced the problem of liquidity and defaults and was forced to borrow from private sources. The chronic deficits of the early modern state drew the attention of *arbitristas* from Tomás de Mercado and Luís Ortiz in the sixteenth century to Manuel de Lira at the end of the seventeenth. They concentrated upon means and resources, or *arbitrios*, to improve state finance, and their analyses pinpointed the structural shortcomings of the economy often with remarkable acuity. At the close of the seventeenth century, whatever the term—contraction, recession, lag, long-term depression, or secular stagnation—of the Spanish economy had been repeatedly diagnosed by Spaniards. By then the grandeur of Spain was in the past tense.

The collapse of Spanish hegemony in Europe was signaled by the mid-seventeenth century settlements at Westphalia, and the "decline" of Spain was magnified by subsequent unequal commercial treaties with Holland, England, and France. The *arbitristas'* problem was three-fold: how to explain the growth of competitive economies in western Europe that lacked imperial Spain's remarkable colonial mineral resources; how to eradicate English, Dutch, and French penetration into the Caribbean, the strategic center of Spain's transatlantic empire; and, finally, how to stimulate within Spain itself an economy capable of utilizing colonial resources to "restore" the nation's lost position of authority. The competitors' development in the seventeenth century grew from new institutions, new attitudes, and new social and economic groups with access to political decision-making. Given Spain's structures—the endurance of privilege, of religious and aristocratic institutions and mentalities, conciliar governance, and the pervasive symbiosis of colonies and metropole—*arbitristas* skirted all notion of dangerous innovation or novelty in their policy recommendations. They searched for the road back to greatness by way of existing, time-tested frameworks. The enduring institutions of the past age of grandeur were, all agreed, basically sound, and all that was needed to recover hegemony in Europe was their renovation. Dutch and English models of growth were held at arms' length: the former because it had taken the form of Protestantism and revolution, the latter because it was associated with regicide as well. In the long run, the model deemed appropriate to Spanish needs was the upscale monarchy of Louis XIV and the *dirigisme* of Colbert. France was monarchical, Catholic, aristocratic, authoritarian—and growth-oriented. Meanwhile the Spanish code words for adaptation to the changing circumstances of commercial capitalism in Europe and America were "re-establishment" and "restoration," and so they remained in the eighteenth century.

In the final decades of the seventeenth century, many high government and church bureaucrats recognized that the reestablishment or renovation of the metropole depended upon control of Spain's colonial resources. They knew that after about 1670 colonial mining production showed signs of recovery: markedly in New Spain, less so in Peru. It is a measure of the colonies' importance that in the sixteenth century Spain's great naval engagements took place in the Mediterranean and English Channel, while in the following century Spanish naval operations shifted to its colonies and the protection of the maritime lifeline stretching across the middle Atlantic to the Caribbean where convoys gathered to carry back to Sevilla the precious metals of Mexico and Peru.

Lacking naval bases in the Caribbean, seventeenth-century English and Dutch shipping concentrated at first on quick seizure and abandonment of fortified Spanish Caribbean ports, and on attacking convoys and individual ships at sea—the age of piracy and the buccaneer in the West Indies. This was the initial stage of their imperialist outthrust into the western Atlantic. The quick raid or *razzia* had long been a tactic in early capital accumulation in the Mediterranean, North Africa, and in the Iberian reconquest itself.[1] In the Caribbean, however, the *razzia* brought at best only occasional windfalls and was not as profitable as the long-term gains from trading European manufactures with the chronically undersupplied Spanish colonies. In the second stage of their imperialist expansion, the Dutch, the English, and finally the French "planted" colonies in the Caribbean to furnish bases for assault and withdrawal. The next step was sustained, illicit, and profitable commercial exchanges—smuggling. The subsequent growth of export agriculture in the West Indies was an unexpected and astonishingly profitable development.

At the end of the seventeenth century, the direct penetration of European competitors into Spain's Caribbean commercial hub coupled with the indirect inroads of the French, Italians, Dutch, and English at the commercial centers at Sevilla and Cadiz threatened to strip Spain of access to colonial resources and thereby destroy the possibility of restoration. Troops under Spanish command had ravaged parts of France and the Low Countries in Spain's age of grandeur; in its age of decline, Spain itself was about to be ravaged by French, Dutch, and English forces, which extended the conflict as well to Spain in the Caribbean. The War of the Spanish Succession had both a European and an American theater. It was Spain's American empire that was the principal issue in the civil and international conflict to be fought in Spain. The colonies played a dual role: American silver had created both the mirage of inexhaustible mining wealth as the measure of economic success and the structures of Spain's immobilism in the seventeenth century. The interplay of silver mining, immobilism, and imperialism goes a long way to explain the coming of the war.

The significance of American silver moving across the Atlantic into Spanish and west European commerce and finance was early recognized by Spaniards themselves. By the eighteenth century, fairly accurate statistics of total outflow from America's mines were available. It is, however, in the last sixty years of the twentieth century that a new phase in the analysis of silver's impact has occurred with emphasis upon quantification via serial data and upon specifying more precisely silver's contribution to change in the west European economy and in that of south and east Asia during early modern times. Now there is a quantitative basis for registered imports until 1660 at the one official entry port, Sevilla, along with approximations of unregistered arrivals both before and after 1660; until more precise data appear, there is reason to rely upon current estimates of rates of change and relative magnitudes of inflows.

Sometime after 1630 the level of Sevilla's registered imports turned downward. They did not begin to recover until the end of the century, although well before the outbreak of the War of Succession. Why imports at Sevilla fell is a matter of debate as is the related question of the effects of infusions of silver into the Low Countries, Italy, France, England, and Southeast Asia. If no longer the main issue, silver remained a principal factor in the so-called crisis of the seventeenth century in western Europe. Earl Hamilton's collection of quantitative data on silver inflows, their correlation with changing price and wage levels, and their combined impact upon the Spanish economy between the conquest of America and about 1660 have clarified why the Spanish economy was in crisis long before the economies of the rest of Europe.

To be sure, the *arbitristas* of the seventeenth century, looking at their country's economic lag amidst arrivals of massive silver shipments, concluded that the mines of Mexico and Peru had induced neither national prosperity nor economic growth and development. In this sense they anticipated twentieth-century analysts. Hamilton has concluded that inflation of factor prices—materials, labor, and capital—sapped the competitive position of domestic producers as compared with Spain's European suppliers, the workshops of the Low Countries, England, North Italy, and France. Foreign woolens, linens, velvets, silks, laces, and metallurgical products entered the ports of Bilbao and Santander, Barcelona, and especially Sevilla, where a high percentage was reexported to the colonies. In return, American silver moved back across the Atlantic in legal channels to Sevilla or illegally (and directly) to English and Dutch smugglers in both Caribbean and Iberian waters. Ultimately this silver paid foreign producers for their goods. The *arbitristas* recognized that imperial Spain was a mere intermediary or "passive" factor in the chain of production and distribution linking Europe and America. In the last quarter of the seventeenth century, *arbitristas* examining mercantilist and developmentalist strategies of Holland, England, and France perceived that they induced growth and development while the Spanish strategy for control of silver from minehead to Sevilla's river banks—bullionism—brought neither capital investment in manufactures nor technological innovation nor an aggressive segment of the bourgeoisie. In the eighteenth century, analysts employed a more modern terminology when they insisted that the Spanish metropole continued to fail in its role in the "colonial compact" as producer of manufactures exported to its colonies.

It is curious as an example of a group mentality shared by the *arbitristas* that none inquired whether Spain had established financial, commercial, and manufacturing institutions *before* the inflow of silver could overwhelm them. Only now are we questioning the assumption that such institutions were in place, subsequent to collapse.[2] It is too much to expect that *arbitristas* ask if their country had been ready for empire in 1500. Then as now, overt criticism of government policy endangered status and career chances. Empire invents its own myths, and the invention of an imagined, glorious past was probably a tactic to avoid critical thinking about the real past.

Spain's decline, sustained stagnation, or simply the phenomenon of immobilism in the seventeenth century reflected more than the attitudes of the ruling class. It mirrored the conflicting realities of empire at the intersection of late medieval and early modern times when interests and instruments of the Hapsburg patrimonial empire coincided briefly with those of what emerged as Europe's first great early modern empire, Spain in America. In the euphoria created by the appropriation of overseas territories rich in precious metals and by Spain's incorporation into the European legacy of Maximilian, bullionism appeared consistent with the interests of Iberia's patrimonial monarchy and its new American dominions. Its elites welcomed their new "power and grandeur"—their expansionist and imperialist possibilities in Europe—readily accepting deficit spending on the promise of future revenues. The precise role of colonial income in total Spanish governmental income in the two centuries after 1500 requires more research, but there is no reason to doubt the proposition that the borrowing capacity of the Spanish state, despite repeated defaults and rising borrowing costs, reflected creditors' faith in the sustained—if often irregular—inflows of colonial silver. If by about 1700 bullionism remained the essence of state economic policy, it was reinforced through a network of public and private institutions and interests which often prospered while the state stagnated. To understand the Spanish imperial system on the eve of the War of Succession, to perceive how stagnation led to crisis, it is necessary to turn to the core of that system, the empire in America—the bones and musculature, arteries, capillaries, and veins of its commercial and mining structures.

Spanish Commercial Structures and Their Atlantic Projections

Production of silver at colonial mines and its flow eastward across the Atlantic into Spain and Europe was the foundation of the complex of economic structures selected and adapted in the sixteenth and seventeenth centuries by Spain's bureaucrats and merchants. Once operative, these structures were carefully maintained with minimal adjustments. The system of trade and navigation between colonies and metropole was characterized by one-port monopoly and within it oligopolistic competition. At the end of the seventeenth century the continuity of these commercial structures and the mentality of their supporters reflected and reinforced the metropole's immobilism.

An imperial trading system often seems the result of a grand design when, in reality, like much of an imperial complex, it represents the culmination of pragmatic selection, adaptation, and application of prior experience and approaches. Drawing upon two historical experiences, geographically distinct, Castilians adapted their late medieval experience to a new situation: the formation and consolidation of a large overseas empire. In the process they constructed a commercial system of extraordinary resilience and persistence.

The initial historical pattern of trade developed in the Castilian economy of the late fifteenth century was the export of Castile's raw wool and to a lesser extent of Vizcaya's iron ores from Cantabrian ports. The southward drive of the Spanish reconquest culminating in the middle of the thirteenth century with the north Castilian occupation of Andalusia and the peninsula's principal urban nucleus at Sevilla opened Castile to extensive shepherding and production of a valuable export staple absorbed by textile centers in and around Bruges in Flanders. By regulating the transhumance of flocks from winter to summer pastures and coordinating clipping, wool exports were concentrated in north Castile.[3] Merchants at the political and ecclesiastical nucleus of Burgos obtained broad jurisdiction for their inland center, extending from Medina del Campo northward through Burgos to the Basque port of Bilbao, where Burgos claimed jurisdiction over its wool trade despite Bilbao's location outside Castile. Burgos merchants bought wool at the Medina del Campo fair, a place for wool sales and the settling of both domestic and international payments. While Burgalés traders did not administer the biennial fairs, their capital and international contacts made them dominant there. Carted to Burgos, the wool clip was washed and then shipped to ports on the Cantabrian coast. Burgos merchants obtained exemption from bridge and toll fees as well as seigneurial and municipal rights for their staple in transit. Early on, they blocked efforts by local weavers to limit raw wool exports in order to meet domestic demand or to curb imports of English and Low Country textiles. Commodity exports took precedence over the needs of an infant industry.[4]

Supervision over the purchase, handling and transport of raw wool to Cantabrian ports constituted one phase of Burgos's control. In the late fifteenth century as a result of its protonationalist economic policy, England reduced its raw wool exports to Flanders, and Flemish demand for Spanish merino wool increased. Burgalés merchants extended their control northward by sea so that they could freight the clip to Bruges. At the same time they competed for the maritime carrying trade with the Vizcayan regional complex centered at Bilbao. The Basques were also entering the European international economy with locally mined iron ore, some crude metallurgical products, and the expectation of participating in the freighting of Castilian wool northward. The often bitter regional competition between the two "nations" was fought not only in Cantabrian ports but also at Bruges where both the Castilians and the Basques maintained factors. On many points the documentation of this competition remains obscure; what is clear is that between 1494 and 1512 Burgalés traders obtained the basis if not the full regulations (*ordenanzas*) of a guild that was formalized in 1553. They thereby extended their control over ship selection, tonnage, registry and inspection of cargo, and collection of a duty or *avería*. The *avería* covered naval protection for convoys carrying wool and ore to Bruges via La Rochelle and Nantes. In sponsoring their own shipping, Bilbaíno merchants repeatedly tried to enlarge their share but had limited success. Latecomers in freighting wool to Bruges and eager to exploit local ores for export, from 1554 to 1560 they competed with Burgos and pressed for the formation of a separate merchant guild or consulado. Regional autonomy from Burgos and Castile has remained a major thread in Vizcaya's history.[5]

The traders of Burgos were not the only ones to gain from its hegemony. Burgos's merchant class, organized in a guild to monopolize handling of a staple, became a convenient revenue source to an embryonic state with limited tax base and fiscal personnel. The ecclesiastical establishment of Burgos gained, too, receiving income both from tithes and from their investment in commercial enterprise. Indeed, the interrelationship of religious and mercantile groups flourished in a variety of ways: elaborate religious ritual and symbol at the annual election of guild officers (prior, consul) externalized the unity of spiritual and mercantile realms, of God and Interest. This pattern was later reproduced in colonial consulados.[6] Further, the consulado's annual almsgiving ritual legitimized private profit making, presenting wealthy merchant princes in a seigneurial relationship with the urban poor. In the merchant guild, in religious pageantry and blending of church and trade, and in forging a legitimate oligopoly controlling the staple trade from Medina del Campo in the Castilian north meseta to distant Bruges, Burgos's consulado represents not so much a waning of late medieval institutions as their waxing with an overlay of early commercial capitalism.

The other historical matrix on which Castilians drew to form colonial trade structures was located in Spain's south Castilian complex, Andalusia and its urban pole of growth, Sevilla. Burgos was a product of the late medieval economy, as the bottled-up peasant communities in the uplands (*montaña*) of the Cantabrian coastal range pushed migrants southward into the heart of Castile's meseta. Burgos first achieved prominence as a way station where the pilgrims' road or *calzada* crossed the Arlanzon river to continue to the shrine of Santiago at Compostela. After about 1300, its prosperity was based on merino wool and, later, on the upsurge of exports at the end of the fifteenth century. By contrast, the south Castilian complex centered on Sevilla was by 1500 already an important part of the western Mediterranean economy. Phoenicians and Carthaginians had tapped its resources from Cartagena to Huelva. Romans incorporated its silver mines, vineyards, and olive and wheat estates into their Mediterranean economy. They colonized the area from Sevilla to Merida, even creating retirement colonies and supporting farms for army veterans. The ruins of Italica and Merida reveal the vestiges of Roman villas, streets, water and sewage systems, temples, and amphitheaters. Then over more than half a millenium of occupation, Muslims developed the Andalusian plain, introduced irrigation systems, the windmill, and the waterwheel and made Sevilla their administrative, religious, and intellectual center. Sevilla's *giralda* symbolized Muslim hegemony, technology, and culture. Then in the first half of the eleventh century, contingents from north Castile and the Basque area began to retake Muslim territory. When they finally occupied Sevilla in the mid-thirteenth century—high point of the reconquest—they became the primitive masters of what had been an advanced Muslim outpost in the western Mediterranean, the largest urban center in southwestern Europe.[7]

Sevilla lay at the heart of western Andalusia. To the northwest were the mines of Almaden, the plains of Extremadura and the Portuguese border; to the south lay Jerez, the port of Santa Maria on the outer Bay of Cadiz, and at the end of a narrow peninsula, Cadiz. The major access route to the Mediterranean from Sevilla was down the Guadalquivir River, the link between the Andalusian interior and San Lucar de Barrameda on the sea. Climate, rolling terrain, and a labor reserve formed the basis of Andalusia's main exports—olive oil, wine, and dried fruits. These and other exports balanced the wheat and gold imports from North Africa and the fine woolen and linen textiles imported from the Marseilles-Genoa area. Most important, the coast from San Lucar west to Huelva and on to Lagos in Portugal contained hundreds of fishermen-sailors. In the fifteenth century these men sailed south into the ocean sea to the Canary and Madeira islands and to the Atlantic ports on the West African coast. In the sixteenth century they sailed to empire in Brazil, the West Indies, and ultimately in Mexico and Peru.[8]

Sevilla, political and ecclesiastical center of the Andalusian area, functioned also as commercial hub, drawing merchants from north Castile and the central meseta, from Portugal, from the Low Countries and the Rhineland, from southern France, and especially from Genoa. Probably Genoese merchants trading with North Africa introduced merinos and galvanized the economy of western and northern Castile. From Genoa also came the commercial techniques of early long-distance trade, and after about 1450, Genoese formed the dominant ethnic group ("nation") in the Sevillan commercial and financial community.[9] But whereas regional interests pitted north Castile and Burgos against Vizcaya and Bilbao, Sevilla dominated San Lucar and Puerto Santa Maria. The men sailing into the ocean sea departed from the epitome of seigneurial and Catholic Spain. Occupation of the Andalusian plain, its human and natural resources and commercial networks, made the north Castilians inheritors (and incarnations, they felt) of the Roman imperial tradition. Castilian gentry and nobility carved out large estates in Andalusia following the conquest of Sevilla, and Catholic military orders, monasteries and convents, brotherhoods, and cathedral churches owned large properties, enjoyed special privileges and rights, and in a variety of ways shared the rewards of participation in the reconquest.[10] Church funds supplied Sevilla merchants with investment capital. Religious jurisdiction—that of the Franciscans, for example—brought reports on maritime exploration to the Canaries and beyond. The Spanish Catholic church, the one "national" institution in the peninsula, as participant in the reconquest, evangelization, and consolidation of the Spains inherited by the Hapsburgs was—as another late medieval institution—thereby prepared for full participation in the conquest, pacification, and "civilizing" of the indigenous peoples of America.

The initial phase of contact in the Caribbean had generated the vision of a trading post or "factory" system comparable to a Genoese or Venetian *fondaco* on the North African coast where protected exchange was possible. For trade with West Africa, the Portuguese had set up a state institution or trading company, the Casa da India, in which the treasury had a direct role; this was the early model for Spain's Casa de Contratación established at Sevilla in 1503. But with the realization that Amerindian economy and society had to be restructured and reoriented to produce exportables and to require imports, and that only private initiative could perform this modification, the Casa de Contratación was transformed into a regulatory agency for private enterprise and state fiscal ends.

The heart of Sevilla's economic activity was its merchants, ship owners, and ship captains: North Castilians, South Andalusians, and non-Castilians such as Basques, Aragonese and Catalans, Genoese (by far the "most powerful"),[11] and a sprinkling of Portuguese, Flemish, and Germans. In fact the Sevillan hub was remarkably cosmopolitan and the colonial commercial pattern in the first half of the sixteenth century remained remarkably open. In 1529 the government opened many Mediterranean and Cantabrian ports (excluding Santander) to direct commercial contact with the American colonies with the proviso that all returning vessels call first at Sevilla. By the early 1540s, however, changes in the domestic and international situation induced reconsideration of what was unregulated or unmanaged colonial trade. First, the presence of many non-Castilian merchants with capital and international connections to producers of Spain's imports could lead to foreign domination of both Sevilla and its colonial world. Second, European competition opened Spanish shipping to attack at sea.[12] By the 1540s, elements of what may be termed the Burgalés pattern of overseas trade were selected and adapted to Sevilla's trade with Castile's American possessions.

Superficially the Burgalés and Sevillan patterns of concentrating in one community the trade flows of a large conglomerate unit have much in common. Both seem to share elements of the staple trade of late medieval entrepôts in which commercial interests utilized the political power of embryonic states to legitimize the hegemony of one urban unit and its hinterland over similar units within a patrimonial monarchy, forming urban and often port monopolies. The history of the early modern state is in one sense the interaction between expanding regional commercial interests and state power explicit in the mercantilism of the seventeenth century. Both the Burgalés and Sevillan systems extended control (or tried to) over shipping to the explicit exclusion of competitor cities' shipping. To single out such common features, however, understates the innovations by state and merchant community at Sevilla in reacting to an unprecedented situation.[13]

In synthesizing stages in the growth and development of Sevilla and its Atlantic complex, one senses the novelty of the merchant community's problem. The scale of operations between Burgos and Bruges—even including the wide Castilian hinterland using Burgos as commercial and financial hub—was by European standards of the early sixteenth century already common. But the sheer geographical magnitude of Sevilla's new overseas operations was unparalleled, and during the first seventy-five years of the sixteenth century those operations expanded steadily to the islands of the West Indies and beyond to the Mesoamerican mainland, then to the Isthmus of Panama and by the early 1530s down to the central Andes. Then, in the last quarter of the century, operations of the Sevilla-based merchants extended via Mexico across the Pacific to Manila and the East Asian coast.

There were two main stages in the organization of the Sevillan merchant community in its consulado, and its ultimate control over colonial trade.[14] The initial stage revolved about the mechanisms of shipping and commercial adjudication. As early as 1522, the community had proposed to the government using protected convoys or *flotas*. First authorized as wartime expedient, escorted convoys to and from the West Indies became a permanent feature after 1561. Once the concept of a primitive state trade monopoly under the Casa de Contratación collapsed, the Casa continued to supervise shipping and briefly assumed the role of commercial court. This role lasted roughly three decades; then the volume of commercial litigation seems to have outstripped the capacity of Casa officials so that in 1543, commercial jurisdiction was diverted to the Sevillan merchants when the *ordenanzas* of their consulado were approved.[15] The Sevillan community was, moreover, already deeply involved with protecting shipping across the Atlantic to the West Indies. Arguably by the middle of the century the Burgalés and Sevillan merchant communities had in fact absorbed two elements of an embryonic state's role: adjudication of commercial cases and provision of naval protection. And just as Burgos had for the moment contained the competition of Bilbao, so Sevilla contained the competition of nearby Cadiz. Furthermore, in the West Indies the Sevilla-based fleets were directed to only two ports for exchange, Portobelo on the Isthmus of Panama and Veracruz on Mexico's gulf coast.

The second stage of the Sevillan consulado's formation flowed directly from close collaboration with and ultimate domination of the Casa de Contratación in handling annual escorted fleets to western Atlantic waters. Burgalés merchants, it will be recalled, had insisted upon the right to charge for the variety of services performed for wool shippers between Cantabrian and their Atlantic ports of call, La Rochelle, Nantes, Rouen and Bruges, a charge covered by an *avería* or duty on cargo value. Apparently Seville began to levy an *avería* on exports to America sometime after 1521. After 1550, as the role and function of Contratación and consulado at Sevilla became interlocked in the preparation and departure of fleets and their return, the structure of *avería* collection took shape. By 1573, as Castilian finance was increasingly tapped to suppress insurgents in the Low Countries, the financial burden of America-bound fleets was formally regulated; two decades later the *avería* emerged as a tax farm or *asiento* purchased and administered by the Sevillan merchant community's guild.[16] Thereafter, concurrent with the expansion of colonial exports and return inflows of American silver, the Sevillan consulado entrenched itself as financial pillar of the embryonic Castilian state in a variety of ways. Some of the *avería* tax farm surplus was invested in long-term government bonds *(juros)* secured on specific customs, such as the income from the export duty *(almojarifazgo)*. It was also used for financial (often government-imposed) "gifts" *(donativos)* by the consulado to the state that became common after 1625 and probably earlier. And between 1624 and 1632, the consulado supplied loans to maintain troops *(infantes)* defending Cadiz or paid reparations for merchants' involvement in smuggling activities *(balbas)*. The consulado protected its interests through such financial contributions and by purchasing key clerkships *(escribanías)* from the state. Clerkships were actually a form of privilege. Clerks registered cargo outbound on escorted convoys.

By the early decades of the seventeenth century the Sevilla consulado had obtained formal control over the mechanisms of trade flows with the American colonies. At mid-century, however, the city's position as the peninsula's sole entrepôt for colonial trade was waning. Larger draft vessels could not easily cross the Guadalquivir bar at San Lucar for the fifty-four-mile upriver sail to Sevilla; and the growing number of foreign resident merchants, eager to avoid seizure of cargo on incoming convoys, preferred Cadiz whose inner and outer bays facilitated smuggling. By 1670 Cadiz had virtually supplanted Sevilla as entrepôt of Spain's transatlantic commercial system.[17]

It is one matter to present a model of the stages of the Sevillan consulado's gradual intervention and ultimate hegemony over trade between Spain and its colonies in the sixteenth and early seventeenth centuries. It is another to piece together the varied instruments of merchants' intervention to form a full mosaic of their guild's operations in the last half of the seventeenth. When Burgos's interests succeeded briefly in curbing Bilbao's participation in wool exports to Bruges, outraged Bilbaíno merchants and shippers immediately labeled the action with the current epithet, *monopodio.* By mid-seventeenth century Sevilla's merchants through their consulado had fashioned slowly but relentlessly within the shell of the state's colonial trade supervisory board, the Casa de Contratación, a hard core of privileged private interest which manipulated the principal webs of trade with the distant colonies. As tax farmers, the city's merchants managed a range of activities from covering the cost of food, munitions, and supplies for the *galeones* and the vanguard and rearguard escorts of *flotas* to New Spain to paying the wages of seamen and soldiers both in Spain and the colonies. Their *monopodio* was on a scale Burgos merchants of two centuries earlier would have envied.

By the early seventeenth century, only Spaniards and naturalized residents could participate directly in shipments to and from the colonies. Since Sevillan merchants had driven upward the value of minimum cargo shipments outbound to such a level that all but the most capitalized merchant firms (largely foreign) were effectively eliminated, Spaniards acted as fronts or strawmen *(prestanombres)* for these companies. In collusion with Contratación officials, the consulado regulated both composition and volume of exports while its notaries and clerks checked manifests and their affidavits.[18] Not only had the Sevillan merchant community early dissuaded the Contratación from setting ceiling prices for goods shipped to the colonies, it had taken the primitive models of the wool fairs of north Castile at Villalon, Medina del Rioseco, and especially Medina del Campo and transformed them into a tolerated system of asymmetrical exchange in American ports on a scale never achieved in western Europe's fairs. Its "loans" and "gifts" to the state were secured by taxes—the *almojarifazgo* and *alcabala* (sales tax)—whose collection Sevilla's merchants or their deputies supervised.

Sevillan merchants' principal activity was handling largely foreign residents' imported goods at Sevilla and colonial exchange points. Since Spanish merchants at Sevilla had little capital to purchase directly through agents in Europe's principal ports, foreign resident merchants ordered what was reexported by their *prestanombres* on the convoys. It is paradoxical that under the Hapsburgs competing foreign import houses at Sevilla operated a system of free trade that Spanish mercantilists tried to "nationalize" only in the eighteenth century. Their merchandise was based upon crude estimates of colonial conditions of supply, demand, and consumer preference, and their sales took two basic forms. They sold on credit to Spanish *cargadores* and earned between 30 and 55 percent (and sometimes more) under optimal conditions; or they aimed at higher returns (40–75 percent) by illegally consigning goods to Spanish cover agents for sale at colonial fairs.[19] Spanish *cargadores* chose agents (*factores, encomenderos, comisionistas*) to accompany merchandise and arrange for sales to wholesale importers attending the colonial fairs. In the seventeenth century New Spain's fair sites apparently shifted among Veracruz, Puebla, and even Mexico City.[20]

At the fairs both *factores* and cargo volume were fixed quantities, and on this basis the *factores* prepared to chaffer with the Spanish and criollo merchants from the colonial capitals of Lima and Mexico City.[21] As Sevilla's agents adjusted their prices to estimates of the volume of hard currency held by potential buyers, bargaining was spread over the six, eight, or more months that the convoys remained in port. All understood that the exchange of imports for silver would proceed slowly in the initial months, accelerate in closing months, and peak shortly prior to the announcement of the convoys' departure. This stripped-down version of Europe's classic fair system had no foreign merchants and needed no moneychangers nor deferred payment arrangements. Once the convoys departed, the level of business activity slumped in the Caribbean ports as European goods were removed for sale. These were only the principal Sevilla-imposed constraints that *en bloc* conditioned the legally ill-defined colonial fairs.[22]

Analysis of the operation of the Caribbean fairs may get to the essence of the Spanish colonial trade system evolving over the first colonial centuries. Prototypical features of European and Spanish fairs are recognizable yet reassembled in a format unique to the Spanish mode of early commercial capitalism. The peninsular fairs were based primarily upon a major exportable, raw wool; at the Caribbean fairs, colonial silver was virtually the sole exportable. Unlike their European prototypes, colonial *ferias* lacked international merchants; instead they were frequented by merchants or their agents from the peninsula and by Spaniards and criollos from the colonies. While Champagne's fairs came under the jurisdiction of local counts, those in the Spanish colonies were part of the commercial armature of the Spanish Hapsburg state. Most important was the supply constraint of the colonial adaptation, the limited volume of merchandise carried to the fairs by the fleet system. To call these functions fairs is a misnomer. They were a distillation of European prototypes on a colonial frontier and at the same time symbolic of Spain's derivative early commercial capitalism.

In fact the Spanish transatlantic system of managed trade extended across the Pacific. Manila's Chinese *parian* stocked Fukienese imports reexported on one annual ship *(nao)* to Acapulco on Mexico's Pacific coast where cargo was landed, dustied, reexported to other colonies, sold in the Mexican market, or moved overland to Veracruz for shipment across the Atlantic to Sevilla. Characteristically at Manila shipping space was auctioned, allocated via a ticket *(boleto)* system open to merchants, bureaucrats (widows included), and religious institutions. So Manila too enjoyed a *monopodio* with a vengeance.[23] Indeed looking at Spain's trade system as a whole, the level of constraint seems to have varied directly with distance from Sevilla, the single designated port in metropolitan Spain managing the empire's main trade flows. And when Cadiz supplanted Sevilla at the end of the seventeenth century, its consulado incorporated its predecessor's control mechanisms as part of the Hapsburg legacy.

Even under the most favorable supply conditions Sevilla's efforts to limit participation in the flow of goods into and out of the colonies inevitably would have attracted Spain's west European competitors. With indicators of Spain's manufacturing incapacity multiplying in the last half of the seventeenth century came an impressive volume of imports of woolens, linens, and silks from England, Holland, France, and Italy—most reexported to the colonial fairs.[24] Inevitably smuggling flourished in the colonial pipeline as the gap between Spain's stagnant economic structures and those of Holland, England and France widened. By the late seventeenth century, Europe's workshops produced in quantity for Spanish American consumers and one good—if price was favorable—readily substituted another. The fact that Lower Andalusia had become a collection point of exports produced outside of Spain for reexport to the colonies as well as point on the return flow of silver, which then flowed out of Sevilla (or Cadiz) to European creditors, dominated *arbitrista* literature of Spain's century of "decline."[25]

As production costs fell, price competition grew. Profit compression in legal exchanges led European merchants to sustained smuggling operations.[26] Smuggled goods appeared as unregistered reexports at Sevilla, or they were delivered directly to Spain's Caribbean colonies by English and Dutch "interlopers" under a variety of guises. Since trafficking in smuggled goods was commonplace and apparently beyond remedial action for over a century before 1700, how are we to explain the persistence of legitimate monopoly paralleling this illegal activity? Examination of Veitia Linaje's classic compilation of colonial trade regulations (1672) suggests innumerable possibilities for what was in fact the parallel economy of smuggling and generalized illegal commercial activity that prohibitions barely disguised. One interpretation is that prohibition became a means of constraining such activities; many financial obligations in the form of gifts or secured loans paid by the Sevillan merchant community ostensibly to ease the cash-flow problem of the state turn out on inspection to be in reality legalized pay-offs to halt criminal proceedings against law-breakers in colonial trade.[27]

The existence of such activity leads to another and perhaps more plausible interpretation: even partial enforcement of Sevilla's port monopoly provided income and profit to a large number of public and private interests involved in its maintenance. After all, Sevilla's merchants and their associates never correlated colonial demand to the formation of manufacturing establishments in Andalusia or other regions of the peninsula or to a policy of early economic development under state auspices (mercantilism). They and cooperative public functionaries designed structures of colonial monopoly only partially to satisfy colonial demand through limited supply at maximum prices; illegal goods would provide the balance. If imperfect monopoly and undersupply sustained a satisfactory level of return to Spanish and foreign investors at Sevilla, illegal commerce was tolerated because the "appetite for large profits" drew all to the colonial trades.[28] Indeed, a cynic might conclude smuggling kept American consumers satisfied with Sevilla's monopoly. In this sense monopoly (or oligopoly) and smuggling—legal and illegal commerce, the formal and parallel economies—were functionally linked in Spain's transatlantic trading system. They were reciprocal structures at the end of the seventeenth century and sustained a level of immobilism as American silver continued to flow into Spain and out to western Europe. They almost suggest a "Spanish mode of production"—a silver-based one.

This conspectus of antecedents, formation, and elaboration of the Sevillan colonial system of managed trade in the first two centuries of Spanish colonialism in America indicates how European elements were retooled for imperial ends. The formalization of the two principal Castilian trade complexes, that of Burgos-Bruges and of Sevilla–West Indies, occurred synchronically during the first half of the sixteenth century—the time lag between their respective *ordenanzas* is too brief to be significant. Both complexes were responses by inexperienced commercial groups to unexpected overseas possibilities. Both shared other qualities: a microregional, even narrowly urban outlook and mentality, and an incapacity to foster a national rather than parochial interest. Just as Burgos tried to curb Bilbao's competition, so Sevilla's merchants tried to exclude both non-Iberians and even non-Castilians from their colonial trade. Their early and enduring success in isolating other regions of Spain from the Atlantic trades gave Sevilla's traders and their associates extraordinary financial power which they methodically transformed into political influence. In this fashion Sevilla's interests came to dominate the Casa de Contratación, the customs house, elements of the colonial bureaucracy, and the Consejo de Indias (Spain's colonial office), absorbing and in fact exercising public functions behind a façade of state regulation. In modern parlance, the private sector manipulated the public sector of a patrimonial state.

Mining: Core of Colonial Structures

The commercial matrix fashioned from Spain's historical experience and adapted to the possibilities of its overseas empire was designed to maximize mining silver and, to a lesser extent, gold in America. Mining in central and northern New Spain and in Andean or highland (Upper) Peru made these the core colonies. They supplied the bloodstream of precious metals that nourished Spain and Europe virtually from the moment of conquest.

Like the structures of colonial trade, those established in mining adapted European elements to meet New World requirements. Through a multitude of direct and more elusive channels, Mexican and Peruvian mining towns linked apparently isolated, obscure, and self-sufficient Amerindian pueblos to Europe's cities, towns, and countryside. In the sixteenth and seventeenth centuries, communities in America and Europe became functioning parts of an international economy that extended to the Indian and western Pacific oceans and the South China Sea. Through one prism, silver mining and trade were instruments of early commercial capitalism penetrating Spain's American colonies; through another, the mines of Potosí

and Huancavelica (Peru) and Pachuca, Guanajuato, Zacatecas, and Somb-
rerete (Mexico) in the sixteenth and seventeenth centuries subsidized Spain's
hegemony in western Europe and in the eighteenth century nourished illu-
sions of renovation or recovery of that lost hegemony.

For at least 1500 years before the occupation of America, southwestern
Andalusia had been a mining zone: copper at Rio Tinto, silver in the Sierra
Morena, and mercury at Almaden near Sevilla. Continuity of mining at
Almaden is evident under Roman, Visigothic, Moslem, and finally Castilian occupation.[29] It was not, however, upon the silver complex of Andalusia that the first Spaniards in the West Indies drew when they encountered surface gold deposits on Hispaniola, their first major island base
in the Caribbean. Trans-Saharan gold flows had stimulated Iberian expansion along the African coast, an aspect of the response to demand for a
medium of exchange as the European economy expanded in the last half of
the fifteenth century. German silver mining at the time was a similar response. Hispaniola's gold placer mines provided major returns on the risk
capital that financed the first maritime expeditions to the West Indies. Labor demands in the placer fields led to the first application of forced labor
legislation, *encomienda,* in which tribute took the form of labor service. The
gold bonanza more than compensated for the absence of trade that had
been confidently expected by the early expeditions to America, and the pattern of mining operations set a precedent for later silver mining, in one
respect a grim precedent. Hispaniola's gold was exhausted by the early
1520s. Its mining was characterized by a minimum of Spanish capital investment and European technology and a maximum of indigenous labor coercion. The application of a labor draft to Hispaniola's agrarian population
coupled with European-introduced epidemic disease and generalized cultural disorganization and anomie induced a demographic hecatomb of unparalleled scope. Since the placer fields were worked out early, disappearance of Hispaniola's male and female work force was a minor consideration
to the newly arrived Spaniards, but one vividly recalled by Bartolomé de Las
Casas.[30]

On the other hand, demands of underground silver mining in Mexico
and Peru forced the adaptation of European technology to a scale of operations unknown in western Europe at that time. This required the importation of skilled European technicians (many German). Spaniards introduced iron and steel tools and lamp oil; German miners erected stamp mills
for crushing ore along with the smelting of ores containing lead. As mines
extended deeper, Spaniards constructed hoists and pumps powered by
water wheels or animals, and to drain and ventilate deep galleries they

designed and opened adits and shafts.[31] Significantly, a Sevilla merchant and a German miner are credited with working out separately the amalgamation process of applying mercury and salt to crushed ore to obtain silver, which replaced smelting. First adapted in Mexico in the early 1550s, it was quickly transmitted to Peru's mines.[32]

Just as basic silver mining technology came from Europe via Spain, so did the mercury first employed in refining by amalgamation. Bartolomé de Medina, a Sevillan merchant, reportedly applied the technique of amalgamation at Pachuca in New Spain in 1554; within three years it appeared in highland Peru where shortly thereafter Huancavelica's mercury mines were opened. The high output of Potosí's silver mines combined with the availability of Peruvian mercury magnified in west European minds the bonanza that was Peru at this time. Until well into the eighteenth century, for example, French merchants were more absorbed with the Peruvian than with the Mexican economy. Meanwhile Almaden's mercury production, under contract (*asiento*) from 1563 to 1645 to the German merchant-banking house of Fugger (which appointed its "administrador y dueño absoluto" at Almaden), was initially exported to New Spain's mines.[33] For the next 250 years silver refining in New Spain and Peru fluctuated directly with the supply and price of mercury produced at Huancavelica and Almaden; and when Almaden's output declined between 1621 and 1641, mercury was ordered from Idrian mines in Croatia under *asientos* awarded to German and Genoese intermediaries.[34]

Expansion of silver production thousands of miles from Europe entailed more, however, than the importation of technicians, technology, horses, burros and mules, and mercury. As with the expansion of Spanish trade from its European context to the West Indies and beyond to the western Pacific, so mining in the Spanish colonies in America dwarfed the Spanish and for that matter the European experience.[35] Over six centuries (from 250 B.C. to A.D. 350) between 40,000 and 50,000 tons of silver may have been mined in the Mediterranean world; New Spain's and Peru's mines produced 40,000 tons in one-third of that time.[36] American silver ores were not as rich as European ores, but they more than compensated for this in volume. Hence the opening of adits and shafts and the construction of dams, waterwheels, whims, and mule-powered *arrastres* to fine-crush ores, and large stone patios for amalgamation. Mexico and Peru each employed roughly 15,000 mineworkers annually, excluding important backward linkages to producers of food, animals, timber and charcoal, salt, sacking, lamp oil, and candles, as well as to muleteers and carters.[37] The scale of opportunity and the probability of large, rapid returns drove both technical adaptation and innovation.[38] Similarly, profit possibilities in silver mining stimulated Spaniards emigrating to America—mine owners, merchants, government bureaucrats, secular and regular Catholic clergy—to rationalize and legitimate the coercion of Amerindian laborers in colonial silver mines on a scale perhaps unknown since Roman times and matched later only by the coercion of Africans transported across the Atlantic to labor on colonial sugar and tobacco plantations in Brazil, Surinam, the Caribbean, Mexico, and Peru.[39]

If the role of the Spanish colonial state was essentially coercive and legitimizing, it was not without rewards. The state contracted through *asientos* for mercury supplies from Spain (Almaden) and the Austrian possessions in the Balkan peninsula (Idria) as well as Peru (Huancavelica). It profited from the difference between the price it paid for mercury and the price it got when it resold the mercury to colonial miners or their suppliers (*aviadores*). It collected a 10 percent tax on bar silver in New Spain (twenty percent in Peru) plus a uniform seignorage fee, not to mention duties on reexport of silver at colonial ports, on silver entering Sevilla, and on silver reexported there. To the Spanish state, its silver flows in bullion and coin—its colonial revenues, "substance and nerve of the wealth of Your Majesty and vassals"[40]—were essential to the maintenance of bureaucracy, the persistence of patrimonial monarchy, peninsular regionalism, counterrevolutionary intervention in western Europe, and the reworking of late medieval or early capitalistic commercial structures and attitudes.

Construction and development of mining complexes in the interior of New Spain and Peru and associated transatlantic trade flows between Europe and Africa, and Europe and America occurred within the parameters provided by a fragile, and embryonic late medieval state on the periphery of western Europe. At the international level the Spanish state legitimated by force and by law overseas territories invaded and organized by Spanish nationals as private enterprise. Mining and commercial activity in the American colonies remained as in the peninsula the sphere of private initiative: effective state-run enterprise including tax collection was still beyond the resources of this patrimonial state. Hence in mining and commercial sectors the private entrepreneur remained omnipresent and omnipotent. A basic input of silver refining, mercury, was supplied by the Fuggers; Peru's Huancavelica mercury mine was farmed out to Spanish businessmen.[41] In both New Spain and Peru the state sold mercury to intermediaries who then supplied those mine owners who had the necessary refining capacity. Over time, intermediaries appeared between colonial mine owner and European silver merchant: capital-short miners borrowed from local merchants (*aviadores*) to whom repayment was made in ore or silver bars, which then were either delivered to royal mints for assaying, taxation, and coinage or clandestinely exported from the producing colony.

Meanwhile, by the seventeenth century, officers of the mints were able to purchase their positions, a practice that could lead to gross malfeasance. Once silver was unloaded at Sevilla, silver merchants bought up both private shipments and those on royal account; they delivered the bullion to the Sevilla mint, then either reexported coined silver to European creditors or sold it within Spain. The multiple stages of the mining process—extraction, refining, shipping along with inputs of iron and steel tools, food, leather, candle wax, and fodder for draft animals in mines and general transport—inserted into the Spanish-American countryside fundamental tenets of the capitalist canon: wage labor, competition and the market, and entrepreneurial risk as justifying immoderate gains and an amoral economy.

Great fortunes generated by the returns on mining enterprise were either reinvested, invested in real estate (often entailed as *mayorazgos*), diverted to charitable foundations (*obras pias*) as a kind of family trust fund (*capellanias de sangre*), or spent on consumption (town houses, clothing, servants).[42] Mine owners also generated fortunes through covert and often not-so-covert fraud that powerful transgressors legitimated or "laundered" by ritualized settlements with the state (*composiciones*) or simply by the state's incapacity or unwillingness to take effective counter-measures.

Nothing exemplifies better the incapacity, even outright complicity of the seventeenth-century Spanish state apparatus as well as the ingenuity and rapacity of Spanish mine owners, merchants, bureaucrats, religious and naval personnel, and merchant vessel operators than the massive, indeed extraordinary hemorrhage of silver bullion and coin past the state's mechanisms of surveillance—a form of early decapitalization.[43] On the basis of two sets of data—five-year estimates of colonial production of silver and gold, together with five-year official registers of Sevilla's incoming receipts to 1660 supplemented by educated estimates for the years 1661–1700—a number of tentative conclusions may be drawn (Table 1). First, average quinquennial production over twenty-five years (1596–1620) reached 51.8 million pesos; after peaking at 77.9 million (1621–25) production over the following quarter-century (1626–50) averaged 55.6 million per quinquennium. Downward inflexion developed after 1660, and for the balance of the century quinquennial American production averaged 39 million pesos, a drop of almost 30 percent. So much for precious metals output in America, mainly silver by amalgamation and smelting. Europe's unprecedented inflow of American silver—perhaps over 16,000 tons between 1500 and

TABLE I

American Precious Metals Production and Spanish Receipts, 1571–1700
(in millions of pesos)

Year	Production	(Spain) Receipts	(Spain) Registered	(Spain) Unofficial
1571–75	21.6	19.7		
1576–80	44.4	28.5		
1581–85	49.0	48.6		
1586–90	61.5	39.4		
1591–95	59.3	58.2		
1596–1600	51.6	57.0		
1601–05	39.5	44.9		
1606–10	43.1	52.0		
1611–15	61.6	40.6		
1616–20	63.1	49.8		
1621–25	77.9	44.7		
1626–30	48.9	41.3	40.8	53.2
1631–35	57.9	28.3	8.0	17.5
1636–40	64.8	27.0	8.4	22.5
1641–45	61.4	22.8	14.2	40.0
1646–50	45.0	19.5	5.9	17.1
1651–55	62.1	12.1	6.3	11.8
1656–60	46.9	5.6	9.8	32.2
1661–65	40.8		25.7	79.5
1666–70	39.9		21.0	40.0
1671–75	53.3		29.4	51.2
1676–80	42.3		50.7	83.2
1681–85	19.4			54.8
1686–90	33.1			71.0
1691–95	43.1		16.0	70.0
1696–1700	39.9			60.0

Sources: (American production and registered receipts, Sevilla, 1571–1660, in pesos of 272 mrvs.) Hamilton, *American Treasure and the Price Revolution in Spain,* 34 table 1; Brading and Cross, "Colonial Silver Mining: Mexico and Peru," 579 Table 1; (Registered and Unofficial Receipts, Sevilla) Morineau, Michel, *Incroyables gazettes et fabuleux metaux,* 232–236 table 39, 242 table 41. Morineau's pesos are probably of 450 mrvs (*maravedíes*).

1650 — led to dramatic economic changes: "one money market after another in Europe experienced successively . . . easy money conditions, . . . abundance of coin . . . cash . . . bills of exchange" with every arrival of silver fleets at Sevilla. It made the *peso de a ocho* "a world currency circulating from America to China."[44]

More significant and generally minimized is a second conclusion. Even allowing for retention in the colonial monetary system and for illicit export to Manila of perhaps 30 to 40 percent of total silver output, there was a constant and growing leakage (a "fraud factor") of silver between New Spain–Peru and Sevilla. Between 1571 and 1595, American production of precious metals totaled 235.8 million pesos while Sevilla registered officially only 194.4—a difference of 17.6 percent. From 1611 to 1635 that difference doubled to 34 percent, and between 1636 and 1660 it doubled again to 69 percent.[45] Using the basis of precious metals' arrivals at Sevilla, Morineau's data for official and unofficial receipts at Sevilla, 1661–1680, shows 126.8 million pesos registered, while informed merchant sources reported 253.9 million, almost 100 percent higher. For just twenty years after 1661, we cannot account for 127.1 million pesos. Some must have remained in Spain (commissions to Spanish agents or strawmen, payment for exports of domestic goods, silver concealed by returning naval officers and crewmen and by secular and religious passengers), while the overwhelming bulk was remitted abroad to settle the accounts of suppliers in France, Flanders, Holland, England, Germany, and Italy. One possibility, offered by Morineau, is simply "massive under-registry, so extraordinarily fraudulent, it was no longer fraud . . . ."[46]

Even if allowance is made for retention of silver in the economy of New Spain and Peru to factor payments for food, clothing, and transport, for the high consumption propensity of the civil-religious hierarchy (merchants and mine owners, bureaucrats, and ecclesiastics), for capital outlays on mine improvements in shafts and adits, hoists, ore-processing patios, smelters, carting and mule teams, or for bequests to religious foundations to furnish fixed income to donors' families and ultimately for church income, a large residual of silver was annually exported. Unregistered silver bullion and coin disappeared between pithead and mint and between mint and ports of export on the Pacific, Caribbean, and South Atlantic coasts.[47] Some flowed from Peruvian ports to Acapulco where it merged with Mexican silver to flow across the Pacific to Manila and on to the Asian continent only to return in Asian luxury goods stocked at Manila by Fukien Chinese. Presumably the largest volume of silver both registered and unregistered was exported from Portobelo and Veracruz on the fleets and aboard *registros* (unaccompanied vessels) for delivery at the Andalusian ports of Cadiz, Puerto Santa María, San Lucar, and Sevilla. Many are the indications that tightly organized and tolerated silver smugglers siphoned away appreciable quantities even before registry at Sevilla by transshipping in coastal waters or at Sevilla and Cadiz for delivery to France, England, Holland, Italy, and Germany.[48]

Equally significant capillaries through which silver leaked into the European economy also developed in the colonies. One led overland from the mines and mint of highland Peru south to the dependent supply area of northwestern Argentina via Jujuy, Salta, and Tucumán. From there silver

crossed the pampas to the Rio de la Plata, and via Anglo-Portuguese intermediaries it made its way to Europe to pay for imports of textiles, hardware, and African slaves.[49] The other leakage developed through contacts at
Portobelo, Cartagena, and Veracruz with the Dutch and English Caribbean
islands of Curaçao and Jamaica.[50] The high incidence of piracy in Caribbean waters in the late seventeenth century was a response to legal and illegal silver flows. It also represents the first stages of aggressive intervention,
private piratical enterprise, against Spain's fragile colonial hegemony. Initially aggression took the form of private attacks against the Spanish empire's trade complex in America, the Caribbean and the ports on its pe-
rimeter; the second stage became national or state enterprise, international
warfare involving England and Holland, France and Spain in the War of the
Spanish Succession.

Mining: Structures, Linkages and Perspective

Recent economic analysis emphasizes the structure and function of agriculture, mining and manufacture and then advances to financial services and
networks of distribution at home and abroad. This analysis highlights basic
structures permitting a degree of model building. In similar fashion a focus
upon the silver sector in Spanish colonial America of the sixteenth and seventeenth centuries may clarify the nature of the colonial economy, its dynamic elements and peninsular and European linkages.

Silver mining's structure, function, and linkages from the mid-sixteenth
century onward shaped the colonial and to a marked degree the European
and international economy. America's mines galvanized local support activities (backward linkages), developed the imperial trade system, shaped the
Spanish metropolitan economy, and ultimately shaped European growth
and development. The interrelationships between mine owner, merchant
and state in the first colonial centuries shaped the direction of growth of New
Spain and Peru as well as their external relations with Spain, and through
Spain with the European world and Asia, a pattern persisting through the
eighteenth century and beyond. The profit possibilities of colonial mining
absorbed the attention of Spaniards in the colonies whether prospectors,
mine owners, merchants and merchant bankers, bureaucrats, or clergymen
as well as Spaniards in the Andalusian mercantile or Madrid governmental
sectors. Inescapably there developed among Spaniards a bonanza mentality,
a unifocal concentration upon getting and spending rather than creating
new sources of wealth. It may indeed be appropriate to term this truly *primitive* accumulation. The focus on maximizing comparative advantage in a

natural resource with a low cost, coercible labor reserve was a key factor in the inability or unwillingness of the Spanish state and Spanish businessmen to modify economic policy in the last half of the seventeenth century when competitive European economies lacking silver mines were penetrating Spain's silver flows indirectly through production and marketing of their manufactures for consumers in New Spain and Peru. So imperial Spain's hemorrhage of silver became Europe's transfusion. For Spain's elites the short-run effects of this position in the international division of labor provided a high level of income; the long-run disadvantages were tolerated and remedial action postponed because silver continued to flow across the Atlantic. American silver mining camps and an exploited labor force, partly coerced and partly salaried, that ultimately included Amerindians, Black Africans, mestizos, and mulattos, created and maintained extraordinary income disparity. They opened up new regions linked by new roads and formed large towns and two viceregal capitals at Mexico City and Lima, impressive by international standards of the time. No doubt, silver—principal export of Spain's two principal colonies in the early colonial centuries— proved a powerful stimulus to the development of commercial capitalism. While the role of silver imports in developing the economies of Holland, England, and France remains a matter for further clarification, it is essential to note that mining brought monetization and commercialization to the colonial economies and forged a link clearly and early between the mining and commercial sectors. Silver mining in New Spain and Peru was one of those New World enterprises that helped integrate different modes of production into the international economy including the variant of commercial capitalism developing in the Spanish colonial periphery.

Commercialization of the Mexican and Peruvian economies occurred in markedly different ways and at markedly different rates. While mining was critical to this general process, it functioned within regional contexts already different at conquest. Indeed, the interaction of conquest and colonialism in Amerindian societies and economies reinforced the heterogeneity rather than homogeneity of the two most developed New World culture areas. Recruitment of mine labor suggests the degree to which the structures of preconquest Inca and Aztec cultures—one a consolidating empire and the other a tribute empire—and colonialism affected the rate and nature of commercialization of the respective colonial areas. On the periphery of commercial capitalism many modes of production bloomed.

It is a paradox that mining, whose direct and indirect labor needs were a major long-run factor in eliminating *encomienda* in New Spain, drew indigenous peoples from their Tlaxcalan, Otomí, Aztec, and Tarascan communities through wage inducements, while in Peru mining led to forced labor drafts that persisted roughly 250 years. The capitalistic nature of American mining operations seems indisputable; equally indisputable is the presence of both wage and slave labor, of free and coerced labor, in the evolution of modern capitalism outside western Europe. It is small consolation that mining drove Amerindians from a communitarian into a competitive capitalistic economy, from a self-contained into an open economy, from subsistence to the market. The benefits of a market economy to Amerindian and other colonial mineworkers must be weighted against the unacceptable morbidity and mortality rates of those exposed to the dust of silver mines and the poison of mercury. As Bakewell has put it tongue-in-cheek, "The Indians . . . must have seemed very distant" to Madrid.[51]

In north Mexico's mining camps at Zacatecas and Parral, there was a rapid transition from tribute to wage labor although it was accompanied by both debt peonage and chattel slavery. A number of factors forged this early transition. Spaniards organized their north Mexican mining operations in a lightly populated frontier zone of nomadic Amerindian cultures; Amerindians there refused to work for mining entrepreneurs, a refusal that seems to have been reinforced by slaving raids that underpaid and often unpaid soldiery initiated to obtain chattels for sale. Forced or tribute labor might have been brought from more densely populated central Mexico where preconquest cultures had formed large urban nuclei. However, the high level of Aztec urbanization probably facilitated the spread of imported epidemic disease, which struck down indigenous nobility and masses alike and disrupted and disorganized Amerindian society. The unprecedented collapse of both coastal and central Mexico's Amerindian population between 1550 and 1620, eliminated a stable reservoir of labor which might have been shifted by long-distance, forced internal migration to mining camps, as happened in Peru. Finally, preconquest Aztec expansion and the ruthless instruments of coercion that Aztec militarism imposed to collect tribute created a pool of discontented subject peoples. Spanish mine owners successfully drew labor from Amerindian groups who had long resisted Aztec expansion and who collaborated with the Spaniards as allies. Early on, Tlaxcalan, Otomí and Tarascan Indian free workers (*naborías*)were drawn to the newly opened mines of Zacatecas (1550) and Parral (1623), a one-way migratory flow attracted by wage payments.[52]

In the long run, the mine operators of north Mexico and of Guanajuato and Pachuca in central Mexico ultimately secured a wage labor force through the gradual recovery of the indigenous population sometime after 1650 and more importantly through the growth of a mestizo population in both central and north Mexico.[53] The idiosyncratic nature of this historical process is suggested by the interaction in New Spain of conquest and epidemic disease. Spanish emigration to the colony and Spanish-Amerindian miscegenation, on the one hand, limited the survival of isolated, relatively autonomous Amerindian communities and, on the other, later accounted for the presence in eighteenth-century New Spain of a growing population in which a significant segment of mestizos and mulattos was responsive to market inducements of wages and prices.[54]

By contrast, recruitment of a labor force for mines in the central Andes suggests how invasion, colonialism, and the needs of the mining sector in the highlands apparently slowed the spread of commercialization at least by comparison with the process in New Spain. The preconquest population of the central Andes was smaller than that of central Mexico. Slower too was the rate of postconquest demographic contraction; the population of Amerindian communities declined gradually to bottom out about 1750, roughly a century later than in central Mexico.

It is difficult to account for the slower rate of decline. It may reflect the isolation at high altitudes of many Andean communities which resulted in less frequent contact with Spanish immigrants and slower exposure to European-introduced epidemic disease and ensuing cultural disorganization.[55] From the viewpoint of culture-contact it is significant that very early the Spaniards resolved to set up a new administrative-commercial center not in the sierra at Cuzco where the preconquest Inca capital had been, but on the coast at Lima. In any event, the apparent relative stability of highland communities of the central Andes along with the survival of the Amerindian (Inca) nobility and its skillful incorporation into the Spanish colonial system as a key instrument of indirect rule kept these communities' homogenous and reliable manpower reserves supplying forced-labor drafts through the *mita* for Peru's mercury and silver mines over more than two centuries. Wage labor did appear in Peru's mines, too, but there is no doubt that under-remunerated *mita* labor kept mining operations profitable.[56] Tentatively one may extrapolate from the handling of mine labor, the lower rate of miscegenation, and the relative isolation and cultural cohesion of Amerindian communities that monetization and commercialization of the central Andes economy as a whole was far less rapid and extensive than in central and northern New Spain.[57]

On balance, then, the impact of Spanish enterprise in the two principal colonial mining areas of America was uneven, greater in New Spain, less in Peru. By the middle of the eighteenth century New Spain's population recovery was noticeable, reflecting perhaps the importance of the mestizo component. Its population was not only larger than Peru's, its rate of recovery was higher, and its expanding demand for imports of textiles, wines, and brandies drew the attention of Spaniards and other Europeans as well as East Asians. In comparison, Peruvian demand for European and Asian imports was relatively stagnant.[58] It is reasonable to conclude that the Mexican population was becoming more commercialized, more market-oriented than the Peruvian.

The nature and scope of mining emphasized the role of merchant intermediaries and, over time, merchant financiers' control over mining. Development and maintenance of mining towns on a large scale set in motion subordinate supply activities, some local, others international. A case in point is the supply function triggered by the development of mining first at Zacatecas and later at Parral. Zacatecas's rapid evolution from frontier to settled community during the forty years between 1550 and 1590 transformed surrounding semiarid grasslands into cattle ranches producing beef, hides for ropes and sacking, large quantities of tallow for candles. More distant forests became lumber sources for mine timbers and smelters. Producers in the fertile Bajío to the south and in the Aguascalientes valley soon satisfied demand for wheat and corn. On the highway (*camino real de tierra adentro*) north from Mexico City hundreds of miles away moved the basic mining inputs of mercury, iron and steel bars, and hardware imported from Europe along with other valuable European imports of Rouen woolens, Breton and Dutch linens, Asian silks, and even Persian carpets. Mine workers bought woolens and other goods and, in fact, were frequently paid in overpriced textiles rather than silver pesos. Cattle ranches along the highway provided oxen and mules for heavy two-wheeled carts and mule teams freighting goods from Mexico City to Zacatecas and beyond and back to Mexico City over a combined distance of more than 1500 miles.[59]

Thus the volume of domestic and imported merchandise, its distribution network, the mechanisms of credit—in brief, the variety and magnitude of distributive functions—early required the presence of merchant intermediaries. Storekeepers (*tenderos*) appeared at Zacatecas with their branches (*dependencias*) in outlying towns; they supplied travelling merchants (*viandantes)* who made the rounds of localities with wares loaded on pack mules. Relations between mine owners and their merchant suppliers (*aviadores*) were close: *aviadores* advanced goods on credit (*avío*) as well as silver pesos for wage payments in return for unminted silver. It was common for mine owners and mine workers to sell their unrefined and refined silver to better-capitalized *rescatadores* who shipped it to the Mexico City mint.

By mid-seventeenth century, however, local *rescatadores* were already subordinated to Mexico City's merchant financiers, the *mercaderes de plata*, with their own representatives in Zacatecas as *rescatadores* and *aviadores*. Although important Spanish local bureaucrats (*corregidores*) supplemented incomes with operations of *avío* and *rescate*, Zacatecas's leading figures in mining had become the distant Mexico City *mercaderes de plata* whose capital and commercial networks linked them to Europe and the Philippines.[60] Through correspondents at Sevilla they imported luxuries—European linens, woolens and silks, Asian cottons, silks and ivories—which they shipped to their far-off *dependencias* in northern mining centers. In the domination of merchants over mine owners appeared that concentration of economic power which made Mexico City merchants and their merchant guild or *consulado* (like their counterparts at Lima) the locus of economic and political influence, pillars of the established colonial order and of its basic industry, mining.

The Non-Mining Periphery

Speculation in mining was profitable but invariably subject to high risk. There were also hidden long-term disadvantages. In maximizing successfully a comparative resource advantage in the early international division of labor, mining overshadowed other resources and enterprises. In the long run, it contributed to forming structures that initially developed and then helped "fix" colonial economies and, in the Spanish metropole, inhibited a developmental strategy. The absence of an imperial strategy beyond colonial mining was responsible for the long neglect of the agricultural and ranching potential of the other Spanish colonies in America. In colonial areas of America lacking mineral wealth, such as Cuba and Venezuela in the Caribbean and the Rio de la Plata in South America, neglect by state and private sectors persisted for almost two hundred years. Development accelerated only in the last third of the eighteenth century.

In light of the eighteenth-century export boom of Spain's nonmining colonies in America, it may seem anomalous that their growth and development lagged so long. For Spain, however, their importance was, for the most part, limited to their ancillary role in the silver trade. In the early sixteenth century Cuba functioned briefly as support area for the invasion of New Spain and Florida, providing soldiery and a base of operations. With the establishment of the convoy system in the second half of the century, Havana became the major crossroad where galleons from Portobelo and fleets from Veracruz assembled for the homeward leg. Truck farms appeared around Havana, and beyond them small and large cattle ranches supplied beef for local consumption and hides as a major exportable. At the end of the sixteenth century the first sugar plantations generated a small volume of exports. These early sugar mills *(ingenios)* were financed by eight-year loans of state capital diverted from the treasury of the colony of New Spain, and their owners could draw upon the technical expertise developed by Portuguese planters in Brazil and upon African labor delivered by Portuguese slavers. Throughout the following century, however, Cuban sugar production virtually stagnated while the Portuguese and the Dutch transformed Brazil's *nordeste* into the world's first major sugar exporting area, and the English and Dutch established plantations in the Antilles. In fact, the first Cuban export of significance was tobacco, especially high-priced snuff for Europe's high-income consumers. Tobacco growers *(vegueros)* were family farmers who worked the most suitable soils, initially in the bottomlands *(vegas)* along streams flowing to the sea.[61] In Cuba and the La Plata—areas lacking mineral resources—the tardy development of exportables was a response to new demands generated in northwestern, non-Iberian Europe.[62]

But Cuba's main function over the first two hundred years of Spanish colonialism in America was as port of call and provisioning point for homeward-bound Spanish shipping laden with the mining output of central and north Mexico and highland Peru along with a small volume of other colonial exportables. Appropriately, subsidies from the colonial treasury at Mexico City financed Havana's fortifications and garrison making the port a naval base, a protected outport on the periphery of the mainland mining colony.

Another zone—a triangle delimited by Tucumán in northwestern Argentina, Asunción in Paraguay, and at the southernmost point, Buenos Aires, on the edge of the South Atlantic—served a comparable peripheral role. Since the strategy of Spanish colonial trade confined contact between Sevilla in the metropole and Cartagena, Portobelo, and Veracruz in the colonies to the Caribbean and North Atlantic routes, the silver mining areas of highland Peru were obliged to trade through Lima and Arica on the Pacific coast, approximately 400–600 leagues by pack mule. This strategy necessitated isolating Potosí from the South Atlantic coast 600 leagues away, with long stretches (350 leagues) feasible for carting. The logic of this strategy led to the colonization of Tucumán, Córdoba, Santa Fe, and Buenos Aires along with Asunción as a series of settlements in the second half of the sixteenth century when Potosí mining developed rapidly.

The logic of strategy is usually undermined over time by the changing pressures of reality. It was not long before Potosí's isolation from the South Atlantic cracked. On the one hand, growth of silver production after the introduction of amalgamation and organization of labor drafts quickly transformed Potosí into a major urban center as population swelled from about 3,000 to nearly 160,000 between 1560 and 1650. A heavily populated mining city at an altitude of over 13,500 feet required a constant inflow of goods to support mining operations, forced and wage labor, bureaucrats, churchmen, mine owners, and merchants. Food, beverages and cocoa, mercury, tools, timber, cattle, sheep, and work animals as well as ordinary and luxury textiles had to be brought in. The area of Córdoba, Mendoza, and Tucumán south of Potosí produced corn and wheat, textiles, cattle, mules, and horses. What imperiled this South American syndrome was the threat of direct commercial penetration of European goods and slaves from Portuguese-controlled Brazil, overland from São Paulo to Asunción and thence to Upper Peru, from Buenos Aires via the Paraguay River to Asunción or via Santa Fe, Córdoba, Mendoza, and Tucumán.

Buenos Aires, however, established as a rampart (1580) against European penetration from the Atlantic, evolved into an entrepôt between the South Atlantic and Potosí. It began this function during the major Potosí mining cycle (1570–1650) that corresponded roughly to Spain's annexation of Portugal (1580–1640) and the Portuguese colonies. In return for Brazilian sugar and rum, European hardware and textiles, and African slaves, Buenos Aires exported some wheat, hides, dried beef, and tallow and, of course, Potosí silver—estimates of smuggled silver vary between 20 to 25 percent of total Potosí output. Portuguese merchants were soon established along the route to Tucumán, Potosí, and beyond to Lima itself. With the separation of Portugal from Spain after 1640 and the contraction of Potosí silver production, Buenos Aires's role receded until hide exports and the brief revival of silver mining became significant at the close of the eighteenth century.[63]

Venezuela typifies another late-developing area of the Spanish empire in America. Like Cuba its coast formed a section of the rim of the Caribbean waterway; but unlike Cuba, Venezuela had no major port, and incoming vessels sailed past the long Venezuelan coast on to Cartagena and Portobelo. Under Charles V, the occupation of Venezuela was contracted out to a non-Castilian consortium of the Welsers of Augsburg, merchant bankers to central Germany's silver miners. The most profitable Welser enterprise in America was enslavement and sale of Amerindians to Spaniards in the Antilles; around 1600 Venezuela was also shipping wheat, cattle, hides, and (with the labor of African slaves) tobacco and cocoa to Cartagena and Portobelo. Tobacco and cocoa exports linked Venezuela to Spain's intercolonial trade and the international economy, mainly a result of Holland's occupation of the offshore islands of Curaçao and Bonaire (1624). Dutch ships brought African slaves and European manufactures, recrossing the Atlantic with Venezuelan tobacco, cocoa, salt, and silver—payment for Venezuelan cocoa exports to Veracruz.[64] Mexican consumers preferred high-quality Venezuelan cocoa to cocoa from Ecuador. Around 1700 Venezuela was within the orbit of New Spain's mining economy, smuggling cocoa, silver, and tobacco in exchange for Curaçao's African slaves and European goods.

What emerges from analysis of Spanish imperialism in the sixteenth and seventeenth centuries is the need for a systemic conspectus of Spain's overseas expansion as part of early modern western Europe's growth and change. In those critical centuries a historic shift occurred in the locus of European dynamism, moving economic hegemony from north Italy to northern France, the Netherlands, and England. This overview demythifies Spain's grandeur and power. Spain, like Portugal, was ideally positioned for maritime expansion at the end of the fifteenth century; yet its economy was and remained agricultural and ranching, its population density was low, its labor was largely unskilled, and its manufacturing capacity was negligible. What has obscured Spain's economic unpreparedness for empire was its facile invasion and occupation of America.

Northwest Europe: Penetrating the Spanish Empire in America

In the second half of the seventeenth century, in the decades between the Peace of Westphalia that ended the Thirty Years War in 1648 and the outbreak of the War of the Spanish Succession in 1701, profound structural changes occurred within the west European economy and within its major area of American interest, the Caribbean or West Indies. The long-term displacement of economic primacy in manufactures (mainly textiles) from North Italy to the Netherlands, southeast England and northern France, ended. Within this new economic heartland of northwest Europe, a secondary displacement occurred when England overtook the United Provinces as Europe's foremost maritime and naval power belatedly followed by France. Expansion of the national economies in this new European economic core was not compartmentalized, for they exchanged goods, services, and people—not always to mutual advantage. All three shared an interest in expanding exchanges with Spain at its south Andalusian commercial complex and across the Atlantic in the Spanish Caribbean trading zone where export-driven expansion offered Europe's producers and merchants the incentive of economies of scale.[65] Neglected by Spaniards for roughly a century and a quarter, the Caribbean islands now became outposts of penetration established first by the Dutch, then the English, and finally the French. Anglo-French competition for predominance in the economy of Iberian America would last for another century and a quarter ending in great sea battles in the West Indies off the "Saints" in the Lesser Antilles (1782) and a few years later off Spain itself at Trafalgar (1805).

The Netherlands had been the first area of western Europe to profit by Spain's expansion into the western Atlantic. By revolting against the Spanish patrimonial empire in the 1560s, the north Netherlands, or United Provinces, assumed the right to trade illegally in the Caribbean utilizing the islands of Curaçao, Bonaire, and St. Eustatius and later to seize and hold portions of the sugar plantation coast of Brazil's *nordeste* until 1654. Around 1650 the Dutch virtually eliminated the Portuguese as the major maritime power in the Indian Ocean and became the main slave dealers to Brazil and the Spanish empire in America by occupying west African coastal supply points. As a result of its manufacturing output, its entrepôt function between north and south Europe, and its expansion into the western and south Atlantic Ocean and into the Indian Ocean, the United Provinces transformed Amsterdam and its immediate hinterland into Europe's leading commercial, manufacturing, and financial center.[66] Forced to abandon control over Pernambuco, the Dutch transferred their expertise in sugar production and refining to the recently occupied English Caribbean. They supplied the islands with African slaves and, for a time, even equipment and other imports in exchange for raw sugar.[67] Meanwhile the economy of the southern Netherlands (Catholic or Spanish Flanders) continued to concentrate around Antwerp, Bruges, and Ostend, shipping textiles directly to the Sevilla-Cadiz complex or indirectly through France's northern ports. After mid-century, however, both the Flemish and Dutch economies gradually lost their dynamism, and their Caribbean operations were quickly overshadowed by the scope and complexity of English manufacturers and traders.[68]

With the Restoration, English shipping and industry (the latter aided by the immigration of skilled Dutch and French Protestant textile workers) expanded rapidly and pressed beyond traditional sales areas in north and central Europe. Like their Dutch competitors, the English were drawn to Spanish silver flows whose importance mounted after 1660 when sustained trade with southeast Asia was initiated.[69] Early in the Thirty Years War English intermediaries as neutrals freighted reexports of colonial silver from northwest Spain's ports to Spanish armies in the Netherlands and between Barcelona and Genoa where American silver moved overland on the "Flanders Road" to the Netherlands. These contacts led to purchase of Spanish wool for the production of the "new drapery" sold to the Iberian peninsula and reexported through the Sevilla-Cadiz complex into the Caribbean and the Spanish colonies. Aggressive exports of "Spanish cloths" to the Iberian peninsula and the Iberian colonies in America, escaping the limitations of income and demand in Europe, spurred the development of English woolen manufactures and export growth markedly in the closing decades of the century. Following the Dutch to the Caribbean, the English established island colonies for smuggling at Providence, New Providence, and Jamaica. Smuggling was complemented by tobacco plantations, which were soon overshadowed at the end of the century by sugar plantations—the seventeenth-century Caribbean's "absolutely unprecedented social, economic and political institution"—and the inevitable linkage to two major Atlantic capitalist enterprises: rum distilleries in Holland, England, and France and the African slave trade.[70]

Over the first 125 years of Iberian colonialism in America Portuguese slavers were the principal intermediaries between American demand for slave labor and the west African slave coast. The Dutch followed them in the seventeenth century, supplying sugar planters in Brazil's *nordeste* and then English planters in the Caribbean. By the 1660s English merchants in a chartered company brought slaves into the Caribbean. It is noteworthy that the Navigation Acts were adjusted to permit ships from Spanish colonies to enter Jamaica and other English island ports to buy slaves in exchange for silver and staples. With sustained demand for African slaves in the Spanish colonies, English merchants—once they had secured slaving stations on the west African coast—also aimed to bid at Madrid for the state-assigned contract *(asiento)*. By the early eighteenth century the slave trade was "an essential part of economic life in England."[71]

This sequential pattern in relentless pursuit of economic innovation, expansion, and profit prepared England—by the end of the seventeenth century perhaps Europe's most "modern" economy—to become the world's largest trader in forced labor in the eighteenth century or, for that matter, in the history of humanity. Around 1700 English merchants and commission agents were established at Cadiz and in the Caribbean. They had surpassed the United Provinces in manufacture and shipping, extended a hegemonic umbrella over Portugal and its colony in Brazil, and through the hoped-for *asiento,* planned to penetrate the Spanish colonies in America. The major obstacle to this grand design was a resurgent and expansionary France.

French economic expansion lagged behind that of England and Holland. Colbert's economic policy was designed to bring French merchants, manufacturers, and shippers up to English and especially Dutch standards in "steady application to work" and in "economie,"[72] and there is no doubt that in the effort to match and surpass competitors, the role of the French bureaucratic elite was decisive. France's size and defensive needs were extensive. Its population was larger than that of other western European nations, and its armed forces required large-scale state intervention for recruitment, training, and maintenance. To meet administrative demands, a large bureaucracy developed that also supervised basic sectors of the economy, namely textiles, shipping, and, of course, the navy. And like the Dutch and the English, the French directed their expansion toward the principal source of Europe's silver supply: Spain and its American colonies.

Two major avenues of penetrating the Spanish economy were open to French merchants. Oldest and expanding in the last half of the seventeenth century was the seasonal migration of farm workers from southwest France over the Pyrenees and down into Aragon, bringing grains and cattle. There were swarms of French peddlers at Madrid and along the Mediterranean coast as far as the silk-raising area of Valencia. A survey of French nationals in Spain in 1680 turned up 65,000 seasonal workers and residents, 10 percent listed as tradesmen. The second avenue stretched from the ports of Rouen, Saint-Malo, and Nantes to the ports of Lower Andalusia. It was via this route that the French exported the woolens of Hainault, Beauvaisis, and Normandy along with Brittany's linens and laces. To Rouen's merchants, "Linens are the real gold and silver mines of that country, for they are imported only for export to those areas whence come gold and silver."[73]

By 1700 French shipping was already prominent at Cadiz while French nationals figured at Sevilla, San Lucar, Puerto Santa María, and Cadiz. The most enterprising and aggressive merchants and shippers were found at Saint-Malo, and their connections to the higher French bureaucracy were close and effective. They dominated shipping between northern France and Cadiz; they extended their operations overseas into the Caribbean; and they were instrumental in the occupation (1697) of Saint-Domingue in the western half of Hispaniola neglected by Spain. Earlier they had occupied islands of the Lesser Antilles (Guadeloupe and Martinique) and, like the English and Dutch, had engaged in piracy. Saint-Domingue, however, furnished what were most desirable, a base for smuggling operations with Spanish colonies and the chance to develop sugar plantations and their associated enterprise, the slave trade. Saint-Malo and Nantes businessmen backed a chartered company to supply slaves to French Caribbean colonies; and on the accession of Louis XIV's grandson as king of Spain in 1700,

French businessmen received the coveted *asiento* for the Spanish colonies. By then Malouin merchants and shippers were prepared to reopen the passage around Cape Horn in order to push into the Pacific directly to Callao and the capital of the viceroyalty of Peru at Lima, the terminus of silver carried down from Potosí.[74]

Analysis of Spain's decline and the structural changes and geographical shifts in the west European economy during the seventeenth century should not obscure the rapidity of the changing relations of power among regions of western Europe. At the time of the treaties of Westphalia, the United Provinces were the leading economic power in the area, while fifty years later they were an ally of England and a contained antagonist of France. In the same five decades the structural rigidities and generalized underdevelopment of the Spanish metropole and its colonies became an international commonplace. Behind the diplomacy and war in Europe in the latter half of the seventeenth century lay the struggle for access to the source of Spanish silver, colonial staples and overseas markets for Europe's manufactures. There was a Caribbean or West Indian counterpoint in the development of commercial capitalism in England and France and the displacement of the United Provinces in the international economy. In this sense, it was inevitable that the French would utilize every instrument available—exports, shipping, then naval and land forces—to take advantage of their asymmetrical relations with Spain and its American empire.

In the 1640s French manufacturers and merchants at Bordeaux and Nantes complained of the volume of imports of Dutch and English woolens and silks. A decade later Foucquet, Colbert's predecessor, created a protective tariff system, and Rouen and Saint-Malo merchants were heavily involved in exporting textiles to Spain and its colonies. Seeking information about "Spain's trade with its Indies as well as all Europe's trade at Cadiz," the French government in 1658 posted a consul *(commissaire de marine)*, Patoulet, to Cadiz via Saint-Malo to "consult with all the Merchants involved in this trade in order to find out the quality and quantity of goods to be forwarded to Cadiz." By the 1670s French diplomats threatened to use gunboat diplomacy at Cadiz to dissuade Spanish authorities from interfering with French merchants illegally trading with America from that port—"Spaniards realize that France is ever-ready to assert itself by force."[75] French naval authorities in 1680 prepared contingency plans for occupying Havana or Buenos Aires. By the 1690s French merchant communities along the Atlantic coast and their bureaucratic connections could appreciate western Europe's stake in Spain's colonial trade ("the largest and richest ever seen anywhere"), they realized the need to dispel fears that their commercial expansion into Spain's colonial trade would displace Spanish vested interests ("grandees who receive income from the Indies like the duque de Alba . . . the Inquisitor and religious communities which participate in trade . . . as well as merchants"), and they agreed on a French policy objective—"to become the masters of Spain's trade in the Indies as well as in Europe."[76]

Over forty years of economic pressure, diplomacy and cultivation of influential elites in Spain culminated in 1700 when Louis XIV's grandson became Spain's monarch and thereby provided the opportunity to transform Spain and its colonies into a "dependencia."[77] Nothing could be more revealing of French policy than the emphasis in guidelines issued to the French ambassador on his way to Madrid in 1698, advising him that "the most important sector of France's trade in Spain . . . the one bringing in the most silver, consists in shipping French merchandise and manufactures to Cadiz, Puerto Santa María, San Lucar . . . to be loaded aboard the galleons and fleets that sail to the West Indies . . . ."[78]

Despite the shortcomings of France's economic performance under Colbert and his immediate successors, the French state had pushed its commercial communities to the point of serious competition with the English for hegemony over Spain and its colonies, making French merchants residing in Spain the "vanguard of French economic penetration." Colbert's policies perhaps never fused what Luthy has called "state capitalism . . . with the spirit of frugality and austerity of the Jansenist bourgeoisie," nor curbed "idleness, alms-giving, pilgrimages, holidays, convents, rentiers, lawyers." Yet even Colbert's flawed success in generating economic growth in the context of a Catholic monarchy would serve as a model for a later generation of Spanish bureaucrats. In the eighteenth century Spanish economic planners or projectors would attempt to adapt Colbert's strategy for inducing growth by privilege, monopoly, concession, and state subsidy to overcome what Bourbon Spain shared with Bourbon France, "a society both Catholic, nobiliary and backward-looking."[79]

2. Financing Empire: The European Diaspora of Silver by War

. . . .

Tracking the diffusion of Peruvian and Mexican silver under the Spanish Hapsburgs involves pursuing strands of the fabric now perceived as the nascent Atlantic economy. The task is complicated, often elusive, and difficult to quantify. As Felipe Ruíz Martín once wrote: "How can one estimate the amounts carried by couriers . . . during periods of limited licensing . . . or lost in the Pyrenees, Alps, and Apennines where bandits lurked. Shipowners and crews were equally involved."[1]

The patterns of silver mining in colonial Mexico and Peru as well as the complementary structures of the "managed" Atlantic trade forged by Spanish colonialism are now generally understood. Some of the conduits of silver into Europe are well known: the open and covert ways by which importers in Lower Andalusia covered chronic trade deficits with their European suppliers of manufactures, the exchange of silver for goods smuggled from foreign Caribbean ports, and the surreptitious ship-to-ship transfers off the Azores, the Canaries, and Cadiz. In tracing the impact of American silver on Castile's relations with Europe, we may begin to understand the creative but "chaotic fluctuations" that invariably followed the irregular arrivals of silver fleets at Europe's commercial and financial centers at Sevilla, Medina del Campo, Villalón, Florence and Genoa, Besançon, Lyon, Augsburg, Paris, Antwerp, and London.[2] Here our focus is on internal and external ramifications of Castile's initial ad hoc financial practices become policy. As early as 1539 analysts in Castilla's bureaucracy had to report that "we have debts about which we know nothing . . . each day come demands for payment, and we have no record nor account books."[3] Clearly Castile's new international projection now required creating a "serviceable, long-term debt at low rates of interest."[4]

What remains to be assessed is silver's dispersion by warfare on the European continent in the sixteenth and seventeenth centuries. In a general sense the development of north Atlantic Europe was a response to the stimuli of war as well as trade. Pursuit of silver for financing war was the leitmotiv of Castile's Hacienda (treasury) operations under the five Hapsburg reigns in Spain between 1517 and 1700. Continuing warfare was the outcome of the late medieval vision of Charles V ("knight errant lost in the modern world") of a universal Catholic empire centered on Europe, a vision received from his grandfather Maximilian, architect of a revitalized Holy Roman Empire dominated by Austria and emperor from 1494 to 1519.[5] He was committed to Hapsburg dynastic expansionism, championship of the Counter-Reformation and opposition to the pursuit by emergent states of economic and political policies that conflicted with those of the Holy Roman Empire. The basic incompatibility of that vision and commitment with the aspirations for sovereignty of the emergent states in France under the Valois, in England under the Tudors, and briefly in the Spain of Fernando and Isabel provided the underlying reasons for European conflict in the sixteenth and seventeenth centuries. Spain fought the various campaigns that constituted the Thirty Years War to preserve the Holy Roman Empire in Europe *and* its colonies in the western Atlantic.

Once initial protonationalist opposition to the accession of Charles of Hapsburg was overcome by suppression of Castile's Comunero rebellion in 1521[6] and, above all, once Peruvian and Mexican silver appeared in volume at mid-century, Spanish officials had to license large-scale export of precious metals to meet the needs of Charles's military enterprises as well as to advertise Castile's capacity to handle the growing problem of debt liquidation when silver flows were interrupted or when demand exceeded supply.[7] Opening these floodgates enabled Spain to subsidize its European networks of Hapsburg power over the following seven decades in Italy, North Africa, Flanders, Germany, Austria, Portugal, Hungary, and the Balkans by attracting investment in the Spanish public debt by "magnates of public finance, members . . . of high capitalism, [and] isolated members . . . of petty capitalism . . . ."[8] At the same time investment in fixed-interest, short-, and long-term government bonds (*juros* offering the attractive rate of 5–7 percent interest, when Genoa's municipal bonds offered 1.1 percent) by Spain's aristocrats, bureaucrats, merchants, provincial gentry, and enriched peasants as well as by convents, monasteries, cathedral chapters, and hospitals furnished continuing sources of relatively secure income.[9] They added to the justifications of religion, political power, and national prestige, and united supporters of Hapsburg policies in Spain and abroad. Silver built consent if not always consensus.

Never before had western Europe enjoyed the buoyant sense of access to such unparalleled financial resources promising liquidity for both private and public enterprise.[10] In 1598 perhaps as much as 4.6 million *ducados* annually were being paid to *juro*-holders from a budget of 9.7 million; in the seventeenth century, the Hacienda of Philip IV managed to expand the public debt to twelve times Castile's annual revenues.[11] Unloaded from incoming convoys from New Spain and South America, silver came to be perceived as a harvested exportable comparable, for example, to the wool exchanged for Flemish textiles. The perception of silver as crop or *fruto* combined with the Hapsburg conception of a dynastic patrimonial empire linking central Europe, Germany, Burgundy, the Netherlands, and Spain in a kind of international division of labor transformed Castile into the financial core of the Catholic order in Europe. In this context, warfare on multiple fronts from the Mediterranean to the Baltic, from the Atlantic to central Europe justified Castile's long-term borrowing capability based on American silver. In Hapsburg cosmography the role of Spain and its colonial world in underwriting Hapsburg dynasticism and papal hegemony in Europe had little to do with the atrophy of Spanish development relative to that of northwest Europe. If sacrifice there were, it was God-ordained.

From *Cambiadores Públicos* to *Hombres de Negocios: Juros* and *Sacas*

Financial policy emerging under Charles V shaped the general patterns of Castilian state finance until the end of the seventeenth century. The financial needs of the Castilian protostate of the late fifteenth century had been controllable, matching an economy of erratic agricultural output, extensive sheep farming, and a low level of manufacture.[12] Raw wool exports to Flanders' workshops constituted the principal source of export earnings and imported goods. Merchant intermediaries financing wool exports then constituted the majority of lenders to the state. They were what Ruíz Martín has called petty capitalist intermediaries, *regatones* and *colporteurs*.[13] Collapse of the *comunero* rebellion in 1521 together with heavy outlays for Spain's campaigns against French competitors in Italy introduced what became

Spain's characteristically ad hoc, disorganized borrowing practices and the pile-up of the Castilian public debt.

With the influx of precious metals from conquest and occupation of Hispaniola, Mexico, and Peru and the initial output of silver mines in Central Mexico and then Upper Peru, the borrowing capacity of Castile's treasury expanded. Charles's treasury officials could now bypass the limited capital resources of Spanish merchant bankers *(cambiadores públicos)* to tap those of German groups like the Welsers and Fuggers (the latter's fortune came from silver mining in central Germany), of the Flemish Schetz bankers and later those in north Italy: the Spínola, Affaitadi, and Grillo.[14] These "cosmopolitan" bankers in turn were displaced between 1538 and 1557 mainly by Genoese who would maintain their role in Spanish Hapsburg finance until at least the third decade of the next century.[15] Unlike Castile's merchant bankers, foreigners enjoyed access to large pools of capital, understood the credit techniques of the time, could anticipate state borrowing needs and—this was critical—could cope with a discernible, predictable pattern of assured (if often postponed) amortization.[16]

Confidence in lending to the Castilian government was grounded on faith in sustained inflows of silver on both public (royal or crown) and private account, although revenue from Castile's domestic taxation was also significant. According to the official registry at Sevilla, between 1526 and 1555, inflows of colonial precious metals jumped by a factor of 6, from 3.2 million *ducados* per decade to 18.4 million. In one decade, 1536/45 to 1546/55, these imports climbed almost 73 percent.[17]

American mining, however, was only one of Castile's main revenue sources. In the 1540s annual borrowing of about one million *ducados* was also secured on provincial taxes from the Castilian Cortes and by revenues in which rising customs receipts from colonial trade *(almojarifazgo de Indias)* figured prominently. About this time, too (1532–41), the Vatican assigned part of its income from Spain's *subsidio* and sale of *bulas de cruzada* to the Castilian treasury—testimony of its support of Hapsburg hegemony.[18] With the state's failure to broaden the tax base to include privileged groups enjoying exemptions, the tax burden rested on a multiplicity of excise taxes paid by the mass of consumers.[19] By 1539 Hacienda officials managed to liquidate most of the outstanding public debt using domestic revenues supplemented at critical junctures by initial expropriations *(secuestros)* of precious metals arriving from America on private account. In the early 1550s the pattern began to change when Hacienda scrambled for funds to finance Charles's ill-fated siege of Metz. Up to this time, mainly Castilian revenues had covered the "inordinately large expenditures on imperial policy," but it was now becoming clear that "credits granted by [foreign] bankers" could be attracted by returns from the overseas colonies and would continue to be.[20]

The Treasury handled incoming colonial metals shipments through three mechanisms. It received the surplus of colonial treasuries *(cajas reales)* at Sevilla's Casa de Contratación plus a tax on remissions in silver. In addition, when Charles desperately needed cash, Sevilla's authorities were authorized to seize *(secuestrar)* privately owned incoming precious metals, offering in compensation interest-bearing government bonds or *juros* of varying maturities. A *secuestro* is reported in 1523, another financed Charles's amphibious assault on Tunis in 1535, when Contratación sequestered 800,000 *ducados,* offering in return *privilegios de juros* at 3 percent annual interest (far below an open market rate of 14 percent or higher). Other forms of security consisted of *consignaciones* (assignments) or claims on specific revenues *(situados)* such as ordinary excise taxes, cruzada bulls, or the sums paid for offices in the military orders.[21] A *secuestro* was ordered in 1551 when Charles directed agents at Milan to procure loans backed by expected precious metals' receipts from America, at which point his Hacienda officials complained that "nothing remains of all these kingdoms' revenues."[22] At Sevilla treasury officers proceeded to commandeer all silver available including 600,000 *ducados* belonging to passengers returning from the colonies. This coincided with Augsburg bankers agreeing to further loans to Castile providing that repayment were made from what La Gasca brought back from Peru. By then Spain's principal creditors were Europe's great German and Genoese financiers.[23]

A main financial instrument used by the embryonic Castilian state to capture funds for an expansive European policy was the sale of *juros.* Like prior short-term borrowing from the peninsular merchant capitalists, sale of *juros* was becoming a common financial technique in the 1480s. By this time, Isabel and Fernando had lowered their inherited *juro* debt by perhaps half. While they subsequently had to augment the volume of *juro* obligations, the volume of such obligations was to explode under their grandson, Charles V.[24]

Juros represented a certificate of the *privilegio* of participation in a royal debt obligation stipulating "periodic payment of annual interest drawn on royal rents."[25] They were issued in various denominations according to term and source of payment, *al quitar, de resguardo, por vida, por herencia, perpétuo. Juro*-holders knew the specific revenue source of interest and ultimate redemption. Although initially payments came from a variety of revenues, over time, colonial income became the preferred source.[26] *Juros* became a fiscal expedient "impelled by money flowing from colonial springs" which attracted *juro* investors from the fair towns of Villalón and Medina del Campo to Sevilla's Casa de Contratación.[27]

Diffusion of *juros* developed in two phases. Until the late 1550s Castile applied *juro* income mainly to domestic expenditures, limiting sales of *juros al quitar* to Castilians. But once the scale of Spanish Hapsburg entrapment in Germany and Flanders ballooned and foreign policy dictated Castile's fiscal and financial policies, another pattern of response developed. In this second phase, Hacienda turned to corporate bodies holding pools of investible funds, to monasteries and convents, cathedral chapters, hospitals, and chaplaincies *(capellanías)*. The investment pool was extended from a few merchant banking houses like the Schetz (Antwerp) and Fuggers and Welsers (Augsburg) to draw upon the larger pool of Genoese capital. Genoese merchants proceeded to market their *juros* in Spain and elsewhere, encouraged by the Castilian government's readiness after 1566 to issue export licenses *(licencias de saca)* covering precious metals exports.[28] By then the assurance of colonial silver backing for *juros* which were "flooding the fiduciary market" had made *juros* the "most coveted form of repayment."[29] By the early 1550s, this instrument of liquidity made it possible for the Spanish Hapsburgs to bypass the *cortes* of Castile, and in five years (1551–55) more than one-quarter of all colonial receipts over a more than fifty-year period (1503–60) were unloaded at Sevilla.[30]

The rising trend of silver shipments notwithstanding, the economic situation inherited by Charles's son Philip II has been painted as "realms wracked by poverty . . . and on the brink of financial collapse . . . ."[31] Already Castile's treasury officials were—and remained—masters of fiscal brinkmanship. The conjuncture of an accumulated public debt of 25 million *ducados* in 1559 (equivalent to 16 times estimated annual revenues)[32] but offset by colonial silver imports inspired Hacienda officials to attempt to convert a regulatory agency of colonial trade, the Casa de Contratación at Sevilla, into a sort of early state bank. Under this plan, Contratación was assigned working capital for investment in colonial trade in expectation that its earnings might help amortize the public debt over a ten-year period. So-called *juros de la Casa de Contratación* would compensate owners of silver subject to *secuestros* in the 1550s. This exercise in state enterprise lasted only fifteen years, collapsing partly due to bureaucratic incompetence, partly (one suspects) because of the covert opposition of Sevilla's commercial corps, and partly because Hacienda officials had to appropriate Contratación funds to finance the forces suppressing insurrection in Flanders (1576–84).[33]

One facet of all these financial activities merits emphasis. Despite repeated bankruptcies, Philip II, like his father, made the payment of interest (if not always capital) on Castile's public debt a cardinal point of fiscal policy. Unlike the French, who frequently repudiated their debts,[34] Philip could afford to honor at least the backlog of interest due on Spanish obligations because the overseas mining colonies from which he always "awaited fresh income" became a major financial prop. In 1557, for example, 70 percent of military operations against France was financed by American silver receipts. The next year, 85 percent of total state borrowing was guaranteed by the same source; and in 1559 Philip, like his father before him, fell back upon what Rodríguez-Salgado has called the "disreputable policy of taking bullion from New World fleets," commandeering all private-sector incoming silver at Sevilla.[35] Here was tacit recognition that state income could be augmented only minimally by what was becoming standard practice—sale of "vassals, jurisdictions, titles" and most public offices, alienation of state revenues "mortgaged to secure immediate cash loans and by *juro* commitments on a scale hitherto unknown." These practices were the genesis of structures later making it impossible for the Castilian state "to persist with real measures of centralization."[36]

To be more precise, the trajectory of Castile's financial policy over the century after 1550 is foretold by indicators appearing between 1553 and 1559. As servicing the public debt rose from 17 to 44 percent of Castile's annual revenues, colonial income (including sequestrations) as share of such income moved from 22 to 32 percent. To finance Philip's initial military operations in 1557 and 1558, Hacienda had to seize 2.7 million *ducados* from an incoming *flota;* for the next campaign, another *secuestro* netted 1.4 million.[37] There is no exaggeration in asserting that American silver in *secuestros* and (briefly) *juros de la Casa de Contratación* represented at one time "enormous fiscal reinforcements."[38]

Second, while the volume of *juro* obligations nearly doubled, the share of the most negotiable and hence desirable type (*juro al quitar*) was 75 percent. Here was a positive correlation between public debt, rising *juros al quitar,* and the role of colonial funds in Castile's revenues.[39] So Sevilla became the main office for handling *juros,* whose volume achieved a "scale hitherto unknown" reflecting the "craving for *juros* as preferred investment." At the century's end, these instruments—now the foundation of Castile's long-term debt—allowed Spain's "clases privilegiadas" to live off interest income, while Castile's Hacienda turned over to the private sector oversight of fiscal operations which "its own ministers had proved unable to handle."[40]

War Finance: An Appetite for Silver

In the half-century (1598–1648) following the reign of Philip II there were repeated financial crises as the domestic and colonial resources of Castile were absorbed in what Spain's political class envisioned as a winnable war—the conflict with the Dutch Republic that was renewed in 1621. This coincided with what became after 1631 a downward inflexion in the already unreliable official registry of incoming silver at Sevilla.[41] War with France commencing in 1635—"año decisivo"—worsened the financial situation. Five years later came uprisings in Portugal and Catalonia that Pierre Chaunu has called "the great crisis . . . that dragged in its wake the grandeur of the Spanish empire." By 1640 it became clear that Spain had receded as the European hegemon, and insiders recognized the country's reliance upon colonial silver to fund warfare. Silver continued to settle perennial trade deficits with Spain's suppliers in northwest Europe and, in particular, expenditures on military forces—wages, arms, food, and transport. A "monetary hemorrhage" flowed from Spain into Europe as "letters from Italy, Germany, and Flanders clamoured for . . . shipments of what was already the sinew of war," and it was obvious that New World silver constituted the security and stability of the Spanish Hapsburg *monarquía,* a bulwark of the public debt including *juro*-based debt held by financiers (*hombres de negocio*), by Spanish noblemen, merchants, bureaucrats, clergymen, and wealthy peasants.[42]

While American silver on royal account was at minimum between 10 and 20 percent of Philip IV's revenues, its significance was multiple. It provided desperately needed liquidity—although *juro* issues alienated Hacienda revenues—and satisfied financiers who avoided debased copper coinage.[43] When *flotas* arrived intact, Madrid would decree holidays in the largest cities; when one was delayed, the premium on silver soared, domestic trade slowed, and it became difficult to subsidize military operations and supporters abroad. Hence everyone "hurled themselves impatiently on that river of silver."[44] The financial roller-coaster of the Thirty Years War was not due, we are assured, to neglect of Hacienda problems by Philip IV who is reported to have developed a "solid understanding of that complicated book-keeping." As he confessed at one point, "Nothing do I regret more than having to seize silver." Options included appeals to officials, clergy, and businessmen in the colonies for gifts or loans, which frequently ended in renewed sequestrations of silver consigned to Sevilla merchants—*secuestros* compensated by at least 5 million *ducados* of *juros* issued between 1621 and 1640.[45]

Broadly speaking, Spain's appetite for silver was a measure of its preoccupation with defending Hapsburg hegemony in Europe and Castilian dominions in America in the course of what has been likened to the first world war.[46] It was an instance of financial policy dominated by external over domestic considerations. This long-term factor was paralleled by the usual current account deficits with European suppliers of basic imports, such as textiles, writing and printing papers, hardware, glass, and even hawkers' goods, consumed in the peninsula and (mostly) reexported to America. In the late 1640s the deficit was exacerbated by the continued fall in wool exports, while profit margins on other traditional Spanish exports—oils, wines, and dried fruits—dwindled.[47] Further pressure derived from Madrid's policy of putting into circulation debased copper coinage. Naturally, foreign creditors insisted on repayment in silver, and as a result, Hacienda officials often fell back on a standard excuse for avoiding payouts, "we have no more silver than what the galleons bring."[48]

With an understandable yet perverse logic, Madrid's fiscal policy concentrated on augmenting the flow of Peruvian and Mexican silver into the peninsula through the port of Sevilla.[49] One element of the strategy was repeated appeal for monetary gifts and loans circulated throughout the two American viceroyalties. These appeared so frequently that by 1647 the Consejo de Indias referred without hyperbole to the "very steady gifts requested in the Indies."[50] Response came from high colonial officeholders, the wealthy merchant communities of Mexico City and Lima, large estate owners, and from religious corporations. In 1628 the Consejo de Castilla took a different tack, linking expansion of colonial trade, merchants' profits, and the silver needs of Hacienda. Colonial trade held the highest priority ("it is so important to keep") for, were it to decline, "the thread of benefits we draw is severed," reducing the already small number of financiers willing to lend to the government. From this analysis flowed a recommendation which would have broken Sevilla's century-old colonial trade monopoly: extend the privilege of colonial trade to other Andalusian ports. Open the trade to Cadiz, Gibraltar, and Malaga, it was suggested. Otherwise Spain's European suppliers would surely expand their smuggling activities in order to satisfy colonial demand. This radical proposal went no further because Sevilla's oligopolists opposed it.[51] Equally unproductive were renewed efforts to persuade Sevilla's merchants to lend to the government. When Hacienda asked why its merchants were reluctant to lend, the Sevilla merchant guild protested that Spanish merchants did not own incoming silver; they were intermediaries, merely *consignatarios* and *encomenderos*.[52]

Hoping to tax the real rather than the officially registered value of the "waves of silver," Hacienda officials in 1630 properly questioned the accuracy of silver imports registered at Sevilla and insisted on copies of silver registers sent from Lima to Portobelo for transshipment to Sevilla. The Consejo de Indias confessed that its investigating officials proved incompetent, even flag officers of transatlantic *flotas* collaborated in silver smuggling, and concluded that "the issue is so corrupted, that few results could be expected."[53] Twenty-five years later, in trying to compel silver hoarders to convert to copper, Madrid officials ordered Sevilla's notaries to disclose the contents of legal documents that recorded silver that Spanish and non-Spanish merchants alike expected to receive for goods dispatched (often through the connivance of strawmen) to the colonies. They backed down before the combined protests of both the Consejo de Indias and Sevilla's consulado.[54]

Liquidity crises during the Thirty Years War and creditors' hardening insistence upon reimbursement in silver obliged the Treasury to turn to Sevilla's merchants for funds or, failing satisfactory response, to further *secuestros*. Invariably, of course, Madrid vowed to abandon the *secuestro* policy, but the promise was always soon broken. In reaction, Sevilla's businessmen took defensive action by concealing assets to protect their colonial trade operations. It was at best a cat-and-mouse game in which both state and society were long-term losers.

Sequestrations were scarcely novel when the Thirty Years War began in 1619; the Spanish Hapsburgs had established the pattern early in the previous century.[55] In essence, Madrid would approach Sevilla's merchant community and, when funds were not forthcoming or the volume was unacceptable, would appropriate private consignments of silver in exchange for government bonds. Philip IV's regime started out disavowing sequestrations but had to change course. In 1625 Sevilla's merchant community offered a 300,000 ducado loan for the siege of Breda and the Flanders campaign; but when one of two expected *flotas* failed to arrive, Madrid expropriated 40 percent of privately consigned silver already unloaded. In 1630 Madrid again requested financing for an Italian campaign. Sevilla's merchants bargained, offering 500,000 in silver and demanding *juros* of 6 percent annual interest plus jurisdiction over the naturalization of alien merchants operating at Sevilla.[56] Over the next decade both parties joined in the dance of credits requested, funds granted, *secuestros* executed—all in return for *juros* backed by prospective silver imports on government account.

By 1641 foreign bankers were insisting on reimbursement in silver only, while Sevilla's merchants underregistered or, more often than not, simply omitted registering their silver. Or they refused to commit cargo to outbound *flotas* "unless assured their funds would not be appropriated." By agreement between *flota* flag officers and Sevilla merchants in 1641, a *flota* sailed from Veracruz with silver presumably to be registered later *(por regis- trar)* on reaching Sevilla.[57] When Madrid again disavowed its sequestration tactics in the late 1650s, the damage was already irreparable. State policy rooted in expediency had disorganized Sevilla's colonial trade, driving mer- chants into a lasting defensive mode of smuggling and fraudulent record- keeping, now tolerable forms of corruption. In 1649 it was clear that "for some years not a single shipment . . . in coin or bullion had appeared in the registers from America." Eleven years later, efforts to insure compliance with regulations for registry of incoming American silver were formally abandoned. By way of compensation in 1660 the merchant guilds of Se- villa, Mexico City, and Lima consented to a fixed annual silver payment to Madrid. The Thirty Years War along with previous international involve- ments had proven to be a "disastrous piece of business for . . . the Spanish monarchy."[58]

At the onset of Spain's participation in the Thirty Years War, *juros* were still viewed as a sound placement for individual as well as religious corpo- rate investors. To judge by an earlier, very proximate breakdown in 1577, investors preferred readily negotiable *juros al quitar* over other types, which explains the observation concerning "how much exchange rates, usury and interest have taken root among so many" in Spain's early commercial capi- talism.[59] For some financiers speculative *juro* profits could be high; witness the case of Genoese speculator Doria who in 1613 bought *juros* well under par, then proceeded to cash them the following year at par. *Juros,* like mort- gages *(censos),* another popular investment, had come to represent high profitability.[60]

The large *juro* debt increases resulting from the financial requirements of Philip IV's regime were invariably underwritten by optimism about con- tinued receipts of American silver to compensate periodic shortfalls in do- mestic revenues and by bills of exchange that some creditors were autho- rized to present directly to overseas colonial treasuries at Mexico City and Lima, bypassing Hacienda's agents at Sevilla.[61] Madrid also adopted new techniques of *juro* sales—forced sales to bureaucrats (obliged to convert one year's salary to *juros*), assigning *juro* quotas by province, and—a last resort—accepting *juros* when *asentistas* bought tax farms.[62] The ballooning of public debt based on *juros* plus the effects of inflation may be gauged by several measures. Between 1598 and 1621, *juro* capital rose 22 percent (from 92 to 112 million ducados); in 1634 *juro* interest payments alone absorbed perhaps half of Castile's annual revenues; while over four decades of inter- national conflict (1621–67) *juro* interest payments grew from 5.6 to 9.1 mil- lion ducados.[63]

The luster of *juro* investment began to dim in the course of repeated fiscal crises and military setbacks during the Thirty Years War and continued to darken once the war was over. A number of factors discouraged further *juro* investment by individuals who had inherited them as well as by corporate bodies endowed with the charitable assignment of *juros*. Among these were the tactics of Castile's Hacienda bureaucrats, who halved annual interest payments between 1629 and 1659, then totally suspended interest in 1645. In 1677 the state decreed a 50 percent reduction in the nominal value of pre-1635 *juros* and a halving of the interest rate on those issued after 1635. By the 1670s when discounting and reduction of *juros* secured on royal rents began, investors' disillusionment was widespread.[64]

Why Castile's Treasury began, after the mid-1630s, to manipulate what had long been a major source of government finance remains open to conjecture. Following the series of treaties at Westphalia with England and the United Provinces (1645–48) and the settlement with France in 1659, Castile's financial commitments abroad began to contract. This appears to coincide with a decline in the level of official government (but not private) receipts of colonial silver at Sevilla, which remained well below the highs of 1590–1620—hardly an incentive to prospective *juro* investors. Reinforcing Hacienda's shifting *juro* policy was the sentiment that long-held *juros* (many now in the third to fourth generation of *juristas*) had been repaid in interest many times over the initial investment, and that—given widespread speculation—the ratio of fixed interest to declining market price was intolerably skewed.[65] It is no surprise that the early Spanish Bourbon regime chose to cut outstanding *juro* principal by one-third (1703) and in 1718 by a further 33–50 percent. This was a curiously silent financial revolution, a sea change by consensus.[66]

Paths of Diffusion: Italy, France, and the Flanders Road

The silver that often guaranteed *juro* investment was a major factor in Europe's expanding regional and international economy well before 1550. Economic expansion after about 1450 had raised demand for precious metals and renewed exploitation of silver mines in the Tyrol, Alsace, Saxony, Bohemia, and Silesia. Then Peru's and New Spain's mines supplied an extraordinary increase in Europe's medium of exchange. American silver—cheaper to produce than Europe's—was reexported from Sevilla eastward to Barcelona and thence to Florence, Genoa, and the Low Countries, and via northern Spain to the Atlantic ports of southwestern France, and then on to Holland and its Baltic correspondents.[67] Flows of American silver into northwest Europe's regional economies accelerated the monetization of Europe and advanced a market-oriented economy there. They were essential in shifting western Europe's economic axis from north Italy and the Rhone valley westward to the Atlantic. They turned Barcelona and southwestern France (Hendaye and Bayonne) into nuclei of "fraude metallique." They transformed late sixteenth- and early seventeenth-century Genoa into the financial capital of the "siecle de l'argent." And they account for a variety of prized silver coins: Segovia's *ocho reales de plata,* Antwerp's *philippes,* Elizabethan England's four reales of silver, and France's *pièces de quatre reales d'Espagne.*[68] While silver transfers from the peninsula paid for Castile's wars, diplomatic maneuvering, and growing trade imbalances, they also bought grain imports during food shortages such as the severe crisis of 1583–84.[69] Many were the roads along which American silver leaked from Spain into Europe; and there were other circuits by which American silver left Spain for the Middle East, India, and China.[70]

For about a century after 1550 Genoa remained a center for diffusing Spain's American silver. Genoese banking houses lending to Madrid along with those to whom they marketed *juros* had to be serviced. More important, Spain's military forces in the Low Countries in the early campaigns insisted on payment in gold (it was less bulky than the silver equivalent), and Genoa capitalized on its network of banking connections and mastery of international exchange to supply it. For example, French exchange speculators would forward gold coins to Genoa to be exchanged for silver delivered by galleys from Barcelona. Genoa's *hombres de negocio* then forwarded gold for Castile's armies in Flanders. Exchange rates oscillated in tandem with those of Sevilla.[71] It is worth noting that one of twenty-six grandee titles created under Charles II was sold to the Genoese banker Domingo Grillo—incidentally an *asentista* who supplied African slaves to Spain's American colonies.[72] The Spanish government's four bankruptcies between 1646 and 1662, however, led Genoese banking houses to lower their exposure in Spanish finance.

Another highway for exiting silver, at least until 1635, led to western France. Most of the silver crossed the border between Irun and Hendaye and traveled on to the commercial center at Bayonne.[73] Also, imports of Breton grains and Anjou linens were covered by silver exports and, in addition, there were the earnings of thousands of Auvergnat field hands migrating each year into northeast Spain at harvest time. The movement of American silver fueled the regional economies of Bayonne, Bordeaux, La Rochelle, Nantes, and Rennes, which served as intermediaries for Dutch trade with Spain when Holland and Spain were at war. Nor should we overlook Madrid's massive subsidies (1588–1606) to the pro-Spanish Catholic League of the Guise in France, estimated at 600,000 *ecus* annually—"an enormous sum of silver moneys" since the League's soldiery was paid in silver *philippes*.[74] Fortunately there are two crude measures of France's silver imports from Spain during the first 130 years after the first large-scale shipments of American silver were unloaded at Sevilla. In only two of the decades (1631–40 and 1671–80) between 1551 and 1680 did the proportion of silver to total coinage of France's mints fall below an average of 65 percent. Furthermore, at the major mints in west or Atlantic France, Bayonne and Rennes, that proportion remained strikingly high, 84 and 98 percent respectively; together these mints produced almost 65 million *livres tournois*.[75]

A third, and perhaps the widest, artery for the diffusion of America's silver from Spain into Europe was Madrid's use of silver to finance the corps of mercenary soldiery from Spain, Germany, Italy, Burgundy, and the Netherlands recruited to fight the Hollanders in Flanders.[76] As this force expanded, it absorbed a growing disproportion of Castilian revenue. In the years 1572–76 alone, it required fully one-quarter of Castile's revenues to maintain an average of 63,000 men in the field; the percentage surely remained or increased when Philip IV's administration was able to muster a peak force of over 88,000 in 1640.[77] Recruits marched along two main highways: one leaving Genoa and Milan (the "Spanish Road") passed through eastern France; the other traversed Tyrol and Alsace. The two converged in Lorraine to reach the Spanish Netherlands. For decades the Spanish government in a vast logistical enterprise moved thousands of troops often accompanied by women and children; contracted for weapons, food, and clothing; and arranged for mules, horses and carts, wagons, and lodging. Arming these contingents entailed arranging *asientos* with suppliers at Milan, Innsbruck, and Liege. In the seventeenth century, all were paid in silver.[78]

Financing this military enterprise were Madrid's domestic and American silver resources. Direct transfers were made through *asientos* or contracts with Genoese financiers. Indirect sources of silver for paymasters at the Antwerp headquarters came from Dutch merchant bankers, who obtained silver from Spanish shipping "at sea, in the Azores or off Lisbon," which represented earnings on indirect merchandise sales to importers at Sevilla for reexport to Spain's American colonies. In point of fact, in the 1640s when the Flanders army was at its peak strength, ships carrying silver were often detached from returning fleets from America and sent directly to Antwerp for settling the *asientos*.[79] Madrid's contracts for wages, supplies, and billeting of mercenaries in the Army of Flanders ultimately put specie in the hands of European peasants who furnished food and lodging at way-stations or *etapes*. Over the decades that Madrid maintained a military machine in the Netherlands to defend its interests there, American silver was diffused from the peninsula into Europe through north Italy and, via the Spanish Road and the Rhine, into the Netherlands. Annual silver fleets entering Amsterdam from Spain after 1648 made that city the center of Europe's international payments system.[80]

Sovereignty and Privatization

Many were the reasons for the ultimate recession of Hapsburg hegemony in Europe, but beyond doubt the sustained effort to suppress rebellion in the United Provinces of the north Netherlands and retain Flanders drained the resources of Castile and its overseas empire. One must recall that during the thirty years of war Madrid was involved in eliminating Dutch outposts in Brazil and the Caribbean as well as the Dutch Republic in Europe. The collapse of Hapsburg power in western Europe followed a relentless drive to mobilize its resources in America and the Iberian peninsula—in Catalonia and Portugal as well as Castile—while keeping at bay its increasingly threatening rivals, England and France.

Such massive European and overseas entanglement had decisive economic and political consequences. In the first place, Castile was obliged to seek specie by multiplying and raising excise rates and extending taxes indefinitely, commandeering incoming silver, and setting aside preferred state revenues to guarantee obligations owed demanding *asentistas* and bond-holders.[81] Of even greater long-term significance was accelerated sale of aristocratic titles and certificates of *hidalguía* and, above all, alienation of elements of national sovereignty through the sale of seigneurial jurisdictions and public offices at all government levels—"a process of atomization and autonomization."[82] As the state privatized revenues and jurisdictions especially in Castile and Leon to purchasers often paying in *juros,* nobility and aristocracy came virtually to control Castile, while the inflation of noble entitlements expanded tax exemptions and other immunities.[83]

Sale of public office proceeded on an even broader scale in both metropole and colonies. In the last phase of the Low Country debacle under Philip IV, the sale of offices assumed an unprecedented magnitude while under the last Spanish Hapsburg most royal income was alienated.[84] Multiple and rising excises squeezed the mass of taxpayers.[85] At the same time, a large proportion of state income as well as authority was absorbed by "administrators, collectors, receivers, treasurers, notaries, bailiffs, and law enforcers." Buyers of office and entitlement came mainly from moneyed groups: merchants, brokers, businessmen. At Sevilla these constituted a majority of the purchasers of *hidalguías* and municipal offices.[86]

The dissipation of effective sovereignty under the later Hapsburgs can also be traced through alienation of a principal revenue source of the *monarquía*, colonial trade at Spain's most trade-centered city and headquarters of its transatlantic trading system, Sevilla. There Hacienda contracted out the customs of Sevilla *(almojarifazgo mayor)* and arranged *asientos* (with non-Spaniards for most of the seventeenth century) to manage customs collection of colonial trade, the *almojarifazgo de Indias*—a major component of Castile's general revenues *(rentas generales).*[87] Given the impressive income of the *almojarifazgo de Indias,* it was a preferred security, guaranteeing interest payments under the terms of *juros de resguardo,* the fall-back when other designated revenues were overcommitted. In 1583 such *juro* obligations already absorbed most *almojarifazgo* income.[88]

And Madrid had to proceed further in parting with elements of its sovereignty at Sevilla. It privatized bureaucratic posts in the Casa de Contratación;[89] It sold to Philip IV's *valido,* the Conde-Duque de Olivares, the post of *juez conservador* along with the lucrative postmastership of the colonial mails *(correo mayor),* which he in turn proceeded to market.[90] It sold *maestrajes de plata* responsible for registry and general oversight of silver shipments from colonial ports to Sevilla and privatized to Sevilla's merchants, through their consulado, collection and allocation of the tax financing the armament of Atlantic *flotas (avería).*[91] Small wonder that the Consejo de Castilla lamented in 1652 that "the keys to our ports are in the hands of Portuguese and foreigners fattening on profits" which facilitated their involvement in "todo lo prohibido." By 1660, in exchange for an annual lump sum assessed among the merchants of Sevilla, Mexico City, and Lima, "the entire machinery of registration, customs and averia was abolished for cargo from the Indies."[92] Further, the process of selling state authority was extended to the colonial administration. Viceregal posts were sold, and the viceroys were empowered to sell entailments *(mayorazgos)* to wealthy landed estate owners, mine owners, and merchants. The lesser colonial posts of *gobernador, corregidor,* and *alcalde mayor* were also sold, easing the path for merchants in the colonies to enjoy a "privileged authority for their business deals, and to defraud royal rights with impunity."[93] Finally, during the Thirty Years War Philip IV repeatedly had to petition both colonial and peninsular elites for monetary "donations" and loans (preferably interest-free). A supplicant sovereign could hardly function as an absolute one.

There are conclusions to be drawn from the seventeenth-century process characterized as the "progressive dispossession of the state for private gain and the consequent rise of a new aristocracy."[94] War finance backed by the liquidity of colonial silver granted Spain the illusory luxury of pursuing power and grandeur in Europe for a century. Selling its authority and alienating sources of state income, the government at Madrid demonstrated an inability to control public finance and to underwrite the costs of an empire whose dispersion made its defense difficult.[95] More significant, sales of provincial and municipal offices undermined the central government by a process fundamentally "incompatible with the practice of 'absolutism.'"[96] By the end of the seventeenth century, Spain's fragmented Hapsburg administration served a fragmented state where vested interests formed a bloc of consensus maintaining what had become a mutually profitable equilibrium: in other words, the status quo. Over time, the dispersion of silver had unpredicted consequences in Spain's double dependence: on Europe for much of what it consumed and reexported to America and on the colonies for the silver to pay European suppliers and cover state expenditures.

3. Westphalia: The Legacy of Unequal Treaties

In the middle of the seventeenth century, the Treaty of Westphalia established the international law of modern times . . . This treaty assigned to each country its proper place . . . it defined relationships of equality, inferiority, patronage.

Hauterive, *De l'état de la France à la fin de l'an VIII*

In spotlighting the prominent role of foreigners in Spain's commercial exchanges with western Europe and its American colonies, seventeenth-century Spanish analysts recognized both the growth of international trade and, tacitly, Spain's deepening economic backwardness. By about 1700 Spaniards had created a colonial economy which in value of mining product was one of the most profitable in the world. At a moment when European demand for manufactures seemed inelastic, wealthy colonial mining centers were hungry for European imports. Annual rates of return from exports to the Iberian colonies varied between 8 and 15 percent, sometimes reaching 30–50 percent or more.[1] Yet merchants in Lower Andalusia could not draw upon the economy of Spain to supply goods to meet that colonial demand. Nor could the Spanish state provide resources to defend its empire effectively from encroachments by competing powers. The definitive transition from power to inferiority occurred around mid-century with the treaties signed in the province of Westphalia ending the Thirty Years War and the sequence of commercial concessions initiated in 1645. In long-term significance, Spain's commercial concessions far outweighed its loss of political power.

The European treaty system of the last half of the seventeenth century flowed from contradictions in Spain's imperial role. Spain, still an essentially agrarian and pastoral economy whose merchants would not (or could not) follow the Dutch practice of eschewing "middlemen and buying out of first hand," had to draw upon European producers and merchant intermediaries to satisfy the needs of its colonial consumers for manufactures.[2] Nonetheless early in Philip II's reign, Spanish policy aimed to deemphasize the cosmopolitan or open posture toward Genoese and other foreigners in Andalusia, so characteristic of the patrimonial empire of Charles V. In the seventeenth century, however, Spanish colonial commercial policy, which was designed to hold down foreign participation, failed to prevent a rapid increase in the involvement of foreign residents in trade with Spanish colonies. For their part, foreign businessmen wanted legal recognition of their presence and their rights and protection for their persons and property.

A propitious moment for obtaining this recognition came at the end of the Thirty Years War, when Holland and England emerged as the dynamic commercial and manufacturing centers of Europe. They were able to legitimate the ambiguous situation of their merchants who supplied imported goods and financed Spain's colonial trade in the Lower Andalusian commercial system at Sevilla and San Lúcar, Puerto Santa María and Cadiz, through an asymmetrical treaty system thinly masking informal imperialism.[3] The treaty system provided a status of virtual extra-territoriality (likened recently to the "*capitulaciones* [which] protected Europeans in Asia"),[4] that was indispensable as the foreign community niched itself into the Lower Andalusian trade complex, extended its prohibited operations, and extracted from the Spanish state a "treatment more favorable than that enjoyed by its own subjects." Extension of this system after 1650 signaled Spain's constant "dread of superior force" and its spiraling underdevelopment.[5]

The Treaty System

Although the Spanish government had long tolerated resident foreign merchants in Andalusia (the internationally linked Genoese had been accepted since the fourteenth century) Spanish legislation granting concessions to foreigners was spasmodic. In addition, concessions were often made to politically weak "nations." Just before the twelve-year truce (1609) between Spain and the United Provinces, Madrid—recognizing that it lacked the expertise and capital resources of more developed west European economies and eager to "attract them to its ports by treaties which then were favorable"—yielded concessions to the Hanse towns that would reappear in subsequent treaties.[6] These included recognition of Hanse merchant houses at Spanish ports and separate status as a *corps de nation,* the presence of consuls representing the community and their own internal system of adjudication, a forerunner of the judges-conservator. Particularly important were provisions permitting Hanse merchants to utilize their own nationals rather than Spaniards as brokers *(corredores)* and—a keystone to the operations of all foreign resident merchants in Andalusia—the right to export their silver earnings. These agreements embodied many, if not all, the guarantees desired by foreign commercial enclaves in Lower Andalusia; where legal ambiguities in the stipulations subsequently appeared, private settlements were arranged.[7] Within forty years, however, the Hanse towns were insignificant in the Spanish colonial economy; far more significant were the victorious exinsurgents of the Spanish Hapsburg patrimonial state, the United Provinces of the Low Countries.

Madrid's treaty with the United Provinces at Münster in Westphalia (1648) implied equality among signatories when in reality there was none. It incorporated and elaborated the earlier Hanse arrangements. The Dutch were to enjoy the Hanse towns' status—"the same rights, franchises, immunities and privileges" in establishing consuls to protect the status of merchants, factors, ship captains, and sailors (art. xvi). In religious observances Dutch Protestants were to "govern themselves with all modesty, without giving any scandal in word or deed or uttering any blasphemies" (art. xix)— a major religious concession by Catholic Spain. In addition, and in cryptic fashion, there was reference to the Dutch as enjoying the "same security and freedom" conceded to the English in "the last treaty of peace" (art. xvii).[8] As a very perceptive French observer would later phrase it, the treaties signed by Spain provided "merchants . . . with the right to establish commercial houses in Spanish ports, to reside under their consuls' protection, in a kind of independence of sovereign authority, to create an ethnic unit, to enjoy a special court for commercial litigation. . . ."[9]

The critical innovation of the treaty with the United Provinces concerned the Dutch presence in what Madrid had long considered its exclusive Spanish imperium in America: now Madrid had to recognize Dutch possessions in the Caribbean and in Brazil (art. v) although there was to be no trade between Dutch and Spanish colonies (vi). Here is evidence of a novel dilemma as Spanish officials had to countenance the occupation of "soft" or lightly populated areas of the Caribbean by expansionist west European powers. Madrid had to acknowledge the Dutch commercial presence and competition in Spain's Caribbean complex.[10] By extending to the Dutch what had earlier been conceded to Hanse towns (art. xvi), Spain weakened its control over foreign residents and would find it difficult to check fraud and "its economic decadence."[11] To the nominal privileges granted earlier to the Hanse, the Dutch had added juridical rights and, more important still, they had the national mercantile structures and business skills to exploit them.

As befitting a commercial and maritime power not yet the equal of the United Provinces that had remained neutral in Spain's early-seventeenth-century conflicts, England made gains in Spain more modest than those of the Dutch, yet still substantial.[12] In 1605 English commercial interests had managed to obtain concessions not enjoyed by the Dutch and the Hanse towns, even exemption from the jurisdiction of the Spanish Inquisition. This gave religious toleration to English Protestants and, even more important, grounds for resisting what were in fact Spanish commercial pressures masked as religious regulations, since inquisitorial action "often was a cover for investigations of an entirely different nature, motivated by hatred or commercial jealousy."[13] As the probability of a general European peace increased in 1645, Lower Andalusia's English merchant community planned to consolidate an enclave status vis-à-vis Spain's transatlantic trade system. Between March and November 1645, pressure from English merchant interests produced three directives or cedulas issued by the Consejo de Estado laying the basis of special rights for English merchants. The 1645 cedulas consolidated the position that English merchants, shippers, and shipping had acquired in Spain's international trade in the first half of the seventeenth century. They were subsequently amplified in the treaties of 1667 and 1670.[14]

The March cedula, issued in return for a 2500-ducat payment, covered "those which do reside and commerce in Andaluzia, principally in the cities of Sevilla, San Lúcar, Cadiz and Malaga." It enjoined the administrator of customs at Sevilla from incarcerating "men of trade" under suspicion of illicit practices. The administrator could, however, "proceed against [their] merchandizes and not against [their] persons."[15] If customs officials insisted on examining English merchants' business records, they had to specify items under investigation; under no circumstance could their records be sequestered. Once English importers had deposited their goods at the Sevilla customs and their duties assessed, their "bales, packs, trunks and chests" could be moved to their shops. The customs "headwaiter" or his substitute were prohibited from then carrying out search (*visita*) of merchants' properties for items not appearing on registers earlier submitted for customs inspection and from demanding bills of lading that ship captains delivered personally to English importers.[16] Finally, to oversee execution of the cedula's terms and to preside over judicial affairs of the English "nation," Madrid appointed a judge conservator for Andalusia, selecting as its first appointee Francisco de Vergara, a member of Sevilla's *consulado*. The road to collusion was opened.

There followed studied reluctance by two public officials of Sevilla (*juez* and *fiscal de grados*, both close to *consulado* interests) to carry out the cedula. A second cedula (June) insisted upon its execution. In fact, the June cedula was not officially issued since the *fiscal de grados*, Juan de Villalva, simply "kept it in his possession." So a third cedula (November) reiterated the main provisions of the March cedula, adding that the English merchant community would select its own judge conservator. There was also a crucial clarification of the judge conservator's jurisdiction: he could take cognizance of cases involving Englishmen and Spaniards only when the English appeared as defendants—perhaps a concession to objections of Sevilla's merchant tribunal.[17] In brief, members of the English "nation" had acquired immunity from judicial oversight by Spanish audiencias and chancelleries, they were protected from inspection (*visita*) even by Sevilla's municipal authorities, and, moreover, they alone nominated their judge-conservator.[18]

In other ways, too, the November cedula amplified earlier concessions. Now customs personnel had to wait three days following a ship's arrival before inspection (*visita*) could begin, thereby providing time surreptitiously to off-load cargo omitted from the vessel's manifest that was delivered to the Spanish customs. Second, in cases where discrepancies occurred between items listed on manifests (delivered to customs) and bills of lading handed to English resident merchants, ship captains rather than the merchants would be responsible. There was another major amplification in the November cedula: the protection against a *visita* in search of items slipped undutied through customs, originally limited to English firms at Sevilla, was extended to those at San Lúcar, Cadiz, and Málaga.[19]

The significance of these cedulas specifying new rules of the game should not be underestimated. En bloc, their details indicate how the English merchant community forged a network of privilege within which to operate in order to protect imports from England and to participate legally (and illegally, too) in Lower Andalusia's colonial trade. The 1645 cedulas consolidated the prominence English merchants, shippers and shipping acquired in Spain's international trade in the first half of the seventeenth century. During a virtual half-century of international warfare, the English had capitalized on their role as Spain's neutral intermediary, somewhat analogous to that of the neutral United States between 1797 and 1808.

Data for isolated years (1605 and 1622) indicate that the English shipped their own merchandise along with those of Dutch merchants to the "treasure ports of San Lúcar and Sevilla." In 1622, for instance, 80 percent of cargo exported from London to Mediterranean ports went to Spain. Most of it (77 percent) was subsequently reexported to Spain's American colonies.[20] In other words, almost two-thirds of England's exports to the Mediterranean were fed into the Spanish transatlantic pipeline. Starting in 1630 and continuing over the next seventeen years, England's role as neutral carrier burgeoned as English ships entered French, Dutch, and Spanish ports.

The most intense activity came in the decade, 1635–45, when not only Holland but also France warred against Spain while England "became the major carrier of Spanish silver coin and bullion to Flanders." As an English contemporary put it pithily, it was a "known truth, that wheresoever silver is imported, the rest of the trade must follow."[21] Dover became the transfer point for English shipping to north and south Europe, the latter constituting the main theater for English commercial expansion. To supply Spanish military operations in Flanders, military contractors *(asentistas)* at Madrid forwarded silver coin and bullion to English carriers proceeding to Dover; there, one-third continued to Dunkirk under English convoy, two-thirds to the London mint where it was sold to English merchants for bills of exchange payable in Flanders. Although perhaps "less than a tenth . . . ever got near the London mint," there was an extraordinary rise in the amount of silver coined in the decade, 1637–47; the highest annual levels at London came in the six years, 1641–47.[22] Meanwhile English ships and crews penetrated the Iberian commercial lifeline to the colonies. They joined Portuguese convoys between Lisbon and Brazil and participated in shipping between Sevilla and the Caribbean because the English offered freight rates "six times lower than the Spanish could provide."[23] The record of these years underscores the importance of the Spanish trade and, through Spain, of America to England's commercial expansion before English mercantilism was formalized in the navigation acts of mid-century. The Dover transit traffic was significant: in 1638 traffic between Dover and Low Country ports, Spain and the western Mediterranean was almost as large by value as all London's exports in 1640. For selected years between 1633–48, Dover's reexports to all Spanish ports formed the bulk (58 to 87 percent) of all shipments to south European destinations.[24] In the decade after 1635 when France was at war with Spain, and French linens along with sailcloth (widely used in Spain's colonial shipping for sails and sacking) were barred from Spain, English merchants resident in Spanish ports purchased lucrative licenses to import prohibited French manufactures.

By 1651 the liquidity of English merchants led them to contemplate engrossing the entire Spanish wool clip to deprive Dutch, Flemish, and French manufacturers.[25] Earnings from Dover's reexports along with invisible earnings in port-to-port shipping and smuggling so augmented the wealth of London's merchants that, despite a domestic recession (1641–46), they managed to lend Parliament funds to equip the New Model army.[26] Here as in other ways, London merchants laid the ground for Cromwell's expansionary policy, penetrating into the center of the Spanish empire in America, the Caribbean.[27]

Over the next twenty-five years English merchants fully capitalized on their Andalusian treaty beachhead of 1645 to protect their commercial operations throughout Spain and simultaneously have Madrid recognize their territorial expansion in the Caribbean. In the 1660s the English economy entered a phase of renewed expansion, political stability was reestablished and the drawing power of Spain's American colonies proved irresistible.[28] Madrid had solid reasons to come to terms with the English, because the occupation of Jamaica (1655) and smuggling activities there had depressed the sales of merchandise freighted by Spain's *flotas* and *galeones*.[29] In two treaties (1667, 1670), the English matched Holland in access to Spain's trade in Europe.[30] The "privileges and immunities" granted the English in Andalusia in cedulas of 1645 were extended to English "trading, buying and selling" in Spain and Spain's European possessions.[31] The formalities of ship arrivals as in 1645 received detailed attention. Unregistered merchandise, discovered aboard ship after a bill of lading had been sent to customs indicating that the whole cargo would shortly go ashore, was no longer subject to automatic confiscation until eight days had elapsed, "to the end that the concealed goods may be entered and the confiscation of them be prevented."[32] Moreover, only unlisted items (not the whole cargo) might be subject to confiscation.

Virtually at the end of the treaty of 1667, "the first and great commercial treaty between England and Spain," came the English merchants' coveted goal, the equivalent of the most-favored-nation status obtained by the United Provinces in 1648 and by the French in 1659—"the same privileges, securities, liberties and immunities, whether they concern their persons or trade, with all the beneficial clauses and circumstances which have been granted, or shall be hereafter granted"(art. xxxviii).[33] Apparently Sevilla's merchants balked at executing article ix (providing for a judge conservator) and at article xxxviii (awarding most-favored-nation status. Consequently Madrid had to issue a cedula in 1670 forcing Sevilla's notary, Andrés Pérez de Mansilla, to register and, moreover, publish the articles, further testimony to the fragility of Spanish "absolutism."

Madrid had to accept another sign of political and economic inferiority in 1670 as well. In the so-called "American" treaty, English interests (like the

Dutch earlier) now obligated Madrid to recognize the altered situation in the western Atlantic, where the English were exploiting Caribbean island footholds to trade illicitly with the Spanish colonies. The brevity of the treaty and of article viii in particular ("The King of Great Britain shall hold and enjoy all the lands, countries, &., he is now possessed of in America") misled no one. And while trade between respective colonies remained prohibited (art. ix), the English intended to interpret this broadly by welcoming Spanish shipping entering their colonial ports for whatever reason.[34]

The changes, first in the United Provinces and then in England, that laid the bases for the policies and institutions of the mercantilist state and economy caused a definitive shift in the locus of Europe's economic development in the seventeenth century. The third nation to follow a pattern of stepped-up commercial development was France. Like their predecessors, the French also focused upon establishing a privileged position for their community in Lower Andalusia and, through it, Spain's colonies in America.

French interest in Spain and its colonies had developed in the early decades of the century. At mid-century, however, while the Dutch and English were at peace with Spain, the French—seeking to expand on two fronts, over the northern edge of the Pyrenees and into the towns and countryside of Flanders—were at war with Spain. In 1646 when the possibility of a settlement arose, the French government called upon the leading merchants of Saint-Malo and Rouen then trading with Spain to formulate the basic issues in contention. Their preoccupations were probably collated by a French consul in Spain, a long-term merchant resident there. Not unexpectedly they resembled those of Dutch and English competitors: choice of community representatives *(protecteurs et directeurs du commerce et navigation)* with internal jurisdiction over the community; protection against arbitrary *visita* by customs officials or inspection of private business documents; confiscation of illegal imports but not of the entire shipment in which they were included; the right to travel and conduct business, including exemption from obligatory recourse to Spanish brokers *(corredores)*, and the right to export silver. Not until 1659 were these objectives realized.[35]

The treaty of the Pyrenees culminated more than fifty years of French commercial growth in Spain and, like the English treaties of 1667 and 1670, laid the legal basis for more than another century of operations there.[36] Under its terms, French merchants, shipmasters, pilots, and crewmen were safeguarded against arbitrary imprisonment (art. ix). Goods illegally embarked for export were subject to confiscation only in the fashion "hitherto practiced in such instances affecting the English, or . . . the Dutch, according to the Treaties made with England or the United Provinces (art. vii)."

Smuggled and prohibited items were liable to confiscation, "but neither the ship . . . nor . . . other properties . . . found aboard the same vessel, may in any way be confiscated (art. xviii)." Business documents could be written in French (art. xxv).

On the other hand, reference to consuls is oddly brief and vague unlike the detailed status stipulated in Anglo-Hispanic treaties, and more curious still, inviolability of domicile and the establishment and role of judges-conservator were omitted. Nonetheless, article vi granted French "subjects, tradesmen, rural and urban residents" the same "privileges, franchises, liberty and security as French merchants." Only in 1662 did Madrid authorize judges-conservator for the French. At the same time, at the urging of French merchants, civil and criminal jurisdiction over their community was assigned to Spain's Consejo de Guerra on the presumption that Spanish military officers would identify with their French counterparts and thereby somehow identify with French interests.[37]

In essence, the security of French resident merchants was strengthened while their involvement in illegal operations became more difficult for Madrid to control. The French in the Treaty of the Pyrenees gained what French consul Catalan called "liberté de commerce."[38] This turned out to be hyperbolic, however. Over the remainder of the century, French traders in Spain remained particularly vulnerable. They formed *the* preeminent foreign trading bloc in Spain's transatlantic system, but during a series of Franco-Spanish conflicts (four in twenty years, 1669–89), their goods remained subject to inspection and confiscation. Freedom from what they considered arbitrary search remained a primary concern.[39]

The Treaties Applied

Microanalysis or *explication de texte* of the treaty system imposed by her trading partners as Spain's economic stagnation deepened in the late seventeenth century can perhaps highlight those clauses essential to the subsequent operations of foreign merchants in Sevilla and, later, Cadiz. The meaning of seemingly parallel treaty clauses on commercial and shipping issues in fact varied with the logic of power between Spain and England or Holland or France. The "privileges" conceded to foreign merchant communities ("nations") covering their rights of residence, consuls and judges-conservator, the handling of their shipping, incoming cargoes, and smuggling infractions did provide protection. In fact, such privileges turned out to be a means of entry for foreigners, beachheads for penetrating Spain's major economic region, Lower Andalusia—more specifically, the Sevilla–

San Lúcar–Puerto Santa María–Cadiz triangle. While Dutch, English, and French mercantile groups all had the goal of increasing their shares in Spain's colonial markets—satisfying the demand for goods and obtaining silver—in other ways they differed. Holland and England, for example, had relatively few nationals in Lower Andalusia; their leading economic sector, the textile manufacture, was advanced relative to France's; their shipping and navies were large. By about 1660, both had established territorial outposts strategically located for illicit ("interlope") activity in Spain's main overseas commercial complex, the Caribbean. France, on the other hand, with thousands of migratory workers in Spain,[40] lacked the maritime resources of its English and Dutch competitors. Only its linen manufacture was well developed, and—a crucial difference—it still had no strategically located island deep in the Caribbean.

These fundamental differences had long-term significance. For example, since France—unlike England—lacked a Caribbean base close to a major Spanish Caribbean port, the French had to exploit relentlessly the "rights" of their commercial enclave in Lower Andalusia. For their part, Spanish merchants and public functionaries tended to overreact to what they interpreted as French economic imperialism. As for the English after 1667, they could and did employ double-pronged pressure in Lower Andalusia and the Caribbean. In this sense, perhaps England's most strategic territorial acquisition in the seventeenth century was Jamaica, intended initially as a commercial entrepôt rather than a plantation enterprise. With the recession of Dutch maritime power counterbalanced by England's export expansion and naval forces, Madrid had to weigh the threat of the French military against that of English naval forces. The international dynamics of the late seventeenth century rendered the Spanish empire doubly vulnerable as Spanish policy-makers foresaw war in the peninsula *and* the Caribbean. It was prepared for neither.

The treaty system, therefore, thinly disguised Spain's growing incapacity as a European and colonial power. Equality of privilege formalized by the treaty system was illusory. In fact the treaties opened the way for both English and French commercial expansion into Lower Andalusia's colonial trade; they were imposed to legitimize illegal commercial activity.

Treaty clauses formed a web of legitimization of fraud in which profits were distributed unequally between foreign mercantile enclaves in Lower Andalusia and the Spanish bureaucracy. Today, we consider external domination without territorial control "informal imperialism;" in this sense Spanish interests in the public and private sectors shared responsibility for

Anglo-French informal imperialism in late seventeenth-century Spain. The political and social status of judges-conservator handpicked by French and English enclaves in Lower Andalusia is revealing. Repeatedly these communities chose prominent, strategically influential Spaniards—governors of Sevilla or Cadiz, captains-general, *oidores* (judges) of *audiencias* and *chancelleries*—"whom low level judges would not dare confront." Characteristically, the office of judge-conservator merited "gifts" *(donativos)* that offered to improvident and impoverished nobility opportunities to restore their fortunes. In return, the Spanish judges-conservator were expected to "favor those whom they sponsored, who thereby could dare to defraud the treasury and break laws on foreign trade."[41]

The pattern of judge-conservator appointees established webs of protective linkages between foreign merchant enclaves and Spanish influence-wielders. At Sevilla, in 1645, the English nominated (and Madrid appointed) as judge-conservator Francisco de Medrano, *oidor* of the Audiencia of Sevilla, who was replaced three years later by another *oidor,* Jerónimo del Puyo Araciel. Appeals of their decisions went to the Consejo de Estado at Madrid. At Cadiz in 1664 the French picked as their judge-conservator the port's governor, Antonio Pimentel; their appeals were channeled to the Consejo de Guerra. It should come as no surprise that at one point the French proposed as judge-conservator the Consejo de Guerra itself. When there were objections, they selected García de Torres y Silva and later José Pardo de Figueroa, incidentally both members of the prestigious Consejo de Castilla and *asesores* of the Consejo de Guerra.[42]

Farming Andalusia's Customs: Báez Eminente

Using the commercial treaty system that established their formal presence in Lower Andalusia's import-export sector, foreign commercial enclaves aimed to insulate their often patently fraudulent activities from Spanish judicial retaliation. Selection of judges-conservator was one technique; another, and perhaps most effective for bypassing colonial trade controls, was infiltrating the regional customs and revenue collection system.

The basic duties imposed by Spanish customs were Sevilla's *almojarifazgo mayor* (5 percent import duty) on foreign trade and the *almojarifazgo de Indias* (also 5 percent) on colonial trade flows. European imports were dutied *ad valorem* based upon official values *(aforos)*. After 1624 the *almojarifazgo de Indias,* under an arrangement worked out between Sevilla's consulado officials and farmers of the customs *(asentistas),* was refined: bales *(fardos aforados)* of high-value imports would pay by weight *(arroba)*, bulkier, low-value goods in chests *(caxones toscos)* by volume.

Curiously, by the 1660s aggregate charges on goods entering Sevilla were higher than at Cadiz, a factor but not the only one accounting for the expansion of Cadiz's traffic at the time.[43] More important was Cadiz's large outer bay, which provided ideal conditions for large-scale smuggling. Directly across the bay north of Cadiz lay Puerto Santa María at the mouth of the Guadalete River, gateway to Xeréz and Sevilla. By mid-century Puerto Santa María was already the preferred residence of Genoese, Navarrese, and French merchant families. Its smuggling role was, if not yet legendary, at least well recognized.[44]

At mid-century, too, Spanish administration of the Sevilla customs house was in flux. In 1647 after the first cedulas covering English residents in Andalusia appeared, tax farmer Simon Rodríguez Bueno tightened administration and modified duties, dispatching employees without forewarning to search commercial records and warehouses, and revising upward official values *(aforos)*. Then in 1661 Madrid abandoned farming out Sevilla's customs. This resulted in a marked fall-off in collections, and two years later Madrid restored the tax farm—yet another indication of the state's incapacity and its long-term tendency to permit private initiative to invade the sphere of the bureaucracy.

Francisco Báez Eminente ("crafty Hebrew") bought the farm of *almojarifazgo* and related tax collections of Andalusia in 1663. This *asiento* remained in his family for the next five decades.[45] A Jewish convert to Catholicism (hence a *marrano*), he was part of the Portuguese merchant banking group with Dutch connections used by the Conde-Duque de Olivares. *Converso* merchants with the name of Báez and Báeza were also in New Spain in the 1640s.[46] Báez Eminente's selection as *asentista* of Lower Andalusia's tax system suggests the Spanish state's dependence upon the financial links and expertise of Sephardic families which, expelled from Spain, had moved to Portugal and then on to Holland. International links, language skills, liquid capital, and command of business techniques made them natural intermediaries between Madrid and Amsterdam. It was not unusual in the seventeenth century to find Sephardic and *marrano/converso* families as tax farmers in Andalusia, consultants to Spanish authorities on the United Provinces, merchants overseas in New Spain, and slave dealers representing the Dutch West India Company at Cartagena de Indias, Curaçao, and Jamaica.[47]

Báez Eminente proved remarkably flexible and effective in handling the Andalusian customs. A conjunction of factors created a climate favoring illegal imports and exports in colonial trade. A cedula (1660) eliminated the official registry of imports from the colonies *(registro de venida de Indias)*, which did not prevent Sevilla's merchants making independent estimates of imports.[48] At the same time, treaty clauses permitted English, Dutch, and French vessels anchored at Cadiz to escape careful monitoring, leading Eminente to complain of virtual floating warehouses *(navires magasins)* loading and unloading without control.[49] Finally, these conditions favored the appearance of gangs of from 50 to 100 men in so-called *compañías de metedores* organized and led by "young gentlemen, second sons of the country's finest households," *(segundones)* whose social status exempted them from local criminal jurisdiction. Cases of smuggling involving them came under the jurisdiction of the Consejo de Guerra (also, it will be recalled, responsible for cases involving members of the French merchant enclave).[50] As a French report summarized the situation: "Formerly there were no regulations covering operations in the bay of Cadiz. Cargo was transferred with impunity from one foreign vessel to another about to sail to the Indies; customarily merchants filed a *guía* in the amount of 200 while loading 1000 [pesos]. Abusive practices were equally widespread in the city, where the purpose of the 'Ministry of *Metedores*' was smuggling in exchange for an agreed-upon fee. The City's leaders, often including the very respectable, engaged in such practices and were held in awe by [customs] personnel fearful of the consequences of carrying out their duty. They were silent spectators of such highway robbery."[51]

Eminente developed a two-stage strategy to reduce incentives for smuggling by Spaniards collaborating with foreigners. He lowered official values *(aforos)* by 25 percent *(cuarto de tabla)*, even changing *aforos* daily (some claimed) or making special arrangements with certain merchants. Duties on imports destined for reexport to the colonies were also cut (to 2.5 percent), while goods entering the domestic market continued to pay 4 percent. These Eminente supplemented with across-the-board reductions on the quantity of imports dutied *(gracia de pie de fardo)*.[52]

He also worked out a solution for the *metedores,* the "really dominant figures in the Indies traffic." Probably at his request, the president of the Consejo de Indias (Pedro Núñez de Prado) removed the official in charge of policing their activities. His replacement received from Eminente 1000 ducados annually to exert his authority over the *compañías de metedores;* rumor had it that the payment came from the 4–5 percent that merchants formerly paid *metedores* to handle their cargo.[53] Overall, through appointments to the customs bureaucracy and influence in the Casa de Contratación and the Consejo de Indias, Báez Eminente created a web of patronage. It is not surprising that his hand-picked administrator of the Sevilla customs later became (1684) president of the Casa de Contratación.[54]

These techniques applied to the foreign merchant enclaves of Lower Andalusia represented the first phase of Báez Eminente's administration. They helped divert foreign trade from Sevilla to Cadiz to such an extent that in 1679 Cadiz merchants supported the *asentista*'s plan to provide a *donativo* to Madrid to move the customs administration from Sevilla to Cadiz.[55] At this moment Báez Eminente unveiled his second stage of customs revamping. A series of private agreements *(convenios)* were made with foreign resident enclaves covering their largest imports. The *convenios* may have commenced with the French as early as 1668; in any event they were in effect with English, Dutch, and French groups by 1680. Under such unpublicized but operative arrangements, for example, English merchants received at customs an across-the-board reduction in official values *(en la hoja)*, and certain imports had their volume reduced by 25–60 percent for duty purposes. These specific duty reductions reveal the well-thought-out and pragmatic nature of Báez Eminente's customs administration. Imports of English woolens, spices, silks, and lace were thus favored, and comparable reductions were granted to French linens, beaver-skin hats, and lace.[56]

The impact of the *convenios* should not be minimized. While imports of cheaper, low-quality Silesian linens remained dutied at 12 percent, better quality French linens paid only 2–5 percent, making the export of Breton and Norman linens "the most valuable branch of their Spanish trade" and laying the foundation for France's capacity to compete with other European producers in Spain's colonial markets. French importers in Andalusia considered these "privileges the foundation of their trade in Spain, without which they could not survive."[57] Báez Eminente's strategy of arranging unpublicized deals with foreign merchant groups at Cadiz was made palatable by conceding to Cadiz and other Andalusian ports a percentage of annual customs revenues, a practice apparently long tolerated (and hardly unknown) by Madrid authorities.[58]

Báez Eminente's *convenios* formed a paralegal pattern of commercial "treaties" paralleling the official treaty system. They provided mutual if unequal rewards. The customs *asiento* was profitable enough that his firm administered it for two generations, and Madrid was guaranteed at least an annual minimal revenue from its most reliable and highly liquid sector, colonial trade flows. The greatest advantages accrued to foreign resident merchants, for combined reductions in the volume of dutiable imports and official values lowered the effective spread of duties to 5–12 percent, well below the 21 to 25 percent that had been charged before.[59] So satisfactory was this parallel system to Báez Eminente and his group that in 1688 Sevilla's *consulado* submitted its own bid for the customs *asiento*, but Madrid rejected it. Sevilla's consortium may have tried to take advantage of an inquiry by Inquisition authorities against Eminente in 1691, but the inquiry was suspended. In fact the house of Báez Eminente survived well into the reign of Philip V.[60]

Further strengthening the parallel system engineered by this *asentista* was the fact that for most of the eighteenth century—actually, down to Spain's first national tariff reforms (1778–1782)—both the English and French governments insisted on maintaining both the official system and the unofficial *convenios: cuarto de tabla, pie de fardo,* and, of course, the much reduced *aforos.*[61] From the viewpoint of the foreign merchant enclaves, treaties and *convenios* were highly effective. In 1686 fully 94 percent of the value of cargo shipped to the colonies on *flotas* and *galeones* consisted of non-Spanish goods.[62] Foreign pressure on Madrid can be explained in large measure by the sheer value of Cadiz's exports to the colonies: estimated at 7 million pesos per annum (1667–68), it equaled approximately two-thirds the value of Amsterdam's exports. Together, paralegal agreements and formal treaties had created an atmosphere in which well-capitalized foreigners in the last half of the seventeenth century exploited Spain's transatlantic trading system at transfer points in Lower Andalusia. "Seen from Cadiz," as Morineau has put it graphically, "exploiting America via the *Carrera* [Indies' trade] was big business involving half of Europe, from Genoa to Hamburg."[63]

Foreign Enclaves in Lower Andalusia

While economic stagnation and some contraction persisted in late-seventeenth-century Spain, foreign and colonial trade through Lower Andalusia's ports remained the motor of the metropolitan economy and by extension of western Europe.[64] Activity in Lower Andalusia continued to oscillate with the periodic departure of convoys to the Caribbean and their return with cargoes consisting mainly of silver. American silver passing through Sevilla and Cadiz favored trade compartmentalization and oligopoly there. Lower Andalusia became a commercial center of Europe, "a rich land, entry point for precious metals . . . a province particularly penetrated by foreigners." In a perverse inverse fashion, "the more Lower Andalusia's commercial role became passive," a recent Flemish scholar has said, "the more Spain and its colonial appendage stimulated Europe's economy."[65] Sevilla and now the bay and port of Cadiz had become the pivot of European and Spanish colonial trade.

Instead of serving as a potential dynamic factor in Spain's domestic economy, Lower Andalusia's trade flows were a magnet drawing non-Spaniards: Genoese, Flemish, French, and English merchants.[66] For many reasons, merchants from Catalonia, patrimonial Spain's most economically developed area in the late fifteenth century, had failed to establish a foothold in Lower Andalusia after the occupation of America. Overland movement of goods was expensive, coastal navigation was subject to North African corsairs, and Castilian bureaucrats treated Catalans from Barcelona as virtual foreigners lacking capital and credit. "The greatest beneficiaries of the treasures of the Indies," Vilar has aptly concluded, "were those who loaned to royalty on the basis of this immense security. Since Barcelona had abandoned its role as banker to the sovereigns by the end of the fourteenth century, they lost opportunities for profit along with power to influence."[67]

Despite banking and financial operations by foreign firms in Spain and their influence on economic policy, Spain's businessmen might arguably have developed a manufacturing capacity in Lower Andalusia to compete with European imports in their colonial trade. However, colonial trade in the sixteenth century provided no stimulus for sustained growth, much less development, to Lower Andalusia's woolen and silk manufacture which—lacking a determined protectionist policy and confronting foreign competition—virtually disappeared by the seventeenth century. Alternatively, over the long run, lacking competitively priced domestic goods for colonial consumers, Castilian businessmen might have ordered through their own agents directly from producers abroad. Here Castilians, despite *arbitrista* hand wringing, would not or could not break into the tightly knit networks of producers and distributors in Europe's early commercial capitalist economy.[68] Foreign merchants, with the capital and business skills Castilians lacked, maximized their advantages to favor artisans in the homelands whence they had migrated and where they returned with savings, business expertise, and connections they could transmit to the next generation who then often completed the circle by training at Sevilla or Cadiz. As was later noted of the guano export enclave in nineteenth-century Peru, " . . . a thriving export industry could operate for decades alongside a stagnating poverty-stricken domestic sector."[69]

Foreign merchant enclaves structured like family enterprise formed culturally and economically hermetic undertakings, maintaining security by relying upon speaking and keeping business records in their native tongue, recruiting among their ethnic group, and buying primarily from producers at home. There was a constant capital drain, therefore, from Lower Andalusia to Italy and the Low Countries, to France and England. No surprise, then, that when the wife of the duque de Medina Sidonia—aristocrat and grand seigneur with jurisdiction over San Lúcar, a gateway to the Indies— entered that town, she was greeted by cheering "cuadrillas de ingleses, portugueses y flamencos."[70]

Great entrepôts, like nature, abhor a vacuum and toward the mercantile vacuum of Lower Andalusia foreign businessmen inevitably gravitated. Data on foreigners in the Sevilla-Cadiz axis over the seventeenth century show a record number of foreigners naturalized "para comerciar a Indias." Flemish (98), Portuguese (91), Genoese (42), and other Italians (19) formed the majority (80 percent) or 250 of a total of 310.[71] The Flemish and Genoese had established a strong presence and early on profited from Iberian expansion into the Atlantic, while Portugal's incorporation into the Spanish imperium (1580–1640) accounts for the Portuguese contingent.[72] Of greater and growing economic importance would be French (23) and English (5) merchants.

More telling is the chronological distribution of naturalizations: fully 58 percent (179 of 310) were issued in 25 years, 1625–49, decades of relative stability in the schedules of colonial convoys just prior to the disrupted sailing schedules of the last half of the century. Unfortunately, chronological distribution by country of origin is not available nor is there a listing of Spaniards trading with the colonies at this time. At best there is Abbé Vayrac who, in 1718, found "Navarrese, Biscayans or residents of the outskirts of Cadiz and Sevilla who sail aboard *galeones* and *flotas* with a small assortment of goods, or responsible for those of foreign merchants, and return from the Indies with considerable wealth." These Spaniards were, however, really agents of Lower Andalusia's foreign resident merchants. As Veitia Linaje had noted earlier in 1672: "Because we neither favored, fomented nor rewarded [Spanish] merchants, most of our trade is now in the hands of foreigners who dominate them, becoming wealthy and ennobled by what we disdain."[73]

In the second half of the seventeenth century, the locus of the colonial and European entrepôt trade of Lower Andalusia was shifting—in fact, if not in law—from Sevilla, on the meandering Guadalquivir 50 miles above its mouth at San Lúcar, southward to the bay and port of Cadiz. Silting of the Guadalquivir and the bar at San Lúcar made passage of large ships of the Atlantic trade dangerous, while the distance upstream to Sevilla and the limited anchorage there caused further impediments to shipping. Other factors dictated the shift: the growing burden of customs charges,[74] repeated state confiscation of incoming silver, and interruptions by war at sea along with the lobbying of Cadiz merchants enhanced the natural attraction of the bay for illegal transfers of colonial cargo.[75] In the decentralized so-called absolute Hapsburg monarchy, local interests at Cadiz could, at their own discretion, enhance the attraction of their port by independently reducing export duties below those of Sevilla.[76]

The Bay of Cadiz was in effect a bay within a bay, a broad enclosed harbor some thirty miles in circuit opening on the north into a larger and more open outer bay with anchorage for many ocean-going vessels. On the west a five-mile tongue of land separated it from the Atlantic Ocean; on the north, it was separated from the outer bay by a headland jutting out from the mainland whose irregular coastline curved south and then west to form the bay's eastern and southern shores.

Seventeenth-century Cadiz, located on the rocky northern tip of the narrow promontory, dominated entry into the wide outer bay as well as the narrow entry into the Cadiz bay. Surrounded by water on three sides, it commanded a broad view of the Atlantic to the west. On the north, across the entry into the outer bay, it faced the distant promontory at Rota; to the east, directly across the outer bay, it was in sight of Puerto Santa María. Cadiz's other link to Puerto Santa María and then north to Sevilla and Madrid was by a circuitous road that wound south, east, and then northward around the bay. And even this link could be severed when storm-driven tides invaded the low-lying channel *(cortadura)* at the base of the spit, temporarily connecting ocean to bay. Understandably the adjacent area was named the Isla de León, while Cadiz was often referred to as the "lsland of Cadiz." Cadiz's peculiar geographical situation played a significant role in the history of Spain's colonial trade and thereby in its relation to the rest of Spain.[77]

The rocky promontory sheltering Cadiz from the open sea sloped down on the bay side where the commercial center of the city was located. The town's main artery, the broad Calle Nueva, began at the shore. Two- and three-storied whitewashed buildings and narrow streets offered some protection from the dazzling sunlight, summer heat, and strong easterlies. Construction was vertical rather than horizontal, since the small walled city lacked space for many permanent residents not to mention the seasonal pressures of crews and businessmen who crowded the port in preparation for the departure of convoys to the colonies. There was a premium on commercial and residential space, and rents and real estate values were disproportionately high. Few European port towns of the time were notable for well-planned sewage disposal and water supply. Surrounded by saltwater, Cadiz lacked adequate drinking water, which, along with grains, meat, fruit, and vegetables, had to be imported. Few residences had their own cisterns; most inhabitants bought water daily from water-carriers, a trade French immigrants monopolized at the end of the century. Cadiz was usually overcrowded, its streets littered and almost always foul-smelling. Beauharnais visiting Cadiz in 1699 found it "poorly located for its residents' convenience." At the end of the century, wealthy businessmen—English, Navarrese, and French from Auvergne and Limousin along with other foreign resident merchants—constructed summer residences at Puerto Santa María. At the Puerto, terrain was level and streets were wide; cultivated lands surrounded the area. Such were Cadiz and environs as this promontory on the Andalusian coast facing the Atlantic became the main staging area for Spain's colonial trade, for flotas and *galeones*. Admirably suited as an entrepôt, Cadiz and its bay were isolated from Spain geographically and economically.[78]

In the last quarter of the seventeenth century, Flemish and French traders were prominent members of the merchant community in and around the Cadiz entrepôt.. Their position was secured by a pattern of residence, business, and social networks and, in regard to the French, a rising volume of transactions. The connection between Flanders and Spain was old, going back at least to the middle of the fifteenth century when there had been exchanges of Spanish raw materials (mainly wool) for Flemish woolens and linens. Stimulated by incorporation under the crown of Spain and by the opening of America in the early sixteenth century, the trade was still strong at the end of the seventeenth century and, although diminishing, continued into the early nineteenth century. With the reopening of hostilities between Spain and the United Provinces in the final phase of the Thirty Years War, Madrid created the *almirantazgo* (an admiralty with naval and commercial responsibilities) to provide cargo vessels and their escorts (in all, about twenty-four armed merchantmen) sailing in convoy between Dunkerque and Sevilla, a kind of *flota* for the "commerce du nord." The principal promoters were Flemish merchants at Sevilla: Nicolas Antonio and Francisco de Smidt, Guillermo Becquer, and Guillen Clore. Their enterprise collapsed in part due to Antwerp interests involved in smuggling in Spain. The Flemish enclave was influential enough to arrange its own merchant guild in 1645 to oversee Flemish commercial contacts with the American colonies—another failed enterprise. In 1697 Flemish merchants in Lower Andalusia offered to organize a chartered company for trade with the Spanish colonies; this, too, failed.[79] Nonetheless, over the second half of the century the Flemish community survived, overshadowed gradually by the French whose government was simultaneously absorbing by conquest parts of Flanders.

French merchants appeared as a significant trading community in Andalusia early in the seventeenth century, and their numbers grew between 1620 and 1640 as ships from Calais, Rouen, and Saint-Malo freighted goods between Flanders and Andalusia.[80] The next phase in their commercial development came when they substituted French linens, woolens, and silks for Dutch and Flemish products. Breton merchants from Saint-Malo became the vanguard of French expansion into Andalusian trade. They carried to Sevilla and Cadiz linen goods of Quintin, Vitré, Coutances, and Morlaix, returning with Andalusian wines, alum and, of course, American silver. Joined by compatriots from Auvergne and Limousin in the seventeenth century, Malouins remained the most prominent among French residents and, in terms of shaping French commercial policy toward Spain under Mazarin, Colbert, and their successors, they were, until the 1720s, by far the most influential.[81] Malouins occupied the Atlantic islands off Argentina's south coast, proved the feasibility of regular entry into the South Pacific via the Straits of Magellan, and penetrated the *Mar del sur* to trade with the Pacific coast ports of the viceroyalty of Peru during the War of the Spanish Succession.

The French and Flemish in Lower Andalusia as agents of merchant-family networks in Brittany, Normandy, and Flanders were advantaged by consanguinal and affinal social ties and common bonds of birthplace, language, and culture. Capital for operating at Sevilla or Cadiz—for the business of importing from Europe, reexporting through Spanish strawmen to the colonies, and finally remitting to Europe colonial earnings in silver specie and bullion along with a few colonial staples—required large sums of money that were often tied up for from three to four years. Such funds could best be mobilized within the extended merchant family. To contain costs, merchants borrowed and ordered through family networks to purchase merchandise directly from producers, thereby avoiding commission fees.

Descriptions and records of French and Flemish firms portray in general a principal house in France or Flanders with branches at Cadiz or Sevilla. Savary described substantial Parisian merchant families "trading with Spain, who avoid agents, sending instead their offspring, brothers, or relatives to Spain. The profession of agent at Cadiz was a virtual training school for French business leaders. As a rule they spent time there and, at the proper age, returned home rich in experience, replaced by a younger relative who, in turn, was trained in trade."[82] This pattern of recruitment and training produced such long-lived French commercial families at late-seventeenth-century Cadiz as Eon, Danycan, Boyetet, Magon, Lefer, and Lecouteulx, many of which lasted well into the eighteenth century.[83]

Analysis of Flemish records produces only minor variations on the

French pattern, differences reflecting perhaps more information. Flemish family firms set up representatives at Cadiz, although there were also independent Flemish merchants, commission agents, and consignment firms *(participation en commission)* serving an international clientele. Consignment and commission houses operated on the basis of contracts *(statuts)* specifying the number of capital shares, duration of the contract, and division of responsibilities. The more important members of the firm usually drew upon Flemings of long residence in Andalusia and upon a constantly revolving group of Flemish trainees; local Spaniards provided the lower-rank employees. In general Flemish business installations were deceptively simple, a *comptoir* (office) and a warehouse. The longevity of the Flemish and French houses produced "veritables dynasties des marchands."[84]

Between the home merchant house and representatives at Cadiz or Sevilla there existed regular, extensive correspondence, which implies that the agents in Spain operated under close family surveillance. Mail couriers' schedules were well organized and rigorously maintained: within twenty-four hours of a courier's arrival, a return courier departed. Cadiz and Madrid were linked by weekly service. Every two weeks a mail courier left Madrid for Burgos, San Sebastian, Irun, Bordeaux, Paris, and Brussels; a letter between Cadiz and Antwerp averaged twenty-six or twenty-seven days.[85] Dependable and relatively rapid communications insured that French, Flemish, and other suppliers learned quickly of fluctuations in colonial supply and demand when special *azogue ships* (which freighted mercury to the mining colonies) returned from the western Atlantic.[86] An efficient mail service allowed foreign representatives at Cadiz to control the cost of warehousing goods ordered for convoy departures to Caribbean ports.

The Import-Export Process

As colonial demand strengthened and the small initial nucleus of Castilian *comprador* or entrepôt bourgeoisie shrank, the function of foreign merchant houses at Cadiz was to order, receive, and warehouse for reexport the principal items of colonial American demand: linen, woolen, and silk textiles. We now recognize that American silver was a major (perhaps even the determining) factor in the development of commercial capitalism in western Europe and that silver represented sales returns on the products of Europe's protoindustrialization: textile manufactures of Holland and Flanders, England, France, Italy, and Germany. Compared to the exports of other European ports, Cadiz's shipments to America were significant.[87] Imported linens were the most important—the better grades for undercloth-

ing, shirting, and trousers, the coarser for baling. From Holland came ba-
tistes, stays, and laces; from Flanders, *brabantes, brantilles,* and *présilles;* from
France's Norman and Breton provinces, *rouens* and *toiles blanches, bretagnes,*
and *crées;* and from Silesia, *platilles, estopilles, bocadilles,* and *napages.* Flemish
linen bleached in Holland (hence, *olan*) encountered heavy competition at
the end of the century from similar French and Silesian products.

After linens came woolens from Holland *(anascotes, camelots, draps)* and
from England *(bayettes* and *sempiternes)* along with taffetas and silk stockings. From Flanders came white and dark serges and woolen stockings. The
same sources forwarded mercery and, of course, mixed fabrics. Even after
French occupation of its major textile centers, Flanders remained "the most
important woolen-producing province" as far as Spanish imports were concerned. This, despite French annexation policy under Louis XIV which
incorporated into the French economy the traditional Flemish skills linked
to Spain's colonial trade through Lower Andalusia, what has recently been
called the Flemish "strong tradition of exports to Spain." [88]

Maritime freight costs between north European ports and Cadiz were,
according to Flemish commercial records, surprisingly low, about 2 percent
of cost of the goods shipped. Flemish and French data reveal that only
about one-third of Cadiz's European imports were diverted to local consumption: 75 percent of this was landed at Cadiz and Puerto Santa María,
while the balance was introduced through other parts of Andalusia.[89] At
Cadiz fully 75 percent of Flemish sales were made to other foreign houses,
the rest to Spaniards. Most sales (60 percent) were on credit payable in
weekly silver installments, only 15 percent in cash.[90]

Total imports from Europe based upon data covering a few years average around 39 million *livres tournois* (1670), falling off in the years 1685–1686
to 35. The largest amount came from France (about 38 percent),[91] followed
by England (18 percent). These percentages, however, are somewhat misleading since the English were concurrently marketing quantities of textiles
directly into Spain's colonies in and around the Caribbean.[92]

Most imports at Cadiz—more than two-thirds—were reexported aboard
convoys (the *flotas* and *galeones*) to supply mainly Peru and New Spain. It
was the practice of foreign firms' agents at Cadiz to inform their European
home offices of imminent convoy departures. The home office would then
dispatch merchandise to Cadiz. When ships arrived with the merchandise
ordered, customs officials in collusion with foreign importers manipulated
treaty provisions for their private ends. Before unloading could commence,
treaty provisions mandated that a consul forward a note signifying approval

of stationing a customs guard ("waiter") aboard to prevent surreptitious off-loading of cargo either by lighter to the shore or to vessels loading for departure in convoy. For his part, a consul might delay his note for three or four days to "allow enough time for merchants to carry out their fraudulent activities."[93] Unauthorized off-loading continued furthermore after the Spanish guard came aboard. For example, merchants bribed waiters at the going rate of 2 écus per bale (ballot) of high-value silks unloaded surreptitiously, which explains the "très petite partie" of imports registered at customs.

While the customs guard and incoming cargo awaited unloading, the ship's captain went ashore personally to deliver to his consul the ship's register (livre de bord). Then importers awaiting their incoming cargo assembled at their consul's residence to decide the number of bales to submit for customs declaration. Each merchant filed a general declaration (estat en gros), usually omitting up to 80 percent of cargo volume;[94] this was then handed to the Spanish customs for official registry, while importers accompanied their merchandise from inspector to inspector. Only then was quantity reported. A bale might be opened and "if by chance a larger volume than declared were found," the appropriate treaty clause might be invoked. Still, customs would not confiscate the bale, "one would merely pay additional duties on what had not been declared." Bales when approved received an inked seal.[95]

This system was designed to check, at least in theory, bales containing high value goods. "At Customs bales of linens and silks alone were opened, rarely those containing other goods." For example, when bales with fine (batiste) linens were examined, customs affixed a lead seal to each bolt (pieza). When about one-third of cargo had been unloaded, customs might be notified that the remainder was destined to another port, whereupon the guard—a key player in the customs ritual—abandoned his post. He was, as French consul Patoulet explained, essential to the process since more than all else he "facilitates the offloading of undeclared goods."[96]

So much for cargo landed at Cadiz, most ultimately reexported. This was a small percentage of what finally went aboard ships convoyed to the colonies since "most cargo [was] trans-shipped without registry, that is, from the foreign vessel to the galleons or the flota, bypassing Customs."[97] Illicit ship-to-ship transfer in the bay avoided both import and reexport duties (almojarifazgo de Indias) levied per bale aboard convoyed vessels, regardless of value. Unregistered bales, however, were conveniently concealed on outbound convoys. Spanish ship captains collaborated in smuggling cargo while Contratación personnel conveniently "avoid[ed] those places suspected of concealed merchandise" or simply chose to forward to American ports the registers of legal cargo for checking when cargo arrived there.[98]

What made large-scale reexport of unregistered or inadequately dutied European merchandise aboard convoys to colonial ports possible was the appointment of convoy officials by a process of virtual self-selection, a key structure in evading controls on undutied outbound freight. Prohibited by colonial trade regulations from shipping cargo to the colonies under their own names, foreign merchants did so through extraofficial arrangements with convoy officers and Spanish strawmen *(presta-nombres, prête-noms)*.

Although the Consejo de Indias nominally controlled outbound convoys to America, the Casa de *Contratación* (its subordinate agency in Andalusia) set export tonnage and hence the number of vessels supplying the ports of Tierra Firme (Cartagena and Porto Belo) and New Spain (Veracruz). The number of 500- to 600-ton merchant vessels tended to increase toward the end of the century. Tierra Firme convoys generally averaged 10 to 12 ships, those to Veracruz, 8 to 10.[99] For permission to proceed in convoy, Madrid charged merchant vessels between 3,000 and 4,000 *écus;*[100] those few ships *(registros)* authorized to sail alone to the Honduras coast or Buenos Aires paid slightly more.[101]

Convoy flag officers—generals, vice- and rear admirals—along with captains of heavily armed escort vessels received monthly salaries from the government, payable on funds in colonial rather than metropolitan treasuries. The salaries were in effect base salaries since officers purchased appointment by making advances to a poorly budgeted state treasury and were expected to recover the advances from charges on cargo protected by escorts. For example, flag officers often advanced up to 100,000 *écus* in buying their offices. These sums were repaid at colonial ports at 8 percent interest—well above the going rate in Spain. In theory, naval commanders could also draw an allowance of 21 silver *ducados* per ton for repairs *(radoub)* and refitting *(agrément)*, also payable on colonial treasuries. To cover these and other outlays, they generally borrowed at Cadiz. Even two years prior to official appointment, a captain might advance 20,000 *écus* for *agrément* plus another 12,000 one month before the departure date to cover ships' stores. These loans (also at 8 percent) were repaid as well on colonial treasuries.

Unavoidably ship commanders, who were as a rule not "gens de qualité," had to borrow. They purchased rank by "the loans made to obtain the preference of *Contratación*'s president and magistrates"; the advances were recoverable by charges on freight, passengers and silver remissions. There are reports that commanders of warships convoying merchantmen may have been forced to borrow from merchants at Cadiz or Sevilla at above the usual rates, binding themselves to repay at 25–30 percent on bottomry *(à la grosse aventure)*. By way of partial compensation, the captains of *flota* escort vessels could register 150 tons of cargo aboard their ships; in fact they often commandeered all the cargo space. Thus royal escort vessels were heavily gunned, overloaded, and unmaneuverable cargo vessels. Indeed, many warship commanders ordered escort vessels built at their own expense to profit from "the right to command them and take them to the Indies on two trips"—another example of private sector enterprise in naval protection involving dozens of people.[102]

Broadly viewed, Charles II's state completed the process of alienating to private enterprise what was a state responsibility: oversight of its maritime link to the American colonies, its principal source of liquidity. Meanwhile, Cadiz's naval installations lacked supply depots, training facilities, and crews (half the escort vessels' crews were non-Spaniards).[103] Small wonder that galleon commanders "take aboard all the fraudulent goods presented," that ships loading for the colonies were not inspected by *Contratación*, permitting thereby foreign and domestic shippers to "conceal all the fraudulent shipments made," and that much cargo outbound for the colonies was registered neither by *Contratación* nor customs. Ledgers of the Flemish firm of Boussemart at Cadiz, involved in exporting goods to the colonies, reveal that on average over three decades (1670–1700) fully 69 percent of its shipments bypassed official registry, a percentage sometimes reaching 90 percent.[104]

Spanish naval officers as well as captains of merchant vessels were responsible for delivery of cargo overseas only to a few Caribbean ports. Foreign merchants at Cadiz still had to monitor at long distance sales of their merchandise in the colonies and remission of silver and selected primary product, such as cochineal and cocoa. Since the Spanish transatlantic system guaranteed, at least in law, exclusive participation of Spaniards (really, only Castilians) and a very few naturalized immigrants, foreigners could neither ship cargo, accompany it, nor supervise *feria* sales in person. As initially formulated, the design of the Spanish system was hardly mercantilist, rather it provided a framework of one-port monopoly and, within it, oligopolistic competition. In practice, foreign resident merchants—already responsible for most merchandise aboard convoys—employed either their few countrymen who had met Spanish requirements for naturalization (twenty years' residence, a Spanish wife, ownership of real estate, a minimum of

4,000 *ducados* of wealth) and as *genízaros* were entitled to travel to the colonies when properly authorized, or as Spanish collaborators, the *presta-nombres*.[105]

Infiltrating the colonial commercial system developed in stages. Until early in the seventeenth century foreign importers at Sevilla or Cadiz sold to Spanish shippers *(cargadores)*. Thereafter a number of factors modified the sales system. An expanding volume of reexports to the colonies required a volume of capital customarily exceeding the resources of Spanish merchants while payment for goods bought on credit could be delayed anywhere from two to four years; Spanish agents or factors who sailed on convoys often disappeared in the colonies leaving uncollectible debts. As colonial trade in the third quarter of the century turned "less profitable and more uncertain," French resident merchants modified their sales management. They settled on transactions partly payable in cash, the balance on a convoy's return at 12 percent. The next phase was full ownership of exported goods by faking sales to Spanish agents *(encomenderos)* or factors *(factores)* who accompanied their goods. In this phase, they netted 40 to 50 percent over principal cost to cover higher risk. Hence the critical importance of the *prestanombre* to the system.[106]

A system of long-distance transatlantic trade flows in which great financial responsibility devolved upon unsupervised agents thousands of miles overseas and in which legal formalities were used as a cover for a system that was manifestly illegal, depended upon trust, upon what Spanish guild merchants termed *verdad sabida y buena fé guardada*. Its operation was deceptively simple. French, Flemish, and other foreign traders in Lower Andalusia covered their shipments by selecting "a Spanish friend of probity and trust, whom they arrange to sign their bills of lading and invoices, and to list the embarked goods for Customs." They carefully selected a Spaniard whose personal holdings approximated the value of cargo shipped in their name so that under questioning he might reply to Contratación's investigators "with every assurance they belong to him." No proof of payment was given the *prestanombre* because "he is a friend of the merchant and offers his services in return for those he has received from him or others of his country of origin." The *prestanombre* signed the invoices *(facturas)* giving in return to the real owner an acknowledgement *(reconnoissance)* that the merchandise was his. The *prestanombre* then distributed the invoices to three Spanish agents *(commissionaires)* on the same outbound convoy so that in case of his death overseas "there is always someone to supervise sales."

On returning from overseas, the Spanish *commissionaire* did not use the *prestanombre* (only an intermediary) but rather reported directly to the foreign proprietor of the goods exported, providing a *compte de vente* and the sales proceeds, "bypassing the Spaniard who had signed the invoice." Acknowledgements and invoices were retained by the foreign exporters "pour sa securité." To minimize the risk of heavy fines for illegal participation, merchants selected "good, responsible people whom they use as agents for goods risked in the Indies."[107] Rare were the occasions when such trust was misplaced. There is reason to believe that for generations at Puerto Santa María across the bay from Cadiz, where foreign merchant enclaves existed, naturalized Flemings along with Navarrese families, such as the Vizarrón and Arraníbar, served loyally as *prestanombres* or *commissionaires.*[108]

Once the heavily laden ten to fifteen merchant vessels in *flota* and galleon convoys had departed along with their equally laden escorts, Cadiz's level of activity subsided, and merchants and treasury officers awaited the returning vessels. Elapsed time between departure and return for either fleet in the 1670s varied from thirteen to fourteen months. Later, especially after 1681, the elapsed time of galleons' round-trips began to lengthen to from nineteen to thirty-two months as a result of a breakdown in the operations of the Portobelo fair on the Isthmus of Panama.[109] For ports on the islands of Jamaica and Curaçao in the last half of the seventeenth century were developing extensive direct sales by English and Dutch merchants who relied far less than French or Flemish merchants on sales at Cadiz.[110] These Caribbean smuggling operations were in the jargon of the time *à la longueur de la pique* because English, Dutch, and French shipping, paying lip service to the treaty stipulations agreed upon at Münster and reiterated in the Anglo-Spanish "American" treaty, stationed themselves just outside Spanish colonial ports (in the roadsteads), where they could "traffic directly, hand-to-hand, in what their vessels carried," a practice made possible by "corrupt Spanish colonial officers whose cooperation they buy."[111] Disruption of the Portobelo fair and the simultaneous resurgence of New Spain's silver exports probably combined to shift foreign merchants' interest from Tierra Firme and South America to the more promising Mexican market.

The counterpart of reexports of European manufactures was receipt (and, ultimately, reexport) of silver coin or bar that represented earnings on colonial sales. Selling in distant colonial fairs was more problematic than in Spain itself, and comparative profit rates reflected this. Flemish business records show returns on sales to Spanish distributors supplying Andalusian consumers yielded 12–15 percent; on sea loans (*a premio de mar,* what the French termed *à la grosse aventure*) to Spanish shippers (*cargadores*) exporting to the colonies, profit margins averaged much higher (40–50 percent). And goods exported on consignment to colonial ports earned even higher rates (40–75 percent).[112] Compared with estimates by a knowledgeable *arbitrista* like Osorio y Redín, these returns seem modest and may reflect bookkeeping designed to mislead Spanish tax inspectors. At any rate, given the high level of returns on colonial operations, foreign merchants were encouraged to maximize the volume of both their registered and illegal reexports to the colonies and to circumvent or weaken Spanish regulations covering imports of silver and staples from colonial ports.

Once returning convoys entered Cadiz bay, the formal apparatus of state control began. Contratación's president, its *jueces* and other personnel boarded the admiral's flagship to post the prohibitions against illegal movement of cargo; officers then visited the vice- and rear-admirals' ships to repeat the ritual. Other personnel remained aboard until the cargo register was prepared. Since this was delayed deliberately four to five days, importers had time to arrange to "withdraw their silver and place it aboard foreign shipping." Of the commanders of incoming galleons it was observed they reported to customs nothing regarding "articles shipped on their account."[113] At best perhaps 50 percent of incoming cargo from the colonies was listed, signifying a high percentage of the most valuable cargo—silver—went unreported. We must recall that unregistered silver was also loaded at the colonial port of exit, registries prepared there were often not remitted to Cadiz, and surveillance of ship-to-ship transfers on the high seas or off the Canaries or Azores was virtually impossible. As for unminted silver put ashore at Cadiz, merchants usually disregarded injunctions to present it at the Sevilla mint in order to save the 6 percent duty.[114]

Metedores solved the problem of re-embarking for west European ports precious metals from shore to ship in Cadiz bay. Merchants called upon the services of these young noblemen,[115] paying them one percent commission for passing silver and gold in carefully labeled packages over the city walls (*por alto*) or from Puerto Santa María. Then it was rowed in small boats to foreign merchantmen or warships anchored in the bay. Local officials, such as Cadiz's governor and aldermen, also received a commission.[116]

Again, a bond of trust existed between *metedores* and merchants, since "a Spaniard would be dishonored and mortified by his countrymen if not faithful to merchants," and for their part, merchants paid punctiliously the agreed-upon commissions. Operations of *cuadrillas* (gangs) of *metedores* were an open secret to officials all the way up to the Consejo de Indias, which "unable to prevent, is obliged to tolerate them."[117] The incentives to continue illegal transfers of metals became even greater at the century's end to judge by generally rising volumes of silver carried by *flotas* inbound from Veracruz. According to Everaert's data, these almost quadrupled from 8.5 to

30 million between 1670 and 1697.[118] Since Saint-Malo merchants then formed the largest single foreign merchant enclave at Cadiz reexporting precious metals and raw materials, they were the most insistent that their government station two warships in the bay year-round to transport silver to French Atlantic ports.[119]

One should not conclude, however, that the carefully structured legitimization of fraud at Cadiz deprived the Spanish state of income from the transit of goods between Europe and America. While the nominal level of duties remained well above the effective rates, and merchants constantly tried to avoid even these, the government often arbitrarily imposed a general levy *(indulto)* on the whole business community in the colonial trades to recover lost revenue. French documents refer to a form of standard levies. There was often an *indulto* of 400,000 *écus* on departing galleons, and this was paid again by merchants in Peru on the galleons' return to Spain. *Flotas* to Veracruz were levied somewhat less (275,000 *écus*) collectible on leaving Veracruz.

Indulto income, which appears to have produced on average about 1.3 million *écus,* netted Madrid half this sum. The balance went to officers of the Consejo de Indias and Contratación (they provided no accountability) as well as to officers of the Sevilla consulado.[120] It was typical of the Spanish state at the end of the century that it entrusted to Sevilla's consulado the assessment and collection of *indultos,* just as customs collection of Lower Andalusia was farmed to Báez Eminente. The two collection devices on the Lower Andalulsian transit trade, *asiento* and *indulto,* were thus complementary. After 1667 *indultos* became more frequent and their application more arbitrary, perhaps indicating Madrid's recognition of the rising percentage of underregistered precious metals imports that rose by a factor between 2 and 3 between 1620 and 1659.[121] For example, in 1677 and again in 1678 *indultos* affected solely foreigners' goods, particularly those of French merchants; in 1682 foreign merchants had to contribute 412,000 pesos, raised in 1684 to 830,000. In 1691 and again in 1697—perhaps reflecting an increase in total value of imports from the colonies—*indultos* amounting to the extraordinary sum of 10 million pesos each were levied on precious metals arriving on private account.[122]

Since the Sevilla consulado's officers were given discretion in allocating *indulto* assessments among Cadiz's foreign merchant enclaves, and since the economic role of the French was paramount there, the French community complained bitterly that Spanish policy was designed to ruin their trade "especially that at Cadiz, the largest and most profitable our nation has."[123] By alienating *indulto* collection to Sevilla, the state shed responsibility for inequity in assessments by claiming ignorance of "what goes on in the Indies trade" while merchants and bureaucrats at Sevilla shared roughly half the proceeds of the levies "to the prejudice of the trade of foreigners who bear the cost."[124]

Managed Trade or Pseudomercantilism?

The contradictory nature of the Spanish colonial trading system functioning in Lower Andalusia in the last half of the seventeenth century, was neatly encapsulated by French consul Patoulet reporting from Cadiz in 1686. "Our merchants smuggle all they can, avoiding duties as much as possible since customs rates are as high as 23 percent. They do the same with the goods they ship to the Indies aboard galleons (these warships are prohibited from loading cargo). They load their goods without registry at Contratación and transfer them from ship to ship. They do the same with the silver they export from Cadiz, or that taken from the galleons. All fraudulent activities are carried on with the assistance and knowledge of Spaniards."[125] The term *pseudomercantilism* best covers this practice, or was it really policy?

Arbitristas' analyses, informed, usually accurate and circulated in manuscript at high levels of policy-making, had little effect on economic growth because Spanish society, supported to a significant degree by a successful colonial mining sector, confronted no compelling need for structural changes. Meanwhile, over the last five decades of the seventeenth century, first England and then France elaborated pragmatic and idiosyncratic structures of protection enhancing economic development which later analysts named "mercantilism." The selection and combination of protective mechanisms generated by post-Westphalian mercantilism whose choice depended upon particular national historical conditions—hence the complex of navigation acts legislated by the English parliament or economic intervention by the French state (*colbertisme* or *dirigisme*). Despite their variety, however, all these mercantilist policies had one thing in common: their prohibitions were manipulated primarily for developmental rather than fiscal ends.[126] Their multiplication became a measure of the growth of the modern state. To the contrary, the prohibitory mechanisms Spain elaborated and applied to colonial trade in the sixteenth century were not designed for national economic development.[127] Bullionist in intent, in practice episodic and ineffective, they undermined the metropole's limited production of quality goods, which were increasingly supplied by Spain's northern neighbors. Over two centuries Spain initiated and then developed on a massive scale colonial silver production and its complex infrastructure, first forcing and then gradually drawing Amerindians and mestizos into a colonial market economy dominated by an elite of mining entrepreneurs, wholesale merchants, estate owners, ranchers, bureaucrats, and churchmen—all eager consumers of old world goods largely produced in Europe outside the Spanish metropole. Consequently the great surge of colonial precious metals exports between 1580 and 1630 and corresponding colonial demand for imports increasingly bypassed the metropolitan economy, stimulating instead Genoese, Flemish, Dutch, English, and French artisans, merchants, and shippers.

This is not to argue that the Spanish system was aimless or, for its purposes, ineffective. A careful reading of Veitia Linaje's classic legislative compendium on the Spanish transatlantic trading system, *Norte de la Contratación,* proves this. It simply did not (nor was it intended to) generate broad economic development, which is what John Cary discerned when in 1695 he commented in a Bristol publication that "One great reason why the Kingdom of Spain still continues poor notwithstanding its Indies, [is] because all that the inhabitants buy is purchased for its full value in Treasure or Product, their Labour adding nothing to its Wealth, for want of Manufactures."[128] Cary, however, was already analyzing English economic praxis through a mercantilist or developmental prism at odds with the obsolescent economic strategy of the Hapsburg patrimonial state. The Spanish Hapsburgs failed to distinguish between the parts of their patrimonial empire, whether Castile (producer of wools), Flanders (center of manufactures exchanged for Spanish wools, dyestuffs, and above all, silver), or Peru and New Spain (silver producers). The vision of late seventeenth-century Cadiz as the "emporium of the world" persisted well into the eighteenth century.

Since colonial silver output during the seventeenth century did not contract markedly (although there was some fluctuation and much illegal siphoning), and since New Spain's population recovery began in the closing decades, the net effect in colonial Spanish America was gradual expansion of a market-oriented economy along with sustained growth in consumer demand. Only a few economies of non-Iberian Europe produced and shipped goods to, and received in return silver from, Spain's colonies in America—the most important regional economy for European products outside Europe. Europe's producers and exporters who expanded operations within the framework of Lower Andalusian trade regulations after Münster had to create an international treaty complex affording elements of protective extraterritoriality for foreign merchant enclaves. The treaties were, at bottom, maintained by threat of retaliation by sea and by the cultivation of Spanish collaborators by land.

The unequal relations between Spain and major economic regions of western Europe in the eighteenth century were expressed in the informal imperialism of the Münster treaty system, which remained an enduring constraint upon efforts by the Bourbon regime to modify colonial trade. The other major constraint on the Spanish state's design to manage colonial trade flows were the foreign merchants for whom the treaty system furnished security. They, in turn, exploited the treaties to the limit and inevitably, like twentieth-century multinational conglomerates, incorporated and manipulated metropolitan and colonial officials and other influential people. In our time, resource-rich but underdeveloped economies draw capital, technology, goods, and services from abroad by welcoming foreign investment. At the end of the seventeenth century, the Spanish state had to create an official ambience tolerant of participatory fraud and smuggling by foreign residents at the Lower Andalusian transfer point of colonial trade. Official corruption became an imperative of survival.

Spain's domestic and colonial economic structures required therefore total involvement in illegality, in toleration of "corruption" and "fraud" in commercial transactions.[129] Prohibitive legislation paralleled by pay-offs or bribes has been described recently as "pseudomercantilism," the "enrichment of legal dignitaries" by extortion applied to the "mere appendages of officialdom."[130] It would be more accurate to argue that the persistence of regulatory mechanisms without a developmentalist core in the seventeenth century illustrates a major facet of Spain's "decline" as stagnation deepened. In an elite consensus, Spaniards in Lower Andalusia and Madrid—merchants and clerics, bureaucrats and noblemen—adjusted to constraints of the treaty system by winking at prohibitions in order to preserve nominal dominance over the American colonies. So Spaniards and foreigners, co-equal collaborationors, developed a sustained interest in illegality. The career of José de Veitia Linaje, who was born into a small-holder family of poor gentry and eventually became a member of Madrid's prestigious Consejo de Indias, illustrates the multiple facets of Sevilla's colonial bureaucracy: its recruitment, its social and religious networks, and its permeability to business interests. It shows the upward social mobility of one befriended throughout his career by well-placed clerical benefactors, and early recognition by churchmen, bureaucrats, and businessmen of the capacity and potential of obscure individuals of lower gentry background. And—certainly not least—it underscores the drawing power of colonial trade opportunities at Spain's then most important urban and commercial center, Sevilla.

Veitia Linaje, born at Burgos (1623), reached the apex of his career in state service at Madrid (1677–1688) but only after decades at Sevilla (1641–77). A succession of posts in the colonial customs service (*almojarifazgo de*

Indias) at Sevilla first as minor assistant to a major official and then as its *contador,* shifting to the Casa de Contratación as deputy to its *tesorero juez oficial* (1649) and later by purchase the *contador propietario de avería* and ultimately *tesorero y juez oficial*—all provided opportunities for public service and self-enrichment.[131] Given his evident bureaucratic endowments and apparent efficiency in handling the responsibilities of office, Veitia found time to draft a monumental compilation of statutes regulating the colonial trading system with which he had been associated over decades. Typical of the practice of the impoverished Hapsburg state, Madrid financed publication of his *Norte* by assigning him one *nao de privilegio,* a license covering one 250-ton vessel transferable to a merchant-shipper forwarding cargo to the American colonies.[132] This type of privilege was becoming standard practice in the Spanish patrimonial state and elsewhere in Europe in the last fifty years of the century. Posted to Madrid where he collaborated with the duque de Medina Celi, a leading political figure of the 1680s, Veitia joined the recently formed Junta de Comercio (1685) and then prominent public functionary serving on *both* the Consejo de Estado and Indias. He died at Madrid eleven years later in 1688.[133]

Veitia Linaje's career has meaning as more than an isolated case of poor-boy-to-prominence by sheer contingency. His success story is more a matter of structures and their relationships, of Castilian society, of the social webs of religion, state service in metropole and colonies, of public office at the colonial trade synapse that was Sevilla and of the range of possibilities of private enrichment in public service there.

A structural approach to analysis of his career is substantiated by many factors. His emigration from Burgos first to Oñate and then south to Sevilla was facilitated by the predominance of north Castilian and Basque families in both ecclesiastical and bureaucratic structures. A once prominent archbishop of Sevilla (Rodrigo de Castro) had family roots in the *montaña* of Burgos. A relative, an archdeacon of Burgos' cathedral (Bartolomé de Castro), taught young Veitia his letters and then arranged for him to accompany a wealthy family member (Juan Fernández de Castro) as servant *(paje)* to the university town of Oñate. Veitia, son of a small landowner in the Burgos area whose sole claim to distinction was Basque "noble" *(hidalgo)* ancestry (Veitia Gasteátegui), subsequently accompanied Castro to Sevilla where Castro's uncle was *administrador general del almojarifazgo.* Jerónimo de San Vitores immediately recognized young Veitia's qualities and brought him into Sevilla's customs administration, the starting point of Veitia's long career in colonial administration and trade. Working under San Vitores (godparent at his marriage) put Veitia at the heart of the Hapsburg state's monitoring of colonial trade and silver flows: the *almojarifazgo* was the "impost on all goods in overseas trade, whatever their destination."[134]

In his first twelve years at Sevilla (1641–53) Veitia married a niece of Sevilla's painter Murillo (perhaps the daughter of a barber),[135] switched from *almojarifazgo* to Casa de Contratación as *teniente del tesorero juez oficial,* and by 1653 could afford to buy (at 60,000 *reales de plata*) the office of *contador propietario* in Contratación. By purchase he could appoint or sell his substitute's office *(teniente);* his office was inheritable (a *juro de heredad*) and convertible into an entailment *(mayorazgo).* This and the subsequent purchase (330,000 *reales*) of *tesorero y juez oficial* also in Contratación were strategic bureaucratic (and lucrative) positions. Sevilla was still the metropole's principal commercial and administrative center where migrants from the Basque country and Burgos figured prominently in colonial trade, administrative cadres, and the religious establishment, and where Veitia could and did cultivate business, bureaucratic and religious networks. He was a great "joiner," associating with fellow Burgaleses and Vizcaínos in the Convento Grande de San Francisco (in 1649 he could already afford to endow there a *capellanía de misas*) and in the Hermandad de la Santa Caridad, a charity hospital. In 1652 he was secretary of the Hermandad's Veracruz branch, an overseas hospital for seamen who went from Sevilla to Veracruz on *flotas.*[136] He developed even stronger links to the mining colony of New Spain: two nephews were in the colonial bureaucracy, one at Mexico City on the *tribunal de cuentas* (Juan José de Veitia Linaje), the other was superintendent of Puebla's mint (José Fernandez de Villanueva Veitia Linaje).

In Sevilla's *Almojarifazgo* and *Contratación* were chances to favor the business activities of Burgalés-Vizcaíno benefactors and friends, and members of the foreign business community. His favored treatment in the Sevilla customs for their outgoing merchandise and incoming silver must have often rewarded Veitia—how else account for the source of the 60,000 silver reales he paid for ownership of *Contratación's* influential *contaduría de avería* and the 330,000 *reales* for its *tesorero y juez oficial* post—in effect, his large investment in the privileges of Hapsburg office-holding? After all, the *avería* was collected on all merchandise outgoing and incoming from the colonies in order to finance the naval forces convoying fleets to the American colonies—a form of auto-financing of state functions. As *contador* and later *tesorero y juez oficial,* Veitia had broad oversight responsibilities: certification of ships' manifests, establishment of differential rates charged on varieties of cargo, checking on the annual balance sheet of the *Avería* administration, including supervision of unpaid duties.[137] Veitia was therefore a key player in the Hapsburg state exploiting overseas mining colonies; he could provide formal toleration of fraud and corruption by Spaniards and their foreign collaborators, of favoritism and payoffs in the ongoing Spanish transatlantic system of trade, navigation and administration.

Veitia survived and prospered at Sevilla moving up the bureaucratic *cursus honorum* by playing by the rules. The patrimonial state readily incorporated those who proved competent, diligent and uncritical of political and social shortcomings. His *Norte de la Contratación* records the state's preoccupation with fiscal control over trade flows for revenue, for liquidity. There is no economic development policy discernible in the maze of statutes he catalogued, certainly no sense of the extent to which Sevilla's foreign resident merchants—French, Flemish, Genoese and others—were systematically subverting the prohibitions compiled selectively in his book.[138] His bureaucratic ascendance from obscurity to prominence, relations with influential segments of Sevillan society—churchmen, merchants, lesser nobility—his possible role as investment counselor to Spaniards seeking to place small funds in colonial trade opportunities,[139] and not least, his blindness toward foreigners' virtual mastery of the Hapsburg transatlantic trading system, underscore the banality of collusion in Lower Andalusia between Spanish bureaucrats and foreign businessmen. Veitia, we must recall, had become an influential member of Madrid's political class shoring up Hapsburg institutions. The boundaries between state and economy, between the business of government and the business of business were blurred.

Decades ago it was hypothesized that the stagnation, recession, and decline that characterized Spain in the seventeenth century was linked to the demographic collapse in the colonies. Loss of population diminished the mine labor force and affected silver production, and as a result, Europe experienced declining receipts of metals from the American colonies.[140] No one questions the collapse of Spain's hegemony in western Europe after Westphalia, the withering of its military and naval forces—its incapacity for further large-scale intervention in Europe. On the other hand, precisely what was the relationship between the situation in the colonies and the stagnation in the metropole? Was there a decline in mining production? Why did Spain's economy stagnate while west European economies grew and developed, and European merchants pressed their penetration into Spain's colonial trading networks? And, finally, how did Spanish interests contribute to and adapt to an economy of stagnation in order to prosper amid poverty? In short, what was the colonial dimension of the "decline" of Spain?

In the early decades of the twentieth century data accumulated that showed that around 1630 registered silver imports at Sevilla began to drop, although critics quickly pointed out that the possibility of significant quantities of unregistered silver reexported to the rest of Europe and, via Manila, to East Asia should not be overlooked. In recent decades as a result of derived estimates of production based upon the relationship between quantity of registered mercury received in America and output from the patio process, it has become evident that while colonial silver production declined, it was not a lasting phenomenon. Detailed analyses of the output of Zacatecas (New Spain) and Potosí (Peru) have refined the conclusion of gradual decline and indicated that New Spain's production recovered in the closing decades of the seventeenth century. In fact, over the century, New Spain's production rose and "remained the basis of the imperial system."[141] Meanwhile, evidence from Dutch *gazettes* revealed that silver imports at Lower Andalusian ports surpassed official receipts by far, a conclusion confirmed as well by the records of Flemish firms at Cadiz. In sum, there is sound basis for the hypothesis that there were ever-growing amounts of colonial silver smuggled into Europe. This hypothesis is confirmed directly by the reporting of French observers and indirectly by the unrelenting pressure of English and Dutch merchants in the West Indies and at Lower Andalusian ports, by reports in Dutch gazettes, and by the anxiety of the French merchant enclave to enter the circuit of colonial silver via trading activity, licit and illicit. No longer can the importance of colonial silver and colonial consumers be overlooked as stimuli to the expansion of key growth sectors of the European economy, such as textile manufactures. As seventeenth-century commentators endlessly noted, Spain's incapacity was Europe's opportunity.

Through the cumulative, piecemeal exemptions to legislation covering colonial trade, Spanish interest groups reached a comfortable accommodation with structures of dependent stagnation. They lobbied to sustain a government-sanctioned monopoly, one of whose effects was the application of scarce resources to unproductive activities. In the first half of the seventeenth century, merchants in Spain's colonial ports obtained exemption in wartime for registry of cargo except on arrival at Sevilla's customs; after 1660 only Sevilla registry at any time was demanded.[142] More significant were exemptions obtained by Sevilla's silver merchants *(compradores de plata)*. In 1647 new regulations provided that their silver could be sequestered only with the specific approval of the president of Contratación; examination of their business records required his approval as well. There was consistent under-registry of silver arrivals after 1645 and probably earlier; the percentage of smuggled silver for scattered years, 1670 to 1700, was probably at least 50 percent of all silver received.[143] The seigniorial jurisdiction exercised by

Spain's noblemen over the port of San Lúcar (Medina Sidonia) and over Puerto Santa María (Medina Celi) masked smuggling in which noblemen and their clientele of merchants and others shared.[144] Furthermore, the sale of strategic public offices to interested individuals offered effective cover for smuggling and fraud in state office. Take the case of Genoa-born Horacio Levanto: after naturalization in Andalusia (as a *genízaro*) he received permission (1629) to export 25,000 *ducados* in merchandise to the American colonies; the following year he furnished naval stores and rations for outbound warships. At this time he also petitioned for exempt status (*jurisdicción exenta*) for property he owned in Sevilla and Cadiz. His petition was rejected on the ground that the properties were positioned "to defraud." But in compensation he was sold two offices, *ensayador y fundidor mayor* of the Mexico City mint and *administrador y tesorero* of the mints of Sevilla and Granada. At his death he left one of the largest personal fortunes of his time (500,000 *ducados*).[145] Levanto's case was symptomatic of how under the Hapsburgs the government chose to turn over to the private sector key areas of the national and colonial economies. Decades later as the scale and scope of smuggling in Lower Andalusia increased, paralleled by the frequency of *indultos,* the Castilian state was selling not only the rank of flag officers of convoys in the *carrera de Indias* but also major tax collectorships at Sevilla, San Lúcar, Puerto Santa María, and Cadiz.[146]

The obverse of the decline of Spain and the impoverishment of the state was the concomitant enrichment of a privileged few among aristocrats, noblemen, bureaucrats, and Spanish and foreign resident merchant groups. Maintenance of the system of fictive colonial trade monopoly kept commodities exchanged at artificially inflated prices, generated super profits, and "off-sided small traders, capable of operating only in a climate of legal commerce."[147] A system of prohibitions theoretically regulating colonial trade, rooted in Spain's economic stagnation, virtual toleration of bribery, and in the affluence of a privileged few and the penury of the state characterized the Spanish state and economy, which was dependent upon the profits of colonialism, upon the silver mines of Peru and New Spain. In the 1680s trade expansion between Cadiz and the colonies and the spread of smuggling with the overt participation of the nobility provided an atmosphere in which the smuggler flourished as folk hero.[148] The colonial dimension of Spain's seventeenth-century crisis seems not so much a sustained drop in silver production and export as its large-scale transfer to the developing economies of northwest Europe.

There was, therefore, no fundamental contradiction between colonial

monopoly nominally reserved exclusively for Spaniards and covert participation by foreigners. Recovery of the colonial mining economy in New
Spain at the end of the century stimulated England and France but not
Spain. To preserve an increasingly contested hegemony over its American
colonies, the Spanish state had to accept constraints imposed by the informal imperialism imbedded in international treaties and the repeated illegal
intermediation of foreign resident merchants. "Toleration or, rather, the
tacit permission that the King of Spain grants so readily to all Foreigners to
trade with his Indies in the name of his subjects," the French consul at Cadiz
noted in 1686, "seems to me rather the result of subtle policy than of corruption and the poor government of his state. It strikes me that such toleration . . . is really necessary, since his subjects are in no condition to profit
from this strong and rich Commerce."[149]

The Later *Arbitristas:* Diagnosticians of Underdevelopment

Analyses by late seventeenth-century Spanish political economists—called
arbitristas because many focused on the problems of state financial resources
or *arbitrios*—captured contemporary perceptions of Spain's problems and
possibilities after decades of stagnation, sectoral contraction, and institutional involution, along with the mentality of the Spanish political class confronting a rapidly changing international order.

Stagnation in proximity to change can never be absolute, above all when
relations of dependence are involved. In the case of Spain, critical thought,
discouraged and suppressed under Philip II, surfaced in unpredictable ways
and unexpected places among clerics, bureaucrats and others of usually
modest social origins. Many seventeenth-century *arbitristas* plumbing the
causes of Spain's endemic problems fell into these groups. Aware of Spain's
economic dependence on foreign producers and its debilitating effect on
the metropolitan economy and society, they focused on different facets of
contemporaneous reality according to individual experience: the country's
lack of commercial expertise, its failure to nurture national manufactures,
its flawed fiscal policies. These diagnosticians of underdevelopment recognized the manifestations of Spain's backwardness, but unable or unwilling
to examine the institutional structures and mentalities underlying Spain's
dilemma, they failed to meet the challenge of their times. Examples from
the latter part of the seventeenth century are illustrative.

Juan de Castro, a cleric with colonial experience and ties to the Genoese
business community in Andalusia, focused in the 1660s on the absence of
statistical data to guide merchants selling in metropolitan and colonial mar-

kets.[150] It was this "laxity in finding data needed to know the condition and balance of our trade" that was responsible for the "subtleties and deceptions of foreigners who had taken control of our trade with America, taking advantage of the lack of sophistication and the downright foolishness of those Spaniards who were merely their strawmen or agents." Not only was there no public intelligence about the composition of colonial demand for imports and the relative proportion of Spanish to non-Spanish cargo sent to the colonies, equally absent was knowledge of the "quantity of gold, silver, emeralds and staples they bring from our Indies."[151] The rank order is significant. As a result he found that duties took the form of Madrid's unpredictable levies *(indultos)* demanded arbitrarily and—here spoke the agent of foreign financiers—in no way proportional to the real value of colonial cargoes. Nor did it escape Castro that the Madrid bureaucracy lacked access to data on the variety, supply, and cost structure of colonial staples and their international price levels in European markets, details that foreign merchants knew well. Spanish statistical shortcomings, Castro argued, were matched only by the perspicacity and subterfuges of foreign traders. Not only did foreign traders marry Spanish women so that their sons might enjoy the "privileges" of Spanish nationals, they shipped their most promising male offspring off to uncles or grandfathers in Genoa, France, and the Low Countries for training in languages and merchandising. On their return these young men were placed in Spain's key economic sector, its colonial trade *(carrera de Indias),* as representatives of their foreign-born fathers, grandfathers, uncles, and associates. Accompanying shipments averaging 200,000 pesos and sometimes reaching 1.5 million to Veracruz, Portobelo, and even as far as Lima, they were well positioned to exploit colonial markets to the disadvantage of their undercapitalized and poorly informed Spanish competitors whose capital averaged 20,000 pesos.[152] Yet rather than bypass dependent Spanish merchants, Castro noted that foreign merchants patronized them in various ways, often lending up to 100,000 pesos to groups of ten to twelve Spaniards at 60 percent payable at the Portobelo fairs. There, moreover, agents of foreign merchants could afford to undersell Spanish merchants since their prime cost was usually well below that of their competitors. Indeed, it could be as much as 45 percent lower. Hence Spanish merchants had to hold out for high prices from buyers at the fairs while a foreigner's agent "has plenty of time to make his sales as soon as the fair begins. And during this period he collects his gold dust and silver in cones, ingots and bars and has finished his business before the Spaniard has even begun to sell." And when *feria* sales lagged, foreign creditors at Cadiz or Sevilla compensated by reducing the Spaniards' debt. Small wonder many Spaniards tolerated dependence upon the foreign business community which Castro compared to a leech that "sucks from Spain without letting go." The point is, Castro had grasped that community's strategy: it was not in its long-term interest entirely to displace under-capitalized and usually poorly informed Spanish competitors.

Another diagnostician of decline and witness to the immiserization of his native Sevilla, Francisco Martínez de Mata, was equally critical of foreign merchants who left to Spain only the "responsibility of keeping [the colonies] while Spaniards are their miserable servants."[153] A champion of Sevilla's craft guilds, he advocated domestic industry since the weakness of the metropole was glaringly visible in the atrophy of its artisanal structures and traditions. He blamed in particular Charles V's regime for opening Spanish markets to Genoese imports in 1518: "the sole cause of our population decline" and of subsequent contraction of domestic production as Genoese as well as French goods flooded Spain and its colonies. For example, to obtain finished linens for export to the colonies "all orders have been directed to France as a result of the malignant trade introduced." The resulting outflow of Spain's specie and bullion, in turn, attracted swarms of foreign wholesalers and retailers "so that 150,000 Frenchmen and 10,000 Genoese can leave loaded down with silver and gold." Unlike Castro who favored purchases directly from European producers rather than from merchant intermediaries, Mata preferred domestic manufactures in order to form an integrated and balanced national economy: "manufacture and trade in merchandise" would link agriculture to industry to capture the added value of manufacture since "as our agricultural products are consumed by manufacturers, their value is raised from one to one hundred-fold."[154] To Mata the road back to the imagined "time of the Catholic Kings [when] Spain was rich and well populated" was feasible by reviving *(restauración)* cottage industry to produce once again silks, linens, woolens, and hats. And Mata was even more innovative in recommending the elimination of foreign tax-farmers and that state revenues be channeled into an investment bank *(erario)* to provide producers *(laborantes)* a line of revolving credits for raw materials and sales.[155]

A third sample *arbitrista* analysis presented to the government in 1686 came from Osorio y Redín, who regretted the end of Spain's once "opulent" trade and the disappearance of its manufacturing capacity as foreigners gained access to its colonial wealth. In his phrasing, "they abandon their thieving at this Court, to rob in all the Kingdoms of the Indies."[156] Osorio aimed to alert merchants and the state to the advantages of controlling colonial trade. He claimed that *if* exports were accurately reported, *if* the average nominal level (20 percent) of export duties were in fact collected, *if* more shipping were available, *then* state revenues might multiply from one to twenty million pesos annually.[157] The analysis is distinguished by a rational calculation of both costs and benefits from controlling the flow of merchandise exported to the colonies. Foreign resident merchants sourcing among their homelands' producers, then reexporting to the colonies through the intermediation of Spanish factors or agents, earned between 250 and 300 percent over the prime cost of imported linens. Part of this return, Osorio argued, could accrue to Spanish nationals once they established direct contact with foreign producers.[158] Currently foreign merchants—although complaining about the high cost of doing business in Andalusia—were cynical, he understood, about payouts of 10 million pesos annually (a rhetorical exaggeration) to those Spaniards *(metedores, cabezas de fierro, encubridores)* collaborating in their smuggling operations.[159]

Osorio's argument hinged upon the accuracy of his proposition that state income might be markedly raised and, in the second place even more significant, that colonial import demand far exceeded the supply provided by the flota system. These propositions would undergird the policy planning and implementation of Spain's eighteenth-century political economists. Osorio's competent, detailed estimates of both composition and value of outbound cargo point either to first-hand knowledge of or at least very reliable information from informed merchants. In any case, they convey a sense of convincing precision.

Following a breakdown by composition and value of the cargo of an average *nao* or ocean-going vessel, Osorio computed the total combined tonnage of the 25 *naos* in annual fleets *(flotas* and *galeones)* at 27,500, assigning to the *galeones* 15,000 (for Peruvian consumers) and to the *flotas* (to Mexico) somewhat less, 12,500. On the other hand, in practice exporters listed on their registers a mere 4–5,000 tons in the case of *galeones.* Multiplying the estimated cargo value per *nao* (6,746,402 pesos) by 25 he arrived at a minimum total value of cargo outbound from Sevilla-Cadiz of about 168 million pesos. In fact, he argued, the real value exported was about 200 million, ten times the assertions of both Spanish and foreign merchants involved.[160] He went further: assuming an export value of about 168 million pesos and an average duty level of 20 percent, revenues could easily yield 33 million or somewhat less. Osorio's allegations of undercounting of tonnage and cargo value are probably exaggerated, but not the tactics he spotlighted.[161]

Equally ingenious was Osorio's estimate of effective colonial demand as well as the respective shares of Andalusian and foreign shippers. He assumed that a *nao* (550 tons) carried slightly more than one million *varas* of linens, roughly adequate to meet the clothing demands of 16,000 men and 16,000 women; 25 *naos* therefore satisfied 800,000 adults of both genders.[162] In reality, effective demand came not from one million but six million "people of distinction." The metropole was neglecting 75 percent of potential colonial consumers and could only load 2 of 25 *naos* with "cloth and staples" of national origin. Again, to employ his phrasing, "fleets and galleons barely furnish one-quarter of the Indies' imports, which makes clear why there is so much fraud." The balance of colonial demand had to be met from non-Spanish sources that operated "illegally in all the ports of the Indies."[163] To dissuade colonial viceroys from tolerating smuggling, it was contemplated offering them salaries of a sole payment of one million pesos—which indicates why viceregal posts were high priced at the end of the seventeenth century.

Like *arbitristas* of his time and *proyectistas* of the eighteenth century, Osorio based his project for national economic recovery and enlarged state income on a metropole equipped to satisfy colonial demand from domestic sources. Influenced by the example of Dutch, English, and French privileged companies, his first recommendation favored one trading company albeit limited to Spanish investors.[164] It would bypass middlemen to purchase directly from foreign producers "until production is available in our country," a process that could eventually lead to a merchant marine of 200 vessels in Spain's transatlantic trade alone. But minus sufficient shipping and an effective royal navy, he warned, "we will lose those possessions, and our monarchy will be destroyed."[165]

There is a strong presumption that the analyses and prescriptions of Castro, Mata, and Osorio were solicited by a central administration concerned with improving the dismal situation of Castilian finance in the closing decades of Hapsburg Spain. Castro, it should be noted, emphasized the lack of reliable colonial trade data coupled to neglect of commercial expertise; Mata underscored the absence of textile manufactures; while Osorio hoped to plug the information gap in government circles with educated guesses of the volume and value of colonial trade flows and profit rates. Foreshadowing later developmentalists, Osorio would charter a single privileged company for the colonial trade but with shareholders restricted to Spanish nationals; this centerpiece of commercial strategy, he was convinced, would provide a backward linkage to textile manufactures and, most essential, lead to a respectable merchant marine and royal navy.

In the work of one of Osorio's contemporaries, Manuel de Lira y Castillo, there is a comparable awareness of colonial and metropolitan reality in the 1690s as both foresaw imminent conflict over the legacy of the Hapsburg state and empire, of imperial society and economy. Lira, however, was a cosmopolitan *arbitrista*—army officer, diplomat, and by the 1690s, an influential bureaucrat. He was part of the group that, at first, supported the conde de Oropesa, admired Dutch economic growth, and sought to maintain close relations with Holland. Hence his interest in a general trading company modeled on the Dutch West India Company and in revitalizing the colonial economy and its staple exports.[166] Lira had entered diplomacy as envoy extraordinary to the United Provinces, ultimately negotiating an alliance in case of conflict with France. In 1690 he broke with the conde de Gastañaga, a close colleague who was then governor of the Spanish Netherlands, over Flanders policy and found himself shifted to the Consejo de Indias. From this vantage point he drafted recommendations for colonial policy in response to issues raised by the marqués de Mancera, a viceroy who had served both in New Spain and Peru.[167]

Mancera had leveled his criticism at colonial, civil, and military administration, colonial finance, and widespread smuggling at foreign colonial ports in the Caribbean, only to have his observations pigeonholed. When the Consulado de Sevilla objected to foreign smuggling operations at Portobelo and Veracruz and to concessions to foreigners made two centuries earlier by Fernando and his grandson Charles V, Madrid—bypassing the Consejo de Indias where Sevilla's influence was pervasive—had formed a special junta to review Mancera's critique and Sevilla's objections. The junta's recommendations, based on the sound premise that the domestic and colonial economies were closely tied ("disorder in the colonies is the root cause of our own"), properly centered on colonial rather than metropolitan conditions. Opening with a bid for a "broad change in the colonies," it came up with measures to curb smuggling in the colonies, to assign the navy to prevent "merchants in the colonies from trading at sea with foreigners," and to register faithfully cargo shipped to Lower Andalusia in order to contain smuggling and the "frauds and monopolies of those who are fronts for foreigners."[168]

Lira received the junta's recommendations, which were accompanied by a request that he offer a view on how to "put trade and finance in Spain and its colonies on a better footing." He came up with an assessment diametrically contrary to that of the junta. Junta members like the *arbitristas* had criticized foreign merchants as well as the Spanish "marchands et commissionaires des Indes." They had (mistakenly in his view) emphasized colonial administrative reform—triennial appointment, a commercial court overseas to prosecute smugglers, naval and military units impressive enough to secure compliance with Madrid's directives. These, he argued, were beyond the current financial resources of the metropole, and would not deter bureaucrats from collaborating with clandestine traders.[169]

Ending colonial irregularities ("disorders"), Lira insisted, had to originate at home and focus on the overall expansion of colonial trade and shipping facilities. Initially, Madrid had to establish a climate of "liberté de commerce," a radical proposition at its time and place. Obviously Lira was impressed by Dutch and English economic praxis. But for him "liberte de commerce" meant lowering tariffs and raising the value of Spanish currency along with the free circulation of foreign currencies in Spain. He also favored imitating the French policy of attracting skilled labor from Italian manufacturing centers, accepting Protestant merchants and even Jews. A privileged trading company, headquartered at Cadiz or elsewhere in Spain and open to foreigners' participation, was the instrumental core of his policy; ultimately it might form a corps of Spanish businessmen ("the veins of the body politic"). Foreigners' participation, however, would not be left to chance. Lira's vision included formal arrangements with London merchants and the directors of the Dutch East and West India companies whereby under the auspices of his "compagnie generale du commerce" English and Dutch businessmen could set up "shops and agents" at Veracruz and Callao. So radical a break with the preoccupations of Lower Andalusia's commercial oligopolists would never be entertained even by Spain's eighteenth-century *proyectistas*.[170]

Novel in Lira's approach is his grasp of dynamic factors in commercial capitalism developing in the United Provinces and England. The Spanish transatlantic trading system based upon the formal exclusion of foreign participation was, he implied, a myth. Since exclusion was a patent failure, and England and Holland had progressed while Spain stagnated, then their paradigm should be replicated. Behind Lira's guarded language is a half-expressed hope of duplicating in Spain an Amsterdam or London. Somehow foreign expertise and capital channeled into the most lucrative sector of the imperial economy—its system of colonial trade and shipping—might rejuvenate Spain's domestic textile manufacture and in the long run help revive economic growth. Here surfaced a theme repeatedly found in eighteenth-century *proyectista* policy: colonial rather than domestic demand could trigger the industrial development of the metropole.

Lira, however, had grasped only the surface reality of his paradigmatic countries, for the legalized participation of foreigners in what was a Spanish commercial preserve could not alone uproot the institutions and mentalities of an imperial Spain rigidified by colonialism and economic stagnation. On the other hand, Lira's radical opening to presumed English and

Dutch cooperation also reflected Spaniards' well-grounded fear of conflict with France. Then Spain would need allies, hence Lira's preference for foreign participation in his proposed privileged company. "The immediate advantage to Spain from this Company and the reestablishment of its trade," he observed at the end of his analysis, "would be that England and Holland will be its firmest Allies in maintaining its integrity and defense, which they will view as their own."[171] Lira represented that faction of Spain's political class which preferred another Hapsburg over a Bourbon successor to the childless Charles II.

Rarely published and clearly not implemented, the late seventeenth-century treatises may be read as reflections on new realities in northwestern Europe, Spain, and America. Westphalia and the privileges subsequently imposed by its commercial rivals made clear Spain's political and economic anemia. These rivals were now freed by the recession of Hapsburg power to compete for maritime and economic supremacy in the Atlantic world. By liberating Europe's developing economies from the mercenary armies and religious and political conformity championed by the Hapsburgs, they opened space for a new phase of commercial capitalism in the rapidly expanding Atlantic trade and manufacturing enterprise and in the social and political transformations associated with these developments.

While Spain's internal weakness had long been apparent at home as well as north of the Pyrenees, awareness of the end of an era began to crystallize in the Iberian peninsula during the last phase of the Thirty Years War with defeat in the Netherlands, loss of Portugal, revolt in Catalonia, and foreign inroads in the Caribbean. For many Spaniards, the Peace of Westphalia marked a moment of truth, a watershed between the dynamism and power that had nurtured the mirage of a "universal Catholic empire" and a Spain submerged in misery and at risk from the very nations which had profited from its achievements as well as its failures. Spanish analysts now had to view problems in a fresh light.

The late *arbitristas'* common discourse, their real message, was the need to come to grips with Spain's condition of economic dependence, immiserization, and overall loss of European status. No longer was it a matter of finding purely short-term fiscal or financial devices to solve the state's illiquidity. Unlike earlier seventeenth-century analysts, they emphasized underlying factors of economic backwardness and perceived—as Spain's rivals had—the importance of America's resources and expanding markets. Through their discourse ran two interlocked themes: the idea of a previous era of prosperity and the conviction that the immediate cause of the collapse of that prosperity and power was loss of control over Spain's transatlantic commercial system at both colonial and peninsular termini. Recovery of lost status focused on reducing the upsurge of smuggling in the Caribbean and in and around the Bay of Cadiz and, at Cadiz, on controlling illegal foreign participation in colonial trade through the use of strawmen and corrupt practices among customs employees. Recovery also required ancillary measures: "restoration" of peninsular manufactures, a reconstituted merchant marine and royal navy, and modernization of colonial port defenses. But there was little agreement on the means to achieve these ends. Particularly sharp were differences over the utility of privileged trading companies as instruments of growth and over which paradigm of development policy to adopt: Dutch, English, or French.

Arbitrista essays changed little in metropole or colonies. They were circulated in manuscript among the political elite (if published at all), and some appeared long afterward under changed circumstances. Spanish policymakers, a small corps of the political class, were generally homogeneous, responsive to vested interests, sensitive to political trends, and often paralyzed by the risks of conflicting alternatives and a deadening sense of victimization by forces beyond their control. For if it had become clear that America was now crucial to the survival of the Spanish monarchy, it was also apparent that America's tropical products, markets, and above all its silver were becoming essential to the economies of northwestern Europe. In their separate ways the beneficiaries of Westphalia were now taking advantage of flagging Spanish power to expand their access to Spain's colonial resources both in Europe and America.

Two centuries of Castilian colonialism in America in tandem with Hapsburg dynastic imperialism in Europe had left a profound, enduring imprint on the Spanish metropole, its economy, society, and political institutions. Not surprisingly, underlying much *arbitrista* discourse of the late seventeenth century was a significant message: if institutional change in Spain was unnecessary or difficult, the colonies furnished a source of recovery just as they had formerly provided a source of power, prosperity, and "grandeur." Westphalia and its aftermath removed a film from the eyes of many hitherto unwilling to recognize the colonial factor as a major element in what historians have come to call the "decline of Spain."

Decline: Perception and Reality

Historians have always been fascinated by the process of imperial decline. As the metropole of the largest early modern empire, Spain has received its share of such attention. Spain's loss of hegemony in Europe and growing economic dependence and stagnation at home have been the source of considerable literary controversy. Spain's decline had multiple facets: economic and political as well as religious, social, and cultural. Often examined as separate phenomena, these aspects of decline in fact formed part of a larger, often contradictory reality that is difficult to encapsulate. When an early *arbitrista* cryptically concluded that Spain was poor because it was rich, he touched on the peculiar contradictions that gave rise to the notion of a nation "bewitched," living outside reality. Although the term decline *(decadencia)* rarely appears in the literature of the time, late seventeenth-century *arbitristas* generally agreed that Spain, once prosperous and powerful, had slipped into stagnation and poverty, political impotence, and even institutional decay.

Detailed analysis of Spain's decline under the Hapsburgs is beyond the scope of this study. Yet understanding subsequent Bourbon failures to overcome Spain's persistent lag in the context of western European development, requires an overview of the political and social consequences of reliance upon colonial silver to reinforce Castilian patrimonialism and Hapsburg dynastic imperialism while inhibiting the effectiveness of the central administration. Thus, the incapacity of the Spanish Bourbon regime in the eighteenth century to advance major reforms at critical junctures, calls into question so-called "absolutism" under the Austrian dynasty. Just as we have implied the existence of a deformed or pseudomercantilism through the agency of a dependent pseudo-bourgeoisie, we posit a pseudoabsolutism— a barely concealed consensus of aristocratic, bureaucratic, and merchant elites sanctioned by the ecclesiastical establishment. In multiple ways the syndrome of silver exchanges tying America, Spain and Europe induced the remarkable proliferation of privilege which sapped the body politic, a process of institutional involution that peaked in the seventeenth century.

The *perception* of decline from apparent prosperity and acknowledged grandeur had its historical context. Europeans still living in a world of medieval cast in the early sixteenth century had been amazed by the extraordinary quantities of precious metals unloaded at Sevilla from the still mythical realms of Peru and Mexico. "Can we fail to ask about those fabulous cargoes unloaded at Sevilla, about the grandeur and fragility of Philip II's empire, about the secret byways taken by the gold and silver escaping from Spain?"[172] Dazzled by the widespread display of "wealth, power and splendor" as bonanzas were transformed into the conspicuous consumption and pursuit of status practiced by Spain's Hapsburg rulers, as indeed by all who profited directly and indirectly from conquest, colonization and commerce, Europeans' images of Spain's wealth and the cultivated iconography of its grandeur were diffused widely in the wake of trade, diplomacy, and warfare. As expenditures outstripped income and Spanish monarchs borrowed heavily from German and Genoese financiers, Europe's merchants and artisans catered to expanding Spanish demand for luxuries, articles of daily consumption, and military equipment. Spain, scarcely unified under the domination of Castile (itself barely emerging from its late medieval past and the last crusade of reconquest), appeared destined under the new Hapsburg dynasty to realize the medieval mirage of a "universal," that is worldwide, Catholic empire.

Income disbursed on imports, on mercenary armies, and diplomatic largesse, however, did not make for sustained prosperity or imperial security. After initial stimulus to peninsular agriculture and manufacture (much of it for export to the colonies), the construction and preservation of empire in Europe and America progressively drained Castilian Spain of its meager possibilities of growth and development. As the locus of economic dynamism shifted to Andalusia and to the center of the colonial enterprise at Sevilla, peripheral zones along the Cantabrian and eastern Mediterranean seaboards, deprived of direct colonial contacts, were disadvantaged. Meanwhile, Madrid—new capital of Castile, bureaucratic nexus of overseas empire and center of the Spanish Hapsburg patrimonial state after 1568— became the locus of an extravagant court and (largely Castilian) aristocracy and bureaucracy. Isolated by geography from Cantabrian ports and population centers, from the Mediterranean littoral, and above all from the Andalusian Atlantic nexus with America, Madrid's role turned increasingly parasitic, consuming an ever growing share of state revenues and aristocratic incomes.[173]

In mythifying a past golden age of prosperity, however, late seventeenth-century *arbitristas* sanctioned the institutions and mentalities resistant to change. Those institutions and mind-sets—products of the flush of colonial income, imperial power, and intensified Catholic orthodoxy in the sixteenth century—dominated the seventeenth century and deepened the absolute and relative disparity between Spain and northwest Europe. Furthermore, as reality mocked an idealized past, as foreign interests infiltrated a supposed system of commercial exclusivism, as metropolitan society and economy became subordinated to Hapsburg patrimonial dynasticism and Castilian religious orthodoxy, acceptance of the fatality of recession or decline further constrained the capacity to reform.

Spain's initial marginality and growing backwardness relative to Holland, England, and France have prompted some historians to characterize imperial Spain as a protostate dominated by late medieval institutions and mentalities, a *sociedad tardo-feudal*.[174] Although overly simplified, such emphasis on the persistence of increasingly outmoded concepts and practices encapsulates a fundamental dynamic of the Hapsburg era. Hapsburg Spain, however, was not merely a "gothic edifice" characterized by "belated feudalism." It was too closely tied to the modernizing states of Europe and to a profitable if inadequately developed overseas empire to be just a stagnating survival of an earlier age. As *arbitrista* literature shows, both the consequences and pitfalls of dependency and immobilism had long been apparent to critical Spaniards, as early as Luis Ortiz's unpublished analysis of 1558. If impetus to change failed to appear under the later Hapsburgs or to make significant headway under the Bourbons in the eighteenth century, it was in large part because exploitation and defense of silver-rich colonies in America had become inextricably involved with defending the dynastic and religious hegemony of the House of Hapsburg in Europe and subsidizing the proliferation of privilege in Spain and America. Maintenance of these interdependent yet often contradictory imperatives reinforced traditional institutions and mind-sets. Spain's Hapsburg regime owed its endurance to the secular interpenetration of mutually self-reinforcing interests, ideals, and rituals.

Elsewhere in Europe the diaspora of silver by war and trade worked to dissolve traditional economic patterns and social relationships to form new constellations of power. In Spain, however, colonial silver reinforced and impoverished an outmoded society. Repeatedly, threats to its empire would force Castile to come to grips with the reality of its institutional rigidities. And, repeatedly, reform confronted the proliferation of formal and informal entitlements—that ultimate legacy so difficult to disown, much more to overcome.

4. Conjunctural Crisis: War and the Utrecht Settlement

\

The complex of treaties signed at Münster in Westphalia at the middle of the seventeenth century signaled the end of imperial Spain's ability to support the waning structures of medieval Europe. Imperial Spain's lone foothold for intervention in the heart of "modern" Europe remained Flanders into which, under Louis XIV, French interests and armies inched inexorably. After Westphalia Spain wrestled with its dual inheritance of medievalism and colonialism, ceaselessly mending peninsular and colonial structures and mentalities, ceaselessly pressured by the developing economies and societies of "modernizing" western Europe. Spain's international position had been slipping, of course, long before mid-century. Recession and stagnation became unavoidably apparent after Westphalia. Once aggressive, imperial Spain turned defensive in its weakness, seeking survival through concessions to major European interests. These—Dutch, English, and French—now focused on the core of the Spanish imperial economy in Lower Andalusia's ports and upon the Caribbean.

In the last half of the seventeenth century, the colonies in the Caribbean furnished the primary overseas dynamism for the growth and development of the principal European economies bordering the Atlantic. The emerging economies of England and France poured capital and personnel into merchant marines and regular naval forces in order to penetrate fully Spain's Caribbean complex, gateway to the markets of Spain's American empire. Like their Dutch predecessors, the English and French probed for weak points in the Spanish Caribbean to develop entrepôts for supplying slaves and merchandise to nearby Spanish mainland ports.[1] The English initiative in occupying Jamaica right after Westphalia (1655) was significant. The French, on the other hand, had to delay four decades before obtaining an equally strategic island base, Saint-Domingue.

Occupation and initial development of these island entrepôts stemmed from the desire to imitate the Dutch pattern on Bonaire and especially Curaçao. The primary function of these bases was to exploit Spanish treaty concessions legitimizing a non-Spanish presence in what had long been considered by the Spanish state as solely Spanish. Jamaica like Curaçao quickly flourished as a smugglers' center for traders from the Spanish colonies—as John Cary later phrased it, "Nor have [Spaniards] so well secured the West Indies but that it is very plentifully supplied by us with Manufactures, and many other things from Jamaica, which is accomplished with greater advantage than when sent first to Cadiz."[2] Of course, the treaty system legalized merely the presence of foreign ships and traders in the Caribbean; their commercial contacts with Spanish possessions remained outlawed. These occurred, however, in response to the needs of Spanish colonial economies. Given the illegal nature of such operations, the twilight zone between illicit trade and outright piracy, and the succession of European conflicts with inevitable Caribbean projections, commercial exchanges continued in a climate of irregularity and unpredictability. Ultimately piracy became a barrier to profitable commercial exchange, which is why the era of the buccaneer lasted in fact only a few decades.[3]

There was one major mode of commercial exchange by non-Spaniards that Spanish metropolitan and colonial authorities had to tolerate in the Caribbean, the *asiento* or supply contract for delivery of African slave workers, origin of one of the greatest population shifts of all times. A recent and admittedly conservative estimate of the migration of Africans to America throughout the seventeenth century is 1.3 million, of which the Spanish colonies imported 292,500 (about 22 percent). On the other hand, if we aggregate Spanish American slave imports (arriving mainly through the Caribbean) with 20 percent of those of the French and English Caribbean, Spanish America imported 29 percent.[4] While an important source of forced imported laborers, the slave supply contracts were also the vehicle for introducing a considerable volume of smuggled goods into Cartagena and Portobelo, Veracruz and Havana.[5] From Curaçao and Jamaica, merchants shipped slaves and goods to Spanish ports, or traders from these ports went to the Dutch and English.[6] At the same time these contacts furnished non-Spanish merchants with scarce commercial data about "goods sold for cash, to whom one may sell on credit, and how to insure payment at pre-arranged times."[7]

The *asiento* in the seventeenth century may be examined from numerous angles. We shall first look at the firms ostensibly receiving the contract. After 1580 Portuguese speculators held the contracts, a pattern enduring until Portugal's separation from Spain in 1640. Then, until the end of the century, Dutch slavers operated overtly or covertly as principal suppliers. When Genoese *asentistas* Domingo Grillo[8] and Lomelin (1630–78) failed to purchase slaves at Portugal's African ports, they turned to an Irish Catholic agent in Spain, Richard White, to arrange slave shipments by the Dutch West India Company from its Curaçao slave depots and by the recently formed English Royal African Company with a base in Jamaica.[9] As a result, the Dutch West India Company sold slaves to Spanish Caribbean colonies for about twenty-one years until Spain awarded the *asiento* first to a Spanish strawman and later to the Dutch firm of Coymans, which had a representative at Sevilla.[10]

From another perspective, the incapacity or unwillingness of the Sevilla merchant guild to fulfill its sole *asiento* underscores the underdevelopment of Lower Andalusia's commercial and financial structures. Only during a brief twelve-year period (1670–82) did either a merchant of Sevilla (García) or its *consulado* even nominally administer the contract. In fact, García fronted for Coymans and the Dutch West India Company, while the *consulado* (1676–81)—like Grillo and Lomelin earlier—had to purchase slaves from the Dutch at Curaçao.[11]

What requires explanation is why more than 150 years after the invasion and occupation of America, Sevilla merchants still lacked the initiative, commercial expertise, capital, and shipping to fulfill the *asiento*. Sifting the history of *asiento* contracts turns up the absence of Spanish shipping and naval forces available for slaving. While García used his profits to finance the construction of escort vessels for the fleets to America, the *consulado* used its earnings in part to hire Dutch admiral de Ruyter and a fleet to attack the Mediterranean port of Messina.[12] Spanish administration of the *asiento* failed. Contrast this incapacity with the dynamism that French latecomers to colonialism with state support displayed in the last twenty-five years of the seventeenth century in producing textiles for the Spanish colonial market, in developing both a merchant marine and royal navy, and in chartering companies to establish slave stations on the west African coast and then pressuring Paris to obtain the *asiento* from Madrid.

French Penetration of Spanish America, 1650–1700

The historic shift of Europe's economic core from north Italy to the Low Countries, northwestern France, and south England was the product of many factors—demography, agricultural productivity, urbanization, innovation and growth in textile manufactures, improvement in ships' hull and sail design, elaboration of commercial and financial instruments and techniques, and the lure of wider regional, national, and international markets. Europe's developing economies—Dutch, English, and French—shared these factors in varying proportions. One of the salient factors lay overseas, the economies of Spain's colonies in America, their growing demand for manufactures overbalanced by their output of silver. In penetrating Spain's Caribbean complex, French merchants aimed to catch up with Dutch and English businessmen. Economic competition led, at the end of the century, to one of the great crises of commercial capitalism: large-scale international conflict for control over Spain's colonies in America.

French expansion can be examined both from the point of view of policy-makers and of regional interests. Overall, instead of conflict there was notable convergence of state and private sectors. What distinguished French overseas penetration were, first, collaboration between central government and regional interests in a primitive *dirigisme;*[13] second, delayed occupation of a strategic Caribbean island base; and, third, state support for the French merchant enclave at the Cadiz entrepôt. There the French state and commercial community converged to support the established Spanish transatlantic pattern of managed trade. Nonetheless, in this respect French bureaucrats and businessmen have been characterized inaccurately as "more timid and backward than the English and Dutch" in exploiting their position at Cadiz.[14]

As the growth and development of mercantile capitalism in France accelerated at the end of the seventeenth century, French businessmen encountered the common problem of late-comers to economic development, the hegemony of economies with more developed commercial structures, maritime shipping and financial services.[15] Initially the United Provinces and to a lesser extent, England, offered a paradigm. French merchants using agents at Cadiz and hamstrung by the "mediocre organization of French trade" had to route their silver through Amsterdam, London or Genoa. Typically, the most comprehensive commercial manual designed for French businessmen, Jacques Savary's *Dictionnaire du commerce* (1672), borrowed from Dutch practice and experience.[16] Like Spanish groups, French producers and merchants had protested in the 1640s about imported manufactures that drained France's precious metals holdings, "seeing that woolen and silk textiles and all kinds of fabrications are no longer manufactured . . . because of those brought by Dutch and English merchants."[17] Mercantilist policy under the Fouquets, Colbert and then Pontchartrain proposed to monitor imports to advance import substitution, reduce reliance upon foreign shipping, and expand the outreach of state power through an enhanced navy. Response was not uniform: legislation for developmental goals touched off complaints by French wine and brandy exporters as well as sugar refiners, whose principal outlets were Holland and England, and by Paris's Six Grands Corps of textile and other importers.[18]

Nonetheless the complaints of established domestic interest groups were diluted as segments of the French Atlantic coast from Rouen, Saint-Malo, Nantes, and Bordeaux to Bayonne explored the vision of an integrated interregional economy dominated ultimately by France and covering Spain and, through Spain, its mining colonies in Peru and New Spain. The colonies were potentially a large trading bloc capable of absorbing French products—linens, woolens, laces, wines—and exporting silver, dyes, and hides. The links of French producers, merchants and shippers to Spain's colonial economy surfaced in 1656–57 when English naval units seized off Cadiz a convoy inbound from Veracruz, setting off immediate repercussions in France's Atlantic ports where "Rouen alone was committed to . . . four millions, Saint-Malo for about the same . . . [so that] no one among us is able to sell, neither in Normandy nor in Brittany." For merchants of Rouen, Saint-Malo, and other Atlantic ports, export growth meant circumventing English and Dutch hegemony in Europe, Spain and its colonies.[19] Buccaneer Oexquemelin sailed from Havre-de-Grace aboard a vessel of the French East India Company to occupy Tortuga off the north coast of Saint-Domingue, and in the 1670s the Compagnie du Sénégal probed for slave depots on the west African coast in order to compete with English and Dutch slavers already established as the Caribbean's main distributors.[20]

Position papers drafted early in Colbert's administration reviewed national interest in light of Spain's overall condition. In 1666 an anonymous memoir centered on subordinating Spain and Portugal to French hegemony, proposing to incorporate them as *dependencias* in the competition with England. First, however, they would have to overhaul Spanish state finance, beginning with the elimination of the plethora of financial intermediaries—tax-farmers, regional corporations and family networks. On this proposed foundation France would formulate a foreign policy. French dynastic claims upon Spain were beyond question, a Bourbon succession there, inevitable. Meanwhile, weakened by "disunity and weakness" Spain continued a policy of compromise and concession to escape the consequences of a war. Along with Portugal and Austria, Spain might be isolated from England; but if Spain refused to link up with France, only then should France resort to war, counting upon the support of thousands of French residents dispersed in Aragon, Valencia, Catalonia, Madrid, and the peninsula's principal ports—"so many columns to support our purpose."[21]

This memoir revealed a quintessentially French international focus, by indirection alone attending to Spanish colonial interests. In the summer of 1670 reports from Madrid to Colbert laid out the basic French preoccupation with English maritime power in European and Caribbean waters. For the Spanish empire held together by its maritime lifeline was now overawed by English naval units that inspired "a constant fear, which has great effect upon the Spirit, on observing daily English squadrons along their coasts." Omnipresent and omnipotent, the English naval presence inevitably impinged upon Spanish policy and molded the attitude of Spaniards expressed in "War with everyone but peace with England."

English naval power made possible the occupation of Jamaica and its conversion into a naval station, a center for distributing goods and African slaves and collecting commercial intelligence, and a channel of regular contact with Spanish colonial officials, according to a French cleric on diplomatic mission. "The profits of the English and Dutch have led them to establish warehouses there . . . from which they flood the Indies with whatever is needed. Profits are large." A poorly united, economically backward, and militarily weakened Spain yielded concessions to French interests in Lower Andalusian ports, and might have to tolerate further English penetration of the Caribbean, further disruption of the Spanish convoy system and threaten French merchants' profitable infiltration of Spain's colonial entrepôt at Cadiz. Logically, the report of the archbishop of Toulouse concluded by recommending that French economic policy support direct sales (smuggling) in the Caribbean, relying upon French shipping, skilled pilots and "merchants who have sailed aboard Spanish galleons and flotas to provide information . . . on how to penetrate that area."[22] Here is a premature, high-level expression of the French thrust into the Caribbean and the Pacific, and a foreshadowing of French interest in the *asiento*.[23]

Competent, protonationalist, high-profile bureaucrats like Mazarin, Colbert, and Pontchartrain, were not the only authors of the policy of state participation in fostering commercial capitalism by exploiting French links to Spain. Policy flowed from the confluence of regional and national interests and their social networks. Colbert's deference to commercial and manufacturing groups in Normandy and Brittany was marked, as were Pontchartrain's connections. In 1698 Pontchartrain, *président* of Brittany's parliament, knew personally major figures behind the Compagnie du Mer du Sud—Jourdan de Grouée and the Malouins Noel Danycan de l'Espine (*connétable* of Brittany), Nicolas Magon de la Chipaudière, and his brother, Jean Magon de La Lande, all wholesale exporters of Breton linens to the Spanish colonies via Cadiz. Magon de La Lande joined others in 1692 to urge Pontchartrain to employ French naval units to convert Saint-Domingue into a Caribbean smuggling center and slave depot.[24] Again, it was Pontchartrain who transformed a merchants' lobby into the national *conseil de commerce.* The president of this *conseil* and ex-ambassador to Lisbon (1685–88), Amelot de Gournay, later turned up as chief executor of French policy toward Spain when ambassador there in the critical years of the War of the Spanish Succession.[25]

Interlocks of family, kinship, and multiple investment in shipping and colonial development, the slave trade, and overseas merchandising are illustrated by the career of Jean-Baptiste Ducasse, born to a petty merchant family of Dax in the Midi. In the 1670s Ducasse was an employee of the Compagnie du Sénégal, procuring African slaves for French indigo planters at Saint-Domingue. There he settled along with other French Basques in clusters connected by "cousinhood and family financial support."[26] By turns sailor, merchant, slaver, and planter, Ducasse began as buccaneer participating in the brief French occupation of Cartagena; his share of the booty consisted in part of portraits of Cartagena's Spanish governors, which later lined the walls of his study at Léogane in Saint-Domingue. He was one of the first planters at Saint-Domingue to shift from indigo to sugar. The French government posted him to Madrid in 1701 to arrange the *asiento* that Madrid assigned to a Saint-Malo company, one of whose directors was Danycan de l'Espine.[27] The interlock of petty bourgeois trading families with the French bureaucracy is highlighted by the fact that one of Danycan's daughters married Amelot de Gournay's son, and Danycan's son married a niece of Pontchartrain.[28] Ducasse's daughter married Louis de la Rochefoucauld et Roye, uncle of French foreign minister Choiseul under Louis XVI. To fellow French Basques, Ducasse confided that Saint-Domingue's overriding importance was as a base "to join to our monarchy those key colonies, Mexico and Peru."[29] Access to the Spanish mainland's silver was the initial magnet drawing Spain's competitors into the Caribbean. From merchant families—Ducasse, Crozat, Danycan, Magon, Eon—many from Saint-Malo, connected to the Atlantic slave trade and to trade with the Spanish colonies in the seventeenth century were to come prominent French bureaucrats of the eighteenth century: Amelot, Maurepas, and Choiseul.

It is difficult to assign relative importance to state and private sectors in the development of commercial capitalism in seventeenth-century France. No doubt state policy reflected ministerial "integrity," competent reporting by zealous commercial and diplomatic agents at Madrid and Cadiz, and in general, consistent pursuit of hard data for formulating protectionist policy—all reflecting "method and order."[30] Ministerial competence, however, was expected to work in tandem with the private sector on the assumption that "trade ought to be free, and rulers ought to involve themselves only to protect it and obtain for their subjects access and increase, spurring them to do what can be advantageous." This policy physiocrat Adam Smith later parodied as "imposed . . . by the sophistry of merchants and manufacturers . . . always demanding a monopoly against their countrymen."[31] The point is, Saint-Malo merchants never lacked state support in extending their commercial operations into Spain and beyond to its American empire.[32] Their initiative over twelve years (1703–15) may have brought to French ports as much as 99 million pesos, in the process doubling France's monetary stock.[33]

Malouin interests served as a cutting edge of French economic imperialism in late seventeenth-century Spain and its colonies. Their prominent commercial, shipping, and financial roles in the War of the Spanish Succession flowed from previous decades of expansion at Cadiz. Here the initial factor was Saint-Malo's role in the growth of French textile exports to Spain and its colonies based upon protoindustrial manufacture of linens *(toiles)* produced in the Breton hinterland. During the 1650s Malouins had obtained from Madrid licenses to freight silver in wartime—the Spanish government's and their own returns on colonial sales—from the Canaries to Saint-Malo. In 1658 alone this netted Saint-Malo 650,000 *ecus*.[34] At Cadiz, La Lande Magon of Saint-Malo was a regular shipper of French manufactures on convoys to Veracruz; in a returning convoy of 1670 from Veracruz at least 25 percent of the silver deposited at Cadiz was reexported to Saint-Malo. Malouins also served in French consulships at Gibraltar (1698) and Malaga (1686).[35] Between 1605 and 1662 the number of French residents at Cadiz rose from 7 to 33; according to a 1714 survey, wholesale Malouin merchants clustered at two points in Lower Andalusia: Cadiz and Puerto Santa María.[36] By 1680 Saint-Malo's shipping resources were impressive, with 120 ocean-going vessels, the number rising to 300 in 1709.[37] When Spain's communications to the Caribbean and the Rio de la Plata were disorganized in the 1690s, Malouin merchant Eon de Villebague[38] recommended a naval sortie to occupy Buenos Aires where Malouins had long been buying hides. Then, to penetrate the South American hinterland to tap the silver mines of Potosí, another Malouin, pragmatic and prescient Magon de La Lande, urged Pontchartrain to "place agents on the Saint-Domingue coast to trade with the Indies, and to establish settlements which will allow us not only to trade through Spanish intermediaries on *flotas* and galleons, but also to undermine their trade and navigation with the Indies."[39] This was still a trader's rather than a planter's conception of Saint-Domingue's economic potential.

Drawing upon the human resources and cottage manufacture of the Breton countryside, equipped with navigators and seaman experienced in Caribbean and South Atlantic waters, knowledgeable of conditions of colonial trade at Cadiz and Puerto Santa María, self-capitalized and encouraged by expansionist-minded French bureaucrats, Malouin merchants in the last decade of the seventeenth century were prepared to bypass the regulatory restraints at both Lisbon and the Cadiz-Puerto Santa María complex. They aimed at direct sales to Brazil at Rio de Janeiro, to Peru via the occupation of Buenos Aires or passage through the Straits of Magellan and up the Pacific coast, and to New Spain and Cuba via the island entrepôt of Saint-Domingue ceded by Spain at Ryswick (1697).[40] Finally, once Bourbons succeeded to the Spanish monarchy, Malouins were well prepared to exploit a major business enterprise of west Europe's merchant capitalism: the Spanish *asiento*. For a brief period it was to bring to Saint-Malo's slave merchants extraordinary earnings and to France near disaster in an interminable war.

Demand for slaves in Spanish America in the seventeenth century came from a relatively small plantation sector, from mining camps and the conspicuous consumption propensities of colonial urbanites of means.[41] Slaving was a profitable enterprise, but in the long run not as profitable to *asentistas* as handling smuggled goods. This dual function under the contract—slaves and smuggling—explains why *asentistas* advanced the Spanish state large sums which, however, it failed to divert, for instance, to subsidize private sector shipbuilding and training of seamen. A thriving shipping industry conceivably might have eliminated the award of *asientos* to foreign bidders among minor powers; in fact they were awarded to Portuguese merchants over most of the seventeenth century. In the 1690s the contracts were distributed in a bewildering fashion. In 1693 a Spanish colonial businessman, Bernardo Marino de Guzmán of Caracas, obtained the contract, banking on the financial backing of residents of New Spain and Peru (to whom he promised delivery of slaves and European goods). However, Marino turned back to the Portuguese, to the Companhia de Cacheu, to meet the contract's stipulations. It was common knowledge that the Cacheu group (which had French stockholders) bought slaves and goods at Jamaica and Curaçao. In other words, Marino and the Cacheu group were only formally the contractors; in fact they were strawmen for the real *asentistas*, English and Dutch investor groups.[42]

In 1692 Pontchartrain planned to support Malouin merchants Magon de La Lande and Eon de Villebague, and Rouen merchant LeCouteulx in using Portuguese strawmen in the Cacheu group.[43] Marino de Guzmán died, however, in 1695 under mysterious circumstances after returning to the Caribbean, and his *asiento* was reassigned to the Cacheu group (and its English and Dutch suppliers). At this time the French Compagnie du Sénégal arranged to purchase slaves at west African depots for shipment to the recently formed Compagnie de Saint-Domingue. In 1699 this enterprise organized by Pontchartrain and numbering among its shareholders La Chipaudiere Magon, tax-farmers Bernard and Antoine Crozat, and (as shareholder and director of its Caribbean operations) Ducasse, was chartered to deliver slaves to the Cacheu group supplying the Spanish Caribbean.[44] If only by indirection, French commercial interests were at last infiltrating the Spanish colonies.

At the end of the seventeenth century as stagnation deepened in metropolitan Spain, New Spain's silver production was beginning a rise that would end only about 1800. The magnet in the west of Mexican and Peruvian precious metals continued to draw the interest of Dutch, English, and French merchants. At best, between the treaty system covering Lower Andalusia and the anarchy of Caribbean "interlopers," there functioned a fragile equilibrium. Leading commercial interests, English (often supported by the Dutch) and French, sought preferment in the peninsula at Madrid, in Lower Andalusia, and at Lisbon. The most destabilizing possibility—a full-blown trilateral arrangement offering direct access to Spain's colonies through non-Spanish shipping in Spanish convoys, through foreign merchants residing in the colonies, and/or the award of the *asiento* to either English or French consortia—threatened to materialize in the late 1690s. As French interests expanded their Cadiz foothold, the English developed their entrepôt on Jamaica. Destabilization came from a political phenomenon: the literal dying-out of the Hapsburgs in Spain followed by the realization of a Hispano-French monarchy promising an economic union of sorts when Louis XIV's grandson was selected Spain's first Bourbon monarch.

The accession of Louis XIV's grandson as king of Spain in 1700, finally cleared the way to the goal denied the Dutch and English. Until this time, no dominant European power had been able to obtain the slave *asiento*. Now the French would no longer have to share the proceeds of the sale of slaves and merchandise with holders of the slave contracts. The *asiento* of

1701 gave French businessmen the possibility of dominating Spain's colonial trading system, or so it seemed. "This would be," wrote Pontchartrain to Malouin merchant Eon, "a proper moment to ship our manufactures directly to Spaniards in America, something we have sought in vain for a long time."[45] Inevitably, the decision of Madrid's political elite to turn to the neighboring Bourbon dynasty, followed by the assignment of the coveted *asiento* to a French consortium disrupted the west European equilibrium, and an international conflict over access to Spain's colonies in America erupted. As Flemish bureaucrat conde de Bergeyck put it bluntly: "Fear of [Franco-Spanish] unity and the loss of trade have been the sole preoccupations of the two maritime powers in this war"—the War of the Spanish Succession.[46]

Crisis and War

The roots of the War of the Spanish Succession were multiple: domestic, international, and colonial.[47] As the government weakened in the last half of the seventeenth century, Spain's regional fissures widened. Influential *grande* family constellations dominated geographical areas—the Portocarreros in Aragon, the Medina Celis at San Lúcar and Sevilla, the Medina Sidonias at Puerto Santa María and Cadiz. Aristocratic factions or *partidos* also developed international projections. The Medina Celi group favored an anglophile policy; Portocarrero and Medina Sidonia sided with Bourbon France.[48] Given the multiple links between the American colonies and the metropole's regional factions as well as the dependence of the metropole's aristocracy, nobility, clergy, bureaucracy, and merchant bourgeoisie upon income from colonial trade, office-holding, encomiendas, pensions, and religious corporations, regional conflict over the heir to the Spanish Hapsburg monarchy (whether Austrian Hapsburg or French Bourbon) and its large overseas empire, raised the fear of civil war in the metropole and, worse, loss of the American colonies to foreign occupation. Broadly speaking, the regional groups leaning toward the Hapsburgs and their alliance with England and the United Provinces sought to preserve regional autonomy. The Aragonese and Navarrese favored a French connection on the premise that French economic and military power properly harnessed might help renovate Spain through a more centralized, efficient, and soundly financed state, thereby leading to a more efficiently administered and exploited overseas empire. The devolution of state power might be reversed.

In the closing decades of the century, the central administration under the conde de Oropesa (an Alvarez de Toledo y Portugal) responded to the needs of defense, monetary stability, and overall fiscal disarray. Oropesa's major efforts were designed to shore up public credit. In 1687, confronting a public debt that continued to absorb half of state revenues, Madrid was obliged to suspend payments on *juros,* pensions, and bureaucratic salaries. Monetary reform, downsizing the state bureaucracy,[49] reducing royal household expenditures, curbing the influence of tax farmers on Hacienda policies—these put Oropesa on a collision course with segments of the aristocracy and nobility. Many had neglected estate management for privileged access to state employment in the military, royal household, and upper bureaucracy.[50] Simultaneously, Madrid encountered pressures from the resurgent peripheral provinces on the Mediterranean coast, Valencia and notably Catalonia. There, merchants and wealthy peasants were consolidating rural properties for production and export of wines and brandies, hopefully to be directed, via Sevilla or Cadiz, to the American colonies, until then virtually closed to Catalan products and traders. Catalan exporters found allies in Anglo-Dutch wine merchants marketing Catalan beverages in northwestern Europe and as eager as Catalans to penetrate consumer markets in the American colonies.[51]

The absence of a direct heir to Charles II (married first to a Bourbon, then a German) put the issue of the Spanish dynastic succession at the center of European diplomacy. Which of the heirs of Philip III, Bourbon or Hapsburg, would inherit the monarchy, and with it Spain, its European possessions, and its American colonies? Hopeful of avoiding war over the issue, England, Holland, and France tried to settle the succession on a non-French royal family. In the process, they agreed in 1698 at The Hague to partition Spain's European holdings. For example, to France would go border zones in northwest Spain (Pasajes, Fuenterrabía, San Sebastian), transit zones for Franco-Spanish trade through the Basque provinces.[52] Details of the partition treaty, modified in 1699, led Madrid authorities to believe there were other, secret articles transferring some of Spain's American colonies to England and Holland.[53] In fact, under the proposed partition, the Austrian Hapsburgs (under Archduke Charles) were assigned Spain and the American possessions. Spain's Consejo de Estado rejected this proposal, supported by the Aragonese aristocratic faction led by Cardinal Portocarrero, and trusting that a Bourbon succession and a Franco-Spanish alliance might preserve the integrity of the empire in America.[54] Contributing to the crisis atmosphere in the peninsula was widespread rural unrest in both Cataluna and Valencia and a palace coup in 1699 at Madrid. The coup, apparently engineered by aristocrats and others threatened by his policies, ousted Oropesa. The leaders camouflaged their participation by inciting Madrid's populace to riot over Oropesa's handling of a subsistence shortage.

Finally, there was the decisive colonial dimension to the crisis of the Spanish Hapsburg regime. Its elements fall into three categories: the threat to transatlantic communications, the threat of Caribbean entry to the overseas empire and, last, the fragility of the empire itself. If Castile had lost Portugal and almost Cataluña, was it inconceivable that Castile might lose New Spain, in 1700 already the economic center of its empire in America.

At the end of the century Spain had a totally inadequate merchant marine and a navy that lacked the ships and personnel to provide reliable protection to the maritime lifeline to the colonies—the convoy system at the core of the *carrera de Indias*.[55] In the 1690s Spanish authorities had to call upon French naval units—another manifestation of Colbert's economic nationalism—to defend *flotas* from English, Dutch, and French international terrorists (the buccaneers) in the Caribbean arena of conflicting European interests.[56] For once Spain's European competitors established island bases there, they proceeded to branch out in many directions: smuggling along the north coast of South America and English log-cutting operations along the coasts of Honduras and Campeche, which also facilitated illegal trading in Central America and through southern Mexico access to silver. Meanwhile, French expansionists operating in the lower Mississippi valley were a potential threat to Santa Fe, Chihuahua, and the silver mining complex of north Mexico.[57]

There were also signs of New Spain's internal instability. In the north between 1680 and 1682 in a coordinated uprising, Pueblo peoples of the upper Rio Grande around Santa Fe forced the withdrawal southward of Spanish colonial authorities, settlers, and their indigenous allies, while at the end of the decade the Tarahumara peoples attacked garrison towns. In southern Mexico native peoples in Chiapas carried on an insurgency that was only contained with difficulty. And then in 1692 in New Spain's capital, urban rioters reacting to a subsistence crisis sacked the symbols of colonial rule—viceregal palace, town council, and public granary.[58]

Foreign penetration of the Caribbean and instability in north and south New Spain and ultimately at Mexico City sharpened the perceptions and anxieties of Madrid's political elite about imperial vulnerability in a core area of Spain's overseas wealth, income, and trade. For New Spain's treasury, based on mining and other receipts, distributed funds *(situados)* to finance Spanish expenditures on massive defensive works and garrisons at Havana, Puerto Rico, Cartagena, Portobelo, and Veracruz as well as the port of Manila in the Philippines.[59] Madrid authorities could not fail to note that despite a rise in New Spain's mining output and expenditures on the area's defense, a growing percentage of returns from trade bypassed legal channels via smuggling in the Caribbean, the Azores and Canary Islands, or in the Bay of Cadiz itself usually with the open collusion of Spanish officials.[60] Moreover, Spanish officials with colonial experience (there were many) knew of the trans-Pacific trade of New Spain and Peru and of intercolonial exchanges that developed as mining operations and urban centers grew. Compared with those in the metropole, businessmen in the American colonies were more dynamic, operated over longer distances, and mobilized and managed larger pools of capital—in brief, they displayed more entrepreneurial skills than their counterparts in Spain. Many had few scruples about dealing directly with foreign traders, even with wartime enemies. Was the diversion of private income to foreign traders a sign of loss of imperial control? Did such practices portend growing colonial autonomy or only willingness to exploit fully flaws in the Spanish transatlantic trading system? Worse, were the metropole seriously weakened in wartime, might colonial elites consider independence?

The twin menaces of partition in Europe and loss of the American colonies came when Madrid's political elites were grasping the importance of the colonies as the economic basis for rebuilding the metropole's economy. Two questions were uppermost: what could be done to improve Atlantic maritime communication (the convoys)? Even more critical, would Spain's political economists, the *proyectistas,* be capable not only of drafting a blueprint for change drawn from existing European models, but also ideating a broad vision of what Spanish America's role might be?

Spain's American colonies were critical in preserving the now delicate European equilibrium. International conflict might be avoided provided they were used—to quote Mesnager, a French agent at Madrid—as "the common territory of all Europe, a source of gold and silver, which should not be the property of any State, rather Spain as always should remain the trustee." On the other hand, if the equilibrium were upset—were French interests to dominate the Spanish transatlantic system—then those Spanish colonies might become "an inexhaustible resource for . . . the conquest of the world."[61]

Viewed from the metropole, there were broadly speaking two principal interest groups. On one side were Catalan and associated Anglo-Dutch interests joined by anxious Spanish privilege-holders who backed the Austrian Hapsburgs, in part because an Austrian succession might open the transatlantic system to their participation. On the other side were Aragonese, Navarrese, and Lower Andalusian factions who tied the integrity of the Spanish empire to collaboration—hopefully equality of collaboration—with French interests, policies, personnel, and power. Such collaboration, symbolized by a Bourbon monarch, might permit the long delayed overhaul of Spain's Hapsburg institutions and policies. Among this Francophile group were also Spanish merchant houses of Lower Andalusia hoping that the French would help preserve their managed trade system. Would French mercantile interests, however, allow Philip V and his Spanish supporters to maintain Spain's secular policy of isolating the colonies from direct access by non-Spanish commercial interests, from the English, for example? Above all, to which foreign interests would Madrid assign the slave supply *asiento* for the colonies?

The resolution of the Spanish succession issue came on 1 November 1700 with the publication of Charles II's testament designating Louis XIV's grandson, Philip, duc d'Anjou, as his successor.[62] Immediately French activity then made clear that French interests would be paramount. First, instead of separating Spain's new Bourbon monarch from France as Charles's testament had insisted, in December Paris reaffirmed Philip in the line of accession to the French monarchy. Some quickly interpreted this decision as implying French hegemony over Spain's domestic and international policy.[63] French influence, it was feared, would legitimate an expanded role for French residents in Lower Andalusia's colonial trade, even the possibility that Madrid might cede parts of its American empire to France.

What in fact triggered open warfare was the decision by the newly installed Spanish Bourbon administration to award the *asiento,* at French insistence, to a French business consortium. In January 1701 the French ambassador at Madrid asked his government to pressure Spanish authorities to assign the *asiento.* "I believe," he baldly advised Louis XIV, "we should lose no time in drawing advantages from our present union that should come to French commerce."[64] Paris then sent to Madrid Ducasse, ex-buccaneer, ex-governor of Saint-Domingue, and now a director of the Compagnie de Guinée. The *asiento* would be the instrument transforming Franco-Spanish political union into an economic one as well. The *asiento* held by the Portuguese Companhia de Cacheu ended the following June, and in August 1701 Ducasse with the backing of French-affiliated bankers Flon and Hubrecht at Madrid, managed to have the contract awarded to his Compagnie de Guinée.[65] It contained as major stipulations: a loan to Madrid of £t. *(Livres tournois)* 600,000; delivery of 48,000 African slaves over a ten-year period to Spanish ports in the Caribbean, to Buenos Aires and (via the Isthmus of Panama) to Peru; the authorization of French agents (and judges conservator) resident in Spanish colonial ports to move into the colonial hinterland on company business; and permission for slave ships to sail from Spanish *or* French ports. These constituted the "first benefit France would draw from its union with Spain." Naturally the Compagnie de Guinée was formally prohibited from using its ships to "unload, introduce, or sell textiles, goods or manufactures . . . or trade or sell other things."[66]

Over nine months French interests had maximized the possibilities of dynastic substitution by collaborating with Spanish bureaucrats to obtain legitimate entry into Spain's Caribbean complex, gateway to the Spanish colonial mainland. Aware of the predictable resistance of the Consejo de Indias and the Casa de Contratación to a French-held *asiento,* France's representatives at Madrid joined with major figures of the Spanish political establishment—Cardinal Portocarrero and the president of the Consejo de Castilla, Manuel Arias—to assign to two officials responsibility for preparing the contract with Ducasse representing the Compagnie de Guinée. The Consejo de Indias was given just two days to suggest revisions; all were immediately rejected.[67] France's breakthrough sanctioned the presence of French shipping and businessmen in Spain's colonial ports, even in the interior provinces of the colonies, creating the "first outline of a commercial pact between the two crowns." Put another way, in less than a year French policy and its implementation confirmed Anglo-Dutch groups' "dread of the union and loss of trade" leading them to conclude that "the chief aim of the French in possessing themselves of Spain [was] to make themselves masters of the West India trade."[68]

Ten days after the *asiento* was signed, London and Amsterdam formed an alliance for joint military and naval operations against France, which commenced in 1702. The ostensible justification was the allies' support of the Hapsburgs and Archduke Charles as successor; yet even a summary reading of the Anglo-Dutch treaty text reveals the underlying motivation. Since French naval units were entering the Caribbean, the "free intercourse of navigation and commerce which the English and Dutch have in the . . . Indies and other places will be utterly destroyed." France and Spain "so closely united and cemented" will now dominate Europe and destroy "freedom of commerce." These threats justified Anglo-Dutch cooperation to the end that the French "shall never get into the possession of the Spanish Indies, neither shall they be permitted to sail thither on the account of traffick, directly or indirectly." Meanwhile, to expand their trade, England and Holland could "seize . . . what lands and cities they can, belonging to the Spanish dominions in the Indies." There can be no disputing the role of colonial factors in the crisis of Spain's Hapsburg regime and the War of the Spanish Succession.[69]

Particularly destabilizing was the transfer of the *asiento* from Portuguese strawmen fronting for Anglo-Dutch slavers to French latecomers in the international distribution of enslaved African laborers. The *asiento,* furthermore, involved more than distributing chattels: slave ships could freight goods for illegal marketing in Spain's Caribbean ports where sales representatives of the Compagnie de Guinée would collect commercial intelligence about the size and composition of colonial demand. In diverting the *asiento* to French merchants, the Spanish state threatened Anglo-Dutch interests in the Caribbean where in the last half of the seventeenth century they had fostered island entrepôts. By 1670 Anglo-Dutch shipping in Spanish Caribbean waters was legitimized by Spanish concession, and Spanish-speaking Sephardic merchants at Kingston and Curaçao communicated with merchants freely entering their harbors from Spain's Caribbean ports. In a period of intense competition among textile producers in western Europe—English, Flemish, Dutch, French, and Silesian—such direct sales to the Spanish colonies offered a major cost-cutting device. The real and imagined demand in Spanish America promised to constitute perhaps the single largest outlet for English woolens and French linens and offered economies of scale as well. In addition, import-export duties, brokerage fees, and other payments at Sevilla and Cadiz could be eliminated.

It was Bristol merchant John Cary, in a port town with a long tradition of trading with the peninsula,[70] who in 1695 voiced satisfaction with the situation of English traders in the Caribbean; "[English merchants] have . . . so well secured the West Indies, but that it is very plentifully supplied by us with Manufactures, and many other things from Jamaica, which is accompanied with greater Advantage than when sent first to Cadiz; for whereas we generally sold them there at Twenty percent advance, we do by this means make at least Cent percent, all paid in bullion. . . . This [is] why our vent for them at Cadiz is lessened, because we supply New Spain direct with those things they used to have thence before." Earlier Jamaica's supply of slaves to the Portuguese *asentistas* had provided English merchants there with "the most profitable of any [trade] we drive." A pragmatist, Cary understood the tenuous nature of Jamaican prosperity for "this profitable asiento or factory hath for some time stood on tiptoe, ready to waft itself to another island."[71] The partition treaties of the late 1690s promised to maintain English traders' advantages in the Caribbean; however, French predominance at Madrid and the *asiento* that was transferred to French Atlantic ports threatened to "waft" such advantages to France's new Caribbean foothold, Saint-Domingue. Now the merchants of Rouen, Saint-Malo, and Nantes might attain equality with their principal European competitors. In fact, England's involvement in a decade of war beginning in 1701, its leonine treaty with Portugal (1703) and with Austrian interests at Barcelona (1707) were intended not for equilibrium in western Atlantic commercial competition but for de facto English hegemony.

In general, France's private sector determined the goals pursued by the French state bureaucracy, first, to gain parity and then supremacy for French interests in the Spanish Caribbean and along South America's Pacific slope. Spearheading the private sector were mercantile and shipping groups in France's Atlantic ports led by Saint-Malo, closely seconded by Rouen and—in the first decades of the eighteenth century—a slower developing Nantes. For Malouin merchants and shippers, the closing decades of the seventeenth century were a moment of expansion into Lower Andalusia and Spain's Atlantic trade.[72] In 1692, Magon de La Lande and Pontchartrain considered turning the northwest coast of Saint-Domingue into an entrepôt to avoid moving goods through Cadiz.[73] The French were hampered by the absence of Spanish authorization to enter colonial ports for protection, repairs, or supplies; but only weeks after the opening of Charles II's testament and possibly through the intervention of Ducasse, recently arrived at Madrid to negotiate the *asiento*'s terms, Madrid granted the needed authorization.[74]

This cleared the path for Malouin interests and by the end of 1701 Danycan de l'Espine and Malouin merchants sent three ships to the coast of Chile and Peru under the pretense they were warships dispatched to defend the area. One vessel returned to Portugal's port of Setubal where agents of Saint-Malo shippers awaited its silver cargo.[75] Thereafter Malouins came to predominate in French shipping to the Caribbean and through the Straits of Magellan to the west coast of South America. In three years, 1704–6, nineteen of thirty-seven vessels exited from Saint-Malo for Spain's American colonies, seventeen aiming for the Pacific and smuggling at Spanish colonial ports. In two years, 1705–7, forty-four French ships sailed to Veracruz alone while in 1709 French shipping returned from trading along the Pacific coast with 30 million pesos in precious metals.[76] All this occurred despite a stream of complaints from disaffected groups at Sevilla and Cadiz but only mild disapproval of the French government.[77]

Beyond doubt connivance among Malouin and other French interest groups joined to the developmental strategy of the French state eased these unauthorized trading sorties into Spanish colonial waters. Inevitably such tactics brought confrontation at Madrid between the French private sector supported by the French state and Lower Andalusian commercial groups backed by Madrid. Malouin interests refused to back down, arguing in 1705 that their ships trading without Spanish permits along the Pacific coast benefited France's domestic economy: "French manufactures have grown twenty-five percent, workers have raised their production, in the hope we will profit hugely from the voyages to the South Sea," wrote Magon de La Lande.[78] Within a month (June 1705), however, he confided to his influential friend, Chamillart, that under pressure he and other Malouins might have to collaborate in the future with Dutch and English competitors in order to penetrate the Pacific. "If we were excluded from that trade, we would have to listen not only to what foreigners propose, but even furnish information, allowing them to profit at the State's expense."[79]

Policy-Conflict and Resolution, 1704–1707

While the interests of France's Atlantic coast merchants and the strategy of the state converged on expansion of trade flows with Lower Andalusia and the Spanish colonies, differences surfaced over tactics. Under Louis XIV, France reorganized its administrative structure. Foreign trade was entrusted to the ministry of Marine, domestic trade to the *Controlleur General des Finances*. In the first decade of the eighteenth century Pontchartrain ran Marine, Chamillart, finance.[80] Pontchartrain posted Amboise Daubenton de Villebois as commercial deputy to Madrid in 1702 to coordinate economic reporting and policy formulation with Amelot de Gournay.[81] To offset Daubenton's activity, and acting on advice from Malouin merchant Magon de la Chipaudière, Chamillart sent his own special agent, Mesnager, a retired merchant experienced in Spanish colonial trade and now a deputy ("one of the most influential") representing Rouen on the newly formed national *Conseil de Commerce*.[82] Mesnager carried instructions to negotiate an agreement on Spanish raw wool deliveries to French manufacturers, and to promote French goods in Spain's colonial trade. More to the point, he probably had orders to undercut Daubenton's efforts to collaborate with Spaniards in restructuring Spain's colonial trading system.[83]

Early on Daubenton concluded that the immediate bottleneck in Spain's colonial commercial system was the state of communications between metropole and colonies. His initial proposal to Cadiz merchants (February 1703) was replacement of a fixed schedule for *flotas* and *galeone* sailings with frequent, unscheduled departures from Cadiz. Ships might depart, for example, as soon as two or more of them were loaded. He omitted the possible use of French escort vessels. Opposition of the Consulado de Sevilla and the Consejo de Indias blocked this proposal, which may explain Daubenton's subsequent antagonism toward Sevilla's merchants.[84] Pontchartrain, probably under pressure from Breton shippers operating through Cadiz, urged Daubenton to put forward another proposal. This time Daubenton first tested his ideas with selected members of the Consejo de Indias, a focus group of veteran ship captains and "fameux" merchants.[85]

Advanced as part of a strategy to break with established patterns based on convoys, Daubenton's second proposal (February 1704) was fundamentally radical. Again, vessels bound for the colonies would depart only from Cadiz but now singly or in convoy, without fixed schedules; he supported rigorous suppression of smuggling. Daubenton's innovation, however, came in recommendations that the Consulado of Sevilla be abolished, its functions transferred to an admiralty court and, equally drastic, that foreign merchants at Cadiz be permitted to forward cargo in their own names supervised by Spanish supercargos (commissionaires espagnols) on Spanish vessels bound for the colonies. Again, no mention was made of the possible use of French escort vessels, presumably since Daubenton wished to provide no justification for an Anglo-Dutch demand for similar treatment under most-favored-nation clauses. This package of recommendations mirrored Daubenton's conviction that survival of the Spanish monarchy depended "solely on freedom of trade" (he meant merely greater participation of foreign merchants at Cadiz) and frequent communication with the American colonies.[86]

Daubenton offered an innovative solution to Spain's disrupted transatlantic trading system. It was logical, laid out new regulations, and was sensitive to Spanish groups suspicious of French economic aggression.[87] Daubenton, however, opposed or simply overlooked French merchants' short-term pragmatism and long-term complacency about their undercover operations. For many French as well as Spanish merchants in Lower Andalusia, and especially at Cadiz and Puerto Santa María, supported the ongoing colonial trading system because circumventing its constraints was tolerated and profitable. Malouin merchants like Magon de la Chipaudière had no confidence in Spanish strawmen, agents, shipping, or escort vessels and consequently no confidence in Daubenton's policy of collaboration. In mid-1704 Magon, drawing on fourteen years of commercial experience in Lower Andalusia, wrote his friend the bureaucrat Desmaretz about the shortcomings of the Spanish convoy system with its "half-rotted galleons, poor sailers badly fitted out." On learning of the imminent departure of a convoy for Portobelo (October 1704) to be followed by a January feria there, he informed Pontchartrain that there was a back-up of six to seven million écus (pesos that is) of Spanish government revenue alone awaiting export at Lima/Callao. Were French merchandise quickly dispatched there, total returns to French exporters might reach ten to twelve million écus. He

recommended obtaining Madrid's authorization for an unannounced convoy departing for the Pacific coast from a French Atlantic port accompanied
by an official Spanish representative, and promised to obtain the consent of
Madrid authorities.[88]

This explains why Pontchartrain, at the end of 1704, forwarded to Daubenton and Mesnager Magon de la Chipaudière's Malouin view of trade
with Spain's colonies, essentially a critique of Daubenton's "liberalization."
Magon rejected Daubenton's recommendation for frequent, unscheduled
sailings from Cadiz on two grounds: First, he claimed, French interests
would gain nothing if they banked upon the "preference" of Spanish merchants who "naturally hate us." Second, Spanish vessels were unseaworthy,
and if the "projected union of the two crowns" in colonial trade ever materialized, the French would have to provide "the shipping facilities Spaniards
cannot maintain." In all, Magon de la Chipaudière calculated that twenty-
four ships annually—roughly three convoys of four ships each to Portobelo
plus two larger convoys to Veracruz—might supply Peru and New Spain,
Buenos Aires and Central America. Cadiz would be designated a duty-free
trade zone for goods in transit to and from the colonies.[89] Magon de la
Chipaudière's counterproposal was far more in line with existing Spanish
colonial trade structures than Daubenton's and superficially appears contradictory coming from a representative of Malouin shippers committed to
illegal trading along the Chilean and Peruvian coasts. Presumably, his critique of Daubenton's mild support for "liberté de commerce" was driven by
profits earned (and to be earned) by continued unauthorized contacts with
the colonies.[90]

In point of fact, widespread and unauthorized Malouin shipping in
wartime along the Pacific coast of the Spanish empire in America interrupted discussion of change in the Spanish colonial commercial system
then under review by the Junta de Comercio in 1705.[91] In May, Malouin
ships, avoiding Spanish ports, returned directly to Saint Malo earning
superprofits from their trade in Peruvian ports. In June, responding to continued appeals from Malouin merchants, Mesnager and Amelot abandoned
principle to urge Paris to support French smuggling operations both in the
Pacific and at the Caribbean ports of Portobelo and Veracruz. Mesnager
conceded that "[this trade] is useful to the State, no matter the origin of the
silver." Malouin pressure-group tactics, combined with exports that drew
upon Breton and Norman cottage industries and paid French export duties,
proved irresistible. In late August 1705, Paris issued unpublicized permits
for French sailings direct to Spain's Pacific ports. According to Dahlgren,
"they were given no authorization to trade there."[92] It was, to be sure, all in

violation of Spanish control mechanisms; the imperatives of state finance and the pursuit of profit by the French private sector had swept aside efforts to mend the Spanish commercial system. Openly Chamillart confessed to Amelot at Madrid that he had authorized the secret sailings. "If you were in my place," he commented, "you would ignore all the great rules of policy, even of propriety, in order to make silver come into France, no matter by what means."[93]

Once the French government yielded to pressure from Malouin and other shipping interests, further efforts of French representatives at Madrid— Amelot, Daubenton, Mesnager—to modify Spanish colonial commercial structures were doomed. In 1706 the French did manage to influence the selection of new members of the Junta de Comercio reviewing colonial trade, Mateo DiCastillo, Antonio Cala de la Vega, José de los Rios, Diego de Murga, the conde de la Torre-Hermosa, Bernardo Tinagero de la Escalera and Juan Manuel de Heredia.[94] Once the Junta recommended (February 1706) changes including authorizing foreigners from friendly nations to ship Spanish goods under their own names to the colonies and establishing a *consulado* at Cadiz,[95] the Consejo de Indias was bombarded with reports from outraged merchants and bureaucrats overseas in Chile, Peru, Panama, and New Spain complaining of widespread illegal French trading along the Pacific coast. The Veracruz agent of Sevilla's merchants complained in December 1706 that thirty-six French ships had arrived at Veracruz and Campeche and he lamented the "marked decline" of New Spain's external trade which "has always made that monarchy so strong" and supplied "the largest part of royal revenues." When Andalusian representatives also complained in force, the Consejo de Indias chose to defer action on the Junta's recommendations.[96]

Events in 1707 only stiffened the resistance of Lower Andalusian groups to modifications in the convoy system demanded by both French allies and English enemies. Since 1701 a minority of Andalusian merchants joined by a few government officials had considered adjusting the colonial commercial system, grudgingly accepted French escorts for Spanish convoys, and tolerated French shipping and merchants in colonial ports.[97] Then in February 1707 rumor spread that the French government had secretly authorized a *flota* of four ships from France's Atlantic ports to sail directly to Veracruz, which the Consulado de Sevilla, Casa de Contratación, and Lower Andalusia's merchant community immediately denounced. They reported thirty French vessels had already entered Campeche and Veracruz, eighty-six were at Portobelo, and another fifteen were along the Pacific coast. They demanded full compliance with Hapsburg colonial trade regulations and the revival of convoys and individual sailings *(registros sueltos)*.[98] As a 1708 report described the unstable situation, "Although Spain has a ready and assured possibility for providing an opulent traffic for its subjects, the country has so deteriorated that its subjects enjoy no ownership, merely the use, of what they produce."[99]

One byproduct of the French *flota* was a comprehensive field report[100] on the economy of New Spain in 1707–8 —*flotas*, external trade, merchants, and silver mines — along with comparisons with Peru based on data collected by Jean de Monségur during his brief residence in Mexico City (1707–9). Monségur, a French Basque, by turn merchant, ship owner, corsair and, at the time of residence in Mexico City, an officer of the Spanish navy, had purchased a vessel at Cadiz, obtained a license for sailing to New Spain, loaded it with Spanish products ("domestic staples"), lost it to corsairs off Santo Domingo, and ended up at his intended destination, Veracruz. Son of a merchant, Monségur understood the importance of first-hand economic reporting to policy-makers such as Pontchartrain and Amelot with whom he corresponded. In fact he intended his memorial to be seen not only by those officials, eager for information about New Spain's economic situation, but even by Philip V. Presumably Monségur also carried to New Spain reports of the favorable progress of Bourbon forces in Spain, which promised the survival of the Bourbon dynasty there. Since the Anglo-Austrians might dispatch an emissary to the colonies also seeking recognition, Philip V's officials hoped to spread counterpropaganda.[101]

Observant and inquisitive, Monségur reflected in his *memoires* the interests of French merchants and their Spanish colleagues at Cadiz, of members of the religious establishment at Mexico City (the Vicar-General of the Orden de la Merced, Antonio de Ocanto, and a Jesuit informant, Juan de Urtasum), and of those prominent Mexico City merchants to whom they undoubtedly introduced him.[102]

Monségur's report made evident that French commercial groups intended to tap fully into Spain's colonial trade, which he valued as "the noblest and at the same time the richest in the world and . . . prime mover of all the trades of Europe and outside Europe."[103] His survey, then, concentrated on major elements of New Spain's economy: prominent figures in Mexico City's commercial community, categorized and ranked by volume of working capital, the sources of that capital, composition of European and Asian imports sold, and the link between transatlantic trade and the mines. He calculated that Mexico City held about 230 merchants whom he ranked in five income categories ranging from a low of 4,000–600,000 pesos. In the highest category (300,000–600,000 pesos) he enumerated eleven, in the next lower (100,000–200,000 pesos) were eight. He proceeded to provide their names for the benefit of French merchants planning to establish "reliable correspondants for their trade" in the two principal commercial centers of the colony, Mexico City and Veracruz.[104] Elsewhere in the colony he located provincial merchants whose capital ranged from 4,000 to 200,000 pesos: at Puebla (70), the mining centers of Parral (55) and Zacatecas (44), Oaxaca (42) and Veracruz (28)—in all, 469 merchants in New Spain's major urban centers.[105]

The impressively large working capitals of the colony's leading merchants stemmed, Monségur must have learned in talking to Vicar-General Ocando and Jesuit authorities, from the symbiotic tie between businessmen, their families, and religious bodies ("for nuns and monks, Widows and Orphans"), all investing considerable financial resources in loans at 5 percent. These "sommes immences" constituted the "very substantial base of Mexican commerce," since in general, trade in the colonies was managed almost entirely in "silver money," especially so in Mexico City. Here Monségur expressed the fears of clerics and merchants who knew that proposals were circulating at Madrid to finance the large wartime expenditures of Philip V's government by expropriating religious funds, paying the affected corporations the current interest rate while requiring immediate redemption of outstanding loans held largely by the commercial community—a forerunner of the *consolidación* process instituted in Spain and New Spain a century later. Depriving Mexico City's *almaceneros* of their major source of working capital, Monségur argued, would simply undermine New Spain's internal and external trade.[106]

There followed his analysis of colonial demand for both European and Asian (mainly Chinese) imports and their price fluctuations. Monségur favored the by-now-traditional Spanish pattern of managed trade and extolled the advantages of curtailing imports of European merchandise at Veracruz as well as Acapulco's Asian import trade.[107] The experience of suspending *flotas* to Veracruz in wartime (1705–8), when the colony had enjoyed a kind of "greater freedom for Foreigners than Spaniards to go to the Indies for trade," had been disheartening. If this continued, he predicted, it would have serious effects on Spain and "one might add, on all foreign trade." The current oversupply of European imports had depressed prices and "impoverished and ruined the Indies trade and of all Spain, too." A combination of uncontrolled imports and ensuing low prices would diminish incentives both to Indian mine workers and "Spanish" mine owners who, as a consequence, "will no longer exert themselves, as has been customary, to mine gold and silver."[108]

Key recommendations were probably added in 1714 to the original manuscript, designed by Monségur to influence the work of a "special junta"—the Junta de Comercio—at Madrid of "very enlightened people" assembled to review the Spanish transatlantic system of "navigation and the dispatch of flotas and galleons."[109] If Spain resumed prewar Hapsburg patterns of managed colonial trade ("founded on sound rules") and cemented its alliance with France, the Spanish metropole would be positioned to supply the total import needs of its American colonies. Monségur recognized in passing, did not explain, and only implied that Spain's colonial trading system differed fundamentally from that of England or France. Adopting a policy of *liberté de commerce* would, he felt, turn out "badly and prejudicial" for the Spanish colonies. By echoing the position of stand-pat factions among commercial groups at Cadiz and Mexico City and their French connections, Monségur was recommending to the junta at Madrid, in effect, that "freedom of trade to the Indies is in no way appropriate."[110] This was indeed a confession that an economic paradigm or model borrowed from Dutch, English, or French practice would somehow be inadaptable to the conditions of Spain's Hapsburg commercial legacy.

The French government now offered to exclude French vessels from Spain's colonial ports, but at a price. Spanish authorities would allow French ships under Spanish flags to enter Veracruz and Portobelo, sailing from either Cadiz, San Sebastian, or Pasajes (in the Basque border zone with France)—a first step toward what some French considered "liberté de commerce" and a compromise apparently advanced by Mesnager. On the other hand, Daubenton, aware of Spanish sensitivity, warned that dividing colonial trade between Andalusia (Cadiz) and Guipúzcoa (San Sebastian) might undermine Andalusian support for Bourbon forces during the war. It would mean, he pointed out, rewarding the virtually autonomous province of Guipúzcoa which "instead of contributing to the king of Spain, lessens his authority and rights as much as possible, using its privileges as pretext." The French proposal was rejected, presumably because Madrid foresaw that French ships returning from the Spanish colonies would inevitably bypass Pasajes for France's Atlantic ports. There are indications that in late 1707 Paris continued to authorize departures to the Pacific from Saint Malo.[111]

Why Spanish policy-makers and Andalusian commercial interests tolerated a ritualized pattern of French proposals for direct participation in colonial trade, rejection by Madrid, followed by renewed illegal activity by the French can be explained by the shortcomings of the Spanish economy: its limited resources in shipping and maritime personnel, its reliance upon French shipping and escorts to bring silver from the colonies, and an obvious fear of English power. To rephrase the issue, although French Atlantic commercial groups were insistent, their commercial penetration of the colonial system was not as fearsome as the projection of English naval power.

English designs upon the Spanish empire were foretold in the commercial treaty that Francis Methuen, London's representative at Lisbon, arranged with the Portuguese government in 1703. It granted English interests a hegemonic position in Portugal's economy and, more important, in that metropole's trade with its principal colony, Brazil.[112] No doubt Spanish interests saw Methuen as representing the English merchant community in general and its "Portugal merchants" in particular. If Spaniards were troubled by the economic designs of their French wartime allies, they were confirmed in their fear of English interests when they learned of the treaty that Methuen's colleague, Stanhope, forced the Hapsburg candidate to the Spanish throne, Archduke Charles, to sign at Barcelona.[113]

Early in 1707 English merchants spelled out the major concessions they expected from a victorious Archduke Charles who, they speculated, would send out new cadres of colonial officers via Jamaica. Predictably the first demand focused upon restoration of the English merchants' prewar situation in Lower Andalusia defined by the treaties of 1645, 1667, and 1670, to which they now added duty-free import and reexport of English goods to the Spanish colonies, and tax-free remission of silver to England. Most significant was the second requirement, transfer of the *asiento* to English investors. Third, they wanted Madrid to open a second peninsular port for direct commercial contact with the colonies—a move probably designed to placate Catalan groups (hitherto excluded from full participation in Lower Andalusia's colonial trade) supporting the Anglo-Dutch-Austrian alliance.[114]

The Barcelona treaty of 1707 incorporated key English demands. It confirmed prior treaties covering an English presence in Lower Andalusia as amplified in 1667, permitted English shipping in trade between southern Spain and Morocco and—a demonstration of hegemony—provided for a joint commission to revise Spain's tariff structure. On the surface, these were hardly major items. In reality, English commercial objectives were reserved for one long, unpublicized article. To form an "indissoluble and perpetual union," England and Spain agreed to set up a "company in the Indies" to mobilize the resources of those "vast, rich provinces." English and Spanish investors would be able to buy into the company to be chartered once Madrid fell to allied armies. Meanwhile, Charles's government in wartime would afford English merchants "the same privileges [and] freedoms to trade in the Indies" as enjoyed by Spaniards by authorizing English warships to convoy annually Spanish merchant vessels as well as ten English vessels with a maximum of 5,000 tons departing from Cadiz or any other designated peninsular port for any Spanish port in the colonies, all returning to their peninsular port of departure. Last, on the plausible ground that French military aggression had been financed by the "great treasures" earned by French smugglers in the Spanish colonies, French investors would be excluded from the proposed company and from trafficking with the colonies directly, or through intermediaries.[115]

No mention of the slave *asiento* surfaced in the public or secret articles presumably because the proposed Anglo-Spanish company implied a commitment in this direction. Sooner or later the joint venture would import African chattels along with English manufactures. In the second place, by assigning to the company the right to ship merchandise, the main objective of an *asiento*—sale of slaves and goods for silver—was assured. "In their dealings with Charles . . . the British got all the commercial privileges and preferences they could desire, save only the right to trade in their own ships direct to the Indies."[116] So drastic were the concessions to English negotiators, Archduke Charles hesitated six months before permitting ratification; French authorities learned of the treaty arrangements by pure chance.[117]

The three years 1704–7 were the midpoint of the war, when the major power blocs still believed total victory was possible. Jockeying for position, neither French nor English interests—mercantile, financial, bureaucratic—respected in wartime what both blocs considered a grossly inefficient and penetrable Spanish transatlantic commercial system. Graphically the war demonstrated the incapacity of imperial Spain as a first-rank west-European state and economy, which is not to say that an imperial Spain lacked the possibility of ultimate survival if it could make necessary adjustments.

By 1707 and increasingly evident over the following four years, a new equilibrium evolved in the Iberian peninsula and the Spanish colonies. English forces now occupied the strategic points of entry into the western Mediterranean: Gibraltar and parts of the Balearics. In the Caribbean neither Jamaica nor Barbados nor Curaçao nor Aruba was seriously endangered. The major outposts in the Mediterranean and the West Indies that the English feared losing to Franco-Spanish forces were preserved, but at heavy financial cost. Warfare on sea and land was expensive, England's public debt had ballooned, and by 1711 England and Holland were resigned to negotiating what they could not obtain by war. At last the English were ready to discuss a general European and colonial settlement, but from a position of power in the western Mediterranean, the Atlantic, the Caribbean, and—key to effective exploitation of the *asiento*—by access to slave depots along the west African coast.

As for the French, by formally occupying Saint-Domingue after the Treaty of Ryswick (1697), they had achieved a quantum jump, shifting from the eastern periphery to the strategic center of the Caribbean. There was an underside to this, however. In exploiting its international and colonial projection in Spain, the shortcomings of the French economy, in particular its shipping and commercial facilities, were highlighted despite some remarkable economic growth achieved in the early decades of Louis XIV's reign.

After six years of the *asiento,* the operations of the Compagnie de Guinée were not promising. Under the terms of the contract arranged by Ducasse and bankers Flon and Hubrecht representing the Compagnie de Guinée, the company had agreed to supply at least 3,000 slaves per annum to Spain's Caribbean ports and Buenos Aires.[118] Initially Ducasse turned for slaves to the Portuguese Companhia de Cacheu, with poor results. Next, the company in effect subcontracted the *asiento* out to designated French ports to supply designated colonial ports: to a Malouin group headed by Magon de la Chipaudière went the subcontract of Veracruz.[119] Again, the results were disappointing. When the first French slave ship arrived at Veracruz with only fifty-two Black children and a large volume of merchandise, the commandant of the fortress of San Juan de Ulua (Andres de Pez, a consistent supporter of the Cadiz *consulado*'s trade positions) refused to permit the vessel to remain in the harbor—its cargo would interrupt, he insisted, the ongoing sale of goods brought by a convoy already there. The insignificant number of slaves for sale suggests the company's poor procurement structure and why it had to request permission from Spanish authorities to buy slaves from Dutch and English Caribbean depots at Curaçao and Jamaica—a petition Madrid rejected.[120]

Without slaves, there was no possibility of extensive sales of merchandise in Spanish colonial ports opened to the slave-trading *asiento.* French investors found that it was not the slave supply contract, but rather Malouin smuggling enterprises in the Pacific (despite Madrid's complaints) that generated profits. Meanwhile, payments by the Compagnie de Guinée to the Spanish government were dissipated on many projects: on military operations, on salaries to important bureaucrats, on diplomatic expenses, on French and Spanish pensioners of the government (including Philip V's cousin, the Duchess of Mantua), on long delayed interest owed to *juro*-holders and even on pocket-money for Philip V (for a wardrobe ordered from Parisian tailors—and for royal wet nurses).[121]

Such were the inadequate performance of French *asiento* holders, the bitterness of Lower Andalusian merchants stoked by unauthorized Malouin commercial expeditions to the Pacific with Paris' tacit approval, and the resistance of Spanish domestic and colonial interests to French economic expansion at their expense that after about 1706 Mesnager opted to compensate for French economic shortcomings. To Madrid he proposed a general commercial company headquartered at Sevilla or Cadiz, chartered for trading to the colonies and open to the participation of English, Dutch, French, and Spanish investors. In 1708, a Flemish diplomat, the conde de Bergeyck, proposed to assign the *asiento* to this international commercial group. To French merchants this proposal held out the hope of retaining a foothold in Spain's colonial trade should Franco-Spanish forces lose to the English.[122] This fall-back position was eliminated after 1708 when the large French public deficit and popular resistance to tax and military burdens complicated by famine, induced Paris to cut off military and financial support for Philip, leaving him to his Spanish peninsular and colonial resources. At the same time, however, Paris made virtually no effort to suspend Malouin trade with Pacific ports of South America.

By 1708, Bourbon Spain and its empire barely survived by default, by an unresolved confrontation of competitive capitalist blocs. In an oddly contradictory way, the very inefficiencies, incapacities, and weaknesses of the empire in America made survival possible. By tolerating Anglo-Dutch contrabanding in the Caribbean, unauthorized Malouin operations on the Pacific coast, and authorized French naval escorts for convoys in wartime, a pragmatic Spanish policy allowed antagonistic blocs to profit from Spain's nominal hegemony while the state and certain Lower Andalusian interests derived some colonial income.

This is not to underestimate Franco-Spanish collaboration, which remained a prime feature of the early years of Bourbon Spain. Yet despite such collaboration at top governmental levels, often in meetings of the *junta de comercio*, it was still possible to insulate the formal core of the Spanish imperial trading system from French penetration. Leading Spanish state servants—Bergeyck, Tinagero de la Escalera, Rios, García de Bustamante, and in the colonies, viceroys Castel dos Rius, Linares, and Moncloa—managed to guard what they considered basic imperial interests. In cooperating with their French counterparts—Orry, Amelot, Daubenton, Mesnager—they were not unconditional collaborators (what a later Spanish generation termed *afrancesados*); rather they were simply protonationalists.[123]

As the loyalty of the principal colonial ports—Cartagena and Portobelo, Veracruz and Havana, Callao and Buenos Aires—to the Bourbon monarchy newly installed in Spain became confirmed along with the incapacity of English or French amphibious forces to seize and hold them, Spanish state policy yielded only what could not be preserved. If the *asiento* had to go to French interests—to Malouin merchants, or merchant bankers like Crozat and Bernard, the French failed to obtain permission to deal directly with the Spanish colonies or to load merchandise registered under their names aboard Spanish ships destined for colonial ports. Secure in the nominal integrity of the principal colonies, ever ready to call upon the merchants of Lima, Mexico City, and Cadiz, upon the Casa de Contratación and the Consejo de Indias to prevent tinkering with the imperial trade system, Tinagero and other high public servants managed to preserve the principle of the convoy system even when it was temporarily escorted by French warships. They scotched the proposal for a privileged colonial trading company open to well-capitalized European merchant investors and repeatedly fended off efforts to transform Cadiz into a free port or to authorize ships returning from Spanish colonial ports to proceed directly to French Atlantic harbors.

The skill of the higher echelons of the Spanish bureaucracy was reinforced by patterns of French and English pressure. While the French government winked at illegal operations by the merchants and shippers of Saint Malo in Spain's Pacific waters, English demands upon a hoped-for Hapsburg-controlled Spanish empire in the Barcelona treaty were no less threatening. The only option for Spanish policy-makers was resistance to the power and special pleading of both hegemonic groups and, when exhaustion and war-weariness led France to abandon Philip V, to coalesce around the symbol of national unity, the new Bourbon monarchy. For Philip and his ministers had resisted French demands for major colonial concessions and only under duress would compromise with the English at the expense of the colonies. In the process Philip V, Bourbon monarch-symbol, became hispanicized. At the same time, many among Spain's aristocracy and church, gentry, and Lower Andalusian merchant community perceived that perhaps only a Bourbon administration might preserve the invaluable resources of the American colonies. Appropriately, the arrival at Cadiz of a shipment of silver from New Spain in January 1710 financed Philip's decision to pursue the war.[124]

By 1711, evidence of French readiness to negotiate induced London to prepare to renew its peaceful penetration of Spain's empire in America, hopefully along the lines of Methuen's recent success in Portugal. After all, as Charles King's *The British Merchant* reported, English factors trading at Cadiz "took off more of our woolen manufactures, and made us greater returns of money than any other trade . . . and paid greater sums for the products of our Lands than any Foreign trade whatsoever."[125] The English

chose what was already becoming an outmoded instrument of early mercantile capitalism, the privileged company, and chartered the South Sea
Company, a title reflecting the persistent mirage in western Europe of the
wealth of Spain's Pacific coast colonies. Presumably the company would
mobilize capital to finance commercial activity in the Caribbean, where
French traders had temporarily reduced Jamaica's trade, and—what was
then critical—to assist in handling the large public debt by lending the English government £10 million at 6 percent secured on selected customs revenues.[126] (Ubiquitous Mesnager went to London as negotiator, alerted
that England viewed Spain's colonies as the "sole resource" for liquidating
the public debt).[127] The South Sea Company would be well positioned to
take over the French-held *asiento* as part of the peace settlement and then
establish slave depots and merchandise warehouses at Veracruz, Havana,
Cartagena, and Buenos Aires, acquiring at the same time invaluable personal contact and sources of commercial information.

The Utrecht Treaty Complex, 1713–16

Chartering the South Sea Company in 1711 represented a pragmatic assessment of naval power guided by a clear-sighted view of wartime goals.
The company was a product of state and private sector collaboration, a
riposte to wide-open smuggling by the French in the Caribbean, Rio de la
Plata, and along the Peruvian coast. It was also prepared, at the end of hostilities, to take over from French bankers and businessmen the long-coveted
asiento. The prominence of this goal among English treaty objectives made
it clear that the negotiating leverage earned by English naval forces would
not be frittered away by the diplomacy of peace-making.[128]

An early and principal objective behind the creation of the company was
the transfer of England's public debt, swollen by military and naval expenditures, to the company whose profitability to shareholders could be assured
by Spanish trade concessions, including a trade monopoly at four ports sit-
uated in an enormous arc from the Orinoco valley southward to Tierra del
Fuego and up the Pacific coast. For their part, French negotiators, desperate to terminate the war, even agreed that Madrid yield to France this and
other commercial concessions only to transfer them to English investor
groups. These extravagant propositions were dropped when one of the negotiators, Mesnager, proposed to his English counterpart, Manassas Gilligan, that the French transfer instead the *asiento.*[129] In hindsight, was Mesnager trying to preserve the Hapsburg complex of managed trade and within
it French merchants' predominant role?

In a remarkably short time—fifteen months between August 1712 and November 1713—English diplomacy reinforced the economic penetration of Spain and its colonial dominions begun sixty-eight years earlier with the treaty of 1645 protecting the English merchant community in Lower Andalusia. The diplomatic process commenced at the end of hostilities (August 1712) and moved quickly to eliminate the long-troublesome threat of a Franco-Spanish coprosperity sphere. Philip was forced to renounce formally the right of succession to the French monarchy (November 1712). Four months later came agreement on the terms of the transfer of the French-held *asiento* to the South Sea Company (March 1713), then a treaty of peace, and at the end of that year the commercial settlement (November). These accords signaled what Argentine historian Ricardo Levene accurately diagnosed as "the starting point for Europe's new policy, no longer turning its back upon the New World, instead looking straight at it."[130] They spelled out what would become, in the long run, subordination of imperial Spain to English naval and economic hegemony.

The principal settlements concerned slaving and trade, and their relative importance is revealed in the chronology of their resolution. Within a matter of months after the armistice, the English government sent merchant Manuel Manasses Gilligan off to Madrid to negotiate the *asiento*. Gilligan had participated in the 1690s in the operations of the Portuguese contractor of the *asiento*, the Companhia de Cacheu, and was known as a "longtime West India smuggler." Gilligan, who later joined the Utrecht negotiations, represented London's "Spanish merchants" and twenty principal members in the "Factory of Cadix" who had forwarded months earlier (August 1712) a list of demands. His commercial savvy may have been responsible for omitting from the treaty duty reductions on English goods reexported at Cadiz, an advantage that would ultimately have to be shared with France and Holland to the detriment of England's "clandestine trade which by the Assiento we have entirely to ourselves exclusively to all the world."[131]

Astutely both English private and public sectors by carefully instructing Gilligan on commercial points managed to incorporate in the "Assiento or Contract for allowing the Subjects of Great Britain the Liberty of importing Negroes . . . to supply the Spanish West Indies with Black Slaves," elements that would not necessarily be shared with French and Dutch competitors. The English government ("the Queen of Great Britain") through the "English Company" was awarded the *asiento* for thirty years; Gilligan's draft of forty-two articles was submitted to three consejeros of the Consejo de Indias and then on to another junta, and accepted despite the strong reservations of some consejeros. In exchange for an advance to the Spanish state of 200,000 *escudos* payable within four months, the "English Company" would send to the "West Indies of America" belonging to Spain over the life of the contract, a total of 144,000 (4,800 per annum) "negroes, *Piezas de Indias* of both sexes, and of all ages." The "Assientists" could employ English or Spanish vessels to deliver "ther Black slaves" to "all ports of the North Sea, and of Buenos Ayres," including Veracruz, Havana, and Cartagena. To the assientists operating at Buenos Aires, the Spanish government allocated "parcels of land . . . sufficient to plant, to cultivate, and breed cattle therein" to feed both agents and African slaves. English or their Spanish agents to the limit of six could reside in each designated colonial port with the right to "send up into the country" a small number of agents on company business. As in the earlier *asiento* with the Portuguese, in "all the ports and chief places of America" the English assientists were to appoint judges-conservator to settle differences between the company and colonial authorities, with the right of ultimate appeal to the Consejo de Indias whose president, governor, or dean would serve as "protector of this Assiento."

For the "support and sustenance" of agents and slaves in Spanish colonial ports, the Company could "keep constantly magazines filled with cloathing, medicines, provisions and other necessaries" imported in vessels of 150 tons burden from "Europe or Her Brittanick Majesty's colonies in North America, directly to the ports and coasts of the Northern Sea of the Spanish West Indies and to Buenos Aires." Asiento ships could sail directly from English or Spanish ports and return with "money, bars of silver, gold, fruits and produce" equal to the value of slaves sold in colonial ports. Further, *asiento* ships in colonial ports might also return in the company of Spanish convoys heading back to the peninsula.[132]

Even a cursory review of the forty-two articles submitted by Manasses Gilligan and accepted by the Spanish state suggests the multiplicity of channels granted the English Company for penetrating Spain's empire in America. Gilligan's preparation insured that in every way conceivable English traders secured "concessions"—"all the favours, freedoms, privileges and exemptions"—present in prior *asientos*.[133] One measure of the sudden projection of England's hegemonic power is the relative timidity shown by English merchants and diplomats a mere six years earlier when in 1706 London officials considered inadvisable inclusion of any reference to the *asiento* in the proposed commercial treaty of Barcelona imposed upon the Austrian Hapsburg leader, Charles III.[134]

The second and beyond doubt most persuasive sign of Spanish subordination to English hegemony was the additional article appended to the *asiento* treaty of March 1713. In this terse addition of about 280 words (diminutive tail to the 42 articles), it was revealed that two weeks earlier (12 March) the Spanish state, "to manifest to her Brittanick Majesty how much [it] desires to pleasure her," had accorded the English company permission to send each year one 500–ton (not 150 ton) ship with "goods and merchandise" saleable only in conjunction with the Portobelo fair and "free of all duties in the Indies." No previous *asiento* had conceded to a European power so broad an avenue of legitimate penetration into the Spanish empire in America. Bernardo Tinagero de la Escalera who countersigned the article as representative *(escribano de cámara)* of the reluctant Consejo de Indias must have recalled bitterly the frequent occasions when he and other consejeros had deflected French pressures for far less comprehensive participation in the Spanish transatlantic trading system.[135]

At this point no overt effort was made to complicate the operation of the colonial *feria*, still a feature of Spain's early modern colonial trading system. If the annual ship arrived *before* the convoy from Cadiz, goods and merchandise could be off-loaded and warehoused "to the end that said goods and merchandise may be sold during the continuance of the said fair only."[136] It is not clear whether the "company of England" ever intended to sell its cargo in competition with convoy sales at the fair, or whether the arrangement collapsed simply because the company's annual ship arrived at Portobelo when a fair had to be postponed because a convoy failed to appear.

Three years later a "convention for explaining the articles of the Assiento, or contract for Negroes" (1716) went far beyond mere clarification, in point of fact making what were substantive changes. The English company now complained that it had lost "prime cost" of cargoes aboard its "permission" ships because there was no "assurance that the fair . . . be held every year, either at Cartagena, Porto-Bello, or Veracruz," nor had notice been announced at which site the fair would be held. If merchants at Cadiz hoped the English company would abandon its permission vessel, they underestimated English merchants' tenacity. In the convention Madrid had to promise an annual and regular fair "either in Peru, or in New Spain" as well as prior notice to London merchants of convoy departures for the colonies—essentially mild concessions. But the Spanish state then yielded more than conceded in the earlier French-held *asiento*. If convoys to Cartagena and Portobelo failed to sail from Cadiz by the end of June, the English company could dispatch its permission vessel either to Cartagena, Portobelo, or Veracruz. And if neither *flota* nor *galeones* arrived within four months, the ship's cargo could be sold.[137] Here was graphic testimony of Madrid's fragile position in negotiating with London.[138] However, concessions from weakness became for Madrid concessions to be canceled. Here were the seeds of the war between Spain and England in 1739 that terminated the *asiento*—along with the 200-year-old convoy system (the *galeones*) to Cartagena and Portobelo, and the Portobelo fair.

The selection of a merchant experienced in the slave trade, equipped with commercial expertise and Spanish-language competence (Manasses Gilligan), the priority given to the additional article (12 March 1713)and to the *asiento* treaty itself, and the insistence upon modifying key features of the additional article (26 May 1716) imply that London traders engaged in direct merchandising of goods and slaves in the Caribbean had developed more political clout than the long established "Spanish merchants" of London and their representatives abroad at their Cadiz "factory." No doubt they were encouraged by London's pressure for access to American silver to supply England's growing trade with the East Indies. "The only means of enlarging the supply was a direct trade with the Spaniard in forbidden merchandise."[139]

On the other hand, the "Treaty of Navigation and Commerce" of Utrecht (28 November 1713) and its brief sequel (14 December 1715) may be interpreted as satisfying the major demands of England's "Spanish merchants" residing in Lower Andalusia who traded with the Spanish colonies through convoys and fairs.[140] Apparently they aimed to preserve the status achieved in 1645 and 1667 because the cedula of privileges granted in 1645 to protect the English enclaves at Sevilla, San Lúcar, and Cadiz followed by the 1667 treaty (but not that of 1670) are inserted "word for word" in this document. The treaty of Utrecht proper is far briefer. It insists that England share the most-favored-nation status granted other nations and attempts to force Madrid to formulate a national rather than its prevailing regionalized customs system and a new tariff schedule ("book of rates") uniform at the ports of Castile, Aragon, Valencia, and Catalonia with rates no higher than those on goods entering or leaving Cadiz and Puerto Santa María under Charles II.

At the same time English commercial interests insisted that the Spanish state confirm special agreements made by London with the port of Santander in 1700 and extend their rights and privileges of 1645 and 1667 to the autonomous provinces of Guipuzcoa and Vizcaya, well-recognized channels for introducing smuggled goods into Castile. While thus confirming their status in Lower Andalusia, London's merchants seemed bent upon extending that status to Barcelona on the Mediterranean and to the Cantabrian ports of Guipúzcoa, Vizcaya, and Santander. The brief explanatory "treaty of commerce" (December 1715) strengthened the Utrecht agreements by depriving the French of a lower level of duties and by perpetuating in treaty the informal duty schedule at Cadiz arranged during Báez Eminente's farm of Lower Andalusia's customs: the *gracia del pie de fardo* and the *quarta de tabla*. What had been manipulated for decades under Charles II without "any formal ordonnance" was henceforth "inviolable law."[141]

Despite statements reiterated in the Anglo-Spanish treaties of 1713–15— "it is by common consent established that the exercise of navigation and commerce to the Spanish West Indies should remain in the same state as it was in the time of . . . Charles II"—the *asiento* put English merchants in a commanding position in Spanish Caribbean ports and at Buenos Aires. Now the French understood clearly that the arrangements covering the African slave trade and commerce with Spain's American possessions, "positioned the English to sell their goods in the Indies 30 percent lower than those brought by Spaniards."[142] Through the *asiento* English agents would now enjoy frequent contact with Spanish naval officers on convoys, with colonial officials and businessmen in ports and hinterland, even with the influential consejeros of the Consejo de Indias.[143]

The Utrecht treaty complex was the result of the application of naval and economic power by what was fast becoming the most powerful mercantile state in western Europe, England, where commercial interests were respected and paramount. These, in association with landed interests, advised a receptive state of its needs and goals, financed a long war on land and sea, and prepared for peace by founding the South Sea Company. Then by treaty with Spain it transferred to that company the right to penetrate with manufactures and African slave labor a colonial market of high-income rural estate owners, mine owners, wholesale merchants, churchmen, and bureaucrats in addition to mineworkers and their families. What English interests reaped in access to the Spanish colonies at the close of the War of Succession, the Spanish state was to spend almost the whole eighteenth century seeking to recover. When Spanish bureaucrats believed at the end of that century that they had at last liberated Spain and its American empire from the network of maleficent treaties with England, they found that liberation evanescent. War at sea, after 1796, again found them going down before powerful English naval forces.

As the English consolidated their position within the traditional structures of the colonial trade of Lower Andalusia and simultaneously opened channels of direct trade through the *asiento,* French commercial interests at the war's end found themselves confined to participation in such trade only through establishments around the Bay of Cadiz. "Since Cadiz controlled by custom and law the metropole's trade with its colonies, a large number of French houses were established there, and France's trade in agricultural and manufactured products flowed there to supply consumers in Spanish America."[144] The English had cut short the expansion of French interests directly into the Spanish empire in America. Only Malouin merchants and shippers were prepared to sustain an illegal Pacific presence, and even this was diminished in the 1720s; by 1730 Malouin shippers had been forced to confine their trade with Spain's empire to Cadiz.[145] Decades later, around 1750, when naval officer Antonio de Ulloa, sent abroad by Ensenada's administration, surveyed Saint-Malo he found it "decadent" in part because the impressive short-term profits of the South Sea trade had been invested in social climbing, in marrying into the nobility, and the purchase of noble office.[146] Yet although French export groups were circumscribed to operations at Cadiz bay, the volume and composition of their trade listed as "with Spain"—in fact, with the Spanish colonies through Cadiz and Puerto Santa María—was still impressive.

Evidence of France's foreign trade in 1716 published in a *Balance du commerce* underscores the salience of Spain's American colonies to the French economy at the close of the War of Succession despite the imperfections of official statistical materials of that time. The balance of merchandise trade was, it must be recalled, already a weapon of propaganda as well as of economic utility.[147] For internal and external use, collection of raw data (not necessarily the printed summaries) measured the effectiveness of mercantilist policies and stimulated national producers and exporters. Reliability was lowered by inaccurate customs reporting where undervaluation, crude categorization, and large-scale omission were both intentional and accidental, and the flow of precious metals was deliberately omitted or grossly understated. This was done to avoid antagonizing Spanish authorities who continued to stress nominal prohibitions on illegal outflows of bullion and coin.

Withal, analysis of the 1716 trade balance leads to a number of conclusions about the weight of Spain and its colonies in France's foreign trade. First, the aggregate value (imports plus exports) of France's exchanges with Spain came to 21.3 percent of France's total foreign trade; official trade exchanges with England, for example, totaled only 13.3 percent. Second, Spain supplied 24.8 percent of all French imports; the categories of precious metals, raw wool, and snuff represented 71 percent of France's imports from Spain, while gold and silver imports alone (most presumably from Spain) represented 17.7 percent of total French imports. There is reason to believe the silver inflow was grossly understated. Manufactured goods such as woolens, hats, paper, snuff, linens, and hardware constituted 65 percent of France's

TABLE 2
France: Foreign Trade with Europe, 1716
(in livres tournois)

	Imports	%	Exports	%	Total	%
Total	*71.043.000*	*100*	*105.669.000*	*100*	*176.712.000*	*100*
Holland	12.071.000	16.9	30.730.000	29.0	42.801.000	24.2
Spain	17.669.000	24.8	20.036.000	19.0	37.705.000	21.3
England	15.419.000	21.7	8.049.000	7.6	23.468.000	13.3
Italy	10.716.000	15.0	23.127.000	21.8	33.843.000	19.1

B. France, Trade with Spain		%
From Spain	*17.669.000*	*100*
Pesos, Wool, Tobacco	12.580.000	71.1
Leather, dyes	2.663.000	15.0
Wine, dry fruits	2.426.000	13.7

To Spain	*20.036.000*	%
Manufactures	13.047.000	65.1
Grain, sugar, cocoa	5.889.000	29.4
Fish oil, whale oil, tar	1.100.000	5.5

C. French Exports to Selected Countries (Manufactures)		%
Total (Selected Countries)	*42.693.000*	*100*
To Spain	13.047.000	30.5
To Italy	17.937.000	42.0
To England	1.029.000	2.4
To Holland	2.338.000	5.4

Source: Arnould, *De la balance du commerce,* tables 1–2.
Note: Totals reflect data for all French trading partners (not just countries listed).

exports to Spain, or 31 percent of all French manufactures exported to Europe and the Ottoman empire (Table 2).

After Holland, Spain ranked as France's largest trading partner. One-quarter of all French imports came from Spain, one-third of French exports of manufactures went to Spain, virtually all imports of silver into France came from Spain. In 1716 Spain's silver-producing colonies appeared integrated with the French economy, supplying silver for France's exchanges with Europe and Asia and, in turn, absorbing French textiles and luxury goods. Although French producers and merchants had been blocked from legitimate direct access to Spain's colonies in America, their stake in Lower Andalusia's colonial trade complex in the Bay of Cadiz remained vital, and expansion there was still possible.

Thus Spain—along with its American empire the principal source of conflict between Europe's two leading economies at the end of the seventeenth century—emerged after more than a decade of war with its nominal sovereignty in America intact. Switching the *asiento* to English interests and abandoning the right of succession of a Spanish Bourbon to the French monarchy bought for Madrid international recognition, at least, of its colonial territorial integrity and brought about a precarious equilibrium between England and France.

Perhaps this outcome is best termed a reprieve. While Spain abandoned its Italian footholds and ceded to the Austrian Hapsburgs sovereignty over Flanders, Flemish merchants, manufactures, and finance remained evident in western Andalusia. And while the early Spanish Bourbon regime introduced French-style secretariats and provincial intendants, they did not replace, but merely overlay the established conciliar administration. When currents of regional autonomy swept Aragon, Valencia, and Catalonia, and French fiscal exhaustion threatened to bring about total English hegemony, Spain's dismemberment, and even the loss of its overseas colonies—*the moment of crisis in the War of Succession*—segments of the aristocracy and nobility joined by merchants and financiers of the Basque provinces and Lower Andalusia forged a common front behind a rapidly hispanicizing Bourbon dynast. They saved Spain from the treatment England imposed upon Portugal under the Methuen treaty.

To survive, Philip and his advisers had to come to terms with Spain's late medieval heritage: agrarian, patrimonial, and ecclesiastical. This heritage had been elaborated in the reconquest of the peninsula, then shaped and sustained by overseas conquest and colonization. It had been complicated by the need to buttress the Holy Roman Empire in the interests of dynasty and orthodoxy, and—above all—by the need to defend its vast American empire against the inroads of Europe's developing commercial nation-states. Since the ruling elites of Hapsburg Spain had failed to adopt an acceptable alternative—a state capable of enforcing "arbitration upon opposing interests"[148]—to its outdated political and economic paradigm, the Spanish Bourbons would spend the first half of the eighteenth century ideating such an alternative and the second half attempting to implement it.

Part Two

Toward a
Spanish-Bourbon
Paradigm

5. Conditions of Growth,

1700–1759

"I will limit myself to revealing and expounding on the causes of this monarchy's decadence and annihilation, and proposing proper and appropriate measures to reestablish it . . . after touching upon the measures foreigners have used to develop their States."
Uztáriz, *Theórica y práctica*

"There are lots of fine-sounding projects on paper, but saddening in execution and damaging in purpose. Projecting has become an art form for many, a science for few."
Gándara, *Apuntes*

The parameters of eighteenth-century Spain were laid down at Utrecht. There the treaties ending the War of the Spanish Succession established an independent Bourbon dynasty in Spain, redefined the monarchy's territory in Europe, formally secured its empire in America, and affirmed the continuity of established Spanish institutions while opening the door to reform along the lines followed by Colbert in France. Utrecht, however, was the outcome of conflict and compromise imposed by a prolonged and ultimately indecisive struggle, which for Spain was also a civil war. It contained elements of instability and further conflict, which hampered efforts to modernize Spain's internal institutions and strengthen its empire in America— its principal objective in supporting a Bourbon dynasty.

The Anglo-French rivalry over European hegemony and above all over access to the resources of the Spanish colonies that was the major cause of the war continued to threaten Spain throughout the century. Despite formal independence from France, successive Bourbon "family pacts" (there were three) made Spain both object of contention and ally of the weaker of Europe's two principal contending powers. The contradictions implicit in this situation would proliferate.

Confident that Utrecht protected the territorial integrity of its empire, Spain did not foresee the use England would make of the *asiento* and its provisions for an annual "permission ship" (which in fact became a floating warehouse) and for ongoing "refreshment" of slaves imported into the principal Spanish colonial ports. Controversy over the implementation of the contract began early and precipitated the longest of five armed confrontations between Spain and England. In the long term, war proved as disastrous to Spain as it was profitable to England.

Alliance with France, it turned out, provided limited protection for the Spanish empire as well as little support for Spain's efforts to reform its internal polity and economy. It soon became clear that French interests did not consider Colbert's mercantilist doctrines a suitable export to Spain except in matters advantageous to France such as rebuilding the Spanish navy; promotion of Spanish manufactures would clearly depress French textile exports and consequently imports of Spanish silver. Indeed, throughout the century French policy-makers consistently gave priority to expanding French commercial privileges at Cadiz. Paradoxically, war between Spain and England often provided French interests the opportunity to participate directly in trade with the Spanish colonies.

Aside from such contradictory implications of the Bourbon accession for Spain's foreign and domestic policies, the arrival of Philip V came at the cost of European territorial arrangements that led to conflict. At the outset Philip refused to renounce his claims to the French succession as well as Spanish claims to Italian territories. Even after he was forced to relinquish formal claims, Philip and his second wife, Isabel de Farnese, pursued distracting diplomatic and military maneuvers aimed at placing their children in Italian principalities—a policy the Spanish Bourbons followed throughout the century. Similarly on Spain's western border, Portugal, which emerged from the War of the Spanish Succession a classic informal dependency of England, remained a focus of Spanish foreign policy. The strategies Spain pursued there were based on dynastic and colonial interests that were frequently at odds with French expansionist designs. Lisbon, now a way-station for English naval forces and entrepôt for the Brazilian trade, also served as alternative conduit for Spain's colonial trade and communications in wartime when Cadiz was blockaded. More threatening (and humiliating), however, was the continued English occupation of the fortress and harbor of Gibraltar, which secured English control of access to the Mediterranean and served as a point of political surveillance and smuggling along the Spanish coast. Repeatedly and unsuccessfully Spain sought to recover what it had been forced to yield at Utrecht.

The first sixty years of the Bourbon monarchy in Spain still lack the historiographical coverage devoted to the era of Charles III.[1] For analytical purposes one may distinguish three phases within this long time-span. First, there were the internal and international conflicts of the War of the Spanish Succession, which ended with the Utrecht settlement, and (by 1717) the recession of French technocratic influence. In a second phase (1717–48) another generation of Spanish leaders undertook to adapt mercantilist practices to Spanish realities while seeking to resolve continuing internal and international tensions. This period ended in another war between Spain and England (1739–48) touched off by Caribbean developments. A last phase (1748–59) under Fernando VI (half-brother of Charles III) brought efforts to maintain neutrality, promote domestic development, and address colonial issues under the marqués de la Ensenada. His ouster in 1754 was followed by stagnation and political division as the reign of Fernando drew to a critical close during renewed warfare between France and England.

Strategies of Economic Development

In the first half of the eighteenth century, Spaniards of the political class who compared the economic condition of their country with that of Holland, England, or France experienced a deep sense of backwardness, inferiority, and resentment as the butt of "sátira extrangera." They saw those economies experimenting with privileged, joint stock trading companies in contact with West Africa, South India, and South China. They saw manufactories (some subsidized by the state, all benefiting from forms of protectionism) producing exportables shipped on a growing national merchant marine (often protected by naval escorts) to their Caribbean or North American colonies. From the Caribbean, ships returned to their metropoles with valuable tropical staples of sugar, tobacco, indigo, coffee, and much silver from Spain's colonies. More galling, foreigners were smuggling goods from Caribbean island ports into Spanish colonial ports on the rim of the Caribbean at Cartagena or Portobelo and along the coasts of Central America and Veracruz, taking in exchange smuggled Spanish silver, even boasting of the success of their clandestine operations. Their chartered companies reexported much of that silver to Southeast Asia and South China in exchange for luxury goods whose price was lowered by Asia's appetite for silver.[2] Spain, its leaders had to conclude, was economically backward. They dated the onset of their country's inadequate performance at sometime after the middle of the seventeenth century when it failed to share in what they interpreted as a great transformation of west Europe's economies. As *proyectista* Miguel de la Gándara viewed the origins of the gap between the performance of England and France versus Spain on the eve of the era of Charles III, "Those countries correctly changed their systems of governance and trade in order to better theirs and destroy ours."[3]

For the countries of western Europe, over the first century and a half of colonialism in America, Spain's transatlantic system had worked efficiently by mining and exporting silver pesos and bullion which entered their economy through many channels. Then a sea change—a great transformation—began after 1650 coincident with the visible recession of Spain's hegemony and the Counter-Reformation it had financed. The new European balance of power, by releasing political and economic energies in the states bordering the English Channel, brought the flowering of commercial capitalism. All exploited Spain's growing weakness not only to exact commercial concessions, but also to challenge Spain's commercial monopoly at the heart of its Atlantic empire: the Caribbean, particularly in the Gulf of Mexico covering the approaches to Veracruz. This second, accelerating phase of commercial capitalism displayed two innovative characteristics. First Dutch, then English and French traders and planters created, in the image of the sugar plantations of northeastern Brazil, an export-driven colonial system providing their metropoles with sustained market incentives.[4] Scarcely less important than the valuable staples of sugar, tobacco, and coffee ferried across the Atlantic for expanding European markets, the new colonies also served as island entrepôts for illegal trade with Spain's mainland possessions—a valuable source of silver for their metropoles. By 1700 European rivals had irrevocably penetrated Spain's colonial precincts in the western Atlantic, in the West Indies.

A second aspect concerns the elaboration of the nation-state. In supporting the commercial speculation of merchant communities, in chartering companies (often buying into them), in encouraging private banking, and in assembling military and naval forces to protect Atlantic sea lanes and Caribbean ports, England and France cemented collaboration between state and private enterprise. This collaboration became a hallmark of what Adam Smith later anathematized as the "mercantile system," the economic underpinning of the early nation-state. To fulfill the needs of developing national economies in terms of what economists label "transaction costs"—enforcing property rights and contracts; financing an infrastructure of roads, bridges, and canals linking interior provinces to port towns; providing protective tariffs; reducing internal tolls; establishing a merchant marine and naval armaments—the state had to augment its personnel and improve its liquidity by tax reforms. In short, the state had to increase its revenue base in response to pressure from nationalist commercial bourgeoisies.[5] Economy, society, and state were driven to respond to the highly competitive, expanding commercial capitalism of west Europe. Trade and war were inextricable and, worse, unavoidable (consider Josiah Child's "all trade [is] a kind of warfare") in late-seventeenth- and early-eighteenth-century European mercantilism.[6]

During the early years of the eighteenth century—what Werner Sombart has labeled the "age of projecting"[7]—a variety of state and private sector initiatives in England and France matched the economic activity and competition in the Atlantic economy, and the power and autonomy of the state. And while there was diversity, there were also common outcomes of public and private economic policy that, viewed in the Spanish mirror, formed a paradigm or model, a set of concepts shared by state functionaries (high- and mid-level bureaucrats-intellectuals) as well as clerics-intellectuals interested in public policy along with elements of a small commercial bourgeoisie. In hesitant fashion, these groups tried to elaborate a national framework, general rather than regional, for domestic and international development. They shared a common interest in the conditions of growth of the national economy, polity, and society. The concept of "nation" was being transformed beyond a regional, ethnic group to cover a larger universe of shared language, culture, and interests. In official documents "nation" was appearing beside "crown" and "monarchy" as a state symbol. This was symptomatic of the evolution of the "absolutist" state during the European Enlightenment. In England and France one source of this sense of identity and pride of achievement derived from overseas trade to ports in the Baltic and Mediterranean, to Southeast Asia and the Far East, and especially to Africa and then the Caribbean plantation colonies. In the seventeenth as in the sixteenth century, "Europe was living on Asia, Africa and America."[8] Colonial markets in America promised new consumers exceeding limited domestic markets for linens, woolens, and silks, the leading products of Europe's protoindustrialization.

In sum, at the close of the seventeenth century, the state in England and France had to respond to pressures from a core bourgeoisie of traders, merchant bankers, and manufacturers whose ambitions overseas growth opportunities unleashed. Collaboration between state and the private sector, between bureaucracy and business, surfaced in England's Board of Trade and Plantations and the Bank of England, and in France's Conseil de Commerce. In Spain there materialized the Junta de Comercio y Moneda. From the confluence of domestic and international pressures and the internal friction between landholding and commercial interests over taxation and expenditure, emerged a limited consensus about a trend, system, or paradigm of economic growth. Within this mercantile system the embryonic nation-state had to elaborate policies for balancing competing interests for the national benefit. The state—to use another formulation—had to find common ground between merchants' individual economic interests and the general interest of the commonwealth.[9]

Suggestive of early policy formulation were late-seventeenth-century commercial manuals like Jacques Savary's *Le parfait négociant* or Pierre-Daniel Huet's *Le grand trésor . . . du . . . commerce des Hollandois.* In multiple editions and translations they familiarized merchants with the proliferating operations of Dutch, English, and French companies chartered for the African slave trade and trade between Europe and India and South China.[10]

It is pointless to discuss what at best is a fictive dichotomy in the concept of mercantilism, to debate whether its purpose was to favor power over plenty, the state over a narrow commercial interest, or the state as end or means. There is no reason to question Charles Wilson's comment that "powerful economic interests represent one of the driving forces behind the [mercantile] system," a viewpoint that matches Heckscher's "mercantilism was not state activity in economic affairs, but private initiative and acquisitiveness stimulated by government measures in the supposed interests of the state." The economic growth policy we term mercantilism served the state by generating new sources of revenue and simultaneously enriched special interest groups which both sought and received state support.[11]

Listing the shared characteristics of mercantilism underscores the compatibility between state and economy, government and enterprise, power and plenty. The agreed-upon ends of mercantilism as a national "project" encompassed growth, wealth, and the projection of power. For growth, policy-makers felt assured, would produce revenues allowing the state to fulfill new functions in its dual role as promoter and protector of a nascent national economy and, as Heckscher once reminded us, help to mold "the medieval framework of European society to new economic and social conditions."[12] The paradigm formulated led, first, to efforts to reorganize and simplify an often bewildering overlay of late medieval fiscal structures: to terminate tax-farming and internal tolls, to unify regional tariff schedules, and to raise the expertise and lower the corruptibility of state finance personnel. Next, the state was expected to reduce outflows of precious metals to cover trade deficits. This meant developing a more efficient agriculture (to keep food imports to a minimum), and stimulating domestic manufactures that wherever possible used domestic and colonial raw materials.[13]

Here we come to the truly innovative aspect (usually overlooked) of growth under the mercantilist paradigm: the critical (and dynamic) function of colonies in western Europe's second phase of commercial capitalism after 1650. Mobilization of colonial staple production translated into sugar refineries in a metropole's port towns followed by reexport of refined sugars, distillates of rum, and other byproducts to other European economies. Other plantation crops such as tobacco, coffee, and natural dyes were similarly reexported. Reciprocally, the output of metropolitan farms and workshops would meet the colonies' import needs—presumably a closed, near autarchic system of mutually beneficial exchange, a primitive pattern of an international division of labor. Undergirding this system were a national merchant marine and naval force (largely constructed in national shipyards and manned mainly by nationals) and minimal direct exchange between overseas colonies and other colonies or their metropoles on the principle that "colonies depend upon the navy, commerce upon colonies, [and] upon commerce depends the capability of the State to generate the most glorious and useful enterprises."[14]

In essence, pursuing a mercantilist paradigm stimulated the extension, penetration, and deepening of merchant capitalism from the mid-seventeenth century onward. It encouraged the monetization of European and colonial economies through capturing and utilizing the silver pesos of Upper Peru and New Spain, and it enhanced an ever-wider market as arbiter of price and resource allocation. State functionaries, as "projectors" cultivating a conspectus of their "nation" and its international role, in collaboration with private interests ideated a model of growth conjoined with development. They integrated their domestic and colonial economies to the ends of public and private wealth and the projection of national power in a highly competitive Atlantic trading world.

These were the elements of a pattern of economic development that Spain's early eighteenth-century political economists (for that is what *proyectistas* were) identified in analyzing the policies of other west European nations.[15] Driven by a psychology of inferiority, they could not avoid contrasting the development of Holland, England, and France after about 1650 with Spain's painfully evident structural malaise, persistent stagnation, and poverty despite the wealth in silver pesos and bullion exported year after year from the American mining colonies to the metropole on public and especially private account. Increasingly, they imagined this backwardness as a fall from Spain's former hegemony.

The Dutch model they were observing, however, was already being overshadowed by the export performance of England. England's maritime capacity was enhanced by the navigation acts ("Parliamentary Colbertism"), by wartime confiscation of Dutch shipping, by a naval establishment nurtured on generous government outlays, and by consensus on the primacy of its trade and colonies in North America and the West Indies. The trouble was, England menaced the basis of Spain's imperial economy, particularly its American colonies in the now "open" Caribbean zone. Spanish authorities, irritated by concessions imposed by the English, could hardly be expected to trust them. Had not an Englishman boasted in 1693 that "a foreign trade managed to the best advantage, will make [England] so strong and rich that we may command the trade of the world . . . and consequently the world itself"?[16]

The rhetoric of universal empire aside, England was neither Spain's ally nor model. Since the sixteenth century the English provided an example of the rejection of Rome's authority. They confiscated and sold ecclesiastical property. Later, they experienced revolution and regicide; and after the Restoration, royal prerogative was subject to restraints by a parliament in which aristocrats, merchants, gentry, and churchmen agreed on the primacy of trade, sea power, and empire at the expense of France and Spain. Indeed, there was an agreement "between a dominant landowning aristocracy and an elite merchant community."[17]

By contrast, Spaniards found in France a competitor of England and an acceptable model of a "patrimonial system efficient and orderly," where Catholicism prevailed and the major contours of society and polity were congenial ("a neighboring Monarchy, so similar to ours in its form of government"),[18] above all where an empowered minister sponsored reforms insuring order, prosperity, and prestige to governors and governed. Assured at Utrecht that Spain would be independent of France, some Spaniards envisioned a time when revitalized imperial Spain would again rank among Europe's great powers.[19]

It is not surprising that some Spaniards looked favorably upon the France whose developmental program Colbert had cobbled together from earlier essays at growth and made more explicit. Particularly attractive was the conclusion that the Colbertian program had stirred France from relative backwardness vis-à-vis the Dutch, indeed, had ended dependence upon Dutch shipping and marketing facilities and helped dissipate among French merchants their sense of inferiority and insecurity. Of course even before Colbert, under Richelieu, merchants of Saint-Malo, Nantes, and La Rochelle had supported the government's efforts to develop a commercial infrastructure.[20] In the generalized national crisis confronting Spain at the close of the century, the apparently successful French model of growth and of "nationalisme de restauration économique" was decisive when Spanish crisis-managers chose a Bourbon, Philip, to succeed the ebbing Hapsburg, Charles II. The first result was the arrival of impressive, energetic bureaucrat-technicians like Amelot de Gournay (trade expert) and Jean Orry (specialist in state finance) to serve at Madrid during the war and briefly afterward.[21]

The Colbertian paradigm was attractive: there were few representative bodies to subvert decisions made at the center (the Etats-Généraux, like the Cortes, were now more symbolic than functional). France had what foreign observers idealized as a well-managed bureaucracy including the recently revamped intendancies to provide control and direction in the provinces, along with secretaries of state with discretionary powers in executing policy—or so it seemed to Spanish outsiders chafing at the holdover baroque Hapsburg administrative maze of conflicting jurisdiction and entrenched privilege. Further, Spanish projectors interpreted Colbert's corpus of legislation and revamped bureaucracy as designed to do precisely what Spain desperately needed, to "to make up for lost time . . . all of us striving for sound planning and more progress in our trades."[22] Just as France had profited from Holland's experience (Huet's *Mémoires sur le commerce des Hollandois* was dedicated to Colbert), so Spain hoped to learn from, and match, the more advanced French.

In the Colbertian model were features believed adaptable to Spanish needs and reality.[23] High priority went to reorganization of state finance by checking the authenticity of pension and interest (notably *juro*) claims on the state, incorporating into state administration key tax farms (the customs, for example), consolidating or eliminating a range of consumption taxes and internal tolls that discouraged business enterprise, and overhauling finance ministry personnel. Consolidating the initiatives of Sully and Richelieu, Colbert's twenty-year administration made essentially qualitative improvements in state accounting procedures, lowered interest payments on the public debt, and, most important, made strides in balancing state budgets. (Between 1661 and 1683 France's net public revenue rose by a factor of more than three).[24] Colbert's achievements in building infrastructure—highways, bridges, interprovincial canals, and port works—showed how state-financed projects could facilitate the flow of agricultural products for both internal consumption and export. This transport infrastructure would also distribute the output of French manufactories, many financed and managed by the state, which tried to set quality controls for private as well as state enterprise. Given the reluctance of private capital to venture into luxury goods production, infusions of state capital proved crucial, even indispensable, in this sector of French manufacture. Might not state intervention work as well in Spain as it seemed to have in France?

Particularly relevant to Spain's colonial empire was the importance that Colbert assigned to construction of a national merchant marine to carry a high volume of traffic in food and manufactures across the Atlantic to the recently occupied French Caribbean colonies and supply an expanding African slave labor force on plantations there.[25] On inbound voyages this merchant marine would return with colonial staples, in many cases partially processed and then reexported to other European ports. In the eighteenth century Colbert's policy for colonial outreach provided excellent dividends as such reexports became the prime source of France's export growth. The next step was formation of a royal navy to protect the sea lanes used by the merchant marine in colonial trade. By investment in infrastructure and shipbuilding, Colbert's policy of comprehensive state intervention employed gainfully a growing population of young workers.

Finally, in pursuing Dutch and English precedents, Colbert took to heart the function of privileged joint-stock enterprise in highly speculative overseas trade. Backed by state subsidies and trading privileges (often monopolies), French overseas trading companies were expected to absorb the high initial capital costs of shipping and crew procurement for long-distance trade. Delayed return voyages could ruin undercapitalized enterprises. Some companies engaged in slaving between Senegal and the Caribbean. Others traded to the South Indian coast and beyond to Canton, invariably picking up, on their outbound voyages, a basic cargo of Spanish colonial silver arranged by French correspondents strategically located in Lower Andalusian entrepôts.[26]

Constraints on Spanish Model-Borrowing

It was one matter for perceptive Spanish *arbitristas* in the closing decades of the seventeenth century to explore strategies of economic development. Quite another was their application to Spain. Two hundred years of imperialism in America and Europe had molded, hardened, and fixed Spanish institutions and mentalities. On the threshold of the eighteenth century, Spanish realities differed markedly from those of Europe's developing states. Conscious that theirs was a long-established empire, many Spaniards were understandably wary of the unpredictable consequences that might follow heavy-handed imitation of foreign paradigms.

Constraints on Spain's mercantilist options were both external and internal, tangible and intangible. They were enmeshed in a web of relationships—personal, group, institutional. The most immediate and obvious constraints on efforts to revamp Spain's economy were external. The commercial treaties imposed by Spain's European suppliers in the mid-1600s deprived the state of a basic tool of mercantilist strategy in the eighteenth century: tariff readjustment at Cadiz, the major Spanish port and hub of its colonial trade monopoly. At the same time, the competitive strategies of England and France militated against Spain's attempts to upgrade its negligible output of the products that had been basic to the transformation of Europe's economies—fine textiles consumed by elites in both the metropole and the colonies. Typically, at the onset of the War of Succession, French policy-makers refused to authorize the drain of skilled French artisans to Spain and quietly advised French diplomats at Madrid to discourage manufacturing initiatives south of the Pyrenees. Explicitly French policy was designed to deprive Spain of "the means to establish . . . manufactures." Ambassador Blécourt was to be less than explicit with the Spanish government, "being careful . . . to take all necessary precautions so that the Spanish do not see into HM's intentions in this matter, or into the motives which influence him."[27]

For its part Spain was neither commercially nor politically capable of blocking foreign participation in its colonial trade as mercantilist strategy prescribed. As we have noted, Madrid had to permit French merchants of Saint-Malo, acting initially under the auspices of the Bourbon alliance, to open the Cape Horn route to the Pacific coast of South America.[28] For their part, English merchants at Jamaican ports expanded their lucrative smuggling networks with the Spanish Caribbean mainland and exploited the Spanish slave *asiento*.[29] Thus an essential factor of Spanish economic development, colonial trade, was being penetrated by competitive mercantilist policies of nations already advantaged in the protoindustrialization of textiles—and their lead was growing.[30] Last, and not least, was the recurrent conflict between Spain and its principal Atlantic coast trading partners caused by European competition for Spain's American markets.[31] War and consequent financial demands upon state and economy—defense outlays, intercepted colonial trade, repeated *ad hoc* fiscal measures—imposed external constraints on adoption of the policy innovations that appeared responsible for the economic progress of France and England.

Equally important were internal constraints on model-borrowing. In the first place, Spaniards had to confront the obstacles of all latecomers to economic growth. Capital accumulation was low, and capital was difficult to attract; savings and investment were not widespread; and banking facilities were rudimentary. Transaction costs—among them, the development of institutions and instruments supporting long-distance overseas trading enterprises; the state's protection of private capital; commercial techniques; and, of course, regular information on current prices and supply conditions, especially at the main colonial ports—were correspondingly high.

In no small measure the persistence of late medieval economic institutions and attitudes in Spain may be traced to the profitable mining economies of Upper Peru and New Spain, which constituted the critical transatlantic link between America and Spain. In the form of the state monopoly of mercury procurement and distribution and a pyramid of taxes (subsoil rights, minting fees, customs duties), American silver had helped finance the hegemony of Hapsburg Spain in western Europe. In addition, silver mining, as we have seen, had multiple functions. It had monetized the economy of many native Americans (quickly forced to pay a head-tax or *tributo* in silver) and, through the intermediation of wholesale, retail, and petty travelling merchants, helped increase sales and consumption of imports of Spanish, European, and Asian origin.

But colonial silver's multiplier effects on the economy of the metropole remained limited. While American silver promoted the staple trades of English and French colonies in North America and especially in the Caribbean, in Spain it enhanced neither employment nor enterprise in processing and reexporting sugar, tobacco, and cocoa. It stimulated neither domestic manufacture nor finance. The Hapsburg state had both created and exploited a cash cow in the form of colonial silver flows, a perennial financial bonanza that over two centuries produced a distorted commercial capitalism, a low-level equilibrium trap or stationary state characterized by negligible economic growth, underemployment, and unemployment—economic stagnation.[32] So Spain around 1700 imported sugar and tobacco introduced by English, French, and Dutch middlemen (the Dutch even supplied Venezuelan cocoa) trafficking in staples of the Caribbean colonies along with European manufactures that Lower Andalusia's entrepôt merchants purchased with colonial silver for reexport to Spain's American colonies. Perception of Spain's anomalous position as recipient of colonial silver transferred to European competitors, as importer and then reexporter of European rather than Spanish manufactures, in theory a metropole wealthy in colonial mining products and in reality oddly impoverished, formed the core of discourse on economic change, that common preoccupation of Spanish analysts or projectors in the first half of the eighteenth century.

There was a further internal constraint, pervasive and enduring: Spain's multifaceted traditionalism, which had contributed to the weakness of the monarchy by tolerating abuses in institutions and customs and by a de facto decentralized polity. What had been inherited and developed in the fifteenth and early sixteenth centuries, particularly under Isabel, Fernando, and their grandson Charles V, remained enshrined, almost sacralized. Change toward something new, an innovation, was in principle unacceptable, an indication that somehow fundamental structures once admirable were failing. Widely accepted and perhaps symptomatic of declining imperial projection was inordinate reverence for past institutions that, presumably, had undergirded an age of hegemony that was still recoverable. That hegemony had slipped away sometime after 1650, it was generally held, coincident with the emergence of European states able to formulate development policies and to intervene in the national economy. At bottom, England's and France's successes were measurable in their recent economic expansion at home and abroad, in Europe and America.

By contrast, Spain's traditional institutions of governance—its polysynodal or multiple conciliar political structure—meant that the early Spanish Bourbons lacked the centralized authority—a controlling state—visible in England and particularly in France. From the outset, they confronted the baroque Hapsburg constellation of interests that a patrimonial state had not centralized. For the Hapsburg patrimonial state had merely stitched together in the peninsula regional entities, each jealous of its "immemorial" rights, privileges, customs, and special *gracias* bestowed upon corporative bodies and individuals. The political process of government by polysynods—notably the Consejo de Castilla ("Spain's most important institution"[33]), the Consejo de Indias (for the colonies) and, in both metropole and colonies, the censorial role of the Holy Office of the Inquisition—provided the space where state policy was in theory harmonized, but in practice usually compromised. The consejos' extended judicial and legislative jurisdictions joined to their operational mode of requesting position papers *(consultas)*, followed by discussion and then often belated decision by a voting majority, stalled action and inevitably opened channels of resistance to much-feared innovation. Always there was the illusion, but not the substance, of centralized authority in the Hapsburg administrative heritage.[34]

Philip V, his French technicians-on-loan (like Orry), and dedicated Spanish collaborators (like regalist, anti-*colegial* and antipapist Melchor Rafael de Macanaz) early on understood that a mercantilist-oriented state to be effective had to emphasize national goals and project the power to implement them. Otherwise, it would not be possible to convince major interest groups and their representatives (often virtual lobbyists) on the *colegial*-dominated consejos to recognize the over-all hegemony of national over regional and particularistic interests. In 1703 Orry reported to Paris that the consejos were at the heart of Hapsburg politics: "They govern the State, assign all the posts, and all the benefits and royal revenues, with the purpose of having the King . . . take no active role in governing . . . ." Since consejos could not be eliminated outright, the new Bourbon government resolved to stack them with new appointees on whom they could depend. These tactics were applied to the Consejo de Castilla between 1706 and 1707 and culminated in the *nueva planta* of 1713. Radical administrative reform of the consejos in the *nueva planta,* ideated basically by Orry and Macanaz, introduced an inner core of five *secretarios de estado y del despacho universal* working closely with the king. At the provincial level, the plan proposed *intendentes de provincia* also on the French administrative model.[35]

Simultaneously, the government stripped the Consejo de Indias and the Casa de Contratación of major functions, among them finance and control of the convoy system. This was done partly in retaliation for the Consejo's failure to support the new Bourbon dynasty in 1706, partly because Philip's key advisors found the convoy system, customs structure, and lack of official registry of incoming colonial precious metals since 1661 incompatible with a projected mercantilist developmental policy.

The Spanish Bourbon government and French advisers monitoring the growth of French overseas trade (in which the Spanish colonies figured significantly) had to address the colonial trade issue. The Sevilla merchant community had long employed money and influence to maintain the fleet system, Báez Eminente's informal customs arrangements, and the Consulado de Sevilla's management of certain funds. In addition, the consulado maintained a sizable slush fund *(gastos secretos)* to lobby the Casa de Contratación, the Consejo de Indias, and the politically influential at Madrid. That commercial guild also relied upon the Consejo in feuding with merchants of Mexico City and Manila, for example over the expanding imports of Chinese silks, linens, and cottons brought annually to New Spain on the *nao de Filipinas.*[36]

The "planta de Orry" aimed to challenge Lower Andalusia's commercial interests at Sevilla and Cadiz, national as well as foreign. Accordingly, in 1713 the government put on notice the Consejo de Indias and the interests it represented of its intention to "create a new structure and regulations for the administration of the Indies trade." It did this by requesting the Consejo's opinion *(consulta)* about "past abuses under the management of the Casa de Contratación and Consulado de Sevilla."[37] This was a warning of what might come, but it was compromised at the outset by an underlying flaw in Madrid's position. A long war had put state finance under extraordinary pressure complicated by the needs of postwar reconstruction in shipping and naval forces to service transatlantic links to the American colonies. Since Lower Andalusia's customs along with income in precious metals entering on royal account from Cartagena, Veracruz and Havana were the largest single category of state revenue under *rentas generales,* Andalusia's businessmen could manipulate the power of the financial instruments they controlled. For its part, the Consejo tried to defend the commercial interests of Lower Andalusia when in its rococo rodomontade it stressed that Madrid had not allowed it time to obtain the input of "knowledgeable and practical" businessmen, and claimed with mock innocence that it had no "special information" about any "abuses and excesses" by Contratación or Consulado.

It is a measure of the endurance of Hapsburg structures that the Consejo de Indias' *consulta* in response to Madrid's request made no concession to the spirit of change that Philip's close advisors shared at that time. To the contrary, the *consulta* reaffirmed the value to the *monarchía* of its transatlantic system in place since the mid-sixteenth century.[38] Restoring that system to its prewar condition as of 1700, the *consulta* said, would permit Spain to recover "what we have lost in the present Cruel Conflict" and predominance as "Europe's arbiter." Europe, the Consejo boasted, depended on America "for the maintenance and increase in its [supply] of gold, silver and staples by which God has enriched" Spain's colonies. In the Consejo's retrospect, the fall from Spain's commercial paradise coincided with the War of Succession. The Consejo then analyzed the commercial situation it had sketched in a *consulta* of 1709, which, it suggested, Philip's bureaucrats overlooked when hastily abandoning Madrid to enemy forces in 1710. The source of evil was "especially" French shipping, goods, and agents infiltrating Spain's transatlantic system once war at sea had virtually suspended the movement of Spanish convoys. This had permitted the French to penetrate to South America's Pacific ports ("those opulent Dominions") as far north as Callao where they had unloaded cargoes of scarce goods and earned superprofits without paying the customary "excessively high duties." They had then withdrawn directly to French ports with their "many millions" in taxed and untaxed *(sin quintar)* silver.

Madrid therefore bore responsibility, the consejeros claimed, for commercial "restoration and expansion" in the Andalusia-dominated colonial trading complex, since "we have no better *arbitrio*" for stabilizing state finance. The first stage of this restoration called for rehabilitation of the disrupted system of fleets. Without this, argued the *consulta,* the colonies would be lost and "the [economy] of these Kingdoms will be distorted, since the revival of both hangs on one principle, that Spaniards take charge of navigation and close the ports in the Indies to Foreigners." This necessitated procurement ("purchase and fitting out of a few ships") of an estimated eight escort vessels which, the Consejo stressed, neither the consulado nor individual merchants could finance since they lacked "funds, wealth . . . credit." However, were Madrid to guarantee loans with the collateral of customs receipts from managed colonial trade flows, then the Consejo felt confident that the consulado's membership could tap other sources of funds. Again, there was a precondition for this service: Madrid would have to certify the accuracy of the consulado's account books *(cuentas)* covering management of taxes on colonial precious metals imports supposedly applied to redemption and interest payments on certain outstanding government obligations, for example, *balbas y infantes*. To quote the Consejo's *consulta*: "Process and settle the Consulado's pending accounts, either punishing accomplices, or absolving and publishing [the names of] those not charged."

Collaboration of the consulado and the Sevilla merchant community in reestablishing the convoy system required, in the Consejo's view, further concessions. First, Madrid would have to continue to collect duties on exports to the colonies when unloaded overseas at colonial ports. Currently, the Consejo was convinced, Andalusia's merchants were in a "wretched condition . . . [with] the principal commercial houses lacking funds or wealth." Only a handful of "ricos" could cover export duties at Sevilla or Cadiz. The majority—among those the Consejo chose for commiseration were "nuns, maidens, widows and other poor folk laboring the year round to produce stockings, kerchiefs, and underclothing"—evidently could not. Second, and more significant, the Consejo underscored the preservation of what had decades earlier been conceded in the 1661 cedula signed by Philip IV, whereby Sevilla's merchants along with their counterparts in colonial capitals covered the costs of royal navy escort vessels in exchange for "freedom and exemption to return to Spain with no further duty on silver, gold, staples and other products arriving on their account, and without their formal registry."[39] The Consejo endorsed this "contrato," which explains the absence after 1661 of official registry of incoming colonial silver and gold shipments, because "everyone has noticed the growth and greatness of that trade, the wealth created and reputation achieved by Sevilla's consulado, Europe's greatest." It meant that wealthy traders, Spanish and foreign, had once had resources for funding the "great needs of the Monarchy," the royal navy, and escort vessels for convoys to and from Spain's colonial ports. As a result of terminating this arrangement between public and private interests and of the disintegration of the convoy system after 1701, "no wealthy merchant has survived, the consulado lacks credit and there are no goods to ship."

In an explicit rejection of the effort by Madrid's reform-minded administrators to modify the pre-1700 transatlantic system, the Consejo de Indias reiterated its terms for collaboration: closing down the recently opened Straits of Magellan route to the Pacific ports of South America coupled with renewal of biennial Spanish fleets to New Spain and Tierra Firme without any participation of foreign *factores* or even crewmen. In return the Consejo offered a vision of its paradise restored: "The Consejo believes that according to what has been laid forth, and on the presumed good faith that what has been stipulated for commerce will be observed, benefits will follow . . . such that at all times Your Majesty will find the funds needed, as on other occasions." The recommended restoration of *flotas* would surely raise "our trades to the highest level" within three years.

Within two years the *nueva planta* was seriously compromised. Orry and Macanaz were dismissed (1715), and the all-powerful Inquisition was allowed to bring charges against Macanaz. Basic reform remained stalled for years although the recently created secretaries of state were retained. The compromise testified to the uphill struggle to modify these and other deeply rooted structures and obliged advocates of change henceforth to emphasize they were merely stripping away aberrations *(abusos)* from otherwise acceptable institutions. The *proyectista* lexicon had to eschew change. The few licensed publications critical of existing structures and mentalities had to accept the official vocabulary; so official discourse privileged "correction of abuses," "restoration," "renovation," or "reestablishment." Simply put, Spain's analysts coming to terms with their troublesome reality cultivated a discourse and vocabulary designed to gain consensus and avoid censorship.[40]

In weighing *proyectistas'* visions of change and their constraints, questions come to mind. Assuming the desire to implement a protectionist policy, was it feasible to expect the early Spanish Bourbon state to have the capacity and expertise to subsidize and manage the vanguard manufacture of that age, textiles, in competition with the woolens, linens, and silks of Flanders, England, France, Genoa, Venice, and Germany, as well as the transpacific flows of high quality Chinese linens, cottons, and silks?[41] And would Spain's hoped-for *fábricas* be able to meet the requirements of a colonial pact, the exchange of predominantly domestic goods for colonial staples? Could the central government at Madrid extract enough revenue from both traditional and fresh sources to finance peninsular industry along with the necessary infrastructure of roads and bridges, canals and ports, and a merchant marine and naval forces adequate to establish a credible maritime presence on the main transatlantic seaways?

To return to the ability of the Spanish state to confront two dominant internal constraints already discussed: could the metropole—assuming the state's capacity to do so—afford to marginalize a major pillar of its imperial economy, the mining complexes of New Spain and Upper Peru? Could the Spanish Bourbon state even venture to tinker with politically influential interest groups, Spanish and non-Spanish, rooted in the Spanish system of managed transatlantic trade?

Fundamentally, Spaniards formulating a mercantilist paradigm had to address the question that all hard-pressed old—as well as modern—regimes must confront: could the late-developing Spanish Bourbon state pursue activity on multiple fronts simultaneously? Or would policy-makers, realizing that "conceiving a policy from scratch is more troublesome than continuing on autopilot,"[42] be constrained to approach change in a pragmatic, piecemeal fashion? Both avenues had pitfalls. The former risked concerted, violent reaction; the latter invited failure by loss of direction and subterranean opposition.

Uztáriz and His Manual

Gerónimo de Uztáriz's classic adaptation of the Colbertian growth paradigm, his analysis of trade and shipping in *Theórica y práctica de comercio y de marina* (1724) remained for more than fifty years *the* manual for imperial Spain to catch up with more advanced and adversarial England and France. Uztáriz, a Navarrese, had outlined his conception of how to stimulate growth seven years earlier in his endorsement *(aprobación)* of Pierre-Daniel Huet's recently published *Mémoires sur le commerce des Hollandois,* just translated by the son of a fellow *navarro* who had made an extraordinarily successful career at Madrid, Juan de Goyeneche y Gastón de Iriarte.[43]

It was not strange that the two early popularizers of Colbertian concepts in Spain were Navarrese. Navarre's ties to France can be traced to the time when as an independent kingdom it had included what is now French Navarre on the north slope of the Pyrenees. Early in the sixteenth century under French rule, Spanish Navarre became a viceroyalty of Castile. Although Henry of Navarre incorporated his kingdom under the French crown as Henri IV, relations between Navarrese north and south of the Pyrenees remained close, cemented by seasonal movements of laborers, sheep, cattle, and by merchandise smuggled across the mountains in exchange for silver from Spain's colonies.

Acquisition of the American empire drew Navarre into the orbit of Castile in many ways. While Navarre retained regional privileges (*fueros*) including exemption from customs duties except at its borders with Castile as well as its own *cortes* and fiscal administration, Navarrese entered into Castile's burgeoning bureaucracy and ecclesiastical establishment, its armed forces, and most important, its colonial trade and administration. By the end of the seventeenth century Navarrese networks of extended families were scattered from Madrid, Sevilla, and the Bay of Cadiz (at Puerto Santa María and Cadiz) across the Atlantic to the vast viceroyalty of Peru (from Lima to Charcas, Buenos Aires, and Santiago de Chile), Venezuela, and New Spain. The eighteenth century was to be the "Hour of Navarre," Julio Caro Baroja's apt title for his study of Navarre's projection in the peninsula and overseas under the Spanish Bourbons.[44]

A constellation of Navarrese linked by blood and alliance, community of origin (especially the valley of Baztán astride the main route to France), commercial networks, state service, and influential sodalities like Madrid's Real Congregación de San Fermín de los Navarros, invested their funds to support government finance in the form of loans, military provisioning and tax farming. Their economic and political weight was substantial from the beginning of the eighteenth century when Goyeneches and Uztárizes supported Philip with loans and business know-how down to the fin-de-siècle crisis of imperial Spain's old regime under Charles IV. In the long interval between these crises, Navarrese entrepreneurs and bureaucrats played key roles in attempting cautiously to adapt Spanish realities to the changing Atlantic world.

Goyeneche, born at Arizcún in 1656 in the Valle de Baztán was older than Uztáriz, born in 1685 near Pamplona.[45] An enterprising businessman, Goyeneche became a financial adviser to the last of the Spanish Hapsburgs and then to the first Spanish Bourbons. As a tax-farmer and financier he formed multiple contacts to the political elite. Uztáriz, equally cosmopolitan, made his career in state service.

Members of the Goyeneche family had preceded Juan de Goyeneche to Madrid. He emigrated from Navarre to study with Jesuits in the capital and became a protégé of the conde de Oropesa, who was then president of the Casa de Contratación.[46] Later as finance officer in Philip V's armed forces, Goyeneche met frequently with French technicians sent to reorganize Spain's state finances, mainly with Jean Orry.[47] His nephew, Juan

Tomás Goyeneche, represented a financial consortium that held military contracts secured on provincial revenues. Goyeneche, a self-made financier, formed part of the Navarrese network, an "economic bloc" that Caro Baroja has suggested represented "capitalismo peninsular."[48] He bequeathed to his heirs commercial and manufacturing enterprises, facilitated their entry into prestigious military orders and the nobility, and gave them access to the metropolitan and colonial bureaucracy.[49] At the time Goyeneche made his will, his family had managed to "monopolize posts in the Palace and other positions of honor at Court."[50]

Unlike other businessmen of his time, Juan de Goyeneche cultivated more than mercantile and financial interests. He helped found the *Gaceta de Madrid* (1697) which later served the early Spanish Bourbon government as official periodical and major propaganda weapon during the War of Succession, and he sponsored publication of the works of Benito Feyjóo, a major luminary of the Catholic enlightenment in Spain.[51] Goyeneche and his family participated in the widely connected Navarrese brotherhood at Madrid, the Congregación de San Fermín, the regional enclave where Madrid's Navarrese community shared political and social solidarity. The *congregación* was probably the locale where Goyeneche met fellow Navarrese Gerónimo de Uztáriz; in the 1720s both served on the national economic advisory board, the Junta de Comercio y Moneda.

More than a passive admirer of French developmental policies, Goyeneche put some into practice. Drawing upon a personal fortune, earned presumably in tax farming and military contracts and through access to government tax and other privileges, he was inspired to replicate French manufacturing enterprise. He built a woolen manufactory, followed in 1716–20 by a woolen and glass works employing French equipment and skilled workers in a model company town near Madrid appropriately named "Nuevo Baztán." Designed as a showcase of private initiative assisted by state subsidies, Goyeneche's experiments in manufacture found few imitators.[52]

A wealthy member of Madrid's small financial bourgeoisie, Goyeneche was more successful in educating his family. In 1704 his eldest, Francisco Xavier, was sent off with a tutor (chaplain to the Consejo de Indias) to France (they covered southern France from Bayonne to Marseille, followed the Rhone to Lyon where they spent a year), and then to Italy (to Genoa and Milan, and south to Rome and Naples). Like his father, Francisco Xavier marveled how a once-backward France (before the accession of Louis XIV), under a well-defined set of government policies managed by a single-minded public functionary like Jean-Baptiste Colbert, had been transformed. In France young Goyeneche was impressed that "the main item of conversation among . . . all classes and professions, was the structure and advantages of trade, the desirability of manufacture, and the benefits of Navigation."[53] At Paris, he found that many were convinced (and very resentful) that Dutch commerce grew at the expense of France. And since Colbert and his circle had seen in more commercially advanced Holland an acceptable model of economic growth, Goyeneche's son translated Bishop Pierre-Daniel Huet's *Mémoires sur le commerce des Hollandois*.[54] It was no mere coincidence that Francisco Xavier turned to his father's friend and fellow Navarrese Gerónimo de Uztáriz to draft an introduction to his translation. Huet's book was an obvious choice: it had already gone through many translations and — it should be noted — well into the eighteenth century many European projectors continued to be dazzled by the performance of the Dutch economy in the preceding century.[55] Less obvious is an explanation of why there was no Spanish translation of what was *the* major handbook for an aspiring merchant class, Jacques Savary's *Le parfait négociant,* whose publication was decades before Huet's.[56]

Like the Goyeneche extended family, the Uztáriz were Navarrese gentry who had been town officials *(alcaldes)* for over three generations. One brother was a deputy to the Navarrese *cortes* (1701) which supported the Bourbons, while another became dean of the cathedral of Plasencia.[57] At fifteen (1685) Uztáriz was residing with Madrid relatives. He then began years of government service abroad that took him to France, Italy, England, Germany, and Flanders. After military schooling at Brussels he joined the staff of the marqués de Bedmar in campaigns against the French who captured him. Uztáriz returned briefly to Madrid but once again departed, on the staff of Bedmar when he became Spain's viceroy in Sicily.

Back in Madrid (1707) Uztáriz filled successive bureaucratic posts in Guerra y Marina, the treasury department of the Consejo de Indias, the Junta de Comercio and — basic to understanding the intricate overlay of the metropolitan tax structure — in Hacienda where he handled the *millones* and tobacco taxes. It is not implausible that Uztáriz had cooperated with Jean Orry at the Hacienda ministry when Orry tried to rationalize the Hapsburg tax system to finance Philip V's campaigns without drawing on the impoverished French treasury. In Hacienda tax records Uztáriz must have come across statistical data on Spain's demography (size, regional distribution) and economy (its productive and non-productive sectors). By 1717 he was a seasoned bureaucrat, proven Bourbon supporter, and cosmopolitan admirer of France's apparent economic turnaround. He was knowledgeable about details of English and French mercantilist legislation and equipped with a fund of information about Spain's metropolitan as well as colonial reality.[58] First in Goyeneche, Uztáriz, and Juan Bautista Iturralde under Philip V, later in Múzquiz y Goyeneche (conde de Gauza) under Charles III, and finally in Garro y Arizcún (marqués de las Hormazas) under Charles IV, one traces the careers of Navarrese in Spanish high finance over the eighteenth century. Their presence is intriguing: mere regional networking or an undercurrent of continuity in fiscal skill and monetary policy, or both?

Two factors help explain why twenty-seven-year-old Francisco Xavier Goyeneche chose to embellish his translation with the *aprobación* of a sixty-one-year-old Navarrese and distinguished bureaucrat, Uztáriz. First, between 1714 and 1717 the prominence of France in Philip V's Spain was receding, accelerated by the arrival of Philip's second wife (Isabel de Farnese) from Italy with her baggage of petty Italian dynastic interests and advisers. Abruptly, French advisers along with their prominent Spanish collaborator, Melchor Macanaz, had to leave. Macanaz—civil servant dedicated to the new Bourbon order, impatient with the decentralized Hapsburg administrative maze, unabashedly regalist and often anticlerical—disturbed supporters of the status quo by his wide-ranging reform interests. For the metropole he envisioned a fundamental administrative restructuring (the *nueva planta* was one effort and a key one), tax simplification (with Juan de Goyeneche he sketched out a single tax, forerunner of Ensenada's later *única contribución*), and incentives to domestic manufactures. For the colonies, he later advocated a "new system for the Indies," by which he meant radical changes in Lower Andalusia's convoy system and one-port monopoly, reduced dependence upon the colonial mining industry, and an end to rampant exploitation of America's native peoples by incorporating them as producers and consumers. Such proposals, many included in voluminous manuscripts prepared in exile in France, suggest how this restless petrel might have upset the old order if retained in royal service. In 1715, the Inquisition was allowed to bring charges against him, forcing him to choose self-imposed exile and personal security in France.[59] With the forced departure of Macanaz and Philip's French core of advisers, the somewhat tolerant climate of overt self-criticism of the "first formative period of Bourbon rule in Spain" evaporated. [60]

Second, by about 1715 forces of the old Hapsburg order were again ascendant. The Cadiz merchant community and allied interests, embittered by aggressive French merchant shipping at Veracruz and Callao during and after the war, were positioned to insist on restoring the Hapsburg structure of convoys and colonial "fairs" despite the consequences of the *asiento* allocated at Utrecht to English merchant groups. To an admirer of the Colbertian model like Uztáriz, a seasoned bureaucrat who grasped the subtext of Macanaz's exemplary treatment *(escarmiento)* entrusted to the Inquisition, what better way to float before Spain's political elite his views about economic change than by inserting them into the *Comercio de Holanda* the focus of which was not on France? Moreover, it is true that Uztáriz's decision to prepare an *aprobación* was also in response to a request by the Consejo de Castilla.[61] Huet's manual on Holland's overseas trade growth with Europe and Asia (it had only the briefest discussion of Dutch operations in the Caribbean and Brazil's *nordeste*) became Uztáriz's vehicle for synthesizing his early vision of the Colbertian paradigm.[62]

Before specifying policy recommendations, Uztáriz advanced fundamental propositions to be elaborated years later in his *Theórica*.[63] There was, he observed, a problem with the Spanish attitude induced by the pervasive negativism of the "malice" of foreigners who found Spaniards (as many had once found the French before Colbert) apathetic ("naturally inclined to an idle and miserable existence") to economic issues.[64] For Uztáriz the main goal of a regenerated Spanish economy was control over the outflow of "the Treasures of its own mines" (he omitted the colonial origin of the silver) to European suppliers to finance its imports of finished goods (he failed to mention most were reexported to the American colonies). Here the defect was Spain's imperfect tariff schedules ("ruination of our commerce"), and now was the moment to draw lessons from tariff policies adopted by Spain's competitors: England, France, and Holland. Under the new Bourbon dynasty, he overenthused, the apparatus of governance was being streamlined ("more concentrated and unified"), had shed its military and financial responsibilities in Flanders and Italy, and was now positioned to provide the "development, assistance and protection" the economy needed.

To the state, Uztáriz assigned a broad interventionist role in creating a hospitable environment for manufacturing. It was to finance plant and equipment, insure inexpensive subsistence for wage workers, and honor men of business. To Spanish readers he held up the example of neighboring France, which, lacking Spain's raw materials base, had nonetheless managed to transform its trade and shipping facilities through "perseverance, appropriate measures and steady protection" under the direction of "that great Minister . . . Colbert." Spain, Uztáriz recommended, had much to learn from its close neighbor to the north.

In Uztáriz's mirror, the growth of the French economy showed that economic backwardness could be overcome by making export-oriented trade *the* engine of growth. This required state support for privileged (in other words, monopoly) overseas trading companies and facilitating production and export of manufactures. The French model had a further advantage. To a Spanish projector hunting for a suitable formulation of national policy, French legislation was clear, comprehensive and logical, characterized by "breadth and formality . . . preciseness." These qualities were absent in the English publications Uztáriz had been receiving.[65] Moreover under Colbert, Uztáriz was convinced, the French state had managed skillfully to circumvent restrictive clauses in commercial treaties in order to protect its infant industries. And since it had been beyond the resources of France's private sector, the state had assumed responsibility for investment in national infrastructure through an ambitious public works program that built roads, bridges, and canals and modernized port works to facilitate the flow of a growing volume of raw materials and finished goods. Products destined for export induced the French state to sponsor naval construction: a merchant marine and (for national defense and that of recently acquired colonies in North America and the West Indies) a royal navy and schools of navigation. What probably startled some of Uztáriz's readers among Spain's political elite was his claim that the French state had committed millions of its funds to subsidize an ambitious economic policy for trade and manufacture.

In his *aprobación* Uztáriz recognized that such broad intervention put a high premium on cleaning up state finance and enlisting private sector cooperation. Colbert had ordered reviews of state finance, formulation of simplified tax codes, and reduction of internal tolls; then he had assigned fiscal experts to probe provincial and local tax records. To augment the capital base of the business community, Colbert reached out to the nobility whom he coaxed to participate in wholesale (but not retail) trade without fear of status derogation. For a dialogue with the business community, he created various levels of state–private sector consultation: at the national level a Conseil Général de Commerce, at the regional level (for example, Rouen and Lyon) assemblies to air the complaints of manufacturers and merchants. Colbert urged wholesalers and retailers alike to forward unanswered complaints to his staff, if necessary directly to him. In Uztáriz's admiring encapsulation of this French growth model, the triad of an interventionist state, cooperative monarch, and activist minister had managed to transform the French people into an inspiring example of "the most diligent, resourceful and hardworking in Europe."[66] Uztáriz had no doubt that Spain, endowed with what he considered a far greater natural resource base, could overmatch France's turnaround, especially in woolen and silk manufactures.

But was there also a hidden agenda behind the censor's approval of a Spanish translation of Huet's favorable analysis of the Dutch paradigm of economic progress introduced by Uztáriz's *aprobación?* Recall that in 1717 there was a quiet but intense ongoing debate within Madrid's political class ("great zeal among some Ministers and other people") over possible reorganization of trade with American mining colonies like New Spain whose silver output was growing and whose treasury department was under repeated investigation.[67] Between 1715 and 1720, Madrid's options were two: renewal of the Hapsburg pattern of managed trade through scheduled convoys or a single general trading corporation for the American colonies modeled on Holland's prospering East India Company and the expectation of "exorbitant profits."[68] Such an innovation would be potentially wrenching for Andalusian interests. In 1720 Madrid chose the first alternative, renewing in the *Proyecto* the traditional Hapsburg convoy system. As for the second option, Huet observed that the performance of Holland's East India Company had induced Colbert to replicate its example in French trading to Asia. Yet Huet had also aptly concluded—this is germane to understanding the motivation behind Uztáriz's *aprobación* and the censor's approval— that "what is good for Hollanders is not always appropriate for others." As long as France continued to import manufactures for reexport, Huet argued, such a company's impact would be dysfunctional. It would threaten to destroy French manufacturing capacity already installed.[69] In sum, Uztáriz's *aprobación* supported Cadiz's resistance to a major innovation, one general trading company in colonial trade.

In this spirit of accommodation Uztáriz seven years later published his *Theórica y práctica de comercio y de la marina* with the clarifying *proyectista* subtitle, "with specific measures adapted to the Spanish monarchy."[70] To analysis and policy-making suggestions, he brought a degree of precision that convinced readers of his reliability. Years in the Guerra y Marina and Hacienda ministries, contacts within ministries, and information supplied by members of the Cadiz merchant community allowed him to discuss authoritatively sources of government revenue, the Atlantic convoy system, Sevilla's and Cadiz's abuse of internal tolls on Spanish products entering their jurisdiction, and the potential shortcomings of monopoly trading companies in the context of the Spanish economy.[71] In light of what he discussed and, equally important, did not discuss, Uztáriz made evident he was no indiscriminate imitator but a pragmatic analyst of comparative developmental strategies.[72] Rational deduction from other nations' experience could insure satisfactory outcomes or, in his own phrasing, "through examination of everything, and the enlightenment of the wise, the truth and utility of example are demonstrated, authorized and reinforced."[73] In neglecting to profit from strategies followed by other states, Uztáriz believed, Spain "keeps itself ever troubled, and somehow scorned for its weakness."[74]

In format, level of discourse and direction of intention, Uztáriz made his *Theórica* a treatise on the shortcomings in economic planning of "this vast and noble Empire" and a strategy for Spain's economic recovery acceptable to Madrid's ministries and to nationalists among Spain's public and private sectors. The introduction as well as the opening paragraphs of his *Theórica* reveal that the fundaments of the conspectus he sketched out years earlier had not shifted nor (to be less charitable) had they brought about a backlash. At the core of his analysis of Spain's economic stagnation remain the composition of its foreign and domestic trade and its inadequate shipping facilities, both of which caused otherwise avoidable outflows of precious metals (mainly silver). Also central are the psychological symptoms of backwardness, "that lethargy that saps [Spain's] natural forces." He promised to offer "appropriate and advisable" policies distilled from the developmental experience of other countries, from their rules, books, and papers supplemented with his own observations made during travel in western Europe. He alerted readers to his preference for the Colbertian paradigm by announcing his intention to discuss France's successful policies for trade and navigation in order to produce for Spanish authorities a "well coordinated plan for [our] commerce and Navy."[75]

The 107 chapters of the *Theórica* divide roughly into four sections, two clarifying the sources and principles of Uztáriz's growth model. First comes an initial survey touching on general factors of growth, on the size and composition of the population of Spain and its governmental revenues, and on problems of lagging growth specific to Spain, which then permits him to formulate propositions basic to his grand design. Exports of domestic manufactures instead of high-value raw materials like wool or silk could activate the economy resulting in retention of colonial silver rather than in its legal and concealed outflows. After this, pragmatically elaborated tariff schedules that would provide indispensable protection for infant textile manufactures. These propositions were then substantiated in two following sections.

The third section elaborates on elements of English, Dutch, and French economic models. In England's case (compressed to three chapters) Uztáriz cites the Navigation Act of 1660 *in extenso* as model legislation for the advancement of commerce and shipping, the exercise of sovereignty ("the decisive fashion in which they determine and order to be executed what is arranged"), and for adroit tariff formulation.[76] In Holland's case (eleven chapters) he again pinpoints the role of protective tariffs but underscores the inapplicability of the East India Company model as a vehicle for Spain's trade with its American colonies—obviously to put to rest "projects outlined for its formation and practice" in Spain. Such a single trade instrument, he warned, could concentrate Spain's transatlantic trade "in a certain number of individuals," alienating to them an undesirable degree of sovereignty. Moreover, Spanish "impatience" *(viveza)* was quite incompatible with the "calm and waiting required by planning and support of such dispositions and affairs, or with the patience demanded by delay in returns, particularly when none are forthcoming in the early years."[77] Such foresight the Cadiz merchant community could readily applaud.

Given Uztáriz's position sketched earlier in his *aprobación* to Goyeneche's translation, it comes as no surprise that he located the most appropriate economic paradigm for Spain in French state planning ("well discussed and better executed") and in praxis developed under Louis XIV ("el Gran Luís XIV") who was "well served by his Ministers."[78] In eight chapters he sketched what he considered the essence of the French economic model: state support of foreign trade, manufacture, and merchant marine that had generated enough revenues to subsidize a navy, huge land forces (300,000 soldiers are mentioned) and ever-rising expenditures on military operations. National economic recovery and national defense were, in his mind, interlocked objectives imposed by the international competition of advanced commercial capitalism for markets in Europe and overseas in the western Atlantic. National security has a long pedigree in the trajectory of modern capitalism.

Major propositions undergirding Uztáriz's analysis were then developed with citations from official documents and widely read classic works. In discussing "experience and examples" he launched into detailed treatment of French techniques for fine-tuning tariffs (1663–1713), tracing the mechanism of low export duties on finished goods and high (or outright prohibitive) ones on selected raw materials. To this discussion he added a review of state programs to control smuggling and contraband handled by any "Merchant, or trader, participating in defrauding royal duties. . . ."[79]

Associated with industrial protection were methods employed by French authorities to expand manufacturing capacity: not only a huge annual subsidy of one million *livres* to manufacturers (previously mentioned in his *aprobación* of Goyeneche in 1717) but also state pensions and other inducements to foreign entrepreneurs and skilled workers alike to migrate to France in order to set up mills to produce woolens, silks, glass, and tapestries.[80] To buttress such intervention Uztáriz quoted from Savary's widely respected manual, *Le parfait négociant* (the recent 1713 edition),[81] on the apparently

successful outcome of French state intervention in manufacturing enterprises at Abbeville and Sedan. The government had sponsored venture
entrepreneurs such as Nicolas Cadeau (French) to turn out Dutch-type
woolens and Joseph Vanrobais (Dutch) to manufacture woolens designed
for Spanish and Dutch consumers.[82] Such specific state sponsorship carried
out during the "long, very prudent and glorious Reign of King Louis XIV,"
Uztáriz noted admiringly, had meshed with other French tactics that he
treated again by drawing on his *aprobación* to the *Comercio de Holanda:* investigation of local tax collection practices, funding infrastructure, and
sponsoring dialogue in local boards of merchants, manufacturers, and bureaucrats to insure collaboration between business and the interventionist
state.[83]

The last section (thirty chapters) of Uztáriz's treatise had an inward-
tending, Spanish focus on growth-related themes he had explored in the
west European context. The basic propositions remained: primacy of trade
in national growth and state power; capturing invisibles—freight, insurance, and commissions—in foreign trade; reduction of labor costs by prun-
ing the tax burden of multiple *alcabalas* and *cientos* levied on workers' subsistence; confining the state's role to finance and related stimuli and to
general oversight of state-sponsored enterprises. In this sense the *Theórica*'s
last section provided Spanish substance and detail to Uztáriz's slant on the
fundamentals of a well-crafted adaptation of the Bourbon model of economic growth.

Nowhere does Uztáriz better fuse his grasp of the French Bourbon paradigm to his mastery of Spanish detail (and his barely suppressed outrage)
than in treating tariff policy specific to Cadiz—Spain's preeminent European
and colonial entrepôt—and its dysfunctional overall impact on metropolitan manufacture. In the Colbertian model Uztáriz saw the state affirming its
sovereign functions—leased via tax farms to the private sector—by incorporating into state administration economic instruments we now recognize
as fundamental to the development of commercial capitalism. Spain's customs administration, he recalled, had been contracted out to well-funded,
pragmatic businessmen like Francisco Báez Eminente, who began farming
the Cadiz customs in 1675; in Uztáriz's time Eminente's descendants still held
it. Uztáriz's understanding of the Cadiz tariff concession reflected his experience in the Hacienda ministry (when at French insistence Madrid had
investigated inefficiently administered revenue sources) and in analyzing
data that knowledgeable and cooperative residents of Cadiz had supplied
him. Overall, his material on the Cadiz *aduana* lent credence to his anatomy
of Spain's economic backwardness and to his prescriptions for growth.

Without explicitly so stating, Uztáriz found that the Cadiz international entrepôt was in fact outside of state control. Effective tariff duties were phenomenally minimal while the virtually uncontrolled influx of European goods for reexport to the American colonies on erratically scheduled convoys constituted a major obstacle to his developmental model. He traced the problem to Madrid's short-sighted decision to alienate the Cadiz customs zone to Eminente and unnamed associated investors in exchange for cash advances on anticipated receipts. In exercising his autonomy to set official values *(aforos);* the percentage *(cuarto de tabla)* of crates, boxes, and bundles dutiable; and tariff rates *(derechos)* below mandated levels, Eminente enabled foreign producers to undersell what Uztáriz deliberately misnamed "Spanish" manufactures shipped to colonial markets.[84] Uztáriz was putting the best face on an embarrassing national deficiency, the absence of peninsular textile production able to supply more than local, low-income demand. The national psychology (or the Spanish elite's response to foreign derogatory comments) would seem to have necessitated Uztáriz's fiction of pressure from Spanish manufacturers for overseas outlets.

Like Sevilla, once the entrepôt of Lower Andalusia, Cadiz was now the major transit point for European rather than Spanish exports to the American colonies. Its customs receipts produced income for the state (and Eminente's tax concession) but were useless for developing domestic manufactures, as Uztáriz made explicit in referring circumspectly to "disarray in the Cadiz Customs." To the detriment of Spain, he claimed, the Cadiz customs operation was the "main source and cause" of the virtual collapse of silk and other textile production once available at Sevilla, Granada, Córdova, Toledo, and Segovia. Here was much hyperbole, little substance; like most *proyectistas,* Uztáriz had to assuage the discomfort of economic backwardness with reference to a fall from former fictive leadership in certain manufactures.

While nominal customs rates on imports averaged 15 percent (by twentieth-century standards relatively low), the effective rates were a low 2–3 percent. On the other hand, when silks from inland workshops entered the Sevilla-Cadiz customs jurisdiction for export, Uztáriz noted, they were dutied higher (at 12–15 percent) despite the central government's legislation prohibiting internal customs. These informal *desordenes* were more than a concern of repressed disquiet among Spain's political elite; Savary's *Le parfait négociant* boasted to an international readership in repeated editions that French velvets on entering Cadiz's customs paid well under even the 2 percent duty per piece of 40 *varas.*[85] Uztáriz's Cadiz informants (his "experienced merchants") summed up how Cadiz's "disorders" kept state revenues low. They estimated that their port's annual imports from European suppliers totaled 15 million pesos (an extraordinary volume for any European port of the time) but paid somewhat less than 500,000 pesos in duties, while a rate of just 10 percent could yield three times that amount (1.5 million).[86]

This situation made neither fiscal nor protectionist sense. Yet for all his revealing details, Uztáriz offered opaque, guarded explanations—"our fatal errors" or "our shortsightedness on the importance of Commerce."[87] He blamed an aborted effort to modify the Cadiz situation (1711) on inopportune timing in trying to "cure deeply rooted ills," on bureaucratic stasis when "long and demanding meditation" was in order and—the most opaque explanation—on internal contradictions when "such matters are under discussion."[88] His closest approach to picking clear targets had a conspiratorial ring: the "tricks and personal ends" of Eminente's group and customs officers, and the "measures of our rivals carried out in complete freedom."[89] Spanish nationalists, like Uztáriz constrained by often xenophobic nationalism, located in foreign interest groups the scapegoats for national shortcomings.

Evidently it was still impolitic, even politically dangerous, to attack frontally powerful national as well as foreign merchant enclaves at Cadiz. Reluctant as he was to take issue with the Cadiz merchant community, however, Uztáriz did lambaste the *aduana* administration there in order to advertise two fundamental tools of the Colbertian armory highlighted years before in his introduction to the *Comercio de Holanda*. By incorporating the Cadiz customs into the central government's administration, he forecast, Madrid could augment receipts at its most trafficked port by narrowing the gap between real and nominal duties. At the same time, Madrid might consider curbing imports of European goods, monitoring exports of high-value commodities like raw wools and silks, and raising duties on imported finished goods while lowering those on exports of so-called Spanish manufactures. This would be tantamount to affirming the state's authority ("the prerogative of Governments") which Uztáriz perceived in England's prohibitions on imports of competitively priced woolens.[90]

Theórica's final two chapters conveniently summarized Uztáriz's basic text—the primacy of trade in what we now see as early capitalist development, and how important it was that trade be "active"—yet another oblique jab at the "passive" mode of Spanish traders at Cadiz. For "active" implied initiating a kind of nationalization of trade whereby Spanish merchants might adopt new patterns of out-sourcing imports, extending their operations abroad in Europe through state-appointed resident factors or agents, or through their own factors, consignees, or partners in foreign ports, operating in the mode set by merchants in France, Italy, England, and Holland.[91] To this came the corollary that shipping and related activities rest in Spanish hands and on "our own account," that is, in vessels built in Spanish shipyards with state subsidy or other benefits in order to retain freight charges, insurance premiums, and commission fees in the manner dictated by England's Navigation Act of 1660 and partially mandated by Spain's own Real Proyecto of 1720.[92]

Uztáriz and Goyeneche, the former a career civil servant and the latter a masterful entrepreneur (merchant-financier-manufacturer), were two representatives of protonationalism in early Bourbon Spain. Both came from the border zone with France; both had traveled in western Europe; both were impressed by what they saw in France as products of the voluntarism of a ruthless monarch and a loyal, persistent, single-minded chief minister: Louis XIV seconded by Jean-Baptiste Colbert. The modern historiography of the France they knew and admired has X-rayed the cracks and tarnish of the once gleaming façade of Louis XIV's reign, revealing initiatives (many begun earlier under Sully, Richelieu, and Mazarin) of state intervention that were often neither productive, efficient, nor as long-lasting as once believed.[93] Whatever France's achievements—considerable, at least to eighteenth-century English publicists like Malachy Postlethwayt[94]—modern historians see them as products of two decades of relative peace for France soon undone by the escalation of international warfare in the latter years of Louis' seven-decades-long reign. On the other hand, to model- or paradigm-seekers in early eighteenth-century Spain, who had collaborated with their French allies in a bitter international (and internal) war of Bourbons versus Hapsburgs and Stuarts, that façade gleamed with lessons to be analyzed, digested, adapted.

Uztáriz, Goyeneche, and other Francophiles in early Bourbon Spain's political class found in pre-1660 France (like the Spain of their time) an economically backward nation, overawed by the dynamic, versatile, entrepreneurial-minded Dutch. Then after 1660 two Frenchmen had transformed their state seemingly overnight into a major, respected European power on the basis of trade expansion, knowledgeable tariff tuning to foster manufactures, a program for gathering in foreign master craftsmen and entrepreneurs, and a merchant marine and navy constructed in French shipyards— all financed by a treasury secretariat that had pruned waste in tax farming and general tax collection. Whatever twentieth-century historians think of state-business relations under Colbert, Spain's early eighteenth-century Francophiles applauded cooperation in local and national councils that brought together bureaucrats and businessmen in an ongoing dialogue. Hence to Uztáriz, bureaucrat and projector, France offered the logical paradigm of economic growth to replicate—up to a point.

Uztáriz did not join to his admiration for French Bourbon patterns a spirit of uncritical imitation. Judging by what he did *not* discuss, we glimpse how he viewed the problem of adapting the Bourbon paradigm to a markedly different Spanish reality. The France of Louis XIV and Colbert contained both a landholding aristocracy and developing regional bourgeoisies at Marseilles, Lyon, Rheims, and Abbeville, at Rouen, Saint-Malo, Nantes, Carcassonne, and Bordeaux. Spain's commercial bourgeoisie, on the other hand, was small, isolated, and too well adjusted to its status in an essentially agrarian and sheep-ranching economy. Hapsburg Spain was hardly comparable to Valois or early Bourbon France, notably in Castile's precocious creation of colonies (no matter that in the Spanish imperialist lexicon they were *Indias* or *Reynos*), in the wealth of their mines, and in their overall impact on Spain. By the early decades of the eighteenth century the Spanish empire had had 200 years to nurture a crippling dependence upon its colonial silver resources, tapped directly by mine owners, merchants, and the state ("Crown") in the colonies. Moreover, ever since the mid-sixteenth century, Spain's normal transatlantic communication had been confined to only one Lower Andalusian port and the few Caribbean ports at Cartagena, Portobelo, Veracruz, and Havana.

No matter that the transatlantic system was not as closely monitored from Madrid as its formal table of organization intimated, a situation advertised by Joshua Child and Pierre-Daniel Huet. For Uztáriz these structures of economy and governance meant that the Dutch East Indies model of an overseas monopoly trading company was unwarranted—on this point Uztáriz was both explicit and accurate. In the 1720s, the merchant community at Cadiz embraced economic "freedom" within the colonial commercial system. This meant an opportunity for Castilians—in a sense perhaps still penny capitalists—to participate in their exclusive transatlantic system, which was managed through convoys that Madrid had restored with some modifications in 1720. This was, Uztáriz argued, far preferable to the other option, a single monopoly company with limited shareholders and capital and virtual sovereign power.

The multi-secular system of managed colonial trade had formed deep and extended roots in the Spanish metropole, linking many overt and covert supporters both Spanish and foreign. It was a structure of colonialism Uztáriz had no intention (although perhaps he had the desire) to confront, much less undermine at that moment. In this context we can understand why he did not criticize *flotas* and *galeones*, except to urge frequent schedules properly adhered to, and why he did not discuss (much less, criticize) the distorting structural repercussions on the metropole of a colonialism based upon mining precious metals. Instead, despite the gravity of the theme and despite his wealth of data and decided views, Uztáriz touched only tangentially and sporadically on the critical colonial dimension of imperial Spain. A full discussion he postponed explicitly to some future *suplemento* or *adición* to his *Theórica*—"I will develop this further," he slipped in at one point, "when I may treat trade between Spain and the Indies." Only in the final lines of his extended 413-page treatise did he promise to cover those "important points" he had judiciously avoided.[95] In one subtext he was unequivocal: his paradigm of growth was built upon retaining within peninsular Spain silver imported from the American colonies. In the ambiance of the *Theórica*'s publication (1724), open confrontation with the Cadiz trade emporium and its many supporters in Lower Andalusia and Madrid would, Uztáriz understood, not be tolerated. This may explain why the first edition of the *Theórica* despite its muted censure of the Hapsburg heritage in trade, manufacture, and shipping—stagnation—lacked a censor's approval and circulated in a limited edition among "amigos" although "the author was caressed, rewarded, and loaded with honours." In 1751 its English translator asserted that copies of the first edition were "destroyed" because the "court of Madrid" did not believe it a "proper season to make it publick;" it was reissued with additions and official approval eighteen years later in the regime dominated by Patiño's successor, Campillo y Cosío.[96] In 1742 Uztáriz's "sad portrait . . . of the deplorable condition to which [Spain] has been reduced," as the Jesuit Joachin de Villareal (the Madrid agent of the "Provincia" of Chile) lamented in his *aprobación* to the edition of that year, was more tolerable and in tune with a despairing conspectus of the Spanish empire's condition.[97]

Nonetheless, Uztáriz's project was a path-breaker for eighteenth-century Spain. It sketched a Spanish mercantilist paradigm of growth and in the figure of the "ever renowned Don Juan Bautista de Colbert, Europe's most zealous and shrewd Minister for the advancement of Navigation and Trade," a prototype of what later became the much-criticized "ministerial despotism" exercised by a generation of Spanish authoritarian pragmatists.

6. Changing Patterns in the Transatlantic System: *Flotas* and *Registros*, 1720–1759

. . . .

"Were I to speak in detail of *flotas*, galleons, mercury ships, register ships, the slave contract and the permission vessel that the English obtained, I would have to prepare a tome about our errors and commercial ignorance."
José Donato de Austria, "Memoria del instituto . . . Veracruz, 1803. Notas"

"Within the British empire . . . the wheels of commerce were kept moving fairly smoothly by . . . the steady influx of new supplies of money through illicit trading with the Spanish empire." Allen Christelow, "Contraband Trade between Jamaica and the Spanish Main, and the Free Port Act of 1766"

A common factor in Spain's three crises in the long eighteenth century was maintaining communications and the flow of silver in the Atlantic system. For Spain's imperial hegemony still depended on uninterrupted access to colonial revenue to insure the liquidity of its finances. At the end of the War of Succession, trade with the American colonies promised to be a reliable source for financing postwar recovery, insuring the stability of Spain's recently installed Bourbon state, and constructing and manning a navy capable of defending the overseas possessions and their trade under conditions of international competition.

"Reformar este comercio . . . constituyó la [tarea] mas urgente."

It should be recalled that during the War of Succession Spanish ministers and advisors made serious efforts to formulate substantial modifications in the transatlantic system once hostilities ended. The negative reaction of the Consejo de Indias, the dismissal of Orry and Macanaz, and other events postponed action until 1719. Now Madrid had to decide: either in-stall a system breaking with the Hapsburg structure of one-port monopoly in the peninsula and utilizing unscheduled, unescorted ships *(registros suel-tos)*, or shore up the traditional system by regularizing convoy schedules, restricting the number of ships in convoy, fine-tuning cargo volume to estimated colonial demand, and raising duty levels on exports to the distant colonies.

A number of factors favoring traditional arrangements were obvious. For one, except for Cataluna's port of Barcelona, which had headquartered Anglo-Austrian forces during the civil war in Spain, no other peninsular port pressured Madrid to share Lower Andalusia's monopoly of colonial trade. Beginning about 1670, Cadiz and its bay had gradually replaced Sevilla as Spain's sole entrepôt between Europe and its America colonies. This situation was recognized formally in 1717 when Madrid shifted the *Casa de Contratación* to Cadiz—not without acrimony between the two cities. By shifting the bureaucratic apparatus from Sevilla to Cadiz, the established mechanisms for management of colonial trade along with commercial agreements with England and France could be maintained.

A restored and now properly managed convoy system could serve two ends. Under the *asiento* ("that reliable and unique key to the Spanish Indies"),[1] Madrid had yielded to the "English Company" exclusive right to sell the cargo of one large 500-ton "permission" ship timed to operate when a convoy arrived at Portobelo or Veracruz and a *feria* formally began. Regularizing the convoy system seemed the obvious tactic to limit English exploitation of the *asiento* concession.[2] In addition, there was a French factor: by forcing French merchants to rely on the convoy system to feed their goods into Spanish colonial markets, Madrid might curtail unauthorized trading activities that the French had pursued during the War of Succession and afterward.

The colonial trade arrangements of the *Proyecto* of 1720—the solution for Spain's trade and communications with the colonies—retained the established practice of escorted shipping: *flotas* to New Spain and *galeones* to northern South America. Convoys were not given a precise schedule. A cap was placed upon a convoy's aggregate tonnage; it was initially set at 3,000, with 66 percent allocated to textiles and the balance (one-third a vessel's cargo space, the *tercio de buque*) set aside supposedly for Andalusian wines and brandies. There was also a provision for unescorted vessels or *registros* to sail unscheduled to the South Atlantic port of Buenos Aires. Assessment and collection of customs duties—critical to Bourbon state finance and part of the important income category of *rentas generales*—were simplified, and payment was accelerated. Shipowners had to purchase licenses at Madrid, paying according to cargo space *(toneladas)*, while export items were dutied by volume *(palmeo)* rather than by weight. Duties were now payable prior to sailing; in exchange, exporters did not have to open bales and boxes of cargo for customs inspection prior to sailing to, or returning from, colonial ports.[3]

There was, however, a fundamental flaw in the system of convoyed shipping to Veracruz over the following half-century. Theoretically *flotas* would operate on schedules designed to reduce turn-around time at Veracruz, thereby lowering the volume and cost of borrowing by exporters from foreign merchant investors at Cadiz in order to finance Spaniards in colonial trade and shipping. In addition, we have to recall, the *flota* system was designed to preserve separate commercial domains or spaces for the exchange of European goods for New Spain's principal export, silver. This it did, beginning in the 1720s, by holding a fair at Jalapa on the road between the port of Veracruz and the capital of the colony of New Spain at Mexico City. As will be seen, the Jalapa *feria* in the eighteenth century could not isolate the sphere or domain of Cadiz merchants and their representatives accompanying convoys *(consignatarios, encomenderos, comisionistas, factores* grouped as the *flotistas* or *comercio de España)*, from that of the well capitalized resident merchants of Mexico City, the *almaceneros* or warehousemen of the *comercio de Mexico*.

The *Proyecto* also contained a developmental design directed to what Spaniards termed the "reestablishment" or "renewal" of textile manufacture, handicrafts *(maniobras)*, and shipbuilding in the metropole. Indeed, the Bourbon state's intentions seem plausible enough. By the law of unintended consequences, however, the *Proyecto* was to prove contradictory. Licensing (taxing) by tonnage led shipowners to prefer a few large over many small vessels, discouraging peninsular ship construction. More important, dutying bales by volume *(palmeo)* rather than weight induced shippers to maximize profit by continuing to load low-volume but high-value textiles, precisely those manufactured outside the Spanish metropole. Finally, even the third of the cargo space allocated to Andalusian alcoholic beverages often consisted of barrels filled with imported drygoods. Maintaining *toneladas* and *palmeo* simply reinforced the prevailing pattern at Cadiz: reexport of English, French, Dutch, Flemish, Italian, and German quality goods. Are we to conclude that they were not intended to generate peninsular economic growth, much less development? As Thomas Southwell would complain decades later, the *Proyecto* "cutting off Spanish industry at the root, harmed its commerce more than the old monopoly."[4]

The incompatibility between Spain's entrenched transatlantic trade system and a French-inspired colonial compact tying domestic manufacture with colonial demand is illustrated by the trajectory of the Guadalajara woolen works, a manufactory initiated, subsidized, and managed by the Spanish state. The project originated early in Spain's Bourbon regime as the joint initiative of Gaspar Naranjo y Romero and French finance expert Orry, who, in 1703, urged the formation of national manufactures in response to demand for military clothing. Naranjo, an Andaluz merchant, was inspired by Colbert's policies and by a vision of Spain's economic development (his code words were economic "restoration") through national manufacture. Left to their own resources, he realized, Spanish businessmen would continue to prefer imported textiles ("even idiots know how to buy and sell") and to find logical and proper the export of raw wool to France and England.[5] Not until 1719, however, when the domestic political situation stabilized, was the Naranjo-Orry initiative followed up. In that year, Madrid turned to Holland's ambassador, Juan Guillermo Riperdá, to organize a woolen mill. Riperdá was commissioned to create in industrially backward Spain what was intended to be one of Europe's modern manufactories. After massive government outlays, the mill ultimately materialized at Guadalajara. In its early years, it used imported Dutch workmen and foreign management.

From the outset, problems braked the progress of the enterprise: English and French exporters deliberately dumped their woolens in Spain. In addition, Madrid's major distributors of luxury-grade imports, the Cinco Gremios Mayores, were unready and even unwilling to accept Guadalajara's *paños* and *sarguetas*. Simply put, well-established distributors favored dealing in English, French, and Genoese fabrics for which demand existed in both peninsula and colonies.[6] There were, furthermore, other internal constraints—predictable in a protomanufacturing economy—which could not be eliminated overnight: poor and frequently changing management, an inexperienced and often uncooperative labor force, and the start-up problems of product deficiencies in weave, color-fastness, and style. Nor can we overlook the mental blinders of a status-conscious society that rejected craft employment as degrading. A contemporary formulated the mentality of Spaniards obliged by falling income to seek employment. When it was suggested that they turn to selling or to other employments they considered derogating, they would usually respond with "Do you expect me . . . to do that? I'd rather beg from door to door."[7] It should come as no surprise that over the first twenty years (1720–39), average annual production hovered around 24,521 *varas* (the equivalent of 751 *piezas*).

The slow rise of output over the first quarter-century of operations indicates the difficulty of marketing Guadalajara's fabrics whose demand had to be fostered despite competition from English and French imports moving through Spain's established channels. Within two years of its establishment the enterprise was forced to set up an independent Madrid outlet for whole-sale and retail sales. These were hardly encouraging since Madrid's influential Cinco Gremios complained of quality, weave, soiled fabrics, and improper sizing. Over two years (1722–24) the Madrid outlet managed to sell only 2.5 million *reales* of fabrics, 14 percent to the military. The large balance was shipped to the colonies.[8] With a domestic market limited to compulsory military purchases and colonial sales at Portobelo, Cartagena, and Veracruz contingent on Contratación and *flota* officials, no wonder sales were stagnant. Ten years after the Madrid outlet opened, it could not dispose of 55 percent of the fabrics received, and in 1744 it was eventually closed down. Opening distribution centers in other peninsular cities made no improvement.[9] Spanish drapers earned larger profit margins on European imports until mid-century and beyond; meanwhile, Guadalajara's managers searched for steady, profitable sales despite the active disinterest of domestic distributors.[10]

For the continued viability of the large royal woolen mill, the colonial option seemed attractive.[11] In all, over the first thirty years (1723–53) Guadalajara's management relied on *flotas* and then *registros sueltos* to ship to the colonies some 220,354 *varas*, more than half during Ensenada's tenure as Hacienda secretary. Examined in another light, until 1739 annualized colonial sales absorbed 24.3 percent of Guadalajara's average annual production (18,000 *varas*) and in ensuing years (1744–53) only slightly less or 22.6 percent.[12]

Despite changes in management and the search for markets at Madrid, in the provinces, in the military forces, and in the overseas colonies, an unbroken string of state subsidies was inescapable. Decades of financial support, oversight of management, an imposing plant (ironically, facing the magnificent palace of one of Spain's largest wool exporters, the duques del Infantado),[13] and the employment of a sizable portion of Guadalajara's population—1,400 workers and their families, perhaps 5,600 people in all—put the state's prestige at risk. Over the first twenty-four years of operation (1720–44), the annual state subsidy hovered between 1.1 and 2.2 million *reales*, rising somewhat over the following decade and matched by an increase in output. Concurrent with increased subsidization came Ensenada's decision to send abroad Ventura de Argumosa—Riperdá's son-in-law—to examine Europe's leading textile manufactories, copying and, where possible, purchasing machinery for installation in Spain. Later Argumosa was appointed Guadalajara's manager.[14] As a result, in 1754, the three-storied Guadalajara royal manufactory operated with 150 looms,[15] and over the decade 1744–54 average annual production rose sharply to 59,620 varas (1651 piezas).[16] Nevertheless, Madrid had to divert to the Guadalajara factory the *rentas provinciales* of Guadalajara, later adding even those of Soria and Cuenca; and when these proved insufficient, colonial income *(beneficios de Indias)* was also diverted to the enterprise. The record shows that, subsidies notwithstanding, the state never recovered its investment.[17]

The trajectory of the Guadalajara royal textile works offers a classic case study of hothouse techniques applied to create an industrial base designed to overcome what Gaspar Naranjo had termed "a century and a half of decadence."[18] *Proyectistas* like Gerónimo de Uztáriz, who inspected the Guadalajara facilities on two occasions, could not have failed to realize what Gonzalez Enciso's recent comprehensive monograph had to conclude: Guadalajara was "completely incapable of auto-financing;" therefore it was a financial "failure" and an "enterprise costly to the nation."[19] Yet Uztáriz and later *proyectistas* might also have drawn at least one positive conclusion: it might still be possible to substitute for diffident metropolitan distributors and consumers at Madrid and Cadiz others in the colonies who could provide an expanding market for the metropole's essays in infant industry. Enforcing an effective colonial compact still remained a possibility; it was not yet pure mirage.

Whatever the intentions of *proyectistas* and others consulted in drafting the *Proyecto* of 1720, they did not introduce a bold initiative to correct the stagnation of Spain in the early eighteenth century and to cushion shocks to the colonial trading system caused by the War of Succession. The *Proyecto* preserved the drawbacks of past practice and projected them into the eighteenth century. As Macanaz once noted, "Age-old ills . . . are not cured with palliatives."[20] But, then, neither polity nor society of early eighteenth-century Spain were fundamentally altered by the Bourbon governments under Philip V and his son, Ferdinand VI.[21]

Why did state policy under the Spanish Bourbon administration, in theory capable of "absolutist" innovation, simply refurbish in the eighteenth century a system for monopolizing colonial trade that was visibly porous in the 1690s if not before, virtually inoperative during the War of Succession, and incapable of germinating much less protecting peninsular manufactures over the previous century? The question is all the more pertinent, since by 1720 it was evident that the conditions of Atlantic commerce were changing rapidly, driven by the growth, competition, and aggressive tactics of English and French manufacturers and merchants seeking to expand market share in North America and especially in the Caribbean. The French,

English, and Dutch traded in smuggled goods with Spain's Caribbean ports, while in addition, the English naval forces threatened to occupy the ports of Cartagena, Portobelo, Veracruz, and Havana.

There seem to be a number of answers. The *Proyecto* sidestepped unpredictable repercussions of a more open trading system that might destabilize structures that had insured continuity. It responded to the inroads of the South Sea Company's "annual ship" under its *asiento,* whose arrival was, by treaty, to coincide with that of Spanish convoys.[22] It supported the economic practices of traders at Cadiz and the ever-present hope of equilibrium in the whole Spanish transatlantic system. Finally, fueling the system since the middle of the sixteenth century was the silver production of Peru and New Spain. Hence a restored convoy system to New Spain and South America contributed significantly to cover the financial needs of Bourbon Spain as it had those of the preceding Hapsburg state.

The financial requirements of the Spanish state were obvious and multiplying in the eighteenth century. Defense outlays on the naval and military establishments and on the extended royal household absorbed most of the primitive budgets. The elaborate convoy system — its superficially tight organization centered in one metropolitan port (now, Cadiz) as well as the limited number of colonial ports where convoys unloaded, its presumed monitoring capacity, and its revenue collection on outbound and inbound cargoes — promised the state financial liquidity and, by extension, stability of the monarchy. This was a quality prized by Spain's bureaucrats, clergymen, aristocrats, gentry, and minuscule commercial bourgeoisie — all committed to the preservation of their ancien regime.

Less obvious were business practices at Cadiz and Mexico City about 1720. At Cadiz, few in the Spanish commercial community dominated by Biscayans and Castilians from Asturias and the *montañas* of Burgos possessed capital assets adequate for independent financing of their commercial operations in the Spanish transatlantic system. The merchandise they shipped to colonial consumers was not produced on any significant scale (if at all) in the peninsula. Early eighteenth-century Spain was no example of protoindustrialization; the Spanish products shipped from Cadiz to America were "only . . . wine, brandy, olive oil, raisins, almonds and silks."[23]

Relying on the drawing power of colonial silver arriving at the Cadiz terminus of their Atlantic system, peninsular merchants had not developed a pattern of sending purchasing agents abroad to seek out producers and export houses in the principal areas of manufacture in England, France, Flanders, Holland, Italy, and Germany. They felt no compulsion to. Over more than two centuries Europe's manufacturers and exporters established representatives first at Sevilla and later at Cadiz to display and market products for sale, especially in the colonies. This mode of operation had always inflated the cost of goods distributed in the colonies, but under oligopolistic competition within the Spanish trading system such costs were passed along to consumers in the colonies—and they paid in silver. A Spanish analyst described it well: Cadiz firms "buy from the last in a line of distributors the foreign goods burdened by all the intermediaries' profits. If they pay cash, they borrow at high interest, and if on credit payable by installments, imports become even more expensive. So they must sell at very high prices to turn a profit. The flota system made such sales possible, it was a monopoly."[24]

By contrast, resident European merchants grouped in their respective "nations" at Cadiz in the eighteenth century could draw upon the capital resources of their parent firms at Saint-Malo, Rouen, Paris, Lyon, Geneva, London, Amsterdam, and Genoa to furnish merchandise to under-capitalized Castilian and Basque merchants. They employed an arsenal of mechanisms. Customarily French merchants (the "French nation") financed the fitting out of convoy ships and paid import and reexport duties. Well-capitalized resident foreigners, French and others, underwrote the operations of Spanish strawmen in the form of the high-risk *prête à la grosse (a riesgo de mar)*, sea loans covering the costs of outbound and inbound runs and duties. Although excluded by law from direct participation in the closed Spanish transatlantic commercial system, foreigners colluded with compliant Spanish merchant collaborators and tolerant state officials in a system best characterized as bullionist and pseudo-mercantilist. It was far from mercantilist, certainly not before the era of Charles III. Within this structure of merchant capitalism in eighteenth-century Lower Andalusia, peninsular merchants at Cadiz remained peculiarly penny capitalists.

Merchants resident in the capital of the colony of New Spain, Mexico City (the "comercio de Mexico" distinct from the "comercio de España"), operated under other constraints. The flow of imported goods into the large colony, whether across the Pacific from Chinese ports via Manila to Acapulco or from Cadiz on the other side of the Atlantic to Veracruz, was concentrated in roughly ten to twenty principal merchant firms owned and operated by warehousemen/wholesalers *(almaceneros)*. Unlike Spanish merchants at Cadiz, Mexico City *almaceneros* were not *prestanombres;* their capital was the product of their own operations, augmented by local borrowing from the funds of chaplaincies *(capellanías)*, cathedral chapters, convents, and nunneries.[25] With rare exceptions these merchant princes—their incomes were indeed princely—were virtually all peninsular immigrants as were their apprentices, clerks *(cajeros)* and the managers *(administradores)* in the colony's other commercial centers.[26] They epitomized a self-selecting, self-reproducing colonial commercial elite whose peninsula-oriented recruitment policy was a factor insuring continuity of Spanish colonial hegemony over New Spain. They traded in both European and Asian imports as well as colonial products, which they distributed throughout New Spain and beyond, to Guatemala, Caracas, Guayaquil, and Callao-Lima. Within New Spain they dealt with wholesalers and retailers in provincial capitals, mining centers, and pueblos. They supplied small retailers in country stores *(tiendas)* and itinerant pack peddlers *(viandantes, buhoneros)* who fed the desire to imitate consumption styles displayed by the colony's Spanish-born and criollo elites.

On the other hand, a shared birthplace *(patria chica)* in the peninsula did not avert intense rivalry between the "comercio de Mexico" and the "comercio de España" when imports were traded for New Spain's basic export item, silver. Peninsular merchants registered *(matriculados)* in the Cadiz consulado intended to remain the sole purveyors of exports and reexports to Spain's new world, and for their part, immigrant peninsular merchants dominant in the capital city of New Spain aspired to remain the sole purveyors of imports within the colony. Both *"comercios"* in this area of the Spanish transatlantic system shared an unbridled interest in oligopoly (their critics termed it *monopodio*).

To this end Mexico City's *almaceneros* mobilized their corporate body, the consulado, created and legitimized by the Spanish state at the end of the sixteenth century, to oblige members of the "comercio de España" who disembarked with their goods at Veracruz to adhere rigidly to the prescribed rules of exchange with buyers residing in the colony. Consistently the elected officers of the Consulado de Mexico insisted upon adherence to such rules in repeated representations to colonial authorities at Mexico City, the audiencia and viceroy, and through salaried agents to the Consejo de Indias at Madrid. Commercial exchanges either at Veracruz or at Jalapa, midway between that tropical port and the central plateau, best suited their objectives. In the late seventeenth century Spaniards accompanying their goods on *flotas* had sold them at a *feria* sometimes held in the colony's capital where they encountered both the capital's *almaceneros* and a range of provincial buyers trying to short-circuit the warehousemen by dealing directly with the *flotistas*. Hence Mexico City's merchants resisted a *feria* in the capital because, to cite a Consulado de Mexico complaint, "once they [*flotistas*, factors, shippers] sense the chance of leaving Xalapa with their textiles for Mexico City, there's no hope of a fair."[27] On the other hand, the Jalapa fair formalized in the 1720s offered mutual advantages to both "comercios." Ideally, *flotistas* could quickly sell off a large volume of imports providing price levels were mutually favorable. This permitted them to return on schedule to their partners or principals at Cadiz with receipts in silver and some high value primary products such as indigo and cochineal. Also there could be savings on crew and ship maintenance in tropical waters, important considerations since sluggish sales in New Spain delayed return voyages.

As for the "comercio de Mexico," large-scale purchases from *flotistas*, particularly when they were constrained to sell and depart within a preset period (the *Proyecto* of 1720 prescribed about seven months for a fair), offered them the leverage to depress the *flotistas'* inflated price levels, to obtain whole lots (a form of forestalling), and to monopolize sales of imported goods of strong colonial demand. In fact, the "comercio de España" and "comercio de Mexico" enjoyed a bilateral monopoly (or duopoly). By limiting the *flota's* stay at Veracruz to seven months and stipulating a departure date (15 April), the *Proyecto* forced authorities to locate New Spain's feria at a point near Veracruz. Evidence suggests that Madrid yielded to pressure from the Cadiz commercial community and finally fixed the fair at Jalapa where its formal existence began in 1728.[28]

There remains another, perhaps most convincing, explanation for the apparent paradox of a convoy and fair system in New Spain revived and elaborated under new and threatening international conditions. Resurgence of New Spain's silver production, a phenomenon already evident in the closing years of the seventeenth century, could predictably sustain trade flows between colonies and metropole despite the inevitable smuggling leakages. New World silver remained a major preoccupation in reviving the convoy system in 1720, confirmed by the results of the *flotas* (if not the *galeones*) and supplemented by mercury-carrying vessels *(azogues)* over the twenty years, 1721–40.[29] Of course one must include the caveat that the data base assembled in Michel Morineau's *Incroyables Gazettes* reflects a prestatistical age and remains subject to future corrections to cover those inflows of American silver at Europe's Atlantic ports which completely bypassed the Spanish metropole.

Two tentative conclusions may be drawn apropos export tonnage and silver imports at Cadiz. Official outbound tonnage figures (much understated) of the five *flotas* to Veracruz between 1720 and 1735 were on average higher than those prescribed by the *Proyecto:* instead of 3,000 cargo tons per convoy, the average is 4,161. Including the tonnage of escort vessels, as Morineau argues, the average rises to 6,000–8,000 tons, virtually double the *Proyecto* limit.[30] As for the peso value of inbound convoys plus *azogue* vessels, it ranges from a minimum of 5.5 to a maximum of 6.6 million pesos per annum, excluding silver smuggled from the Veracruz coast via England's Caribbean possessions and from Acapulco across the Pacific to Manila. More significant, the admittedly proximate data on returns in silver from all the Spanish colonies in America over this fifteen-year period suggests that of a grand (in fact, extraordinary) total of 187.2 million *pesos fuertes* received in Spain and Portugal, 58 percent came from Veracruz-Havana, and 42 percent from South America.[31] The growing preponderance of New Spain's silver mining in the Atlantic economy is self-evident.

If the resurrected *flotas* to New Spain after 1720 seemed profitable by comparison with the moribund *galeones* to Cartagena and Portobelo, still there were grounds for diluting the optimism of contemporaries about long-term results. The theory that there were economic spaces or compartments mutually respected by Cadiz and Mexico City oligopolists generated friction when put into practice as the oligopolists, then as now, competed for larger profit margins. Mexico City's *almaceneros,* well supplied with Asian goods (both legal and smuggled) from Manila and smuggled French and English goods, often rejected prices initially set by *flotistas* of the "comercio de España." Unsold merchandise had to remain at Jalapa when *flotas* were scheduled to depart Veracruz for Cadiz. *Flotistas* reacted by refusing to remain confined to Jalapa as prescribed by *Proyecto* regulations. They faked sales to justify moving their goods from Jalapa fairgrounds to Mexico City where they could sell to competitive buyers. In turn, Mexico City's *almaceneros,* to undercut *flotistas'* control of European imports, shipped their funds to agents in Cadiz to purchase goods on their own account, also violating *Proyecto* regulations. The Cadiz merchants then lobbied Madrid for an order prohibiting the transfer of funds from New Spain to Cadiz unless the funds were sent to peninsular merchants registered with the Cadiz consulado. In addition, they urged regulations mandating that goods aboard convoys to New Spain be consigned only to *flotistas.* The ministry of colonial affairs under José Patino complied. By the late 1730s a shared oligopoly at Jalapa did not satisfy the respective "comercios," which is not to say the commercial interests were prepared to opt for an alternative system—the somewhat more radical "comercio libre" contemplated by projectors like Macanaz and later Bernardo Ward and Pedro Rodríguez Campomanes.

The revived convoy system was suspended in 1739 by the outbreak of war between England and Spain triggered this time by the aggressive tactics of English traders in the Caribbean. International war was again the main fac-

tor forcing tradition-minded Spaniards to try to come to terms with changing colonial and transatlantic realities.

Interregnum: The *Registro* Phase, 1739–55

The slave supply contract had figured prominently in the origins of the
long War of Succession. Once again, the *asiento* was at the root of the conflict between Spain and England that began in 1739. Madrid was determined
to eliminate two major concessions to English commercial pressures it had
made at Utrecht: the right to supply African slaves and the *navío de permiso,*
both instruments of commercial penetration that English merchants now
exploited to the full. Spanish interests were understandably unnerved that
the *navío de permiso* at Portobelo leaked English goods from the isthmus to
flow north into their principal mining colony of New Spain, a threat heightened by English Admiral George Anson's expedition along the Pacific coast
during the war.[32] Linked to these issues was another: the perception of English manufacturing and commercial groups that French export interests still
maintained a commanding presence at Cadiz *inside* the Spanish transatlantic
system. For their part, French analysts concluded that the English were pursuing their grand design, "an operation which would bring the English to
the coasts of Spanish-dominated America."[33] Both English and French perceptions were compatible with reality, as Spaniards were quite aware. They
understood it was now a war over "the trade . . . and navigation of the
Indies."[34] Six convoys had left Cadiz for Caribbean ports in the 1720s. The
number dropped to four between 1730 and 1737, and the suspension of both
flotas and *galeones* in 1739 caused no profound shock. Spanish bureaucrats
and businessmen had already foreseen, as English historian William Robertson interpreted the suspension later, the need to devise "some method of
supplying their colonies, different from their ancient one."[35]

Of course, the critical problem for the Madrid authorities in 1739 was
still finance: how to cover skyrocketing defense expenditures. Immediately,
they cancelled the convoy scheduled for New Spain (its cargo had to be unloaded) but retained all prepaid export duties, perhaps the equivalent of 25
percent of invoiced cargo. This action by the Spanish state fell mainly on the
largest interest group involved in the *flota* to Veracruz, French merchant
investors.[36] In addition Madrid then imposed two forced loans *(indultos),*
repeating a traditional instrument of state fiscal desperation that had exas-
perated peninsular and foreign merchants since the 1520s. First they demanded 500,000 pesos from all shippers involved in the cancelled convoy,

prorated by percentage of outbound cargo. This was followed by another demand of 500,000 pesos (reimbursable from future customs receipts) from the Consulado de Cadiz in exchange for authority to license individual merchant vessels sailing unescorted to the colonies *(registros)*.[37] (Later, it appears, the government insisted upon the 300,000 pesos that the consulado had presumably collected in licensing fees.) In all, Madrid laid hands on from 1.3 to 2 million pesos—a measure of the American colonies' continued contribution to the metropole's financial liquidity in war and peace and of Madrid's awareness of Andalusian merchants' practiced skill in undervaluing and concealing cargo.

Indultos, however, could not long serve as policy. At this juncture, Madrid had to resort to what had been legislated under the *Proyecto* of 1720 for supplying selected ports hitherto not served by the convoy system, for example, the *navíos de registro* dispatched to Buenos Aires. The Spanish state did so, however, adapting Spanish *registro* practice to wartime conditions because it could not effectively defend its merchant marine at sea. Now it proceeded to license *neutral*-flag carriers (which turned out to be predominantly French) as *registros.* This ended when France, too, became a belligerent.

Suspending the revived convoy system in order to supply the American colonies, at least for the duration of the war, was an act of desperation. But once *registro* licensing got underway, the new system continued to provide some control over colonial trade. It also provided the opportunity (to some, a promising innovation) for more peninsular merchants to go into colonial trade, and it even ultimately reduced their dependence upon foreign merchants for capital and credit.[38] The greatest advantage of the new system was soon recognized by a chronically underfinanced state: *registros sueltos* on a large scale unexpectedly generated more income than the far less frequent convoys.[39]

Merchants pursued *registro* licenses at Madrid paying fees based upon tonnage *(toneladas)* of freight capacity. As wartime freight rates rose, so did license fees. In practice, licenses were another form of purchased privilege, "a special grant bestowed by favor and subject to endless delays, inspections, and other bothersome formalities."[40] French merchants, the single largest ethnic group ("nation") involved as neutral-flag carriers supplied 42 percent of all foreign-built *registros.* They complained bitterly about the baroque formalities the Spanish state continued to impose, its charges for "dispatch, costs, delays, constraints, guarantees of every sort, sentinels aboard, transporting officials" not to mention the "constant threat to confiscate shipping."[41] Like the temporarily shelved convoy system, *registros* could only sail from Cadiz and had to return there.

Despite the complication and cost involved in petitioning for licenses and fitting out vessels, Spanish merchants, duly *matriculados* in the Cadiz consulado, pursued licenses because they were readily negotiable with third parties.[42] For example, the *permiso* for a *registro suelto* to Veracruz was transferable to an investor in exchange for a half-share of profits and free fitting-out. This produced a saving of, on the average, roughly 60,000 pesos. Licenses, therefore, became a preferred form of speculation, profitable to businessmen and corporate bodies like Madrid's Cinco Gremios Mayores, the Compañía de Zaragoza and even the naval academy at Sevilla, the Colegio de San Telmo (to which Madrid authorities assigned licenses in lieu of other financial support).[43] Inevitably entrepreneurs on the trail of *registro* licenses resorted to bribes of between 12,000 and 15,000 pesos per license in addition to the formal fee per cargo ton. Depending on the vessel's hold, this varied between 30,000 and 50,000 pesos.[44] Robertson hardly exaggerated in reporting that a license from the Council of the Indies could cost a shipper "a very high premium."[45] Despite Madrid's intention of using *registros sueltos* to broaden the small circle of merchants engaged in colonial trading operations, *registros* continued Cadiz's port monopoly: licenses had to be registered with its consulado, and *registros* were dutied in the fashion of the suspended convoys. "The trade monopoly . . . was once again re-established," in effect "linking trade to a limited number of wealthy merchants."[46]

In fact, however, the formalities of the convoy system had always been subject to manipulation by Andalusian merchants, a normal defensive reaction embedded in their business culture to the arbitrary financial demands (*secuestros* and *indultos*) that officials of the Hapsburg and early Bourbon regimes in Spain frequently imposed upon the merchant communities. In the 1740s abandonment of the convoy system for unscheduled *registros* to the colonies and the resort to neutral-flag shipping multiplied opportunities for profit-taking by both Spanish and foreign commercial interests. Neutral shippers who obtained *registro* licenses through third parties proceeded to load cargoes not at Cadiz but in neutral European ports whence they sailed directly to Spanish colonial ports.[47] Despite the colonial trade legislation, the cargoes of *registros* were usually (and illegally) the property of French rather than Spanish merchants—which explains why French businessmen were upset when "commercial correspondence from the Indies contained in sealed boxes as a sacred, ever-respected trust" were "opened on several occasions."[48]

Wartime conditions also favored manipulation of maritime insurance by Cadiz merchants. A Cadiz merchant might insure a vessel and its cargo but fail to load the insured cargo, or he would substitute goods cheaper than listed on its manifest. Then once at sea, its captain might put up no resistance to English corsairs or, on nearing his colonial port of destination, sink his ship, then file an insurance claim. Ironically the fraudulent nature of the claims was sometimes uncovered in unexpected fashion as when English corsairs searched the holds of their neutral-flag prizes *(registros)* sailing under license to Spanish colonial ports only to find they were "filled with rags."[49]

Foreign operators of neutral-flag carriers with so-called Spanish cargoes were no less manipulative in maximizing the profit possibilities of Spain's transatlantic trade. Saint-Malo shipowners registered their tonnage without advising Spanish port authorities that a Malouin ton was twenty percent larger than its Spanish equivalent.[50] Or French shipmasters returned to Cadiz with a high volume of unregistered or undervalued silver: "One does not list in Cadiz's registers and Customs the real amount of money, but rather according to what one wants to pay in royal duties; this is accomplished by sacrificing a small percentage in gifts, and much fraud."[51] Many French register ships simply bypassed Cadiz to return directly to French Atlantic ports as they had in the War of Succession.[52]

Foreigners participating in what was normally an exclusive Spanish trading enclave found their conduct criticized. "The tale of those register ships under French flag," it was reported with some overstatement, "left a lively impression in Europe. . . . It should have been preferable had captains, shippers and all involved followed the customs and rules, even with respect to the King of Spain's legitimate duties." The prime error in Spanish policy, an analyst observed years later, was the licensing of neutral shipping which "had the effect of stimulating and revealing how to engage in illegal trading." Neutral shipping—French, Dutch, and Swedish—disregarded Spanish regulations to sail "without schedule, by various routes, and to different colonies." Since Spaniards desperately needed foreigners' wartime participation in clandestine trade, they had to tolerate foreigners "who purchased their goods in foreign lands and shipped them directly to America."[53]

The results of almost sixteen years of *registros sueltos* licensed by an imperial government dedicated for almost two hundred years to the ideal of an exclusively Spanish convoy system were mixed. Despite a soft statistical base, evidence indicates that over the years, 1740–56, Madrid officials licensed 164 *registros*, 119 (73 percent) to Spaniards, 45 to non-Spaniards (of whom the French accounted for between 24 and 40 percent) supplemented by 24 *aviso* (mail) ships.[54] Moreover, there is reason to believe investors at Paris, Rouen, Saint-Malo, Bordeaux, Lyon, Marseille, and Geneva financed many of the 119 Spanish licensees.[55] For its part, the Spanish government gained not only from Cadiz customs receipts and related revenues, but also from other fees. Assuming an average tonnage per *registro* of 500 (probably an understatement), at 50 pesos per ton the yield was 25,000 pesos per licensee.[56] Although average annual receipts of Spain and its allies (1741–45) initially fell to 5.7 million pesos (three million under those of the preceding five-year period) they rose spectacularly in the following two five-year periods to 17.7 and 16.5 million pesos respectively. To quote José de Gálvez, "more funds came to Spain than under the former *flota* system."[57]

The use of *registros*, which brought such impressively large silver imports after 1748, led Madrid to attempt to tighten its exchange controls. The government had always sold to Cadiz merchants a percentage of silver shipped from colonial treasuries on royal account, much reexported. Also, much received on private account went abroad—at times "almost all the returns from Spanish America." In attempting to reassert control over the reexport of precious metals after 1748, Madrid under Hacienda minister Ensenada insisted upon additional formalities: exporters had to transfer silver at the government's exchange rate, for which it charged a 3 percent commission, and accept its bills of exchange *(libranzas)* collectible abroad. This was a big change from the former ease with which silver had been exported. The French business community at Cadiz complained that the government's exchange rates and commission inflicted serious losses, and they viewed the rigor in executing policy as "beyond words."[58] There were, however, unexpected benefits. As strawmen for French investors in Spain's colonial trade during the *registro* phase, a few Spaniards at Cadiz earned enough in commissions to set themselves up in postwar years as self-financed traders, "full owners rather than agents as was formerly the case."[59]

From this perspective, the performance of *registros sueltos* in the fifteen years after 1739 seemed to support recommendations for a more open imperial trade system by eighteenth-century projectors like Macanaz and by Hacienda minister Ensenada (1743–54). Consider the performance of shipping from Cadiz to Veracruz: comparing shipping and tonnage of two periods—1717–39 and 1740–56—the number of vessels rose from 112 to 169 (51 percent), total tonnage from 30,699 to 54,659 (78 percent) while tonnage per register vessel increased from 274 to 323 (18 percent).[60] The American colonies would figure large in Ensenada's nationalist policies which favored continuation of *registros* over convoy resumption, the imposition of exchange controls, and a program of naval construction to protect the colonies and their trade.[61]

On the other hand, at the microeconomic or firm level there were mixed results. After the scheduled or regulated system of escorted convoys, inevitably the regime of unescorted *registros* produced a sense of disorder exaggerated by tradition-minded traders. Some Cadiz shippers profited hugely by a 50 percent increase in freight rates. Wartime profiteering on sales in New Spain was common, and the performance and personal responsibility of Spanish factors and encomenderos who accompanied cargo from Cadiz left much to be desired.[62] Time, distance, and greed caused losses to other Cadiz merchant-shippers and their French partners. Many *factores* and *encomenderos* managed to sell European merchandise directly to buyers in the populous, wealthy colonial capital of Mexico City where for some of the "comercio de España" the attractions proved irresistible. They then misappropriated sales revenues to spend on lodgings, alcohol, and women, on "gambling . . . and . . . other criminal diversions that consumed other people's funds." Some speculated in mining ventures with funds in their trust and "since this activity is both uncertain and risky, they buried in mines funds for which they bore responsibility."[63] Others made contact along the Veracruz coast with smugglers operating out of Jamaica in order to transfer their silver holdings to English and French ports in Europe.[64]

These activities might have been dismissed as unavoidable consequences of abrupt abandonment of the trading system restored in the 1720 *Proyecto* and tolerable, as a Cadiz merchant wrote Prime Minister Ensenada, "because the times so required."[65] Once the war ended, however, pressure from commercial groups surged at both terminals of the transatlantic system. These interests preferred the advantages of escorted convoys: managed undersupply, the likelihood of rapid turnover at the Jalapa *feria* site, and mutually shared profiteering. From consulado officials of Mexico City and Cadiz, complemented behind the scene by French businessmen at Cadiz, came repeated petitions to Madrid to restore the convoy system which "alone can restore this commerce to a level fitting the general interest."[66]

Unscheduled *registro* arrivals at Veracruz carrying large shipments of European textiles supplied New Spain's consumers with a wide assortment but brought lower-than-expected earnings to the "comercio de España"—a reflection of the scarcity at Cadiz of up-to-date commercial intelligence about colonial supply and demand, a situation that "upset and frightened everyone."[67] Mexico City's merchants analyzed their situation: "When some register ships bring what is already in stock, and others what is needed, no one ventures to buy since he risks fresh supplies introduced by subsequent register vessels, lowering the prices of what he has bought and causing him losses."[68] As a result, the stock of unsold goods mounted (in 1754 it was estimated at more than 600,000 pesos) and *flotistas* grew impatient to return to Cadiz and reluctant to extend more credit to underfinanced provincial traders in New Spain. There were reports of a greater than normal rate of bankruptcies in Mexico City, probably among medium and small traders.[69] Unable to arrange quick sales, some *encomenderos-factores* chose to remain behind to dispose of their goods under acceptable conditions. Beginning in 1744 reports from Mexico City filtered back to Spain concerning the illegal overstay of the "comercio de España," and in 1755 a viceregal survey (requested by Ensenada's administration) turned up about sixty *encomenderos-factores* from Cadiz (including three Frenchmen) residing in the colonial capital alone. Some had been in residence for twenty years, although most had only been there one to three years.[70] No doubt even more were dispersed in the provinces. The segmented Atlantic trading system of two separate commercial spaces reconfirmed by the Jalapa fair schedule in 1728 seemed to be collapsing.

Prime Minister Ensenada temporized over the issue of renewal of convoys or their complete abandonment on receiving petitions from Cadiz and Mexico City for resumption of *flotas* to Veracruz in July 1749, immediately after the peace of Aix-la-Chapelle.[71] In 1750 he invited a group of six Cadiz merchants to submit recommendations about "how to fix the trade of the Carrera de Indias." In a letter of invitation, he implied his reservations about resuscitating the former convoy system managed by Cadiz. "Our hope is that no monopoly bind nor constrain freedom to participate in this Trade, for we want every vassal to be able to participate on a plane of equality."[72] Still a few conferees insisted on resuming convoys to Veracruz, Cartagena, and Portobelo, assigning cargo tonnage to Veracruz at between 5,000 and 6,000 tons, or virtually double the level specified in 1720—a fairly reliable indicator of real growth in New Spain's import capacity. Apparent agreement of the conferees was achieved when it became clear that some Cadiz businessmen were willing to jettison the convoys to Cartagena and Portobelo in favor of an unlimited number of *registros* rounding Cape Horn to reach the Pacific coast ports of Chile and Peru.[73]

Significantly, the decision to renew the abandoned convoy system, but only to Veracruz, came four years later following the mini-coup that forced Ensenada's dismissal, the abandonment of many of his policies, and his internal exile until the accession of Charles III and the intervention of his leading minister marqués de Esquilache.[74] Ensenada's replacement, Ricardo Wall, and the junta he assembled agreed that the *flotas* to Veracruz depart on a biennial rather than annual schedule as some had proposed—precisely what the Cadiz consultants had proposed.[75] Now through the lobbying of two very trustworthy agents dispatched to Madrid, Francisco Xavier Gamboa and Francisco de la Cotera, the Mexico City consulado, alleging an over-supply of textile imports in the colony, managed to have the first *flota* to Veracruz since the late 1730s delayed until 1757.[76] This was completely to the satisfaction of the French merchant community at Cadiz, one of whose prominent members from the port of Saint-Malo, Magon de la Blinaye, chortled that "It is a pleasure to learn that Spain's new minister [Wall] has finally yielded to the wishes of commerce, by reestablishing trade with Veracruz on its old basis."[77] French commercial interests at Cadiz were as confirmed traditionalists as their Spanish colleagues. Ensenada's delaying tactics and the decision of Wall to resume *flotas* to Veracruz in 1755—a decision favored by Francisco Fernandez Molinillo and Colonial Secretary Julián de Arriaga, both veterans of colonial service and close to the Cadiz commercial community—suggest the cross-currents among merchants and bureaucrats on the critical issue of the imperial trade system.[78]

The decades following the peace of 1748 were comparable to those after Utrecht when the Bourbon state confronted the troublesome transatlantic trade issue. In the second decade of the eighteenth century the full power of commercial capitalism in England and its naval outreach could not yet be fully envisioned, and it was still reasonable that Spaniards hoped to revive pre-1700 trade patterns. By 1750, however, Spanish state officials realized how effective the aggressive tactics of Jamaican smugglers along the Caribbean coast from Veracruz to Portobelo had been and recognized the ability of the English navy to mount simultaneous assaults on Portobelo and Cartagena, synapses of Spain's South American trade.[79] In the early 1740s Admiral Vernon's campaign against Cartagena (although it was unsuccessful), his brief occupation of Portobelo, and the destruction of its harbor defenses joined to English smuggling there removed the possibility of resurrecting the *galeones* convoys, despite the insistence of most Cadiz traders. Further, *registros*, authorized to sail to Buenos Aires since 1720 and sustained during the war, had reopened the South Atlantic route via the Rio de la Plata to gain access to the consumers and silver of the vast viceroyalty of Peru. The Rio de la Plata became an open back door to the mining centers of Upper Peru, beginning the drive of the Buenos Aires merchant community for economic hegemony in the Plata area.

New Spain fell into a different category. Veracruz was the only major port on the colony's Caribbean coast, and it had impressive defensive works. Unlike Portobelo, it was not a *feria* site; rather, the fair was inland at Jalapa protected from surprise attack by English forces. By the mid-eighteenth century, the colony's population was recovering from the awesome post-conquest demographic collapse and emerging as the largest single market for

European (and Asian) imports in the Spanish empire in America. Here commercialization of the colonial economy had progressed in tandem with the production of its silver mines, which at the end of the eighteenth century would attain levels never before achieved in colonial America (around mid-century its silver exports already surpassed by far those of the Central Andes). After 1748 the performance of New Spain's economy more than confirmed that colony's role in the Spanish imperial system. Between 1748 and 1753, Abbé Raynal's data revealed, New Spain furnished 51 percent of all colonial silver and primary products imported by the Spanish metropole and 50 percent of its silver receipts.[80] Over a slightly longer period, 1746–56, New Spain provided 63 percent of the metropole's precious metals imports, some retained for state expenditures, but most reexported to western Europe.[81]

No doubt Madrid policy-makers banked on New Spain's growing economic importance in the Spanish empire, hoping that the convoy system to Veracruz along with the Jalapa fair would remain feasible despite leakage by smuggling. The fact that commercial groups in both Mexico City and Cadiz had petitioned for restoration of convoys and that the Mexico City consulado had dispatched two deputies to Madrid to press its position (although seeking to delay the arrival of the first convoy) suggests as well that they hoped that former friction between the two "comercios," highly visible during the *flotas* of the 1730s, might subside. The attraction of the old bilateral monopoly between Cadiz and Mexico City was still persuasive; worse, it bred complacency. Probably the principal obstacle to convoy resumption evaporated with the coup of 1754 against Ensenada who believed *registros* and not convoys could best handle trade in the Spanish-managed transatlantic system. Although he had terminated the South Sea Company's *navío de permiso*, he had pressed Madrid's well-capitalized Cinco Gremios Mayores to participate in colonial trade monopolized by the port of Cadiz, where such participation was not welcome.[82] Meanwhile, the decade after 1739 drove home to a few young civil servants the need to reconstitute the shattered royal navy, overhaul the metropole's fiscal system, stimulate economic growth in the peninsula's peripheral provinces by authorizing many peninsular ports for direct contact with colonial ports, and—most essential—modify the structures of colonial trade.

On Ensenada's forced departure, however, interlocked traditional interests once again managed to block effective change. Delayed until 1757, the first postwar *flota* to Veracruz sailed from Cadiz under the marqués de Villena, opening what would be the last phase of a two-hundred-year-old pattern.

7. Critical Voices,

1720–1759

"[our] agriculture enfeebled . . . the most respected and honorable positions exercised thoughtlessly . . . commerce unknown . . . the learned rejected, manufactories unsupported, industry forgotten, religious orders influential . . . the navy without ships, common trades [are] monopolies and profiteering respected . . . privileges many . . . reality loathed. . . ."
Campillo, Lo que hay de más y de menos en España

"Gold and silver mines, far from making the nation opulent, render them miserable. Commerce is the mainspring of the monarchy . . . we will be the masters of our wonderful mines, and the slaves of European powers who have none."
Macanaz, "Auxilios para bien governar una monarquía católica . . . ,"

"As our competitors advance each year, we fall further behind."
Gándara, Apuntes sobre el bien y el mal de España

Uztáriz's *Theórica* ideated only how a Colbertian growth policy might impinge on the Spanish national economy. There were solid reasons for his reticence about Spain's colonial world: to engage in open contestation with the extended complex of interlocked colonial interests could have serious consequences for one's career chances. Moreover, to grasp all the changing conditions in the post-Utrecht Atlantic world and formulate a suitable colonial policy required far more data than at his fingertips.

The prominence of the *asiento* indicated that economic policy for the colonies had to shift, if only to match the Caribbean enterprises of Spain's colonial competitors. Colonies once peripheral—Venezuela and Cuba in the Caribbean and the Rio de la Plata in South America—promised to produce exportables of sugar, tobacco and hides for which European demand was expanding. An elastic slave labor supply could insure in many areas that desirable increase in non-metallic exportables, one of the major objectives of the French-inspired paradigm. Further, the adjunct to the *asiento,* the permission ship, in the hands of English traders revealed their capacity to exploit a growing demand for European finished goods in Spain's American colonies. For the first time ever, one group of English traders operated legally inside areas of the Spanish colonial trade system, bypassing Lower Andalusia's commercial complex.

Driving the sustained pressure of English, French, and Dutch merchants to expand their participation in the Spanish trading system was the insatiable demand of Atlantic and international trade for American silver. In a very real sense, silver demand in Europe and Asia was turning more globalized than in any previous period. Europe's internal exchanges were multiplying, matched by trade expansion to South India and on to the South China coast. Both were based upon the reliable, mutually acceptable monetary foundation that only Spanish American silver *pesos fuertes* provided. As Spaniards knew at the time, "No country is more examined than ours . . . think of the many who count up the millions we receive from the Indies; that they are many, none can deny."[1] For its part, East Asia's demographic growth and trade translated into silver imports partially met by trans-Pacific peso movements from Acapulco to Manila and on to Canton in exchange for Chinese silks, linens, cottons and porcelains freighted by the Manila *nao.* Japan's suspension of silver exports to China in 1668 had only exacerbated shortages on the East Asian continent.[2] To put this in perspective: precisely when convoys to Caribbean ports were reinstituted by the Real Proyecto of 1720 to restore systemic stability, a number of developments—the *asiento* in English hands, European imports into the colonies from Cadiz and from European colonies in the Caribbean, trans-Pacific Asian imports—were draining the silver production that was surging at New Spain's main mining centers at Zacatecas and Guanajuato. For those involved in silver transfers, only more goods in both the trans-Atlantic and trans-Pacific pipelines insured a satisfactory supply.

To support commercial interests at Cadiz hoping to stabilize both the Atlantic convoy system and Madrid's income from the colonies, the state moved to supervise more closely tax farms and the management of the Mexico City mint. Bureaucrats like José del Campillo y Cosío, returning from the colonies to Madrid in the 1720s, reported widespread mismanagement in Mexico City's colonial administration. Knowledgeable returnees indicated collusion between Mexico City's customs officers and the capital's wholesale merchants *(almaceneros);* in addition they noted concealed profits accruing to the Consulado de Mexico from its *alcabala* tax farm. More vexing were complaints about the silver content of the coinage of Mexico City's mint farmed by a small group of wealthy, well-connected *almaceneros*, including some who bankrolled mine owners. While Madrid ultimately absorbed the mint as a state operation, it was unable (or unwilling) to absorb the sales tax farm at that moment. Nor did Madrid manage to reduce the volume of unregistered (and undutied) East Asian imports at Acapulco, nor the funds well above the legal maximum of 500,000 pesos smuggled aboard the *nao* on its return trip to Manila.

Overall, Madrid's policies seemed geared to maintain the colonial status quo, avoid confrontation with the Cadiz merchant community, and dampen regional networks and factional infighting among *almaceneros* in the Mexico City consulado. Virtually all were Spanish immigrants aligned by kinship and birthplace into moieties, one of Basques *(vizcaínos),* the other of those from the montañas de Burgos *(montañeses).* Perception of the reality of bitterly contested biennial elections to high offices *(prior* and two *consules)* in the Mexico City merchant guild led Viceroy Fuenclara, Pedro Cebrián y Agustín (his wife was a niece of minister Patiño), to mediate between the factions. To his intervention Fuenclara brought the prestige of his former ambassadorship at Vienna and his role in arranging the marriage of Philip's son Charles (later king of Spain) to a Savoyard, María Amelia. Fuenclara managed to impose what became known as the *alternativa* that provided alternation in elective office between *montañeses* and *vizcaínos.* Madrid also directed him to open an inquiry into a sensitive area, the Consulado de Mexico's handling of the *alcabala* contract.[3]

Intervention by the Spanish state brought only minor adjustments in the Spanish colonial system. Perhaps the sole feature of the Colbertian developmental paradigm early incorporated by Madrid was the chartering in the 1720s and 1730s of monopoly trading companies in the peninsula's peripheral provinces, which were assigned designated peripheral areas for their operations in America. The companies had the additional charge of encouraging production of colonial exportables, such as Venezuelan cocoa by the Compañía Guipúzcoana. They were, however, deliberately excluded from access to the mining colonies serviced by convoys, the ports of Cartagena, Portobelo, and Veracruz—another concession (a sales preserve) to the Cadiz merchant community which consistently opposed competition from monopoly companies, which they considered an infringement of their "freedom." Here is an example of how the French model that assigned to monopoly companies responsibility for colonial economic development (at least in the initial stages) was fitted to Spanish structures. Spain's mining colonies in America were too fundamental, too well developed economically and administratively to be entrusted to a circumscribed number of stockholders for exploitation.

On balance at the close of the 1730s, only minimal implementation of Uztáriz's grand design of a Colbertian developmental model had materialized in the metropole. In finance the Spanish state had made some progress in reducing interest and principal owed on its bonds (juros), a major legacy of the Hapsburg era;[4] yet, Uztáriz's data on rentas provinciales showed an unexpected surge of 46 percent in outstanding juro indebtedness over the decade 1714–24.[5] In state administration shifts at the senior levels proved more cosmetic than real. French-type secretariats or ministries under titular heads still only foreshadowed the cabinets typical of the later age of Charles III. The traditional polysynodal consejo structures—Estado, Hacienda, Marina e Indias, and above all, the Consejo de Castilla—still remained functioning elements of state administration. A sense of decades of foregone opportunities for change was sharpened by the unexpected (and hardly predictable) inroads of the English permission ship under the asiento. The presence of this ship at the Caribbean ports of Cartagena and Portobelo (1720–38) invariably disheartened the Cadiz merchants and factors who, arriving on galeones, found their merchandise uncompetitively priced in comparison with goods offered by the English navío de permiso.

Field reporting from a young naval officer, Antonio de Ulloa (he and Jorge Juan accompanied La Condamine's French scientific expedition to Ecuador, a "cover" for gathering data on conditions in Spain's Pacific coast colonies) confirmed the worst suspicions about Madrid's management of colonial affairs. In fact Patiño, not the Consejo de Indias, handpicked Ulloa (then 19) and Juan (22) to join La Condamine's expedition. Along with Juan, Ulloa was an early graduate of the naval academy (Academia de Guardias Marinas) that minister Patiño had organized.[6] Their instructions, drafted by the president of Cadiz's Casa de Contratación and signed by Patiño, directed them to gather materials on navigational and defense details of South America as well as on flora, soils, manufactures, and native peoples.[7] Of the spectrum of colonial maladministration that benefited private rather than state interests, Ulloa emphasized in his reports overt collusion between colonial officers, asiento operators, and other smugglers in ports and coastal waters; the corrupt practices of corregidores (district officers) who managed Indian affairs; and the exploitation by merchants and colonial bureaucrats of native peoples on the presumption that indios would not respond to the inducements of wage labor and the marketplace alone. Two years earlier, an agent of Peru's native peoples had published at

Madrid a moving, painfully graphic depiction of exploitation by colonial officials and their collaborators.[8] Campillo must also have seen an anonymous critical manuscript with a graphic title, "Political State of the Kingdom of Peru, a government without law, of treasure and poverty, a fertile land uncultivated, wisdom unappreciated, armed forces without honor, courts but no justice, theft not commerce, integrity considered madness."[9] It was probably Ulloa who sent informally to navy minister José del Campillo y Cosío in the late 1730s disquieting details on inhuman labor conditions throughout the Potosí mining zone of Upper Peru.[10] A toned-down version of the joint field investigation by Ulloa and Juan, the multi-volume *Relación histórica del viage a la América meridional* (1748), was published with government approval.[11] But Ulloa's subsequent devastating critique of the South American colonies of Spain, "Discurso y reflexiones políticas sobre el estado presente de los reinos del Perú," written at the request of the marqués de la Ensenada (protégé of former minister Patiño, and himself a patron of Ulloa) circulated for decades only in manuscript within a few Madrid ministries.[12]

On the outbreak in 1739 of another war with England over the American empire in the Atlantic with its inevitable pressure upon state finance, realization of the few superficial efforts to escape the cycle of stagnation in metropole and colonies combined with continued lack of an effective naval force in the Atlantic magnified the Spanish political elite's underlying sense of despair of Spain's ability to catch up with France and England. Few Spanish civil servants–political economists expressed the national mood more despondently than minister José del Campillo in a manuscript of 1742 where he listed "commerce unknown . . . manufactories unsupported, industry forgotten."[13]

Campillo: Sources, Issues, and Manuscripts

When in 1741 forty-six-year-old José del Campillo y Cosío drafted the first of two manuscripts on Spain's persistent stagnation and relative backwardness, he occupied high bureaucratic office, overseeing—like his mentor, Patiño—three ministries (Guerra, Hacienda, and Marina e Indias). His career, like that of Patiño, presents a classic model of how the Spanish Bourbon monarchy advanced and incorporated those of ability, merit, loyalty, and dedication into state service regardless of their humble social origins.

Precocious son of a country schoolteacher who gave him a primary school education, Campillo was thirteen when his father died. He left home to serve a cleric (Antonio Maldonado) at Córdoba. Maldonado recognized his intellectual acuity and supported his study of theology and philosophy for five years. In 1713, however, Campillo abandoned a religious vocation. At some point after that (it is unclear when and under what circumstances) he worked briefly in the Cadiz merchant house of Leghorn-born Sebastián Lasqueti, whose operations were ultimately to span Leghorn, Santander, Havana, Veracruz, and Mexico City.[14] In 1715 Campillo became the personal secretary of Francisco de Ocio, *intendente general de Aduana* at Córdoba. Patiño, no stranger to Cadiz, also recognized Campillo's abilities, perhaps encouraged by a recommendation from Lasqueti. Once Patiño became *intendente general de Marina* in 1717, he brought Campillo (and later, Cenon de Somodevilla) into the naval ministry, forging a line of reform-minded naval administrators stretching over more than a quarter-century (1720–54).[15] A close connection developed quickly between Patiño and Campillo, who carried out "varias comisiones" earning him four unsolicited promotions. Between 1719 and 1724 one commission entailed a "long maritime voyage" to Cuba and New Spain, an experience that must have shaped his views of colonial affairs.

Aside from isolated and elliptical references in a brief autobiography Campillo drafted when intendant of Aragon to defend himself against politically motivated charges by the Inquisition, little is known about his years in America. As *comisario de marina* he was instructed to evaluate construction of a state-owned shipyard at Havana.[16] There, with the assistance of another promising bureaucrat, Antonio José Alvarez de Abreu, sent from Caracas to serve as his *asesor* (legal adviser), the young *comisario* recommended construction of the shipyard with funds, material, and prison labor from Spain's key colony, New Spain. The project, one of several ideated by the new Bourbon regime, was in operation by 1725 "thanks," we are told, "to José de Campillo y Cosío's reports."[17]

Since the success of the Cuban project depended upon subsidies from Mexico City's colonial treasury, Campillo's assignment took him to New Spain, where shipyard expansion was also contemplated. He may also have been instructed to evaluate the condition of the maritime *presidios* guarding access to Veracruz. One may glean from fragmentary sources that on assignment in New Spain Campillo acquired valuable insight into the situation in the viceroyalty from his own personal observation and from those he later termed "knowledgeable and trustworthy informants." One dignitary with whom he forged an exceptionally close tie, Francisco Garzarón, acted toward him, in his own words, "more as a father than a superior."[18] Garzarón was resident inquisitor of New Spain. In 1716, he had been appointed *visitador-general* of the colony charged with investigating "tribunals and *presidios.*"[19] One of Campillo's unexpected informants was Diego Joseph González de la Herrán y Mier (adopted son of Pedro de la Herrán y Mier and probably a *paisano* and kinsman). Employed in Mexico City's customs house like his adoptive parent, Gonzalez was a whistle-blower, who in 1726, alerted Patiño and Campillo to the profitable on-going scam of the *alcabala* farm by the Consulado de Mexico.[20] This issue surfaced years later when Campillo, wary of the well-funded and influential consulado, instructed Viceroy Fuenclara in 1741 to ascertain *sub rosa* the real volume of *alcabala* receipts collected by the consulado.[21]

A number of local problems made Garzarón's commission urgent, and he went to work immediately.[22] The first issue he addressed was the unstable condition of the northern frontier missions and maritime *presidios.* The California missions had long lacked adequate funding; and in 1719, the garrison of the Texas *presidio* and its mission had withdrawn south to Coahuila.[23] More worrisome were foreign movements along the Mexican and Florida gulf coasts. Lacking support from Mexico City, Saint Augustine had briefly been occupied by English colonists from South Carolina. Meanwhile Pensacola, also short on munitions and food, had fallen to the French who, from a new settlement at the mouth of the Mississippi, were also establishing commercial contact with the *presidio* on the Rio Grande in Nueva Vizcaya (modern Coahuila).[24]

Although Valero dispatched a new governor (marqués de San Miguel de Aguayo) to reestablish and resupply the settlements, disturbances among the native peoples in the northern reaches of New Spain raised new problems as Spanish operations expanded. The perennial issues of native policy reemerged: gradual assimilation into the Spanish colonial economy and culture versus forced pacification. The question and its solution were dramatized during Valero's administration by the public burning of a skeleton found in a Nayarit cave. The skeleton was reputed to be that of an ancestor of a Nayarit *cacique,* Tonatiuh, who had recently gone to Mexico City to petition that his community be permitted to supply salt to Zacatecas' silver mines. Apparently he hoped to barter Christian conversion and recognition of Spanish sovereignty for the salt trade.[25] Valero, anxious to incorporate Nayarit territory where repeated military expeditions had failed, agreed to Tonatiuh's petition on condition that *presidios* and a Jesuit mission be established. The Nayarits, however, rejected Tonatiuh's deal and denied the Spaniards entry into their territory.[26] The symbolic *auto-da-fé* organized by the *provisor de indios* with considerable publicity on grounds of Nayarit rebellious activities and the refuge they granted to "outlaws," carried a subtext to Amerindians, settlers, and would-be settlers alike. It may be interpreted as an act by the colonial state, stripping native people of the chance to enter colonial society as uncoerced producers and consumers, as equals in the marketplace. Valero was awarded *grandeza de primera clase* soon afterward.[27]

Behind the problems of frontier defense, *presidios,* and Indian unrest, lay the fundamental need for "curbing abuses that had appeared in that large colony, which was not easy."[28] In his *instrucción* to orient his successor (marqués de Valero), Viceroy Linares had noted the rampant administrative corruption that had permitted *presidio* commanders to accumulate large personal fortunes at the expense of colonial treasuries by withdrawing funds ostensibly to cover soldiers' pay and garrison supplies. Administrative collusion also allowed district officers *(alcaldes mayores)* to enrich themselves in partnership with merchants through the forced sale of services as well as overpriced and often unnecessary merchandise to their Indian communities, practices repeated on an even wider scale in the viceroyalty of Peru.[29]

By 1722, when he sailed from Veracruz, which the Consulado de Mexico noted,[30] Campillo was surely aware of the handling of the Nayarit Indians, of the mistreatment of the native peoples by district officers, and of the extent of maladministration in the tribunals of New Spain, especially in its Audiencia and Hacienda offices.[31] In addition, from Garzarón and Herrán y Mier, Campillo had learned of Indian issues and the tactics of mulcting the colonial treasury on which Madrid had come to depend. Moreover, he could hardly ignore rumors of fraud in the management of the large *alcabala* tax farm of the Mexico City district by officers of the Consulado de Mexico and complaints from European as well as Chinese and East Indian silver merchants about the unreliability in weight and fineness of pesos coined in the Mexico City mint.[32]

Campillo must have examined the caustic listing of the spectrum of New Spain's shortcomings *(dolencias)* detailed by outgoing Viceroy Linares in 1718 in his *instrucción.* Campillo had further opportunities to discuss conditions in New Spain after his return, since Campillo's Madrid residence virtually adjoined the town house built by Valero on returning from Mexico City.[33] Two major themes covered by Linares concerned native policy in the colony—the treatment of *naturales* and the colonial treasury. While Linares, a European cosmopolite and obvious colonialist, had a low opinion of the people he found in New Spain ("I discern no outstanding qualities . . . from the lowliest Indian to the highest gentleman . . . in the Indies the rule is fabrication or hypocrisy"), he was troubled by the exploitation of Indians in urban workshops *(obrajes)* through the mechanism of debt slavery.[34] As he put it graphically, "If an Indian dies or flees, they seize wife or children as slaves; these, barely catechized and worse fed, suffer in the land of Christians what Barbarians do not inflict." In the countryside this situation was no better, since district officers "tyrannized" the Indians by forcing them to purchase goods and services *(repartimiento)* at monopoly prices.[35]

The other theme reviewed the multiple demands on the Mexico City *caja real,* the colonial treasury. In the War of Succession, its funds had supported the struggling Bourbon government in Spain at critical junctures. Now Linares had to fulfill Madrid's directives to continue subsidizing the vast Spanish colonial establishment in and around the Caribbean, as well as the Pacific outposts. The Mexico City treasury was running an annual deficit of 800,000 pesos to cover such obligatory disbursements on "subsidies and garrisons, missions . . . the Barlovento fleet." Military garrisons had to be paid, supplied, and reinforced on the colony's northern frontiers, in the Gulf of Mexico and the western Pacific—Veracruz, Havana ("the most important strongpoint in the Indies"), Saint Augustine, Puerto Rico, Santo Domingo and Cumaná, Manila, and the Marianas. In New Spain itself *presidio* soldiers were paid by their commanders in kind: in food and clothing (often including women's skirts and silk stockings) reckoned at "scandalously high prices."[36] This system gave leeway to commanding officers to arrange a supplier *(aviador)* to collect their soldiers' pay from colonial treasuries at Mexico City or Zacatecas. In addition, Madrid insisted Linares forward annually one million pesos and honor other drafts *(libranzas)* payable to European creditors drawn on the Mexico City treasury, a bureau Linares compared to "a bankrupt trader."[37]

What Linares' *instrucción* elided were reports from the ongoing investigation of colonial Hacienda personnel, which uncovered that Zacatecas's provincial treasury officials followed the practice (they termed it exercising their *regalía)* of skimming anywhere from 33 to 50 percent of all *libranzas* presented for payment while officials in the main office at Mexico City raised their self-assigned *regalía* rate to between 50 and 60 percent.[38] Linares knew the treasury's account books were misleading, and he promised later to inform Madrid authorities "in person . . . of what I have learned ex-officio."[39] When Campillo sailed home, he must have left convinced that New Spain's administrative personnel, from the Audiencia's *oidores* and Hacienda bureaucrats down to district officers and provincial treasury officials, needed thorough investigation and overhaul—a *visita general*—and that only a drastic reorientation of colonial native policy might draw large numbers of exploited *indios* into a market economy. Surely in New Spain he had grasped the potential of native people to become yeomen farmers, producers of a promising variety of export staples and, more important, consumers of

European imports. Antonio de Ulloa's reports on Peruvian conditions in the late 1730s must have confirmed Campillo's experiences in New Spain.[40]

Back in the metropole after five years in the colonies, Campillo remained in the naval ministry under Patiño, and made the acquaintance of a brother of the translator of Huet's *Mémoires,* Juan Ignacio de Goyeneche, participating in his Madrid *tertulia* (salon). Then followed two years of service in Italy under the duque de Montemar (1734–36) after which Campillo was recalled to Spain as intendant of Aragon. He brought along as his private secretary Jorge Astraudi, a nephew of his former Cadiz employer, Lasqueti. From 1741 until his unexpected death in early 1743, Campillo held down multiple ministerial portfolios, Hacienda, Guerra, Marina, Indias.[41] Apparently he was responsible for the selection of the conde de Fuenclara (Pedro Cebrián y Augustín) as New Spain's viceroy in the 1740s and, in particular, Fuenclara's administrative secretary Francisco Fernández Molinillo.

Campillo was observant, dynamic, and nationalistic, but, as one of his secretaries, Miguel de Múzquiz, later reported to financier Francisco Cabarrús, some also found him uncommonly critical, aggressive, and impatient.[42] A bitter anonymous critic censored his "outspoken way of talking, his strong bent for prohibited books, since he neither sees nor reads others"—habits which inspired opponents to call upon the Inquisition to bring charges against him. Since he had achieved high status despite mediocre social origins, detractors claimed he was motivated by greed, since in the very short span of his ministry he had managed to acquire a "respectable fortune." "No river," they said, "rises with clear water."[43] At the peak of his career in 1741, Campillo's life had spanned the first four decades of Bourbon Spain and the inconsequential record of failed initiatives in pursuing a model of economic growth.

Campillo's manuscript, "Lo que hay de más y de menos en España," opens with a convoluted expression of hope that a frank discussion of Spain's shortcomings might stir Spaniards from a mood of lassitude ("ninguna aplicación") and irresponsibility ("no importa"). The essay would be complemented, Campillo promised, with "España despierta" ("Spain Awakened") and there are references to a third contemplated manuscript, a "Nuevo sistema de gobierno económico." How a Madrid minister nominally holding down many key secretariats found time to work on these materials over two years remains a mystery. Multiple responsibilities of office probably explain why the essays lack the organizational logic and critical insight of the prominent *proyectista* work then available (in the limited edition of 1724), Uztáriz's *Theórica.*

Organized in alphabetical order—Campillo's manuscript begins with "agriculture" and closes with "virtue-vice"—"Lo que hay" presents no discernible economic model, much less developmental policy. Rearrangement of its entries, however, reveals the bare bones of an essentially negative paradigm emphasizing what Spain still lacked. Campillo viewed agriculture as fundamental, but found Spanish farmers rack-rented, often ruined by inflated costs of inputs—plow mules, for example. Equally basic for a sound economy, in Campillo's view, was trade; yet he found (as did Uztáriz) that Spain continued to export valuable staples like raw wools and silks only to have them return in the form of imported high value-added manufactures. From Campillo's perspective, Spanish middlemen were a disreputable (*vil*) lot. He lamented that they lacked an ethical sense and suborned the civil service by financing those who purchased colonial district posts *(alcaldías mayores),* expecting to earn 300 to 400 percent of the price of their office— details probably derived from Antonio de Ulloa's field reports and letters.[44] (He cited especially the case of the post at Charcas in Peru.) Distrust of businessmen's ethics lay behind Campillo's order jailing corrupt civil servants in the Cartagena customs and his directives designed to "intimidate men of business with the result that they always try to hide their goods, funds and papers to protect themselves from his furious indignation."[45]

Two entries in the work, at the heart of any developmental strategy, were given the most extended treatment: colonies *(Indias)* and manufactories *(fábricas).* Despite auspicious beginnings including state subsidies and considerable management oversight, the woolen mills of Guadalajara, Segovia, and Chinchón (Spanish examples of the Colbertian developmental model) Campillo correctly diagnosed as virtual failures. In no small measure, he judged, this was because Spain's high-grade wools were bought up by English merchants, leaving to domestic manufacturers inferior grades suitable only for low-quality products. Spain's organized sheepmen alone profited from this structure of international dependence. Similarly Campillo faulted Valencia's raw silk exports which French manufacturers returned as finished cloth lacking, he asserted, the durability of comparable Spanish goods. Overall, Campillo highlighted two factors accounting for the disappointing performance of Spain's policy for infant industry: inveterate reluctance to hire foreign textile and other technicians, and disturbing discontinuity in the policy goals of successive ministries.

Campillo's analysis of Madrid's colonial policy was comparably caustic. Here surfaced critical flashes of insight on the underlying significance of colonial mining as a decisive factor in Spain's economic stagnation. Since other European economies produced the manufactured products imported by Spain's colonies, the empire represented profit to them but not to Spain, which explained why "so many nations calculate how much they are getting from Spain's Indies."[46] Without the attraction of colonial silver mines, Campillo hypothesized, the Spanish metropole might retain those 14,000 Spaniards (an exaggeration), who he calculated emigrated annually to the American colonies and, instead, develop national manufactures.[47] Meanwhile—here one detects Campillo's personal colonial field experience—native Americans were oppressed, and colonials resented the "yoke of Spain."

Six months after drafting "Lo que hay" Campillo finished its promised complement, "España despierta," where he laid out recommendations for removing the obstacles cited in his first essay.[48] Now, however, there was a pervasive undercurrent of exasperation at the minimal impact of developmental concepts, a condition that he traced to bureaucratic inertia that any dynamic minister had to contend with. The country's situation continued to deteriorate, he concluded; whatever the merits of an earlier growth model, conditions for progress were now bleak. He ticked off the dispiriting situation of major sectors of the economy concluding with "[our] Indies, stepmothers of the Crown when they could be the basis of its grandeur." Spain had abandoned hope; it was locked into a profound reverie *(sueño)* from which state intervention joined to suitably motivated leadership alone might awaken it. Hence the title, "España despierta."[49]

Further distinguishing "España despierta" from its predecessor was Campillo's stress upon careful selection of civil servants at the highest levels, the secretaries of state in Spain's Bourbon-inspired civil service. Probably sensitivity to endemic bureaucratic obstructionism by multiple *consejos* lay behind his lament about their "malice tied to ignorance." Meanwhile his efforts to improve recruitment for the civil service inspired the charge that he packed the bureaucracy with "Montañeses, relatives, and friends." Like later critics in eighteenth-century Spain, Aranda for example, Campillo found the most effective instruments of change in competent, dedicated civil servants, "the poles of the monarchy, [while] the bad ones are the ruination of the State."[50] Secretariat by secretariat he listed qualities most desirable in high officeholders, citing those indispensable in ministries critical to economic policy. Hacienda demanded competent grasp of all the "parts, funds, and needs" of commerce, since it was the "index" of the national economy. Above all, the Hacienda secretary needed practical experience in all treasury departments. As for the colonial office, it required a "great statesman" who understood the colonial world, the forms of *opresión* exercised over indigenous peoples, as well as the "vices and unjust authority" of colonial elites and the way colonial differed from metropolitan legislation.[51]

"España despierta's" second part became Campillo's vehicle for suggesting ways to improve the performance of the alphabetical entries in "Lo que hay." Certain themes were emphasized, for example, manufacturing over commerce. In particular, Campillo proposed as the foundation of a viable textile industry at least five *fábricas* for producing medium-quality woolens of mass consumption. In his model the viability of these and other workshops of cottons, silks, laces, yarns, and hardwares depended on broad-based, sustained *dirigisme*, as the Colbertian paradigm demanded. The state would bear responsibility for building and—at least initially—operating workshops and attracting qualified immigrant technicians from England, France, Holland, Flanders, Germany, and Italy to manage mills and train Spanish workmen. It would underwrite start-up costs until workshops proved transferable (under terms favorable to the state) to the private sector, either to well-capitalized guilds like Madrid's Cinco Gremios or private companies. In Campillo's model, state-sponsored manufactories would concentrate first on the domestic market. Then, he hoped, in the next stage of their development, they would augment production to meet the demand of colonial consumers, whose incomes would be improved, he was sure, by "my new system of economic governance for America (*mi nuevo sistema de gobierno económico para America*)."[52]

Campillo's third projected manuscript, a development of his "new system of economic governance" may have been among the personal papers removed by his private secretary, Astraudi, who turned them over to Campillo's successor, Ensenada.[53] No doubt concepts of the new system circulated among Ensenada and his associates including Astraudi's replacement, Agustín Pablo Ordeñana, and *proyectista* Bernardo Ward. Note that the second half of Ward's *Proyecto económico* (1779) subsequently appeared as *Nuevo sistema económico para América* (1789) with questionable attribution to Campillo. In any case, Campillo's germ of a "new system" in which the colonial market might function as incentive and challenge to metropolitan economic development was a major contribution to colonial reform in the second half of the eighteenth century.

Campillo's Ambiguity

From the standpoint of economic model-builders and policy entrepreneurs, Campillo's two manuscripts offered little novelty. They lack the structured mercantilist policy of Uztáriz's *Theórica*, although elements of a growth paradigm surface intermittently.[54] Instead, one finds pessimism over how little progress Spain was making in catching up with English and

French competition, a tendency to admire England over France, and above all a careful skirting of the issues of Cadiz's one-port monopoly, Spain's basic convoy system, and its managed transatlantic trade. A career civil servant who had served at Naples, Campillo must have reentered Spain eager to initiate long-overdue changes by drawing on the Neapolitan reform experience under Charles, king of the two Sicilies and later Charles III of Spain. Nevertheless, as he must have recognized, Spain was not the Two Sicilies; Madrid was hardly Naples. There was no Cadiz consulado in young Charles's Italian kingdom. In fact there is little in Campillo's two manuscript essays, aside from reference to a third forthcoming study, to suggest the rigor and vehemence of what may have been his promised "Nuevo sistema de gobierno económico para América."[55]

Campillo's caution on colonial matters is ambiguous on several counts. His executive role at Madrid involved decisions affecting the colonies. He approved an inquiry into the Consulado de Cadiz's disbursements to government bondholders of funds (balbas e infantes) collected on imports from the colonies and withdrawals (gastos secretos) from those funds to subsidize its lobbyists at court. Second, since the onset of war with England in 1739 followed by England's patrolling of Atlantic maritime routes imperiled Spanish maritime movements, Campillo chose to authorize individual ship sailings (registros sueltos) from Cadiz and other peninsular ports to America. This decision was vehemently protested by the Cadiz consulado, which pressured the Casa de Contratación to question Campillo's authority by declaring it would execute such authorizations only under direct royal order. By way of compromise, the consulado then agreed to lend Madrid one million pesos provided no registros sueltos were authorized until the loan's redemption. Once the funds materialized, however, Campillo insisted (September 1741) that his ministry continue to license register shipping despite petitions by the consulados of Cadiz and Lima joined predictably by Contratación.[56] And so for the second time in the eighteenth century, Spanish convoys were replaced by individually licensed Spanish and neutral shipping. Hence the complaint that Campillo had "not kept faith with the public, because of his many permissions in the American trade, [which allowed] our worst enemies, the English, profiting from the disarray and permissions in which they are involved through third parties, to engage openly in the trade of Your Majesty's Indies, [even entering the Pacific Ocean] despite what has been stipulated and agreed upon with the merchants of Cadiz."[57]

Third, attentive to the importance of New Spain's silver exports and trade, Campillo assigned the conde de Fuenclara the post of viceroy in expectation that he would improve the situation in what was now clearly

Spain's major mining colony in America. Fuenclara was accompanied by a highly empowered *secretario de cámara,* Francisco Fernández Molinillo, *oficial mayor* in the Consejo de Indias and—to give his rank weight—promoted to *consejero de Indias* just before departing with Fuenclara for New Spain's capital. Evidently he would be the ministry's watchdog.[58] Campillo ordered Fuenclara to treat his secretary with "full confidence and esteem" and to consult him on all matters internal to the colony. For his part Molinillo was authorized to sign Fuenclara's official correspondence, countersign all letters of exchange (*libranzas*) presented for payment at the Mexico City treasury, and conduct an inquiry into the accounts of the Veracruz treasury and customs.[59]

In this light Campillo's reticence about writing explicitly and fully on colonial issues becomes comprehensible. Surely he knew that the Consulado de Mexico had tried to marginalize critics like Herrán y Mier as "greedy malcontents" who questioned unreasonably the "honor" of consulado officers ("persons of esteem and considerable wealth"). Those officers managed to have the Consejo de Indias reject Herrán's charges even when substantiated by Mexico City's *tribunal de cuentas.*[60] Reports available to Campillo must have confirmed his experience in Cuba and Mexico two decades earlier and probably inspired his ambiguous references, for example, to merchants who financed an *alcalde mayor* in the viceroyalty of Peru (Charcas) and to the *opresión* of native peoples by "españoles" who misused their authority. We must recall that Campillo's successor, the marqués de la Ensenada, who requested that Ulloa and Juan draft an unvarnished situation report on conditions in Peru, also guarded that devastating document, the *Noticias secretas,* from publication as did succeeding prime ministers until it surfaced in the 1820s.

Ambiguity was a defensive tactic forced upon a critically minded, high-profile bureaucrat like Campillo at Madrid in the 1740s. The fate of that earlier outspoken critic loyal to Philip V, Melchor Macanaz, committed to analyses of Spain's sensitive colonial question and of deeply rooted structures in the metropole, remained an implicit warning of persecution awaiting immoderate, nationalistic critics. The tactic of calling upon the Inquisition to block Macanaz's bureaucratic career in 1715 was repeated against Campillo in 1726, but without success. Logroño's inquisitor warned him of charges that, to quote Campillo's interpretation, "I read prohibited works, communicate with heretics" (purportedly he had questioned "la pureza virginal de María Santísima"), and "hold different views." Campillo credited the accusations of the Inquisition partly to envy of the career advancement of a person of "lowly origins." More likely it was due to his "opiniones disonantes"—his readiness to question aspects of the status quo.[61] And there was explicit warning, too. In December 1742 Campillo received a death-threat that he had to take seriously. Although aides dismissed the anony-mous note as "the plaything of one of the many jokesters who filled Ma-drid," Campillo ordered his coachmen always to drive at a fast pace. When he died unexpectedly four months later he was, interestingly enough, eulo-gized overseas at Mexico City.[62] There his correspondents valued him.

Campillo and Bernardo Ulloa: A Comparison

Was Campillo's reluctance to criticize Lower Andalusia's powerful com-mercial interests (as Uztáriz had done for Spain's domestic situation) and the evident shortcomings of an old colonial trade policy shared by Spanish contemporaries? One way to settle this question is to turn to the published (hence officially sanctioned) analysis of Bernardo Ulloa's *Restablecimiento de las fábricas, tráfico y comercio marítimo de España* (1740), written while his son Antonio was on his commission of inquiry in South America.[63]

While Campillo had a northerner's *(montañés)* critical perspective of the condition of Spain, Bernardo Ulloa's view was colored by his upper-class Sevillan roots. His family had held, as *juro de heredad,* a permanent seat on Sevilla's town council since 1649. Bernardo had approved financial assis-tance to Philip V during the War of Succession; and in 1735 he became Sevilla's *procurador mayor* at the court of Madrid.[64] Bernardo's manuscript had the placet of the Consejo de Indias' cosmographer (a Jesuit) and was authorized by Madrid's Junta de Comercio y Moneda, proof to the politi-cal elite that it offered no startling condemnation nor unsettling innova-tions.[65]

The domestic sector of Ulloa's growth policy was pure Uztáriz, as Cam-pomanes (and surely others) later perceived.[66] Industrial development, he believed, was hobbled by perennial high cost factors—inflated food prices, inadequate transport networks, and worst, layers of excise imposts *(alca-balas, cientos, millones)*—a maze of internal tolls and badly skewed tariffs. Ulloa's sole occasion to criticize Cadiz's interests came when he surveyed Andalusia's oddly effective customs wall, crafted intentionally, he implied, to discourage the entry of domestic textiles for reexport to the colonies. For example, legislation issued (1717) to eliminate customs barriers not far from Cadiz at Jérez de la Frontera and Lebrija was systematically ignored; and at Cadiz itself, he noted that domestic textiles paid 8–19 percent duties while comparable imports arriving by sea paid 2.5 percent, often less. It was a duty structure designed "to prevent our textiles from arriving at the pier." It was typical of Spain's Bourbon state where "every hamlet was an independent sovereignty."[67] Following Uztáriz (whose *Theórica* was republished in 1742, now with all the apparatus of official approval), Bernardo Ulloa based manufacturing development on consolidated internal taxes, tax exemptions and protective tariffs framed to block raw materials exports and to raise duties on imported manufactures.

It was in the second section of his *Restablecimiento* where he offered analysis and recommendations for colonial trade growth that Ulloa went beyond Uztáriz. Sevillano to the core, Ulloa was nostalgic for Lower Andalusia's pre-1650 colonial trade patterns (a time, he fantasized, of "opulence and good faith"), whose most profitable American colony had been the viceroyalty of Peru with its Potosí silver and its commercial links to the Caribbean ports of Portobelo and Cartagena.[68] In Ulloa's prism, the silvered age of *galeones* and fairs was doomed once Spain's European competitors penetrated the Caribbean to convert its "most sterile and useless" islands into plantations as well as centers for other nations' clandestine trade and when Spain, at Utrecht, had to assign the *asiento* to English businessmen.

Bernardo Ulloa (like his son Antonio) found open collusion among colonial civil servants, merchants, and Jamaica-based smugglers whose activities also provided English traders invaluable commercial intelligence.[69] Obviously irritated, he cited disapprovingly data he had found in a Spanish translation *(Los intereses malentendidos)* of an English publication on the volume of Jamaica's annual returns in Spanish colonial silver and dyestuffs shipped to London. They were in the alarming range of 6 million pesos. Furthermore, how could Cadiz's interests, he complained, ever hope to compete when most of Spain's so-called merchant marine was in fact foreign-built and foreign-owned and when Spanish merchants at Cadiz were usually strawmen fronting for the foreign resident merchant community there?

Nothing in Ulloa's recommendations for an effective growth policy could seriously ruffle established interests, public or private. Primary among his suggestions were English-type navigation acts to form a merchant marine manned by Spanish crews. Next came termination of the Cadiz customs farm—Eminente's contract at the close of the seventeenth century (considered a give-away to foreigners in Spain's colonial trade) was no longer tolerable.

In addition, Ulloa pointed out that customs inspectors *(vistas)* needed retraining to be able to discriminate between old and new types of fabric imports, their composition, lengths, and current prices.[70] On the controversial issue of the most efficient instrument of colonial trade—whether convoys, individual *registros,* or joint-stock companies—his position was unequivocal: in typically *sevillano* fashion he rejected register ships and companies. His "primer subsidiario remedio" involved annual convoys, with *galeones* to service Peru and *flotas* to New Spain including permanent warehousing facilities at Jalapa (presumably to replace the fairs there).[71] Meanwhile, he overlooked the importance of New Spain's rising consumption of imports, as population recovered from the seventeenth-century trough and silver output rose dramatically. For him, Lima's trade remained—erroneously, as it turned out—paramount.[72] A reorganized convoy system, he optimistically predicted, would respond to colonial demand once Madrid decreed "the total prohibition of any foreign textiles in America."[73] Behind these recommendations lay a strong regional bias: vessels from Manila via the Cape of Good Hope would be permitted to bring only raw silk for Sevilla's workshops.[74]

Ulloa's *Restablecimiento,* like Campillo's two brief essays, both drafted twenty years after the limited first edition of Uztáriz's *Theórica,* skirted confrontation with the influential Cadiz merchant community and its constellation of national and foreign interests. Significantly, the bleak national perspective of prominent (if controversial) cabinet minister Campillo remained in manuscript, locked in his files.[75] His manuscripts, pessimistic in tone, were copied and circulated but not published. By contrast, Bernardo Ulloa's optimistic analysis easily passed Spanish censors. Yet both shared one key element. Neither Campillo nor Ulloa ventured to criticize, much less undermine, the two fundamental structures of Spain's colonial system: dependence upon the mining sectors of Peru and New Spain and the one-port monopoly now at Cadiz. Instead, tradition-bound authorities of the Spanish Bourbon state preferred to view the condition of the colonies through rose-colored glasses just when the convoy system virtually collapsed for seventeen years (1740–57). Public display of optimism covered but could not erase underlying unease.

Legarra, the Caribbean, and Cadiz

There was an abiding, underlying strain of malaise, of frustration with the inadequacies of economic policy and practice that was kept underground in manuscripts more critical, sometimes more radical in analysis and recommendations than Uztáriz's *Theórica,* Ulloa's *Restablecimiento,* or Campillo's two unfocused manuscripts. The manuscripts of Legarra (1719), Macanaz (the mid-forties), and Gándara (1759) were radical to the degree that they dared criticize what the published *proyectos* avoided, which is not to say they were immoderately critical. Spain's old regime, we must remember, put its intellectuals under great state censorship: the Spanish press was "fundamentally supervised by government authorities."[76] So Legarra remained unpublished, and only a fraction of Macanaz's manuscripts and the "Nuevo sistema de govierno económico para la América" (whose authorship remains questionable) were published, and this only at the end of Charles III's reign. Gándara's *Apuntes* surfaced in print in 1804—for reasons still unclear.

Juan de Legarra's "Representación . . . sobre el estado actual de los Comercios de España e Indias" of 1719, one of several position papers circulating among Madrid's high civil servants then debating the future of the transatlantic trade system, confirmed the bleak perspective sketched by the *consulta* of the Consejo de Indias in 1713.[77] Miguel Fernandez Durán (marqués de Tolosa), secretary of Marina e Indias and Guerra and one-time collaborator of French finance expert Orry, had asked Legarra to draft an analysis of the situation, not least because of Legarra's experience in the Buenos Aires section *(negociado)* of the Consejo de Indias.[78] Legarra was troubled by the collapse of the convoy system supplying the Caribbean and South America during the War of Succession and the consequent uncontainable collusion in smuggling between French, English, and Dutch merchants and Spanish colonial officials. He was shocked at the extent of that collusion (what Antonio de Ulloa would later document in extenso), recommending that "some royal officials at Buenos Ayres, Cartagena, Veracruz as well as the governors of Santa Marta, Caracas, and Trinidad, should be deposed, others suspended, for complicity in illegal trade." The situation was aggravated by the escalating scale of English operations from Jamaica, French activity from Saint-Domingue and Martinique, and in the South Atlantic, by Anglo-Portuguese commercial inroads in the Rio de la Plata.

Legarra seemed especially au courant of the Caribbean situation, of Dutch involvement in Caracas's cocoa export trade, of Cuba's potential for sugar production and export, and in particular, of the details of the convoy system to Veracruz.[79] The prominent characteristic of Spain's colonial system, he found, was massive leakage of colonial silver to foreigners first in American waters, and then at Cadiz. At Cadiz alone, he estimated (with exaggeration) that 12 million pesos were transferred annually to European textile suppliers.[80] No small responsibility for the disruption of the convoy system operating until 1700, he argued, resulted from lobbying by the "three men without funds or skills," the prior and two consuls of the Consulado de Cadiz, a corporate body lacking "authority, standing, and rules."[81] Legarra, however, grossly underestimated the *"autoridad"* of those three consulado officers.

Legarra's analysis diverged markedly from the conservative *consulta* of the Consejo de Indias and the cautious *Theórica* of Uztáriz in its approach to economic policy formulation and its execution, particularly in matters affecting Lower Andalusia's colonial trade. Legarra's initial (and perhaps most ambitious) innovation targeted the roadblocks to policy changes formed by the Hapsburg maze of overlapping jurisdictions. On the one hand, he found many well-intentioned "knowledgeable and active ministers" among Madrid's upper-level bureaucrats, but they were scattered around in the Consejo de Indias and Consejo de Castilla, the Junta de Comercio, the Junta de Asiento de Negros, the Junta de Azogues, and the Navy. On the other hand, he found notably lacking one central administrative body devoted exclusively to the "maintenance and expansion of the trades of the Indies and of Spain and its workshops" and responsible for oversight "of all the trades." A more representative "Consejo de Comercio," replacing the Junta de Comercio and other competing jurisdictions, could be inserted, he thought, as another bureau (*sala*) in the Consejo de Indias. It would have eight directors (one for each Spanish province) and be installed at Cadiz. This *consejo* would formulate a national economic development policy including highway construction linking other provinces to Cadiz and incentives for agriculture and manufacture. Perhaps most essential, it would circumscribe the dominant role of foreign merchants in Lower Andalusia's ports.

This ambitious, clearly Bourbon-inspired administrative innovation Legarra would pair with a single chartered company unlike, he hastened to explain, English or French models. Stockholders would be limited to Spaniards ("Spaniards from Spain"), which implied excluding the capital of foreign investors and surely of residents in the colonies. Then, in what seems an aside designed to minimize its explosive significance to Cadiz interests, Legarra let drop that he would assign to this new "national" company oversight of the "trades . . . for which the Consulado de Cadiz is currently responsible." This was no minor innovation. It spelled a head-on confrontation with the Cadiz commercial complex whose Spanish members, Legarra underscored, put themselves under the "protection of foreigners, influential in all our commerce." This pattern enriched foreigners ("because they are well informed") while impoverishing Spaniards ("because of their poor management"). His proposed privileged company would provide opportunities for Spain's peripheral provinces like Galicia and Catalonia to participate at last with their own products in the colonial trades from which they had been systematically excluded by Spanish and non-Spanish commercial groups alike, "perhaps due to the opposition of Andalusia's commerce in which foreigners play so prominent a role."[82] Furthermore, his proposed company offered an additional national advantage: provincial businessmen participating in colonial trade might, unlike foreign merchants, reinvest earnings in domestic product improvement. Properly motivated, they might abandon their "passive" business mode for an "active" one and then venture abroad on their own account to purchase goods below prices demanded by foreign merchant intermediaries resident at Cadiz.

Two other structures of colonial trade, Legarra was convinced, also had to change. First, Cadiz's main export taxes—the tonnage fee *(toneladas)* levied on shipowners and the undiscriminating duty based on volume *(palmeo)*—had to go. His reasoning was explicit: to deter the ingrained practice of undervaluing exports on their passage through customs since "most cargo of *flotas* and *galeones* is packed in bales wrapped in sacking, and only the owners know the contents." Second, the convoy system would have to be changed. Legarra would have his major administrative innovation, a new *sala* for the Consejo, reprogram the traditional Hapsburg convoy system by staggering *flotas* and *galeones* in alternate years while sending individual ships *(registros)* to the "permission port" (Cartagena) frequented by English slave traders under the terms of their *asiento*.

There is no doubt about the fate of Legarra's innovative design to consolidate in Colbertian style policy and execution in one administrative entity designed to absorb two fundamental Hapsburg trade structures: the Junta de Comercio and the Consulado de Cadiz. As coordinator of the early Bourbon government's review of colonial policy, Fernandez Durán passed Legarra's proposals to the politically prominent, wealthy, and traditionalist *andaluz* Acevedo y Hermosa (conde de Torre-Hermosa) for his opinion. Surely Fernandez Durán must have anticipated Acevedo y Hermosa's categorically conservative stance—"I neither am, nor ever was, tolerant of innovations, nor is there a greater admirer or follower of the ideas of our old-timers." Acevedo, a member of the influential Consejo de Castilla, spotted immediately the threat to the Junta de Comercio and to the commercial interests operating through the Consulado de Cadiz. Flatly opposing Legarra, he claimed that the proposed *sala* could not be staffed adequately since "ministers who may understand this matter are either few, scarce, or none at all." Furthermore, the proposed administrative procedures ("styles, forms and judicial procedures") would "ruin the *sala* at the outset, even destroy the best established [bureaus] in the world." In Acevedo's hands, Legarra later noted, his representation was fated to go nowhere.[83]

Spain's transatlantic trading system had virtually collapsed during the War of Succession. Legarra's report and other solicited *informes* form part of the early Bourbon government's package of cautious initiatives to sound out interest groups, then coax bureaucrats and businessmen to adopt fresh procedures to revive it. This intramural debate ended in the *Proyecto* of 1720 that restored the Hapsburg dual convoy system but modified it to include individual register ships to Buenos Aires. There was to be no privileged trading company nor new economic policy-making body.

For all his criticism of Cadiz's three incompetent men and his proposed *consejo* or *sala de comercio*, Legarra was, at bottom, really not all that iconoclastic. Just recall that he would restore the convoy system to Veracruz, Cartagena, and Portobelo along with fairs, all tightly scheduled, His detailed description of the *flotas* to New Spain was remarkably accurate—revealing but uncritical. As for his *sala de comercio*, he proposed to incorporate it in the Consejo de Indias precisely where Lower Andalusia's native and foreign commercial interests maintained an entrenched and well-financed lobby. Legarra's *representación* was quietly shelved. Obviously he had underestimated the consulado's *"autoridad."* Bureaucratic channels of the Hapsburg administrative maze were manipulated to disregard his explicit criticism of Cadiz's consular officials along with his suggestion for the proposed *sala.* His opponents used the strategy of requesting further evaluation by the very politically influential people Legarra had criticized: Fernandez Durán (president of the Junta de Comercio), Gaspar Fernandez Montejo (Cadiz' representative at Lima), and a group of Cadiz traders—Ysidro de Heraso (consulted three times), Francisco Victor Bandin, and Andrés Martínez de Murguía. Predictably they recommended reconstitution of the convoy system; and they succeeded in silencing Legarra—another indication of Madrid's repeated abdication to entrenched interests, spearheaded earlier by Sevilla's and now by Cadiz's consulado.

Macanaz and the "Discurso"/"Nuevo sistema"

Approximately twenty-five years later came an analysis from the exiled Melchor Rafael de Macanaz, one more profound than Legarra's. Macanaz's view was rooted in his career: in his early jaundiced conspectus of Hapsburg institutions and attitudes that had sparked resistance in Aragon, Catalonia, and elsewhere in the peninsula to Philip V and to the new Bourbon dynasty and all it represented.[84] It also mirrored the mentality of a dedicated civil servant forced into exile in 1715 when opponents, stung by his unrestrained regalism on behalf of the newly installed Bourbons, his combative antipapalism, and his critical stance toward the Jesuit Order, used the Inquisition to fabricate charges against him. With reason Antonio Valladares, his editor in the 1780s, warned readers long after Macanaz's death not to be put off by his "arrogance and the headstrong aggressiveness of certain of his propositions."[85] Once in exile in France (1715–48) Macanaz cultivated unflagging interest in the peculiar economic dependence of the Spanish metropole upon its American colonies fostered by centuries of Hapsburg imperialism.[86] An inveterate, prolific writer (he left 232 manuscript volumes), Macanaz's colonial interests were public knowledge. We know that Gonzalez de Bárcia asked him for an autobiography to include in his *Historiadores primitivos de América*.[87] All of which implies that Macanaz's controversial views on domestic and colonial issues, even though they were locked up, as it were, in manuscript, were known and shared by members of the Spanish political class.[88]

Macanaz's reflections on colonial policy for the benefit of Spain's high-level civil servants were drafted at a time when France and England, Spain's Atlantic competitors, were enjoying the profits of their Caribbean colonial enterprises and the African slave trade. At that time sugar exports from the French Caribbean were booming. They represented the main growth sector of the French economy and were attracting international attention as a remarkable example of successfully engineered colonialism and the working-out of the colonial compact to the great benefit of the metropole. The fullest exposition of Macanaz's colonial perspective, his manuscript "Discurso sobre América Española," is in the collections of Madrid's Real Academia de la Historia.[89] Complicating its attribution, however, is what appears to be another version, the "Nuevo sistema de gobierno económico para la América," found among Macanaz's papers but published in 1789 under the name of José del Campillo y Cosío. The attribution to Campillo has been seriously questioned.[90]

What seems clear is that both the "Discurso" and "Nuevo sistema" were drafted in the early 1740s. Further, sporadic observations on the American colonies, notably an impassioned and virtually unique (for its time) condemnation of the legacy of centuries of silver mining in Peru and New Spain, surfaced in Macanaz's "Auxilios" finally published in Antonio Valladares' influential and widely read periodical *Semanario erudito* in 1787.[91] Both the "Auxilios" and "Discurso" or "Nuevo sistema," in their treatment of mining, native American peoples, and Lower Andalusia's merchants, and in their recommendation of radical change rather than cosmetic reform of the Spanish transatlantic trading system, reveal Macanaz's unconventional conception of a Spanish Bourbon growth paradigm at mid-century. Spain's colonial system, he postulated at the beginning of the "Discurso"/"Nuevo sistema" demanded a "new method whereby we may take advantage of our wealthy possessions."[92]

Underlying "Auxilios" and "Discurso"/"Nuevo sistema" is an implicit perception of the paradox for Spain created by the dynamism that Anglo-French development of Caribbean export agriculture had injected into commercial capitalism in Atlantic-coast Europe after about 1650. While Spain's American possessions were far more extensive and populated than those of any of its competitors, Macanaz had to conclude that England's Barbados and France's Martinique profited their metropoles far more.[93] The root causes of Spain's comparatively poor performance were two: First, he listed the long-term "greed for mines"—Spain's obsession with silver mining, that ever-present yet unspoken safety net of Spanish Hapsburg and now Bourbon state finance.[94] Few *proyectistas* of his time or earlier, even those writing for the drawer, dared paint as grimly the legacy of silver—a linked series of "calamities, misfortunes, deaths, tyrannies, oppressions, and cruelties that our mines have cost us to date." Clearly this was an allusion to mine owners' unrestrained exploitation of native labor in Peru and New Spain. *En bloc,* the effects of the colonial mining syndrome had been negative since "the *flota* system does not operate effectively, and an abundance of silver curbs trade, employment, and manufacture, the principal supports of glory and opulence."[95] Along with the silver complex came a cultural analog, the Spanish colonists' overpowering "spirit of conquest" which, joined to their conviction of the "total inferiority" of native peoples, justified in turn the "worst tyranny, misery, and oppression." Moreover, conquest had led to widespread land monopolization by colonists who "do not themselves farm, but use Negroes and Indians." As a result: "He who labors does not harvest, nor does he who harvests, enjoy the fruits."[96] Macanaz's sweeping condemnations of Spanish colonialism were not published in his lifetime.

The second cause, according to Macanaz, was that mining and land-monopolization had led Spaniards to underestimate the benefits of trade, that "productive mine rendering the commerce of England and others thriving and respected."[97] Spain's transatlantic trade had long ago turned into a broad-scale monopoly *(estanco general)* under "the government of the past century" (shorthand for the Hapsburgs) whose commercial policy was fashioned primarily by Andalusian interests, "narrow-minded men" gathered in a "self-interested, short-sighted guild" rather than by "statesmen of sound policy."[98] They persisted in maintaining the managed trade of convoys and an export duty structure *(palmeo)* that privileged bales ("neither opened nor appraised") of expensive imported textiles. These they then reexported to a minority of high income consumers in the colonies where in reality were millions of "poor . . . [who] need common, ordinary goods."[99] To satisfy strong local demand for common types of cloth, colonial authorities in Peru and New Spain had tolerated the operation of "thousands of looms" producing goods for sale not only to "poor Indians but also American-born Spaniards of moderate resources." Small wonder merchants in the colonies traded *sub rosa* with nearby foreign colonies such as the English in the Gulf of Mexico.[100]

A revamped commercial policy, Macanaz argued, would have to end the perennial fixation of colonial elites on mining enterprises, on great rural estates, and the conquest mentality if only to maximize a major colonial resource that English and French colonies lacked, a broad base of potential consumers among low-income *naturales*. Native peoples responding to market inducements promised such a "large and promising demand that, if well managed, would absorb the staples and manufactures of this Kingdom, even if the Indies were to develop their own manufactures."[101] To transform *naturales* from tutelary status into independent subjects *(vasallos)*—from self-sufficient producers into market-oriented consumers of imports—necessitated that the state distribute land "in fee simple to our Indians." Macanaz reminded Madrid's high-ranking civil servants and the political class in general that America's native peoples were the real, "the great Treasure of Spain," hence a comprehensive official tour of inspection *(visita general)* would have to focus its "zeal, application, love, insight" on the Indians themselves.[102]

This brought Macanaz to his main recommendation—extending to Spain's colonial world projects designed ultimately to better conditions in the homeland, thereby rendering the American colonial enterprise profitable to its metropole at last. His fundamental proposition—the "resolve to open up the colonies"—would require eliminating the burdensome *toneladas* and *palmeo,* and "enabling anyone who so desires to trade without constraint, to go to the Indies." This "libertad" was the very "soul of all improvements proposed for agriculture, manufactures, and other Spanish problems."[103] At the centerpiece of this policy proposal was his "new system for the Indies" formulated to advance the commonweal—the "Interests of everyone, from the King down to the lowliest day laborer"—by stimulating "consumption of Spanish products in every one of those Provinces."[104] Otherwise it was fruitless to complain when a "Jewish merchant of London dispatches goods to a Spaniard of Cadiz to be shipped in the latter's name, paying him a commission; or when a Spaniard asks a Jewish merchant to buy goods for him, or forward some." Spain's fundamental problem remained unequal exchange, since the "goods are always English, and England gets most of the final price, leaving to the Spanish merchant or commission agent a small profit."[105] From French colonial policy Macanaz would borrow the principal link between metropole and overseas colonies—virtually duty-free exports to the colonies according to the principle of "comercio libre."[106]

A series of measures introduced in stages would test the practicality of Macanaz's vision.[107] While maintaining the convoy system solely for the wealthiest colony, New Spain, and keeping prohibitions on intercolonial flows of goods shipped from Spain, Madrid could innovate by opening its metropolitan ports to direct trade with the colonies, only insisting that ships first touch at Cadiz on their return voyages. His plan also favored further expansion of New Spain's trade with the Far East through Manila (a proposition, he thought, Mexico City merchants would surely find acceptable). Overall, his proposed *comercio libre* would, he predicted, lower maritime freight rates, supply a range of exports for a broad spectrum of consumers, and stimulate production in the metropole, "creating employment, developing industry, and enriching our nation: this is a chain of causes and clear effects."[108]

Macanaz was, of course, mindful of the mentality of tradition-bound members of the merchants' "guild" of Cadiz, ever insistent that "in Spain and America people prefer the current Method, since the whole machine of trade is geared to it, and introducing this innovation would unhinge it." To these doubters he would reply that there was no point in keeping to a "method that has minimized our American commerce and transferred to Spain's competitors the riches of Mexico and Peru."[109] With such doubters Macanaz bartered a concession: continuation of convoys to Veracruz and obligatory return of Spanish shipping to Cadiz in exchange for the cooperation of knowledgeable merchants willing to wait for the long-term benefits of his "new economic system."[110] Excited by the possibilities of his proposed freedom, Spanish traders might develop hidden business talents. They might become, he opined optimistically, merchants transformed, "arranging reliable correspondents in the Provinces of America, and just as soon as they hear an item is in short supply, ships will be able to leave at any time to supply it."[111] Macanaz's vision of what might be was really a muted critique of Cadiz's commercial monopoly and, by extension, of Spain's commercial underdevelopment.

Macanaz shared with Legarra a number of key concepts. Both were mercantilists, which is to say, both supported growth-oriented paradigms—initially with government subsidy and monitored management—formulated to develop their metropole's manufacturing base. Both condemned the one-port hegemony of Cadiz over Spain's transatlantic trading system because its merchant community lacked the commercial skills, vision of national interest, and willingness to forego current for future benefits. Spanish traders lacked, we would say today, characteristics basic to the making of late commercial capitalists, those some English merchants of the time cultivated as "fast followers."[112] Yet neither Legarra nor Macanaz would dismantle abruptly a basic, long-running structure of managed trade: Atlantic convoys to the colonies. On this critical point the otherwise radical Macanaz was markedly prudent, conciliatory, even meliorist. He would leave to official quarters or to a new Junta de Mejoras decisions about sensitive issues such as whether Spanish goods "may be shipped from any peninsular port to any in the Indies, if ships may depart at any time, alone or in convoy, the cargo capacity of each ship, whether all or only part" of the crew were Spanish, or whether "every vessel would have to leave and return to Cadiz or only on returning [from the colonies]." This was pure rhetoric. For Macanaz, there was really no choice because he believed in "complete freedom to leave, requiring only that all return to Cadiz to pay . . . duties on colonial products."[113]

Recognizing the role of New Spain's silver production and its thousands of potential consumers of imported goods, both would restore *flotas* on the run between Cadiz and Veracruz while opening Spain's other colonies to individual register ships from all major metropolitan ports—a kind of halfway measure. In one salient feature, however, Macanaz proved more innovative, daring, even radical. He pictured a "nuevo sixtema de Yndias" at whose core he grasped the potential of human capital that had been marginalized by the conquest mentality and mining syndrome. He would Europeanize millions of America's *naturales* (in his felicitous phrase, "industriar a los Yndios") through land reform, distributing to landless masses the means of production, thereby facilitating their participation in a marketplace formed and dominated by Europeans where they could sell their products and above all satisfy their import needs.[114]

However, just as in the initial phase of his career Macanaz had thrown himself regardless of personal consequences into the struggle to reduce aristocratic and clerical constraints upon the formation of a more centralized (and presumably better administered) state, so in his "Discurso," he made recommendations for modifying colonial policy that were too radical. As Liberal nineteenth-century historian Ferrer del Rio encapsulated Macanaz's propositions, "Macanaz's recommendations were fine, except that in his zeal, he failed to note they would hurt many concerns and overlook problems."[115] Another oblique comment on the Hapsburg legacy?

A View from Naples: Gándara's "Apuntes"

Another critical and unpublished *proyectista,* Miguel Antonio de la Gándara, drafted his "Apuntes sobre el bien y el mal de España"[116] at Naples in mid-1759, that critical juncture in Spanish history when Fernando VI's death was imminent and his half-brother Charles, king of the Two Sicilies, would shortly succeed as Charles III. Between 1750 and 1757 Gándara as *agente de preces* had represented Madrid at Rome where he reported on relations between Spain and the Vatican. A dedicated regalist like Macanaz, Gándara participated with Ventura Caro in negotiating a concordat (1753), and he remained at Rome supervising its execution.[117] He was counting on what he considered a promised appointment to the Consejo de Hacienda, a hope that vanished with the death of Prime Minister Carvajal y Lancaster in 1754 and the subsequent removal of his patrons Ensenada and Padre Rávago (Fernando's chaplain and confirmed patron of *montañeses* like Gándara). From Naples, Charles, his secretary of state Tanucci, and other collaborators monitored closely developments in Spain and the empire, especially the situation of public finance. They were preoccupied with the pervasive sense of drift during Fernando's last years, the dangerous distancing between Madrid and Paris, the widening gap between the Spanish economy and that of leading competitors. They were also worried about the menacing outreach of expansionist English interests in the Caribbean.[118]

Particularly troublesome was the hemorrhaging of colonial silver leaking out through channels in the Caribbean and Lower Andalusia to England, France, and other European countries and by large transfers of church revenues, originating in the American colonies, from Cadiz to the Vatican.[119] Earlier in the decade when Tanucci needed data on monetary transfers from Spain and its colonies to the Vatican, he had contacted Gándara to draft regulations (what Gándara called "antiexport legislation") to stem such remittances. The general results of Gándara's research on export controls informed the body of his "Reflexiones sobre quindenios."[120] Gándara's grasp of details and his efficiency in handling assignments probably induced Tanucci in the late fifties to urge him to expound his views on Spain and the American empire that Charles was about to inherit. Thus materialized notes or *apuntes* (dated July 1759) for what Gándara intended later to expand into a "Discurso sobre el bien y el mal de España." Like other aspirants to high appointment in the incoming reign, Gándara hoped to improve his dossier and the possibility of a prestigious post in Madrid's civil service.

Gándara aimed to lay out, he made quite explicit, in one overview the roots of Spain's backwardness. This would be complemented (if solicited) by a list of recommended measures *(arbitrios)* along with how "to execute the plan in his 'Apuntes.'"[121] His "Apuntes" offered, he warned, no philosophical discourse, no "political verse," no "imagined republic" in the vein of a Plato, Thomas More, or Abbé Fénélon. Rather the manuscript was aimed at those "noble spirits" who reflected on Spain and its problems and had the "capacity and breadth of mind" of "Campillos y Macanaces."[122] The nuance of his reference to such critical and unpublished paragons should not be minimized. In fact, concepts advanced in Macanaz's "Discurso sobre América Española" and (in what has been attributed to Campillo) the "Nuevo sistema de gobierno económico" resonate repeatedly in the "Apuntes." They bear witness to the velocity of circulation of such manuscripts and the regard in which they were held.

On close reading, the underlying argument of the "Apuntes" becomes explicit. By this time it was hardly original although accurate to argue that possession of overseas territories, the first stage of European colonialism, had so warped the Spanish economy that it was now falling dramatically behind Europe's advanced nations. "As our competitors advance each year, we slip further behind, as they rise, we fall.[123] Consequently silver, the principal colonial staple, had not and would not contribute to the metropole's development. Instead, Gándara calculated, a mere fraction (about 6.6 percent) or 2.5 million of 38 million pesos annually produced by Peru's and New Spain's mines was retained by the metropole. The balance (except what the colonies retained) disappeared through licit and illicit channels "in a thousand ways and a thousand forms" (Table 3).[124] Textile imports might easily be substituted by peninsular workshops using domestic raw materials such as raw wool and silk that, on the contrary, were exported. This pattern of economic dependency—exporting raw materials, importing finished goods, then covering trade deficits with reexports of silver from the colonies—had crystallized, Gándara was convinced, since about 1650. It permitted Spain's European suppliers of finished goods, he said graphically, to "bleed us." A sound economic policy would not permit "anyone to drain off our substance."[125]

Spain's most threatening trading partner was England which drew off the "very substance of Spain and its Indies," silver, and seemed intent on taking over "everything on earth, cutting, drawing lines, and dividing up" the possessions of Spain and France. Still, toward England Gándara showed a hate-love attitude for he, along with many Spaniards, felt there were lessons to be learned from English statesmen who had persisted over decades in elaborating what Gándara deeply admired, an integrated national and nationalist policy founded on the "political arithmetic of their commerce, workshops, agriculture, consumption, merchant marine, colonies, plantations, taxes, and the real interests of the Nation and its navigation."[126]

While Gándara discounted France's current economic performance and life-style ("gallicisms, simpering ways, cosmetics . . . affeminization of the mind"), he conceded much could be learned from seventeenth-century France. There he found a determined minister of state, Colbert, building on Richelieu's system and on English example, who had demonstrated that sound economic policy could blend colonial trade under conditions of freedom (the "heart of trade") with initial state financing of domestic manufacture.[127] He took pains to clarify that he was not recommending mindless imitation, only hoping to conform to the "current mentality of the dominant nations." A considered developmental policy covering the requirements of both domestic manufacture and colonial trade demanded that policy-planners select judiciously from European models and praxis, from the "most educated . . . skilled and informed" nations.[128] Economic backwardness, however, could be used to advantage. In what was tacit recognition of English preeminence in Europe and Spain's need to preserve (while restricting) its alliance with France, Gándara urged Madrid to pursue a policy of neutrality during the ongoing Seven Years War so that "victory will tip the scale in Spain's favor."[129] Economic inferiority might be capitalized as an international bargaining chip.

To overcome Spain's backwardness Gándara advanced what were two sets of recommendations to cover both metropole and colonies. Nothing less than a "new form of governance in keeping with present-day Europe" would suit Spain's circumstances. In both Hispanic worlds he found a debilitating factionalism mirroring the interests of "party and provenience, school and university" that his new system would contain by imposing "one coinage, one law code, one oversight, one measure, one language, and one religion." To this Gándara added an essential factor, leadership of a prime minister of "action, great understanding, and creativity, who has studied Spain and the Indies from their roots."[130]

A second set of recommendations consisted of by now commonly recognized measures for national growth in agriculture and manufacture and for fiscal and monetary policies to harness America's silver resources to national development in the same way that Spain's European competitors had managed America's staples to develop the "wealth of their dominions."[131] In effect Gándara was projecting a role-reversal for silver which down to his time had sufficed only to "strip us of our commerce, skills, manufactures, and industries." Now from the colonial world "should come resources for our needs." His was a vision of a closed, economically autonomous imperial economy, a version of the colonial compact.[132]

These measures could be effectively (if belatedly) tapped by applying the principle of "freedom" to Spain's transatlantic commercial structures and to its colonies. This meant opening more peninsular ports to trade with the overseas possessions, eliminating at Cadiz the pyramid of import and export duties, and setting up a reliable, scheduled maritime mail service for the flow of commercial data. For colonies no longer to be viewed as "lands of conquest," he advocated a blend of tradition and innovation. The traditional economic core of the Spanish colonies, silver mining, could be enhanced by larger mercury shipments from Europe and by technology transfers he believed were available in Sweden and Central Europe. More significant, his principal colonial recommendation (following Macanaz) was the cultivation of millions of potential consumers of European products among America's native peoples. While he drew back from expatiating on agrarian law in Spain ("no need to speak of this here"), he was explicit about the colonies. In America native peoples did need both "freedoms and land ownership."[133] Once they became independent farm owners, they would expand production to export dyes, cotton, and other colonial staples, and with their rising incomes, they would turn to dressing *a la castellana* in common Spanish textiles, the initial products of an infant industry whose quality would then improve. Gándara did not overlook the social aspects of colonial rule, for he grasped the essence of potential imperial social integration by class. Some *Americanos,* "wealthy merchants, distinguished people of letters, and the military," should be encouraged to migrate to Spain. Better still, encouraging the sons of America's colonial elites to settle in the metropole would be the best way to "draw to Spain that wealth commerce has failed to provide."[134]

There is an encouraging coda to this threnody of suppressed paradigms of a national growth policy by Legarra, Campillo, Macanaz, and Gándara. Macanaz was kept in internal exile at La Coruña (1748–60), Ensenada in the south at Granada (1754–60). But within months of his accession, Charles III (no doubt with the agreement of his minister Esquilache) recalled both to Madrid. This signaled the new reign's approbation of the reformism that Macanaz and Ensenada had symbolized, at least to those of Spain's political class at mid-century who examined their manuscripts.[135]

8. Toward the Mid-Century Crisis: Ensenada, 1743–1754

· · · · · · · · · · · · · · · · · · · ·

"As long as Spain lacks a competent navy, its closest rivals, France and England, will not respect it."   Ensenada to Fernando VI, "Representación, 1747"

"The expences of Spain have been very extraordinary during the late war . . . they have no Resource but their American Indies; nor need they a better."
                    Malachy Postlethwayt, *Considerations on the Revival of the Royal-British-Assiento*

Campillo's two manuscripts epitomized a literature of despair. They were written for the drawer, left unpublished yet allowed to circulate among Madrid's political class. His and others' contemporary manuscripts mirrored a sense of disillusionment, of inferiority, of lost opportunity, of Spain's social inability to meet the challenge of west Europe's competitive nation-states. Censors blocked critical publications, uneasy about public reaction to unfavorable judgments in print "because this would authorize . . . criticism of government and its ministers."[1] As we have seen, by the early forties little progress had been made in realizing a Bourbon growth model like that described by Uztáriz for the domestic economy. The transatlantic convoy system had barely been changed, and English publicist Postlethwayt proclaimed that Spain's transatlantic trade was the main source of the "Royal Revenues of the whole Spanish Empire."[2] Most Spanish monopoly companies trading to the colonies had gone bankrupt. A few state-sponsored textile factories like those at Guadalajara and Sevilla survived with difficulty, suffering from poor quality, inefficient management practices, unpredictable shifts in consumer preference and very competitively priced imports that could not be blocked.[3]

While the state financial administration was gradually simplified and centralized, systems of revenue collection remained substantially unmodified.

As late as 1739 the largest single source of government income, the customs, were still farmed. Although that revenue grew in the 1740s, government financial needs were not met.[4] And, last, reform of civil administration at the regional level through the Bourbon-inspired intendancy system was effectively instituted only after 1749. In administration, finance, trade, manufacture, naval forces, and merchant shipping, many Spaniards in the fifties sensed that their country had not merely failed to catch up with competitors — the gap was widening, and few "dared to point it out." "What does it mean," Gándara asked rhetorically, "not to go backward when others march ahead?"[5]

Bernardo Ulloa' *Restablecimiento* had tried to fill the obvious lacunae in Uztáriz's paradigm by inserting the all-important colonial component. Yet, although troubled by the state's incapacity to disrupt flourishing smuggling networks in the Caribbean, Ulloa went along with Spain's ongoing transatlantic system. He was at best a cautious, nationalist critic of the status quo. It was as if by 1740, after the initiatives of French technocrats, their Spanish collaborators, and Uztáriz's model-crafting, the burden of the Hapsburg legacy had reasserted itself. The first of Spain's eighteenth-century crises seemed to have subsided in somnolent stagnation.

The Atlantic and the War of the Austrian Succession

The War of the Austrian Succession followed, after what was only an eight-year truce, by the Seven Years War, locked Spain into conflict at sea with England, and over two decades, 1739–59, Spain's second great crisis began to loom. Its strands were many. First, expansion of English export sectors and exchanges with their North American and Caribbean colonies were evident in an impressive merchant marine and the efficient performance of the English royal navy. Between 1739 and 1748 English superiority at sea, reflecting parliamentary foresight behind massive naval outlays, became uncomfortably clear. English naval units attacked Spanish ports and sea lanes in the Caribbean and Pacific. Anson seized a Manila-bound *nao* with its cargo of registered and unregistered silver from Acapulco, while Vernon attacked Portobelo, Cartagena, and Santiago (Cuba).[6] More than ever, Spain's Caribbean islands and mainland areas were penetrable by English smugglers and Spanish collaborators. Jamaica's ports became entrepôts for trade with Spanish colonies; they were convenient points whence to reexport silver to Europe, bypassing Cadiz's import and reexport duties and leading some English observers to gloat that "Great are the advantages accruing to Britain from the trade between Jamaica and the Spaniards of Mexico."[7]

In the second place, suspension of escorted convoys led Spanish authorities to turn to *registros sueltos*, licensing Spanish and neutral shipping—French and other—to sustain trade and communications with the colonies.[8] As a consequence, for French manufacturers and exporters, the two decades after 1740 (particularly after 1748) were the highpoint of France's legal and illegal trade with Spain and its colonies, as Raynal's data later verified (see data in table for note 11 [p. 318]).[9]

A combination of increased volume of non-Spanish goods reexported from Cadiz to the Spanish colonies, and illegal direct commercial exchanges between colonial merchants and Jamaican suppliers heightened the visibility of New Spain's silver outflows to western Europe.[10] Commercial intelligence had long kept French exporters informed about New Spain's economy, the capital resources of leading Mexico City merchant houses, and the colony's real and potential demand for imports. This is the kind of information French naval officer Jean de Monségur had reported so extensively in 1709 after his sojourn in New Spain. His data were corroborated decades later by Raynal who underscored New Spain's capacity to absorb exports (and reexports) from Spain.[11] In addition, English reports of Jamaican smuggling operations multiplied as did data on Cadiz's imports of colonial precious metals, which were widely publicized in Amsterdam's periodicals.

Trade expansion by Europe's exporters to the Western Hemisphere and the Far East brought a renewed focus upon Spain's mining colonies, especially New Spain. A case in point: the English East India Company's shipments of precious metals to the Far East peaked at 398,041 kilos (1751–55) for the fourth time over the century 1660–1760.[12] In 1740 Bernardo Ulloa boasted that "at no time in this century have our mines been better managed and more productive."[13] This was not hyperbole: in the immediate postwar years (1748–53) Europe's receipts of colonial precious metals, 115.7 million pesos (an annual average of 19.3 million), were up 33 percent over a comparable peacetime era (1730–37) when average annual receipts were 14.3 million. New Spain alone accounted for between 69 and 79 percent in the postwar era (Table 4).[14] Small wonder that an official in Mexico City (1746) enthused over its mint as "the very heart of our various trades, where the blood of silver and gold is purified before flowing through the nations of the world." Campomanes wrote in 1762 that the colony of New Spain had become "one of the Crown's most essential and valuable possessions," and in the same vein, France's ambassador at Madrid urged his government to

TABLE 3
Silver Receipts from Spanish America, 1741–1745
(in pesos)

Year	Spain and Allies		England		Total
1741	4,110,000		70,00		4,180,000
1742	2,395,812		*		2,395,182
1743	8,214,500		1,550,000		9,764,500
1744	1,924,024		2,490,000		4,414,024
1745	12,000,000		8,700,000		20,700,000
Total	28,644,366	(69%)	12,810,000	(31%)	41,454,336

Source: Morineau, *Incroyable gazettes,* 377, table 57.
*No data available.

concentrate on Mexico "as the precious touchstone of the Spanish colonies, and the main support of French commerce via Cadiz."[15]

Ensenada's *Reformismo*

On Campillo's death in 1743, Philip V and Isabel Farnese, on the advice of high level civil servants who had also patronized Campillo, called to Madrid the marqués de la Ensenada to take over several ministries in the fashion of his predecessors Patiño and Campillo. By then Spain was at war with England over smuggling in the Caribbean. By then, too, the maritime outreach of English naval units was rapidly expanding. In a series of pincer-like moves against the Panama area from the Atlantic and Pacific Vernon attacked Portobelo and then Cartagena, and Anson sailed around Cape Horn, up the Pacific coast, and then into the western Pacific. The English strategy had only limited success, but it was brilliant in conception if not execution, a rehearsal for worldwide naval operations by both England and France in the next great international conflict, the Seven Years War. The danger of war at sea to Spain's lifelines to its American colonies was never lost upon Ensenada, a career officer in naval administration ("in which I grew up," he once confessed proudly).[16]

Uppermost in the strategy of Madrid's ministerial group in 1743 was national defense. They emphasized both immediate and long-term financing of all aspects of an ambitious naval rearmament program: ship design and construction in peninsular and Havana shipyards; the development of arsenals at Cadiz, Cartagena, and Ferrol; the undertaking of defensive works in the peninsula and overseas in the Caribbean at Veracruz, San Juan, and Havana; and the recruitment and training of naval officers and crews. So ambitious a program led directly to overhaul of all aspects of state finance ("finance," Ensenada was convinced, "is the axis of government").[17] Ensenada encouraged Hacienda personnel to review the padded rolls and accounts of the large royal household and court mandarins who defended privilege, perquisites and patronage.[18] (He pictured them as "Palace magnates, whose invariable principle is, make Ministers fear and respect them in order to gain personal ends.") He hoped to obstruct the Vatican's stratagems designed to "delude us into transferring more and more money there."[19] He pushed reform of the imposts *(rentas provinciales)* and assembled a vast national statistical database of wealth and income (the remarkable *Catastro de Ensenada*) in preparation for a single tax *(única contribución)* on income. And he tightened revenue collection and accounting procedures in the metropole and overseas in the American colonies. Last and not least, he established a government bureau *(Real Negociación del Giro)* for settlement of Spain's international payments in American silver.[20] Ministerial cadres under Philip V in his later years and now, at last, under Fernando VI had an opportunity to implement colonial as well as domestic elements of the Bourbon growth model sketched by Uztáriz and supplemented by

TABLE 4
Spain: Average Annual Receipts of American Precious Metals, 1730–1753
(in pesos)

Year	Annual Receipts
1730–37	14,281,477
1748–53	19,298,945

Source: Morineau, *Incroyables gazettes*, 369, n. 22 (1730–37), 385–388 (1748–53).

Spain: Receipts of American Precious Metals, 1748–1753
(in pesos)

	Total	From Veracruz*	Veracruz (%)
1748	4,816,752	3,316,722	68.9
1749	34,866,801	25,793,722	75.9
1750	30,149,112	26,051,627	86.4
1751	7,643,866	4,751,345	62.2
1752	25,392,598	11,728,231	46.2
1753	12,924,541	8,766,834	67.9
Total	115,793,541	80,408,481	69.4

Source: Adapted from Morineau, *Incroyables gazettes*, 385–89, table 58.
*Veracruz, Havana, and Cartagena.

Bernardo Ulloa to meet the financial demands of war and to counter the Spanish elite's sense of despair expressed in Campillo's two pigeon-holed manuscript *cris-de-coeur.*

Philip and his advisers recognized the necessity of implementing the policy orientation of Patiño and his protégé Campillo. In Ensenada they picked a well-qualified appointee, experienced in the complexity of state finance, cognizant of the international situation and Spain's exposure in it and capable of driving overdue changes without unnerving the many lobbyists networking the ministries of Hacienda, Guerra, and Marina e Indias, as well as the Consejo de Castilla. Ensenada hoped to put bureaucratic recruitment on a new basis by reducing the number of appointees drawn from the self-selecting elitist *colegios mayores* in order to favor non-*colegiales,* the *manteístas.* Promotion in the civil service, Ensenada believed, should be a measure of ability. It should be controlled neither by "seniority nor *colegial* factions," nor "should *manteístas* be considered inferior."[21] This, he was to find, was more easily said than done.

Ensenada at forty-one seems, in retrospect, to have been groomed as Campillo's successor, for he was appointed on the day Campillo died. He came from the lower gentry of La Rioja and Guipúzcoa. On his father's death, young Ensenada moved to Madrid where an uncle-priest sent him to clerk in a Cadiz merchant house. There, in 1720 when he was eighteen, Patiño spotted him and initiated his career in naval administration.[22] In 1726 he served under Campillo (recently returned from the colonies) at the Guarnizo shipyard. In 1730 he was at the Ferrol naval arsenal, and in 1732 he went to Italy, first in the naval forces (as *intendente de marina*) supporting Charles's occupation of Naples, later in the administration of Charles's brother, Philip, at Parma. Charles bestowed the title of marqués de la Ensenada on him in 1736.[23] Ensenada was at Parma when Campillo died unexpectedly and his patrons at Madrid, Aníbal Scoti, Sebastian de la Cuadra and Philip's confessor Padre Rávago, and at Naples by Charles's confidant the duque de Losada, immediately recommended his appointment as Campillo's successor. No doubt they shared the appraisal of a member of the royal household that "no one was better informed about Campillo's thoughts and projects, nor more able to carry them out."[24] Four months later (1737) Philip V bestowed another mark of distinction, secretaryship of the century-old *Almirantazgo,* facilitating his intervention in both commercial and naval affairs.[25]

At Madrid he fashioned a small network of influential advisers ("few, because the good are rare"): Padre Rávago, Agustín de Ordeñana (secretary of the Consejo de Estado), Bartolomé de Valencia (director-general of

Rentas), Josef Banfi y Parrilla (*oficial mayor*, Consejo de Indias), and at Marina, Alonso Pérez Delgado ("Ensenada's right arm").[26] Supported by key members of the political class at court and fed data and advice by well-informed officials,[27] Ensenada could hope to fulfill his ministerial responsibilities under Philip V and then his son Fernando VI during the ministry of José de Carvajal y Lancaster, an anglophile aristocrat, who was a descendant of Moctezuma and had siblings in the church (bishop of Cuenca) and army (a colonel in the Spanish Guards).

Ensenada, now a prominent bureaucrat although of lower gentry social origins, former clerk in a Cadiz merchant house who had no university education (hence, was not even a *manteísta*), holding down four ministries under a nobleman like Carvajal, could not avoid tension. Here was more than conflictive compatibility between strong personalities, since Carvajal and Ensenada symbolized major fissures in the Spanish polity of Fernando VI. Social origins and career patterns aside, Ensenada and Carvajal differed on critical issues, notably foreign policy: whether to maintain Spain's alliance with France confirmed by the treaties ("family pacts") of 1733 and 1743 or lean toward England.[28] It was the recurrent dilemma of a dependent European state.

José de Carvajal Moctezuma, Alencastre y Noroña (and, later, the conde de Aranda) were the only prime ministers whom Spanish Bourbons in the eighteenth century recruited from the aristocracy.[29] A number of factors seem to have rendered Carvajal reluctant to tinker with Spain's colonial trading system. For one, he understood that "the core of Spanish power [was] its large, wealthy American possessions . . . the sinews of our power."[30] The family's encomiendas in New Spain (Tenango and Tacuba in the Valley of Mexico) had been converted long before by the imperial state into an annual pension of 4,000 pesos, by Spanish income levels (60,000 *reales*) a very respectable sum. Drawn on the net proceeds of the state monopoly of mercury sales to New Spain's silver refiners, it was paid to him even during the deficit spending of the war years, 1743–48, despite general suspension of such payments.[31] A *colegial* at Salamanca, he was appointed seven years after graduation to the *Chancillería* of Valladolid (1729) and nine years later moved up to the Consejo de Indias. When the Consejo's president, conde de Montijo, who had served as Spain's deputy to the South Sea Company in London, went to Frankfort for a meeting of the Diet of the Holy Roman Empire, Carvajal went as his deputy. And when Montijo left the Consejo's presidency, Carvajal replaced him. Philip V, who knew of Carvajal's admiration (perhaps exaggerated),[32] multiplied his appointments, adding posts in the Junta de Comercio y Moneda and the Consejo de Estado, where he specialized in foreign affairs. In 1746 Fernando VI picked him as his *primer ministro de Estado.*

Ozanam, who edited Carvajal's correspondence with fellow nobleman duque de Huéscar (later, de Alba), believes Carvajal hoped to contain Philip's Italian ambitions and Francophile leanings in order to concentrate on developing the resources of Spain and its colonies.[33] This meant shifting toward a moderately anglophile or at least publicly "vigilant" neutral stance if only to minimize the threat of English naval and commercial power to the Spanish colonies. England's Ambassador Keene was ready to reorient him. "I can't make him as English as I would like," Keene is said to have observed, "but I daresay he'll never be French."[34] Tilting toward England implied improved relations with Austria, which may have drawn to Carvajal those Spanish factions (mainly Aragonese) still preferring Hapsburg patrimonialism over French-style centralization. Both Carvajal and Ensenada were undeniably nationalist, but Ensenada's orientation favored French praxis if only to counterbalance an equally expansionist England. On the other hand, it would be misreading Carvajal's foreign policy to overlook his hope that Spain might distance itself from major rivals in the Atlantic in order to protect its empire in America. London and Paris, he observed, perceive "our ignorance and negligence" and have made "an informal agreement among themselves for each Nation to enjoy whatever is most convenient without prejudice to what the other wants."[35]

Other issues point to the tolerated incompatibility of Carvajal and Ensenada. If Ensenada attended no university, Carvajal and his three brothers went from their family's estate in Extremadura to Salamanca as *colegiales* of the well-endowed and prestigious Colegio de San Bartolomé, thereby tracked for bureaucratic prominence or church eminence, in *casa real* or *iglesia.* In Carvajal's Salamanca class of 1722 figured other notables whose shared social and educational background formed a natural network of interests, attitudes, prejudices, and goals when they entered government service under Philip and later his son, Fernando. Second, Ensenada worked with bureaucrats of pro-Jesuitical persuasion (Basques like Villarias and Montiano y Luyando among others) and defended the Spanish Jesuit missions in the disputed border zone between southern Brazil and Spain's Rio de la Plata; it was an attachment Ensenada continued later under Charles III. Significantly, the Luso-Spanish treaty of 1750, which shifted some Spanish Jesuit missions in Paraguay to Portuguese control in exchange for the port town of Sacramento (*the* Anglo-Portuguese smuggling center on the Rio de la Plata) was negotiated by Carvajal apparently without Ensenada's support.

Ensenada's fiscal housecleaning policy, a third issue, probed the claims (sometimes real, often fabricated) of long-term holders *(juristas)* of state bonds and put into question the aristocracy's privileged access to public revenues, those ancient and multiple life-support systems of an old patrimonial state. Finally, there was Carvajal's heightened sense of bureaucratic territoriality: he remained convinced that the prime minister rather than the secretary of Hacienda (Ensenada) should control the Junta de Comercio, Spain's economic planning board, and hence have the power to shift state subsidies, for example, from the large-scale Guadalajara woolen factory (one of Ensenada's pet enterprises) to the other new but small-scale textile enterprises favored by Carvajal at Sevilla and Brihuega.[36] That there was tension, perhaps creative tension, between these two powerful bureaucratic personalities was predictable; that the two did not part company during Carvajal's eight-year tenure, which ended with his death in 1754, is, on the other hand, surprising.

Ensenada's major situation reports *(representaciones)* of 1747 and 1751 were comprehensive, insightful, and hard-hitting but often tantalizingly short on detail.[37] The subject matter covered in most detail is predictably Hacienda and foreign affairs while coverage of the colonies (Indias) is schematic. He was critical of bureaucratic corruption, nepotism, and intellectual arrogance (too many civil servants "believe that everything is taught, studied and known at the University"). He castigated tax farmers, but his criticism of the Cadiz commercial community is noticeably muted and, where made, oblique rather than explicit.[38] Trade he considered an honorable profession, defending it eloquently in his *Representación* of 1751: "What kind of mentality is it that holds that the earnings of trade and commerce are demeaning, while robbery in wartime is considered noble and honorable?"[39] Alerted by informants at Madrid, Cadiz, and in the colonies, he respected the political clout of the Cadiz consulado, its overseas supporters at Mexico City and Lima, and their considerable lobbying funds.

The first five years (1743–48) of Ensenada's eleven-year tenure were a phase of wartime damage control with few reform initiatives. Only after the international settlement at Aix-la-Chapelle (1748) could Ensenada emerge as an activist bureaucrat seeking to implement key elements of a Bourbon growth model. He could now focus on major long-term preoccupations: finance at home and in the colonies, naval rearmament, and colonial trade. These issues had been broached by *proyectistas* but implementation, where it had occurred, had been half-hearted. At the accession of Fernando VI, a new administration made "renovation" a real possibility.

Perhaps it is distorting reality to systematize what was more likely *ad hoc* decision-making, yet one may discern a pattern in Ensenada's activity. He began with a specially convened finance junta to review accounts.[40] Like his predecessors at Hacienda, Ensenada knew about gross misappropriation of state revenues by tax-farmers (*arrendadores*) and the burden upon business-men and consumers alike of sales taxes (*alcabalas*) and the *cientos* and *mil-lones* imposts of *rentas provinciales*. One of the first imposts farmed by "los hombres de negocios" (*arrendadores* who manipulated them "despotica-mente"), which Ensenada brought under state administration, was *alca-balas*.[41] His most innovative tax initiative, however, was a projected single tax on income of landlords, manufacturers, merchants, artisans, and certain church revenues. It was designed specifically to eliminate the multiple *rentas provinciales*.[42] Sifting the experience of such a tax in France, Savoy, parts of Italy, and Catalonia, Ensenada concluded comparable success was possible in Castile despite the predictable resistance of "financiers and their associ-ates who would try to frustrate such an initiative." Its first stage would be a carefully planned economic census to collect data on national wealth and income and its distribution, a plan to "'cadaster' the Castiles" as he phrased it in 1747.[43] This remarkable project executed with the cooperation of bu-reaucrats, local authorities, notables, curates, and others, generated data that recently has been reworked to analyze the economic structure of mid-eighteenth-century Castile.[44]

Interest in colonial finance was less explicitly demonstrated by Ensenada, who found it in worse shape than that of the metropole. Colonial treasury surpluses were, at best, "contingente." They were sizeable but irregular in arriving at Cadiz, especially in wartime. Campillo had been aware of mal-administration of the profitable *alcabala* farmed by the Consulado de Mex-ico since the end of the seventeenth century, and Ensenada, who also noted the "terrible alcabala administration," pressured Viceroy Güemes y Horca-sitas (first conde de Revillagigedo) to put that farm under state administra-tion.[45] In addition, to curb the exploitation of native American consumers, increase sales of imports and locally produced goods, and improve colonial tax collection, Ensenada's administration prepared price schedules for goods and services sold by *corregidores*, *alcaldes mayores* and their *tenientes* in collu-sion with local merchants in the viceroyalties of Peru and New Spain.[46]

While the connection between fiscal reform in the metropole and the colonies was not spelled out, occasionally Ensenada expressed it by indirec-tion. For example, elimination of *rentas provinciales* could induce a tempo-rary revenue shortfall to be compensated, he suggested, by raising customs rates and tobacco taxes in Spain.[47] On inspection, however, these measures were another reflection of the colonial economy: the level of colonial trade affected customs revenues at Cadiz, while the tobacco factory at Sevilla (then under construction) processed Cuban and other tobaccos purchased with transfers from New Spain's treasury. Irregularity of colonial funds aside, the potential improvement of Spanish finance through better fiscal performance in the colonies fascinated Ensenada. Income from colonial treasuries, he once calculated, could readily be doubled, from 3 to 4 million *escudos de vellon* to at least 6 million per annum; in fact, he believed, the real gross of colonial treasuries totaled perhaps double that estimate, or 12 million. Incoming silver transfers may have been *contingente* in his view, nonetheless they proved an invaluable resource in covering deficits incurred by his ambitious naval rearmament program. To curb the influence of the Cadiz consulado over handling customs receipts and the surplus of colonial treasuries in the *Depositaria de Indias,* Ensenada shifted management of these funds from the Casa de Contratación to the Hacienda ministry in 1751.[48]

His administration had several objectives in augmenting treasury revenues. He planned to reduce the public debt swollen by borrowing during the long War of Succession. That debt totaled about 100 million *escudos de vellon,* roughly equivalent to four times annual government revenues. By refinancing, he aimed to lower large interest payments owed to domestic and foreign creditors, those "powerful banking houses at Madrid and abroad."[49] By verifying the "authenticity and legality" of claimants of interest on *juros,* Ensenada's administration managed to invalidate part of the public debt.[50] In addition on his agenda were large-scale public works projects, completion of the Sevilla tobacco factory, the long contemplated Canal de Castilla to ship the grains of north Castile's *tierra de campos,* and two major highways, one through the *montaña* to the Bay of Biscay, the other over the Guadarrama mountains northwest of Madrid to link the two Castiles.[51]

By far the most pressing objective of Ensenada's financial reorganization was funding an ambitious—to England, dangerous ("our naval construction . . . has and ever will have no other purpose than to counter England")—naval program (he planned fifty warships over eight years). This was a reaction to the impressive scale of English naval operations in the Caribbean early in the previous war and to the availability, when hostilities ceased, of only twelve operating Spanish warships (a "rickety fleet"), some so unseaworthy they were sold to Cadiz shipowners for the colonial carrying trade.[52] In 1751 the Spanish navy listed 18 major warships (to England's 100), but by 1754, Ensenada's program raised that figure more than twofold to 45. In addition, it was responsible for stockpiling of naval stores (masts, canvass, cables); improved dockyards at Cartagena, Cadiz, and Ferrol; and a pool of 40,000 seamen.[53]

At Ensenada's direction Madrid sent abroad to western Europe for further training foreign-born naval officers Luís Godin (later, director of Cadiz's Academia de Guardias Marinas) and Thomas Southwell, and for reporting on maritime and commercial developments in Europe, Antonio de Ulloa and Jorge Juan. The latter were part of a state-sponsored program that also supported publication of the controversial *Teatro crítico* of Feijóo (a favorite author of Charles III), José Antonio Gutierrez de Rubalcava's *Tratado historico, politico y legal de el comercio de las Indias Occidentales* (published on the naval ministry's press at Cadiz),[54] a guide to the Escorial's impressive Arabic manuscripts collection, and other cultural activities. Juan, who studied naval architecture, was responsible for recruiting English naval construction experts to supervise Spanish shipyards.[55] This was an ambitious effort to prod Spain into the wider flow of information and ideas of mid-eighteenth-century Europe.

Naval rearmament was intended primarily to defend Spain's possessions in America to which convoys had been suspended in 1739 because the navy could not spare the necessary escort vessels. As Ensenada articulated his conspectus of 1747, "without a Navy the Spanish Monarchy will neither be respected, retain control over its dispersed States, nor develop this peninsula."[56] Driving his pursuit of international respect was a practical dimension, a hoped-for renewal of Spain's projection in Europe. There was, to be sure, another dimension. Ensenada foresaw renewed conflict between France and England over access to the resources of Spain's American colonies. A respectable Spanish naval force could serve Madrid's strategy under Prime Minister Carvajal y Lancaster to remain neutral and play mediator, honest broker between the two superpowers. But there was a down side: the English might interpret Spain's rearmament as potential reinforcement of French naval units which, when combined with Spanish units, might contest England's domination of the Atlantic maritime routes. It was a possibility never discounted at London.[57]

The clarity of the program of reform in Spain and its relationship to the international situation and naval rearmament contrast with Ensenada's infrequent and invariably cautious official references to colonial affairs in his major situation reports of 1747 and 1751. Probably this reflects reluctance overtly to tamper with the vital core of the Spanish empire, its "comercio de Indias." A realist, Ensenada recognized that commerce demanded "much experience . . . much examination of the situation in many areas inside and outside Spain," all the more since in his time trade patterns seemed to have lost any fixed rules.[58] His caution is not explicable by lack of current information on colonial conditions. He and Alonso Pérez Delgado closely monitored the naval construction program at Havana (an early and abiding interest of his predecessor, Campillo) under contract to the Basque-Navarrese privileged Real Compañía de la Habana from 1745.[59] No doubt Ensenada had discussed the situation of both Cuba and New Spain with Campillo at Guarnizo where he had served under him. He could also draw for colonial data upon experienced, informed merchants like Juan Antonio de los Heros Fernandez (marqués de los Heros) and the in-depth reporting by young naval officers Antonio de Ulloa and Jorge Juan on contraband-running, administrative corruption in the colonial world, and the abuse of Indian tribute-payers by colonial officials and their commercial allies in the American colonies of Santa Fe, Ecuador, and Peru. Ensenada, it must be recalled, supported publication of the sanitized *Relación histórica del viage de la América meridional* (1748) of Ulloa and Juan, then directed them to draft their far more critical and explosive "Discurso y reflexiones políticas sobre el estado presente de los reynos del Peru," long a closely guarded but often-consulted manuscript.[60] And from New Spain came the reports of Viceroy Güemes y Horcasitas which filled in Ensenada's grasp of conditions in New Spain, by now Spain's wealthiest and most populous colony. These were summarized in Horcasita's lengthy *Instrucción* that in 1751 Ensenada had to remind all outgoing viceroys to prepare.[61]

Since Horcasitas had prior colonial experience as governor and captain-general of Cuba before his posting to New Spain, Ensenada had grounds for trusting his grasp of colonial conditions. A reading of Horcasitas's final report from Mexico City may account for the relatively low overt priority Ensenada assigned to colonial matters in his formal *representaciones* as well as the muted criticism he introduced. The *instrucción* is no Macanaz-like call to minimize the colonial economy's mining fixation and its distorting consequences, no attack upon Cadiz's managed trade monopoly, no explicit criticism of the performance of the influential merchant communities of Mexico City and Cadiz. Horcasitas, whose wife came from a well-placed Andaluz extended family (Padilla) with members settled in New Spain, knew how to navigate in political waters and in the process to accumulate a very respectable fortune during extended colonial service.

Horcasitas put silver mining and the Mexico City mint at the heart of his economic review.[62] New Spain's mines were the "main source of the wealth supporting this kingdom and all those in Europe" while Mexico City's *casa de moneda*—recently put under state administration and dazzling in its new installations—was the "pearl of the royal crown" whose "abundant riches" had created its "renown . . . in the four corners of the world." He reminded a revenue-enhancer like Ensenada that the new mint ("one of the finest buildings gracing this city") was a prime source of revenue through the 2.5 percent fee that in 1753 alone produced over 700,000 pesos net every year. Analysis of New Spain's mining sector led him to discussion of the linkages between mining and trade and of those Mexico City merchant capitalists who ventured their capital in mining enterprise, a significant additional source of their profits.[63]

Horcasitas avoided referring to the consulado as such, only mentioning the "*cuerpo*" of merchants, and he did not discuss the bitter electoral infighting between the factions of *montañeses* and *vizcaínos* that had forced the intervention of his predecessor, Viceroy Fuenclara. Instead, reflecting cordial relations with the city's wealthy *almaceneros* he reiterated their complaints about the destabilizing effects of Campillo's and Ensenada's wartime innovation *(registros sueltos)* upon pre-1739 trade patterns: the "reglas del comersio" had been violated. No longer could they manage the volume of New Spain's imports. There was neither price stability nor observance of the traditional ground-rules that prescribed that imports and exports be exchanged at Jalapa. He reported that the fifty-or-so agents (so-called *registristas*) of Cadiz's exporters were abandoning the Jalapa *feria* without authorization to market their imports at Mexico City and provincial centers and were even trading in local products.[64] Horcasitas's solicitude for the problems of the colonial capital's merchants marked his deference to their impressive (and always welcome) financial assistance (about 4.3 million pesos) in grants, loans, and *alcabala* tax payments to Madrid during the recent War of the Austrian Succession.[65] And in the long-festering friction between Mexico City and Cadiz interests over the volume of transpacific Asian imports at Acapulco, Horcasitas sided with Mexico City's *almaceneros*, recommending raising the value of authorized trade each way. Still, wary of alienating either of the two influential merchant communities, Horcasitas advanced no basic recommendation apropos the "reglas del comersio" other than that Madrid agree upon appropriate regulation—a truly Solomonic opinion. Meanwhile, he reported that he was checking the licenses of foreign merchants recently arriving at Veracruz.[66]

On the conditions and treatment of Amerindians under Spanish colonial rule, which Macanaz had castigated, Horcasitas was ambivalent. Native peoples were indispensable to the smooth functioning of the colonial economy, "for . . . Indians farm, pasture cattle . . . work the mines, construct the buildings," furnishing food and craft goods "with their sweat and . . . low wages." Yet these lower social orders *(vulgares, plebe)* were congenitally "vile and vicious," a "monster as many-headed as there are castes," with a marked propensity for crime and alcoholism.[67] The security of the colonial system required their control by New Spain's 148 district officers, the *alcaldes mayores*. Only their internal disunity and fear of colonial officials and soldiery—the power of the colonial state—kept them in check.

Still, there was Horcasitas's ambivalence: the "stupidity, dejection and extreme poverty" of native peoples, he wrote, deserved compassion and the alleviation of their exploitation by the district officers, the frequent and most visible targets of their complaints.[68] This brought Horcasitas to what he recognized as a long-run contradiction in the colonial service. Since *alcaldes mayores* were assigned no formal salary, they were authorized to appropriate a percentage of the head tax *(tributo)* paid by native peoples. In practice, they supplemented the share of *tributo* by exploiting those in their jurisdiction, usually through a virtual monopoly trade. So Horcasitas (along with his counterpart, the viceroy of Peru) felt obligated to recommend legalizing such unauthorized practices while regulating the kind of goods supplied and their prices, adjusted to the income level and needs of each *alcaldía mayor*.[69] Overall, the subtext of Viceroy Horcasitas's comprehensive *instrucción* to Madrid and to his replacement was that New Spain's mining and commercial sectors needed only fine-tuning, certainly no radical change of direction—a message Ensenada must have taken seriously.

Horcasitas handled Mexico City's *almaceneros* and their influential consulado with calculated circumspection. Their many shortcomings were left unmentioned: illegal trade practices in collusion with transpacific Manila counterparts; confrontational interethnic politics in consulado elections that Viceroy Fuenclara recently had to settle; mismanagement of the mint that had forced Madrid to take control; and, finally, the practices of consulado officers in skimming the *alcabala* tax farm for decades. On the contrary, he went out of his way to applaud with hyperbole the charitable investment of *alcabala* surpluses by their Mexico City leaseholders in behalf of "widows, maidens, and other kinds of the poor."[70]

For supplements to Horcasitas's reports, Ensenada could rely for information about colonial conditions on experienced civil servants in the metropole: at Madrid, José Banfi (who once claimed that almost everyone posted to high colonial office since 1731 "knows me more or less confidentially"); at Cadiz, Francisco de Ocio, the *administrador de rentas* (the French consulted him on "everything connected to its vast trade"), and Julián de Arriaga, recently recalled from Venezuela to become president of the Casa de Contratación at Cadiz.[71] Given such sources of information, ignorance does not explain Ensenada's circumspection on colonial affairs in his two principal *representaciones*. In no ambiguous terms Banfi, for example, had warned him to sidestep "colonial affairs" in official reports because "many are the uncomfortable invitations to receptions which disguise deals, agreements, and other invitations to corruption. . . . [and] how risky it [is] to make promises that might soon have to be honored."[72] Hemmed in by domestic and foreign interests, many of them hangovers of the Hapsburg legacy, Ensenada's administration, recognizing Spain's naval, military, and manufacturing shortcomings, had to move cautiously in suppressing smuggling in the Caribbean by English and French merchants, for whom Spain's colonial trade "is the most important."[73] As long as exports of Spanish products to the colonies remained patently insufficient and Spain could not "handle all its American trade or protect it," colonial silver would have to remain a "a good shared with others."[74] Awareness of such national shortcomings obliged a pragmatic Ensenada to espouse a policy of tolerant compromise acceptable to colleagues and later echoed by José de Gálvez and, in particular, Manuel de la Gándara who put it well: " Look away and dissemble with foreigners, letting them share in our Americas, if only to remove their rivalry, even the possibility of their invading them."[75] The policy could implement Ensenada's vision of refashioning Spain into a well-armed international honest broker. As he never failed to reiterate, "as long as Spain lacks a competent navy, its closest rivals, France and England, will not respect it."[76]

This, however, is not to imply that Ensenada's was a policy of benign neglect in colonial trade. On the contrary, his approach seems incremental, unobtrusive, lacking formal coherence, but pursued on many fronts. A number of initiatives suggest an underlying intention to modify elements constraining Spain's transatlantic trading system. The South Sea Company's *asiento* was not renewed. Instead Ensenada backed a Spanish merchant's proposal to transport 5,000 African slaves from the Guinea coast aboard properly authorized English vessels, a project that was not pursued.[77] In mid-1747 his administration chartered the San Fernando textile company at Sevilla, authorized to export its products from Sevilla (bypassing the port of Cadiz) to any colonial area except Cuba and Venezuela.[78]

Far more significant and controversial, Ensenada extended Campillo's wartime expedient—licensing unescorted shipping *(registros sueltos)*—by allowing any ship to sail from any port in Spain to America in order, he explained, perhaps with tongue in cheek, to form a pool of Spanish seamen. In 1749 Ensenada boasted that his administration had licensed "any petitioner to sail with Spanish-registry vessels" to the colonies—no way to mollify Cadiz's commercial interests.[79] And after the war, he went further, reopening the long dormant shipping route between Cadiz and Callao via Cape Horn (the first such ships may have carried French pilots who had pioneered the route from Saint-Malo during the War of Succession).[80] Finally, Ensenada's administration assembled a group, including representatives from Cadiz, to harmonize views on restructuring the colonial trade system, presumably using register vessels. To France's veteran commercial agent at Madrid, Beliardi, the maintenance of *registros sueltos* departing from many peninsular ports signaled Ensenada's long-range intention to open somewhat the Spanish transatlantic system in order to encourage more participation by peninsular businessmen.[81] This opening gesture, Beliardi noted, ran into Cadiz's resistance.

Whatever the rationale for register ships in wartime, continued licensing after 1748 irritated Cadiz traditionalists. Increased shipments and, by 1753, an inevitable postwar slump in prices and profits in colonial markets led Cadiz merchants ("extremely downhearted . . . dismayed and distressed") to claim that the transatlantic system without scheduled convoys was unmanageable.[82] Equally disturbing was authorization from Madrid allowing merchants in the colonies to forward funds to Cadiz to cover their own shipments or to receive goods on consignment.[83] These developments signaled an estrangement between Madrid and Cadiz over the key issue of "space" between Cadiz's representatives and merchants in the colonies, something other Ensenada initiatives did nothing to heal.[84]

Merchants in colonial trade at Sevilla and later at Cadiz had invariably opposed chartered companies like those in the overseas trade of Holland, England, and France on the ground they prejudiced commerce in general.[85] Uztáriz' strictures against chartered companies were consonant with this opinion in the Cadiz community. In authorizing the management of Sevilla's San Fernando *fábrica* to bypass Cadiz in trading with the colonies, did Ensenada expect to reduce subsidization of state-sponsored textile manufactories in the metropole whose products, like those of the Guadalajara enterprise, did not sell well in the domestic market? Subsequently his administration at one point did order that vessels outbound for the colonies carry a sizeable percentage—by value—of cargo in domestic products.

In the event, his solution for unprofitable state-sponsored manufactories was partial privatization, turning over plant management and product distribution to Madrid's Cinco Gremios Mayores with a guarantee of "complete independence from ministers at Court." Members of the Cinco Gremios knew the product line, their organization attracted investment capital, and they had a distribution network. Under the arrangement, agents of the Cinco Gremios would warehouse stock at Cadiz, selling to local *cargadores para Indias* who would then assume full ownership of the goods, the risks of maritime transport, and final sales to merchants in the colonies. Ensenada was supported by Hacienda officials, one of whom (Francisco Carrasco, critical of Cadiz's colonial trade exclusivism) commended him for encouraging the Cinco Gremios to extend their operations to the colonies.[86] The representatives of the Cinco Gremios, however, mindful of the predictable resistance of Cadiz merchants to handling domestic textile products, insisted on an additional proviso: the government order had to be generalized so that "no ordinary vessel nor register may use a license for the Indies trade if it carries less than one-third or one-fourth of its cargo in Spanish manufactures." The participation of the Cinco Gremios in colonial trade would, however, only materialize in the early years of the era of Charles III.[87]

Another initiative further estranging Ensenada from Cadiz and (to his regret) probably from Madrid's Cinco Gremios was the formation of a special subdivision (*Real Negociación del Giro* or simply *Real Giro*) in the Hacienda ministry to process government silver transfers to Europe's financial centers.[88] For instance, Ensenada was openly critical of the uncontrolled outflow of church income from colonial sources to Rome via the *Depositaria* at Cadiz.[89] The state, he was determined, should monitor and, moreover, tax such international transfers. Merchant bankers generally charged between 8 and 24 percent for this service as Ensenada had learned when, *intendente de marina* in the military expedition that led to Charles's occupation of Naples (1734), he had to have funds transferred from Madrid. By 1747, the War of the Austrian Succession had required transfers of more than 60 million *escudos* in specie from Spain to European capitals.[90] In fact, partly to hinder English financial operations during the war, Ensenada ordered Havana officials to retain an estimated 16 million pesos on public and private account destined for shipment to Cadiz.

The *Real Giro,* initially authorized to transfer funds from Madrid to cover diplomatic and related state disbursements, subsequently was empowered to handle all private transfers at 3 percent commission for bills issued on Paris, Amsterdam, Lisbon, Rome, and Naples. In 1753 alone the *Real Giro* shifted 100 million *reales* (about 7 million *pesos*) of colonial silver to European financial centers.[91] The transfer fees, while opposed by both Madrid's Cinco Gremios and Cadiz's *cambistas,* were paid mainly by foreign rather than Spanish merchants, Ensenada noted with satisfaction. The *Real Giro,* he boasted, despite the "distrust, even dislike, on the part of reputable men of wealth," had done away with the "tyranny of the bankers"—the *cambistas.*[92]

Ensenada's purpose in trying to modify incrementally the transatlantic system, while simultaneously reducing foreign intermediation at Cadiz, was buttressed by his hope of terminating the constraining Hapsburg legacy of unequal commercial treaties, which he characterized as "unseemly legislation imposed by France and England on the commerce of Spain."[93] Hence his administration avoided further commercial treaty negotiations and refused to tolerate English shipping in Spain's colonial waters. Earlier in the reign of Fernando VI the administration had ruled out concessions of "libre navegación" to English shipping in Spanish waters, claiming it would be tantamount to abandoning the colonies—as Ensenada put it dramatically, it would "wipe out the Indies" along with their "treasures." To prevent illicit logwood cutting along with smuggling on the Campeche and Belize coasts of Central America, Ensenada secretly ordered naval units to seize English smugglers freighting dyewoods there.[94] Those who feared antagonizing English interests (and there were many among Madrid's political elite including Prime Minister Carvajal) accused him of discarding a "prudent approach to so powerful a nation," by exposing Spain to international conflict and the possibility of considerable losses. In support of this influential bloc of internal opposition, which included the duque de Huéscar (later, Alba) and Ricardo Wall (Spain's ambassador to London), English ambassador Keene, skillful manipulator of Madrid's political factions, admonished the Spanish government that continuing Ensenada's aggressive naval tactics would poison Anglo-Spanish relations.[95]

A Quiet Coup: *Escarmiento* as Political Ritual

It was only a matter of time before opposition to the international, domestic, and colonial policies of Ensenada and his collaborators coalesced to force his ouster. To be sure, during the six postwar years (1748–54) under Prime Minister Carvajal y Lancaster, Ensenada enjoyed a charmed life. In perspective, the eleven years of Ensenada's administration were a breathing space for Spain to prepare for renewed conflict between England and France. To its credit Ensenada's administration placed a high value on preserving neutrality between a calculating ally in France and a powerful antagonist in England. (The administration was convinced that England pursued the goal of "universal empire.") The price of neutrality, however, came high: extraordinary outlays on naval rearmament by an imperial Spain which in 1748 had only twelve major warships to defend an extended empire in America.

Ensenada's ambitious economic program—actually the first sustained effort to adapt elements of French-model mercantilism—achieved only limited success partly because of limited government revenues. Madrid had to borrow on the security of specified revenues, many still farmed by the private sector. Servicing the public debt still absorbed a significant percentage of state revenues as did the ostentation and conspicuous consumption of the large royal establishment—the separate, over-staffed households of royal family members at the *reales sitios* used by the royal family at different seasons of the year—that was impervious to budgetary stringency. Despite state subsidies and other incentives to domestic manufactures, import substitution remained minimal.

The output of Spanish workshops came nowhere near meeting the demand of metropole and colonies. Nor had progress been made in developing an "active" trade with Europe or devising a transatlantic trade system capable of supplying adequately demand in America with national products. In the first half of Spain's first Bourbon century "anachronistic and ineffective" forces along with an attitude of "somnolent and self-satisfied unconcern" that had consolidated under the Hapsburgs, managed to stall major innovations.[96]

On the other hand, Ensenada's program should more properly be measured by what it attempted simultaneously and unevenly on many fronts. It rebuilt Spain's naval forces and repair facilities and began to bring under direct state control hitherto privatized imposts *(rentas provinciales)* of *cientos, millones,* and *alcabalas.* By verifying the authenticity of the outstanding *juro* debt, it managed to invalidate a significant portion and laid the bases of a contemplated single tax to be levied on income from "land, mortgages, *juros,* industrial production, and commercial earnings" in order to shift part of the tax burden to groups, especially large landholding interests, that had always rejected it.[97] It tried to introduce discipline in colonial accounts and rein in the virtually uncontrolled exploitation of native American peoples through price controls on the *reparto de mercancías.* Not least, it managed to maintain through large-scale licensing of *registros sueltos* contact with the colonies during and after the War of the Austrian Succession, while postponing what Cadiz really wanted, restoration of the 200-year-old convoy system. By authorizing as register ships neutral as well as Spanish shipping in the colonial trades, Ensenada's administration saw average annual customs receipts from colonial trade and remissions of colonial treasury surpluses rise by an impressive two-thirds between prewar 1732–38 and postwar 1748–54.[98] On balance there were reasons for Abate Facundo de Mogrevejo to praise Ensenada for "his many benefits to our trade with Europe and the Indies."[99]

Ensenada's representations of 1747 and 1751 clarified his priorities of governance: defense, revenues, taxation, administration, and colonial affairs.

They demonstrated his stance on the inflated costs of the royal establishment and on the patronage power of its high officials—on clientelism and networking of the high civil service's *colegiales* and *manteístas*. He was critical of profiteering by private sector tax-farmers at public expense and—the target of so many Spanish projectors—the troublesome volume of illicit capital transfers of colonial silver to other countries. His carefully drafted *representaciones* were intended for circulation in the upper echelons of Madrid's bureaucracy and were interpreted (or misinterpreted) depending on one's commitment to moderate change or to immobilism. They generated some support, more opposition, and among most, simply toleration or resignation. It is easy to imagine how senior officials of the Consejo de Castilla along with rural oligarchs who dominated municipal governments reacted to one of his memos, "Puntos de Gobierno." Here he faulted pointedly the Consejo de Castilla for failing to exercise one of its major responsibilities, oversight of the cities and towns of Spain. The Consejo, he complained, approved local budgets without full examination, tolerated blatant judicial favoritism for protégés ("ordinarily the most powerful and intemperate"), left unchecked illegal monopolization of municipal office by those who "do anything for personal gain," and avoided investigating gross mismanagement of local granaries. Here Ensenada was attacking frontally what was probably the most important legacy of the Hapsburg era, the political armature of Castile's integrated elites, the *Consejo Real*.

English and French diplomats scanning his representations and memoranda had to conclude that one century after west Europe's remarkable economic surge beginning in the mid-seventeenth century, Spain could no longer realistically aspire to great-power status. It could only try to preserve its overseas empire by a policy of armed neutrality. Loss of empire would bring full second-class status for Spain in Europe. Deconstructing the subtext in Ensenada's approaches to Paris and London, those governments realized that in his optic Spain had one major long-term interest—preservation of its American possessions. A well-founded preoccupation with English commercial and naval expansion in the Caribbean hub of the empire induced Ensenada to support a naval operation—a sudden sweep against English smugglers—presumably to be executed with French support. Inevitably, copies of the secret orders to authorities at Havana and Mexico City were obtained by Ambassador Keene, and London immediately demanded Ensenada's dismissal.[100] Ensenada's policy of protecting Spain's transatlantic trade from penetration by foreign merchants was a major factor in Keene's antagonism.[101]

By early 1754, Ensenada's position was eroding before gathering opposition, some apparent, the rest to be inferred. What was apparent (and many have emphasized this) were the international repercussions of his national-ist program. London felt threatened by the buildup of a respectable Spanish navy now up to forty-five modern vessels,[102] and, most of all, by stepped-up Spanish naval patrolling in the Caribbean. Furthermore, it was common knowledge that Ensenada, who did not conceal his relations with the Jesuit order, was dissatisfied with the delineation of Spanish-Portuguese borders on the Paraná-Paraguay rivers in the La Plata area and with tariff conces-sions to English products.[103] Rumor circulated that Ensenada had once remarked that Spain's concessions were due to Carvajal's incompetence, that he "let Mr. Keene lead him like a child."[104] Through the trusted secre-tary of the Neapolitan embassy at Madrid, Facundo de Mogrovejo, Ense-nada complained to Charles's confidant at Naples, the duque de Losada, and Charles then expressed his personal misgivings to Madrid. For his part, Keene tried to bribe Spanish officials to change state policy, using the Ma-drid banker Patricio Joyes as intermediary. For instance, Ensenada's collab-orator on the Consejo de Indias, Banfi, rejected a bribe by Keene, while Ensenada (of whom Keene noted "The marqués has not wished to be a friend") refused to let his daughter accept a set of diamonds offered by the English embassy.[105] On the other hand, Keene kept a cordial relationship with the duque de Huéscar, a prominent figure in the anglophile aristo-cratic faction and a supporter of Spain's ambassador to London, Ricardo Wall.

Diplomatic friction over South American boundaries, Spain's apparently Francophile stance and, above all, London's exaggerated fear of Spanish naval rearmament were symptomatic of international instability developing by early 1754. They were but the tip of the iceberg. Within Spain, dissatis-faction with domestic policies promoted by the Ensenada administration ran deep in many quarters. The *Real Giro* took away commission fees from many exchange dealers *(cambistas)* at Madrid and Cadiz.[106] Former and cur-rent tax farmers (Ensenada labeled them "that financiers' guild") foresaw termination of profitable leases, many held by members of Madrid's Cinco Gremios Mayores who insisted on renewing their "unfair contracts based on fictive loans at outrageous and damaging interest rates." As an anony-mous backer of Ensenada's program noted, in Spain "to engage in public finance" was *the* "way to wealth."[107]

Within the Cadiz colonial trading establishment, Ensenada's initiatives for the Atlantic trade system alienated many, including members of the in-fluential Cadiz consulado. When the consulado complained that allowing the ships of Sevilla's Compañía de Comercio y Fábricas de San Fernando to bypass the port of Cadiz would increase precious metals' smuggling, Ensenada's Junta de Comercio recalled the well-known smuggling operations in Cadiz bay, adding sarcastically "nothing is more notorious than the enormous quantity of silver and gold, goods and staples, brought into the bay which are then shipped abroad."[108] Ensenada's administration kept open many peninsular ports for trade with the colonies; it continued to use *registros sueltos* and did not restore the convoy system. It drew the Cinco Gremios into colonial trade and did not refute rumors that it intended to oblige Spanish strawmen in the colonial trades at Cadiz to open their account books in order to ferret out those Spaniards posing as independent merchants. Meanwhile across the Atlantic, Mexico City's *almaceneros* complained to Viceroy Horcasitas about the impact of unscheduled register ships and the neglect of the rules separating the Cadiz and Mexico City commercial domains at Jalapa. They had dissuaded Viceroy Fuenclara in 1742 from calculating their real returns from the lease of the *alcabala* farm, but they could not block Ensenada's decision in 1753 to suspend further *alcabala* contracts and to incorporate their profitable tax farm into state administration.[109] There is no question that the peninsular and colonial poles of Spain's managed transatlantic system were lobbying for reviving Hapsburg patterns of transatlantic *flotas*.

The collapse of the deteriorating position of Ensenada's administration occurred in three months: April to July 1754. In April, Carvajal y Lancaster died. Huéscar and the aristocratic faction ("reactionary minority with its aristocratic preoccupations"), opposed to Ensenada's Francophile tendencies, urged the appointment of Ricardo Wall. In mid-May Wall was recalled to Madrid where he took over from interim Prime Minister Huéscar (*mayordomo mayor* of the Royal Household).[110] Now Ensenada understood that he, his program, and his circle of collaborators no longer enjoyed support among the resurgent aristocratic and increasingly anglophile faction led by Huéscar and Wall, and he immediately resolved to exit high office with dignity to avoid the ritual ostentation of the patterned dismissal by higher authority.[111] Twice he offered his resignation, once directly to Fernando VI and once indirectly to the anglophile queen; both efforts were rejected. So Ensenada resigned himself to the inevitable: an abrupt, ritualized disgrace and internal exile to be orchestrated by the new governing faction of Wall, Huéscar, and Carbajal y Lancaster's brother Nicolás, lieutenant-colonel in the Spanish Guards regiment (and marqués de Casa Sarría) in complicity with the Consejo de Castilla.

Under cover of night on 20 July, Huéscar with the collaboration of Wall removed Ensenada along with his immediate supporters in a surgically efficient operation.[112] He dispatched two members of the *sala de alcaldes* of the Consejo de Castilla along with an officer of the Royal Guards to the home of Nicolás de Carvajal y Lancaster who furnished written instructions signed by Wall to seize Ensenada and escort him to internal exile at Granada. Ensenada was permitted neither to gather his private papers nor correspond en route. Swept up with him and also dispersed in internal exile were Agustín Pablo de Ordeñana, Josef Banfi, Alonso Pérez Delgado, and Facundo de Mogrovejo.[113] Three days later the operation was quietly closed by a terse announcement in the official *Gazeta de Madrid* of Ensenada's removal and of new appointments to Wall's ministry: Hacienda to the queen's *primer caballerizo* the conde de Valdeparaíso (José de Gauna y Portocorrero), Guerra to Sebastián de Eslava, and Marina e Indias to Julián de Arriaga.

All were known quantities and knowledgeable in colonial affairs, a competence prized in light of imminent decisions on colonial matters. Eslava, a Navarrese, had commanded the Cartagena garrison against Anson's naval forces (1740) and had been New Granada's first viceroy. One of his brothers was an *oidor* at Bogotá, another had briefed Antonio de Ulloa about the misuse of *reparto de mercancías*, which Eslava nonetheless supported as the only means of overcoming Amerindians' "laziness, carelessness, and sloth with respect to any work whatsoever, inclined as they are to idleness, drink, and other vices."[114] Arriaga, a naval officer, had been sent as governor to Caracas in 1749 to investigate *criollo* grievances behind their uprising against factors of the Guipuzcoan Company, arrange a settlement, and recommend measures for improving the colony's external trade.[115] Gauna y Portocarrero had served on the Consejo de Indias since 1740. In the semiotics of the time, these appointments signaled to Madrid's political class the policy directions of the newly installed Wall ministry. It would be nationalist in a markedly traditional style, avoiding unsettling innovations that might ruffle comfortably established domestic and colonial interest groups. In international affairs, it would pursue a distancing from France that some interpreted as anglophile.

On one level there would seem to be nothing uncommon about replacing a prominent cabinet officer over policy differences, executive style, or plain incompatibility with influential members of the political elite. Ensenada could have been eased out, it is arguable, before July 1754—witness his two efforts to resign. Instead, acting Prime Minister Huéscar directed Ensenada to continue to handle diplomatic correspondence relating to the ministries for which he was responsible. Was this a symbol of reassurance or a device to retain Ensenada until Wall had returned from London? On another level, then, one must ask: why was Ensenada's resignation unacceptable?

One explanation involves the ritual of dismissal in the political process as it functioned in Spain's old regime in the century of enlightenment.

Ensenada as high-profile policy-maker remained invulnerable as long as Carvajal lived, and the royal family—king and consort—retained confidence in Ensenada's policies. This was the platform on which elite politics in early Bourbon Spain operated. Were Ensenada allowed to resign his multiple secretariats *following* a period of public criticism, inevitably questions might arise about Carvajal's (and the royal family's) long tolerance and apparent support of the most influential figure, the personification of policy, in the embryonic cabinet system. It was common knowledge among Madrid's political elite that Padre Rávago (Fernando's confessor, a Jesuit) rated Carvajal's competence low, an opinion Ensenada shared. Nonetheless, the political process called for the semblance of "absolute," discretionary power exercised by the *primer secretario* in the king's name. The fact that the king did not enjoy absolute authority and that the first secretary lacked the unalloyed respect of immediate subordinates had to remain masked from public view. Monarch and ministry seemingly cooperated without friction—so mandated the ritualized process of governance.

This explains the political style in eighteenth-century Spain for discarding the real architect of what influential factions might consider questionable national policy. Since the political process conjoined policy and its principal architect inseparably, once the architect's patron disappeared, the policy became disposable. Debate over policy was not a public affair—press censorship took care of that—lest the "absolute" authority of the monarchy be questioned. For public discussion might provide an opportunity to mobilize a crowd or "people's" movement in support of a leader such as Ensenada—this was the subtext of political discourse. Rejection of policy, therefore, called for the ritualized, brutal, surgical removal of the bureaucratic embodiment of the rejected policy. The minister and his policy required simultaneous "disgrace." The embodiment of the disgraced policy was to remain incommunicado and—at least to the public—impassive and uncomplaining, loyal and obedient.[116] Of course, he could not remain *in situ;* under cover of night he had to be arrested and packed off under guard. The decision by Wall and the aristocratic faction was cloaked, of course, in royal "absolutism" indisputably correct and just. Still, the ritual needed a patina of public support. So the Consejo de Castilla's *alcaldes de casa y corte* tolerated or encouraged posting on Madrid street corners of anonymous manuscript *pasquinades*—the product of professional pens-for-hire—vilifying the deposed minister by citing personal frailties: over-display of wealth by one not to the manner born, his corruptibility, clientelism, nepotism, favoritism—character assassination as proof of incompetence. The surface discourse portrayed a trusting but distant monarch poorly served by a corrupt, self-serving civil servant.[117]

The ritual of deposition included an indispensable fall-out, aftershocks of a sort. Ritual mandated that Ensenada's "disgrace" be matched by the "disgrace" of advisers and confidants in his entourage, hence their immediate internal exile, too. Abrupt removal of minister and collaborators signaled the intended root-and-branch elimination of Ensenada's policy as well as the persistence of an "even deeper reality, of the mentalities and behavioral patterns of the 'closed society.'" At the same time their ouster also laid bare the fundamental flaw in Spain's Bourbon regime, the "internal fragility of reformist structures," for their *reformismo* was the product only of the "voluntarism of intellectuals and technicians," not of pressure from "an emergent class."[118]

Now, in the critical five years before Charles left Naples for Madrid as king of Spain, Wall, Huéscar, and Valdeparaíso in a kind of aristocratic resurgence had their moment to prove their competence or incompetence when, in 1756, Anglo-French conflict flared again over empire in America and South Asia, and Spain scrambled to preserve a still inadequately armed neutrality.

The policy-directions of the new ministerial cadre were soon apparent. Convoys to Veracruz were authorized in 1755, then postponed for two years by petitions of the merchants of Mexico City joined by Cadiz, claiming oversupply in the colony. Second, despite the impressive amount of data gathered by Ensenada's *catastro*, Valdeparaíso and subordinates at Hacienda ignored the *única contribución* as the basis of a more equitable tax structure. They were also responsible for severe financial and operational problems in the regime's industrial showpiece, the Guadalajara woolen manufactory complex.[119] Third, under Wall's direction, foreign policy tilted away from France and, when warfare between France and England recommenced in 1756, toward a precarious neutrality. The policies of Wall, Huéscar, and Valdeparaíso would bring Spain to "one of the great crises of its history in the eighteenth century."[120]

Bourbon Spain's Second Crisis, 1756–59

Once again an external factor—aggression over colonies in the age of high commercial capitalism—opened Spain's second major crisis of the eighteenth century. As the war widened, it became a confrontation between Spain's structural involution and immobilism and England's commercial dynamism and naval aggression in the western Atlantic. France's collapse in Canada heightened fears of further English expansion southward from its North American colonies into Florida and then via the Lower Mississippi Valley to the Gulf of Mexico and even beyond to the northern frontiers of the mining colony of New Spain at Santa Fe and Durango. The French had no reservations about the importance of New Spain, for the "preservation of the Kingdom of Mexico is a matter of grave consequence for Spain, while for France . . . the danger . . . is obvious and imminent."[121]

Recognition of the power of English naval units had recommended to some in the cabinet of Carvajal y Lancaster a minimal distancing of Bourbon Spain from Bourbon France. Perhaps the Colbertian paradigm of national development was losing luster for those Spaniards shifting their admiration toward what they interpreted as exceptional English skill in fine-tuning tariffs and in protectionism—a different form of *dirigisme?* Or perhaps the Spanish political class began to accept the uncomfortable reality that, lacking a solid base in human resources and capital, development of the metropole's manufactures and an effective colonial compact were both "artificial and idealistic?"[122] The prospect of English aggression was pushing Madrid toward neutrality in another Anglo-French imperialist conflict.[123] Once omnipotent in the late seventeenth century, France, after the loss of Canada, seemed "feeble, flabby, and decadent" to Gándara, a Spanish anglophile in the 1750s.[124] Ensenada's ouster closed the first sustained effort to adapt the French model of growth to Spain.

To call Ensenada's ouster a "quiet" coup risks minimizing its significance in the political evolution of eighteenth-century Spain. It was the third resort to the political object-lesson or *escarmiento* in the Spanish political process since the 1690s in order to remove a leadership that promised to effect overdue change. The first had eliminated Oropesa in the 1690s. The second followed twenty-five years later with the removal of Orry and Macanaz. Because of these events, Patiño and then, all too briefly, Campillo along with many *proyectistas* who were troubled by the absence of visible movement on many metropolitan and colonial issues had to move circumspectly.

What separated Ensenada's experience from that of Oropesa and Orry-Macanaz was a radically different international context. The war ending in 1748 revealed an England that was far more powerful than it had been three decades earlier at Utrecht. It was entrenched in the Indian subcontinent and was a commercial giant backed by the largest (and probably the most efficient) naval force in the Atlantic world. Ensenada's Spain was no longer a leading power. Now its "grandeur" lay outside itself, overseas in its American colonies, precisely where heightened competition between English and

French blocs was ominously evident. What Utrecht had created, a space and time for a Spanish *renovación,* was disappearing by 1748. This is what impelled Ensenada and his group to try to move on both peninsular and colonial fronts—as it turned out, at great risk. As Fernando VI's government drifted during his terminal illness, members of Madrid's political class contemplated a paradigmatic shift of policy toward effective action on national and colonial issues under his successor. Vital to this development was the prospect that key personnel and appropriate policy changes would be undertaken by Fernando's half-brother Charles.

To some at Madrid, it was clear that change in Spain and its empire would require the reigning monarch's unequivocal and sustained support, willing to move on multiple fronts simultaneously, confident that committed civil servants would execute policy without foot-dragging. Those espousing change longed for an unquestioned, a real rather than nominal absolutist authority and, above all, leadership at the ministerial level personified by a "secretario . . . de acción," who in ruthless authoritarian fashion might adapt the mercantilist concept of the colonial pact to new realities in metropole and colonies by eliminating multiple and costly commercial formalities, convoys, and Cadiz's port monopoly.

Since seven decades of uncoordinated essays at a Spanish developmental paradigm had failed, the incoming regime of Charles III would have to decide quickly which Hapsburg legacies to modify or abandon, where to assign priority, and who would be the enthusiastic as well as dependable collaborators. A tall order for Charles and Squillace (Esquilache) when news of Fernando's death came to Naples in late 1759. Anyone giving a close reading to the history of Bourbon Spain and its overseas empire had to realize that change in the guise of "renovation" or "reestablishment"—today's modernization—was always a hazardous operation. Here was a situation crying for change yet making change itself impossible. To select for Spanish conditions elements of other nations' praxis was taxing enough; to apply them could become a violent process.

Now one can appreciate the factors that made the task of Spain's projectors a difficult balancing act and that explain the Spanish paradigm of tardy mercantilism. On the one hand, pressures from the international economy of late commercial capitalism demanded that European states develop their economies rather than rely upon growth alone. The early interventionist state was expected to stimulate population growth, channel "surplus" labor into gainful employment, raise agricultural output of food and raw materials, and foster an industrial plant that would export semi-elaborated and finished goods preferably to a managed market of colonial consumers who also produced marketable staples. But here was the first dilemma: such developmental (and, inevitably, protectionist) policies in the short run threatened the ever-necessary flow of income derived from customs duties, especially from colonial trade. They might even precipitate retaliatory action by more powerful aggrieved powers.

A Spanish paradigm had to incorporate its unique, enduring colonial factor: silver mining benefiting the private sector in the colonies and metropole, as well as the state. Here surfaced a second dilemma: private and public silver earnings had nourished for generations the very structures that in the eighteenth century inhibited development of the Spanish economy. Torn between the requirements of national development and financial liquidity as state outlays on defense and bureaucracy rose uncontrollably, Spanish policy-makers found short-term pragmatism preferable in order to protect the product of the silver mines of New Spain.

Finally, there was a third dilemma. At the middle of the eighteenth century, Madrid's ministries believed that an explicitly articulated protectionist developmental policy for the metropole would endanger neutrality in the tension and conflict of the cold and often hot war between England and France. Protectionism and outright prohibition of selected imports invariably antagonized English and French manufacturers and exporters as well as their respective governments. Strengthening Spain's naval and military forces also antagonized both the English admiralty and the French war ministry. At the same time, it remained moot whether a massive financial commitment to expanding Spain's navy could effectively protect colonial shipping.

Thus what seemed simple solutions to problems of growth and development were complex and interrelated, inextricably weaving together colonial, peninsular, and European factors. Put another way, in the long run, a policy conjoining neutrality and development might prove more costly than alliance with France and stagnation. This clarifies the caution of the published *proyectistas,* their piecemeal approaches and maddeningly belated adjustments. They recognized the granite-like outcrops of the Hapsburg legacy. In hindsight we know that only an unexpected conjuncture of internal and external pressures could open the way to rapid change. Change of direction by empires, however, has always been a wrenching process. This the political elites of Spain and its empire would learn the hard way over the next half-century, beginning with the ill-fated *renovación* pushed by Charles III's initial Hacienda minister, the marqués de Esquilache.

9. By Way of Conclusion

 ·

Until recently the historiography of Spain since the age of Fernando and Isabel divorced metropole from colonies, minimizing the repercussions of colonialism as Spain emerged from its late medieval chrysalis on Europe's periphery to play an unexpected, crucial, hegemonic role in western Europe until the middle of the seventeenth century. While seminal studies by Clarence Haring *(Trade and Navigation)*, Earl Hamilton *(American Treasure)*, Ramón Carande *(Carlos V y sus banqueros)*, José López Larraz *(La época del mercantilismo en Castilla)* and, more recently, by Jaime Vicens Vives, Antonio Domínguez Ortiz, Guillermo Céspedes del Castillo, John Elliot, Henry Kamen, Josep Fontana and Antonio García-Baquero adverted to the importance of the Spanish empire, they were counterbalanced, even overbalanced by studies emphasizing *Europe*'s expansion, *Europe*'s hegemony, *Europe*'s contact with what *Europeans* called their "new" world whose culture and technology, we now belatedly recognize, were already thousands of years "old." It is time to reconsider the evolution of the Atlantic economy from the Spanish and Spanish colonial vantage point and to examine the major elements of the legacy of the two-centuries-old Hapsburg dynasty and their projection into Spain's early Bourbon era.

Through mechanisms of conquest, occupation, and consolidation in the western Atlantic, late medieval Spain contributed in unique ways to the growth and development of commercial capitalism in its pre- and post-1650 phases. The influx first of Caribbean gold and then massive remissions of silver, mined, processed, and minted in the viceroyalties of Peru and New Spain, accelerated production and exchange in western Europe and expanded its trade with north, or maritime, Europe and the eastern Mediterranean as well as trading posts in west Africa and then in southeast and east Asia. Mines, mine workers and mine owners, merchants and artisans of Potosí, Oruro, and Huancavelica, of Taxco, Zacatecas, and Guanajuato fueled the growth of market-based and market-shaping institutions spreading from local to provincial to national and ultimately to international levels. They created the first stages of what we now, on the threshold of the twenty-first century, term a global market-based economy, penetrating everywhere.

The consequences in the colonies were different from those in the metropole. Silver pesos and bullion enriched a few, impoverished many. Colonial elites both peninsular and criollo neglected the export potential of the American continent's staples as well as the natural fibers that skilled pre-conquest native artisans had turned into cotton and woolen fabrics extraordinary in weave, texture, and design. Merchants in the colonies preferred to import European and Asian high-value textiles, leaving the low-income market to local producers. They paid no attention to the skills of indigenous metalsmiths from Colombia to Central America, preferring to seize, melt down, and then export as gold bullion extraordinary products of the goldsmith's craft. Sugar plantations in the Caribbean islands of Hispaniola and Cuba already in place in the first half of the sixteenth century were not developed. The cocoa bean, which Spaniards first encountered in New Spain and was widely cultivated in Venezuela, was initially popularized and distributed in Europe by the Dutch, not the Spanish—and this does not end the list of roads not taken. By the same token, resources in the metropole itself in the form of fine merino wools and raw silk, while forming the basis of a briefly expanded textile manufacture in the sixteenth century, were subsequently exported to Europe's manufactories only to return to Spain as finished European imports.

Silver, however, as we have noted, did not flow gravity-driven from inner Peru and central and north New Spain to Europe and the Far East. It had to be siphoned off by primitive market mechanisms, mainly exchanged for imported goods whose composition was quickly dominated by the products of west Europe's leading-edge industries: woolens, linens, and silks fabricated in workshops in Holland and Flanders, England and France, and Italy and Germany. As American silver flooded into western Europe in the 1550s then peaked in the three or four decades after 1590, there came a counterflow of merchandise from western Europe through Lower Andalusia directed to the small yet growing mass of consumers in the Spanish colonial economy unevenly becoming monetized. At first the awesome demographic consequences of Spanish occupation depressed the aggregate level of colonial demand for imports—the mining nuclei and the capital cities of Lima and Mexico excepted. But once population recovery commenced at the end of the seventeenth century and New Spain's mining output surged,

Europe's exporters pressed merchants at Sevilla and Cadiz to augment the flow of their products to increasingly market-oriented, commercialized consumers in the cities, towns, and provinces of colonial Spanish America. Now, in addition, the colonies received a rising volume of Asian linens, cottons, porcelains, and other luxury goods shipped from Manila across the Pacific to Acapulco and thence distributed to other Spanish colonies.

Moreover, the flow of European goods into the Spanish transatlantic pipeline formally anchored in Lower Andalusia also leaked informally, illegally, and uncontainably into Spain's colonies through Dutch, English, and French Caribbean islands, mostly occupied and developed after 1650. The original purpose of those colonies was to serve as entrepôts whence smugglers could operate. The subsequent transfer by the Dutch of sugar production techniques from northeastern Brazil to Caribbean islands about the time they withdrew from Pernambuco coupled to Dutch control of the west African slave trade at that time, transformed first Antigua, Barbados, Martinique, and Guadeloupe and then, in the first half of the eighteenth century, Jamaica and Saint-Domingue into extraordinary engines of commercial agriculture generating sugar, tobacco, indigo, and coffee for an expanding mass of west European consumers further enriched by American silver inflows. This innovative complex—plantation colonies relying on gang labor, an elastic supply of forced labor funneled through the African slave trade to produce valuable exportables whose declining prices enlarged consumption and, finally, sustained smuggling with Spanish ports in and around the Caribbean—stimulated capitalism in western Europe. This complex joined to American silver was, in large measure, responsible for the flowering of commercial capitalism that ended in the first industrial age in western Europe.

The Bourbon dynasty inherited an imperial Spain forged during the initial phase of commercial capitalism by the persistence of late-medieval structures of polity, society, values, and religious orthodoxy associated with the Hapsburgs ("Los Austrias"). A patrimonial polity, a Castilian agricultural and ranching economy of large landed estates and impoverished peasantry, a system of cultural beliefs attuned to an already defunct concept of Catholic universality—all sustained by silver income from the American colonies for the public and private sectors—undergirded imperial Spain's hegemony in western Europe from roughly 1520 to about 1650.

Over the following fifty years, an informal consensus on the politics of change in northwestern Europe was unavoidable. Somehow the requirements of evolving commercial bourgeoisies in England and France had to be fitted with those of emerging nation-states. Consensus on national policy took one of two forms. In England, there was regicide and the imposition of limited parliamentary institutions. In France, there was expansion of central authority through formidable military forces and an enlarged state bureaucracy. Both forms of consensus expressed the objectives of their emerging national bourgeoisies. In Spain, however, small and dispersed bourgeois nuclei cultivated a local or regional rather than a national vision; they found comfortable niches, opportunities for upward social mobility, in Spain's patrimonial society. Unlike England and France, Spain had to undergo a long, painful quest for both a paradigm and appropriate instruments of growth as it wrestled with the burden of the Hapsburg legacy.

Meanwhile, with the evolution of England and France and their eclipse of Holland, the stagnation of imperial Spain deepened, and the gap between involuting Spain and its principal European competitors widened. England and France, traveling separate and idiosyncratic paths, became late "model" monarchies in the course of the second and last phase of commercial capitalism still propelled by American silver mining. Each cultivated the conditions of sustained economic growth that turned into development by pursuing rational growth policies, overseas trading partners and colonial enterprises, and by tapping into the ever-growing volume of silver that now came largely from New Spain.

The source of the longevity of the Spanish empire—the first great colonial empire of modern Europe—can be found in the logic of its *ad hoc* responses to unpredictable challenges. The responses met the goals of a precocious colonial power limited by budget and personnel in harnessing the people and resources of advanced paleolithic cultures in two vast viceroyalties, New Spain and Peru. There Castilian overlords redirected native cultures toward a Spanish variant of the west Europe culture that emphasized a combination of monotheism and polytheism in religion, and whose economy was shifting toward the individual and away from the communal.

It was indeed an encounter in which a patrimonial European state ruthlessly subordinated indigenous, less well-armed cultures. In fact, Castilians put in place in their transatlantic trading system a form of early commercial capitalism more "managed" than in Spain itself. If Castile's economy displayed a seigneurial façade at times, it was hardly feudal. While American silver financed the brief hegemonic role of Hapsburg Spain in Europe, at the same time it undergirded a Spanish society of involuting aristocratic values, a pervasive and invasive ecclesiastical and bureaucratic establishment, and a polity that was hardly "absolutist." The involuting Spanish state, society, and economy survived as long as expansionist states did not seriously threaten the empire in America. Spain's civil servants and merchants, relying upon the reality (and mirage) of colonial silver, did not enter upon the road to development taken by England and France. Money earned in colonial mining did not spur development in the metropole—it created an illusion of wealth and power. Reexporting silver required no social change. As nineteenth-century liberalism affected historians, it was inevitable that the historiography of eighteenth-century Spain should reflect the belief that the Hapsburg-to-Bourbon dynastic transition somehow marked a clear progression from stagnation *(decadencia)* to "reform." In fact, the first seven decades of the same century received little academic attention: the integrated elites' resistance to innovation offered only case studies of failure.

In probing for elements of a growth paradigm in *proyectistas'* works of the first half of Spain's eighteenth century, several patterns surface. The longer a social system involutes by adapting to stimuli without making fundamental structural changes, the greater becomes its capacity to deflect subsequent pressures to change. Philip V's bureaucratic collaborators and French technicians believed that administrative changes could minimize, perhaps erode, traditional structures and mentalities. They were mistaken. Their few innovations—isolated elements of a mercantilist policy—were quickly blunted, since dynastic change from Hapsburg to Bourbon by itself was incapable of sidelining the core structures, value system, mentality and—perhaps key—the personnel who had managed the Hapsburg order. At bottom projectors aimed only to adapt structures to a changing reality; in accepting the framework of existing society, they had to accept the logic of Spain's old regime. That regime survived while breeding disillusionment among policy-ideators and policy executors alike.

Long minimized is *the* factor that fed the persistent involution of Hapsburg structures: silver from America's mines—in the eighteenth century from the mining camps of Zacatecas and Guanajuato in New Spain. Silver pesos and bullion leaked from the Caribbean and from Lower Andalusia, leakages tolerated even as they became more pronounced after 1715. Madrid, transferring its *asiento* under duress to English interests in 1713, grossly underestimated English merchants' market-driven ingenuity in exploiting that contractual innovation, the annual register vessel, the "permission" ship. The equilibrium between formal channels of silver flows and informal leakages visible between 1660 and 1700, however, seems to have remained stable until London declared war in 1739 precisely over Spanish contestation of growing English smuggling activity in the Caribbean. Then the equilibrium collapsed. English naval units attacked ports frequented by the *galeones* at Cartagena and Portobelo (and later at Santiago de Cuba off Jamaica's northwest coast) and threatened to establish permanent footholds on the

Spanish mainland, and Madrid, in wartime, turned to French and neutral merchant shipping to supply the American colonies and maintain transatlantic communications.

The mid-century despair after years of *proyectista* speculation, a few censored publications, the inability of the Spanish state consistently to pursue basic elements of a delayed development policy and Ensenada's desperate eleven-year effort to refashion state finance, colonial policy, and national defense, were complementary and comprehensible. They responded to the growing production of silver in New Spain's mines, the deepening market-orientation in the colonies, and the uncontainable smuggling that were also sharpening international competition of expansionist French and English interests. At the same time, incapacity to match colonialist competitors in providing the Spanish colonies with domestic products aggravated Spain's sense of inferiority and dependence and fostered a disheartening awareness of the gap between developing northwest Europe and underdeveloped Spain. By mid-century *proyectistas'* vision of harnessing colonial resources to their metropole's development in a colonial compact was fading—the consequence of roads not taken by Spain under commercial capitalism since the age of discovery.

Invariably it was implicit in *proyectista* discourse that two hundred years of the Hapsburg regime in the metropole joined to dependence upon American mines and neglect of the colonies' broad range of human and natural resources had blocked the flowering of assertive commercial bourgeoisies like those in late seventeenth-century Holland, France, and England. Neither at home nor in the colonies did Hapsburg Spain nurture the type of mercantile interests that by 1660 had managed in England to push aside the once hegemonic merchant adventurers sheltered behind privileged companies or, in France, were eager to market abroad Lyon silks, Breton and Normand linens, or Amiens, Rouen, and Beauvais woolens. By contrast Spain's commercial bourgeoisies in the early eighteenth century remained isolated nuclei at Sevilla, Cadiz, Madrid, and Barcelona. Their activity was circumscribed mainly to procurement and marketing of imported goods. Theirs was a traffic of intermediaries, of buying cheap and selling dear, financed by foreign resident communities better supplied, informed, and connected internationally, who delivered to Spain's merchants goods produced outside Spain.

One legacy of Hapsburg involution was a Spanish variant of a comprador bourgeoisie that avoided domestic products which—when available—they considered to be of poor quality, outmoded, and overpriced. Once the transatlantic trading system was set in place by the mid-sixteenth century,

Lower Andalusia's merchant community cooperated with (and coopted, too) state officials in the Casa de Contratación and the Consejo de Indias to maintain a system that by 1650 had for them no viable alternatives. The opportunity costs were not negligible. To high civil servants, as to seventeenth-century *arbitristas* and eighteenth-century *proyectistas* fell the responsibility of a national policy for adjusting Spain and its American empire to a rapidly changing international scene. Many were bureaucrats of vision (some indeed visionary), but they lacked a supporting commercial bourgeoisie with a national vision willing to challenge the structures and interests that were in place. Consequently *proyectistas* turned to the state to initiate and manage change, emphasizing the role of a competent minister supported by *the* source of authority in the *monarquía,* the crown. In fact they had to ideate and mythify the absolutism of a mercantilist state directed by an authoritarian executive. Was the Spanish state in 1759 that "absolutist?" The inability of a carefully selected leading minister to carry out a policy of even moderate change in the metropole and colonies was symbolized by the failed enterprise of Ensenada, perhaps the most activist "reformer" in Spain in the first half of the eighteenth century. His ouster revealed the limits of the Bourbon state, the shallowness of its "absolutism."

It is gross oversimplification to blame the absence of the enterprising bourgeoisies found in northwest Europe in the late seventeenth and early eighteenth centuries solely on the antibusiness value system of a society dominated by a landed aristocracy of seigneurial privilege. Closer analysis shows that factors supporting merchants in post-1650 France, England, and Holland—investment pools, joint-stock companies, banking and credit facilities, informational networks, judicial systems enforcing contractual obligations against the extra-legal pretensions of the holders of privilege—were largely absent in Spain. There were savings, but they tended to flow toward government obligations offering attractive interest rates or to rural and urban real estate, which conferred security and status. Businessmen have always appraised risk factors in deciding whether to modify operational styles, accept new product lines, or send abroad purchasing agents. For Spanish merchants, the risks (now termed "opportunity costs") of change seemed too great when foreign resident merchants in the export enclaves at Sevilla or Cadiz readily provided competitive goods. Still, *proyectistas* from Uztáriz to Gándara were drawn to elements of Colbertism because they believed that French merchants at Rouen, Nantes, and Bordeaux, who before 1660 felt inferior to Dutch merchants, had somehow caught up with the foreign competition under Colbert and Louis XIV.

While the mentality of Lower Andalusian merchants in the colonial trades remained immobile when external conditions began to change rapidly after Utrecht, even the best-adapted structures and attitudes were endangered. So it seemed to some among Spain's political elite between 1740 and 1760. Meanwhile, Cadiz's merchants only dimly envisioned the extraordinary international shifts as a consequence of the fast-moving market-driven expansion of the west European economy after mid-century. These were at the root of the second crisis confronting imperial Spain.

Proyectistas were not businessmen, although they often drew upon business expertise. They prided themselves on their broad national conspectus of the interests of the commonwealth, not those of a privileged core of merchants. This is why frequently one encounters in *proyectista* literature a carefully drawn distinction between a business-oriented, localistic policy *(política mercantil)* and a nation-favoring one *(política comercial)*. The *proyectistas* projected a vision of the state-that-might-be; Lower Andalusia's merchants insisted on the state-that-existed, already providing security for established interests that they shared, of course, with others in Spanish society. In the long run, initiative for change by careful adjustment still lay with the state bureaucracy whose members—hardly a *clase dirigente*—might try to bypass traditionalists at moments of acute crisis. This is what happened between 1759 and 1766, the initial years of Charles III.

Notes

. . . .

In preparing this volume, the authors consulted manuscript materials in the following repositories:

AAEPar   Quai d'Orsay (Paris)
AGI   Archivo General de Indias (Sevilla)
AGN   Archivo General del la Nación (Mexico City)
AGSim   Archivo General (Simancas)
AHN   Archivo Histórico Nacional (Madrid)
ANPar   Archives Nationales (Paris)
BMus   British Museum (London)
BNMad   Biblioteca Nacional (Madrid)
BNMex   Biblioteca Nacional (Mexico City)
BNPar   Bibliothèque Nationale (Paris)
BRAHM   Real Academia de la História (Madrid)
BRPal   Biblioteca del Real Palacio (Madrid)
MN   Museo Naval (Madrid)
NYPub   New York Public Library
AE   Affaires Etrangères
CP   Correspondance Politique

   Manuscript collections utilized include the following: (Mexico City) AGN: Consulado, Archivo Histórico de Hacienda, and Historia; BNMex: Reales Ordenes; (Sevilla) AGI: Indiferente General, Audiencia de Mexico and Consulado; (Madrid) AHN: Consejos and Estado; BRPal: Ayala collection; BRAHM: Mata Linares collection; and materials in (BNMad) and (MN); (Simancas) AGSim: Dirección General de Rentas (2a remesa) and Marina; (Paris) ANPar: B I and B III of Affaires Etrangères; BNPar: Fonds Français and Espagnol; AAEPar: Correspondance Politique, Consulaire and Mémoires et Documents; (London) BMus: Egerton and Additional Manuscripts; (New York) NYPub: Rich collection.

1. Spain, Europe, and The Atlantic System, 1500–1700

1. Góngora, *Studies in the Colonial History of Spanish America*, 2–3.

2. See Kamen, "The Decline of Spain," 24–50, the critical response of Israel, "The Decline of Spain," 170–80, and Kamen's, "Rejoinder," 181–85. Careful reading of Ramon Carande's *Carlos V* and José Larraz López's *La época del mercantilismo*, both published decades ago, suggested such structural weaknesses in the Castilian economy as early as 1500, if not before.

3. On the origins and development of sheep ranching and raw wool exports, see Vicens Vives, *Economic History of Spain*, 241, 250–52; the recent summary by García Sanz and Sanz Fernandez, "Agricultura y ganadería," 29–30, 32, 35; and Ubieto et al., *Introducción a la historia de España*, 167–68, 206–7. Ubieto suggests that the early prominence of churchmen and noblemen in the sheepherders' guild (*mesta*) led to preference for luxury imports from the Low Countries, the weakness of Spain's woolen manufacture, and the small size of the Spanish bourgeoisie. Ibid., 163–68, 254–55.

4. García de Quevedo y Concillón, *Ordenanzas;* Basas Fernández, *El Consulado de Burgos*, 29–33; and Suárez Fernández, *Navegación y comercio*.

5. The Burgos-Bilbao rivalry over the carrying trade to Bruges is covered by Basas Fernández, *Consulado de Burgos*, 36–46; Guiard-Larrauri, *Historia del Consulado y Casa de Contratación*, 1:15–21; and Smith, *Spanish Guild Merchant*, 67–74.

6. Cf. Basas Fernández, *Consulado de Burgos*, 51–54, 81 ff.

7. Vicens Vives, *Economic History of Spain*, 101–21.

8. Chaunu and Chaunu, *Séville et l'Atlantique*, vol. 8, pt. 1,chaps. 1–2.

9. On foreign resident merchants at Sevilla, see Pike, *Enterprise and Adventure*, and Sánchez de Sopranis, "Las naciones extrangeras en Cádiz durante el siglo XVII," 639–77. There is also the fine monograph on Sevilla as Castile's principal commercial hub in the late fifteenth century by Enrique Otte, *Sevilla y sus mercaderes*.

10. On the mentality of the early Spanish emigrants to the New World, see Chevalier, "En lisant les 'novelas,' 105–30; Canny and Pagden, eds., *Colonial Identity;* Altman, *Emigrants and Society*, and Elliott, *The Old World and the New*.

11. Otte, *Sevilla y sus mercaderes*, 186.

12. Haring, *Trade and Navigation*, 3–24, 201–9; Chaunu and Chaunu, *Séville et l'Atlantique*, vol. 8, pt. 1, 196, 253. See also Antúñez y Acevedo, *Memorias históricas*, which notes how, after 1529, Malaga and other peninsula ports were deliberately isolated from Spanish colonial trade.

13. On one-port monopoly, an early stage of mercantilism according to Eli Heckscher, see *Mercantilism*, vol. 1.

14. Smith, *Spanish Guild Merchant*, 91–100.

15. Haring, *Trade and Navigation*, 21–32, 43–44; Veitía Linage, *Norte*, bk. 1, chap. xvii, para. 26.

16. Céspedes del Castillo, *La avería*, 25ff. This model monograph's conclusions (136–40) bear careful examination.

17. Smith, *Spanish Guild Merchant*, 105–9; Haring, *Trade and Navigation*, 51–53, 73; Domínguez Ortiz, *Orto y Ocaso de Sevilla*, chaps. 7–8.

18. For stipulations on volume of outgoing cargo per convoy, see Veitía Linage, *Norte*, vol. 1, chap. xvii, para. 34; for minimum cargo required, vol. 1, chap. xxix,

para. 10; for the consulados's privilege to choose the *escribano de sacas* and define his function, vol. 1, chap. xvii, para. 32; chap. xxvii, para 19; and vol. 2, chap. vii, para. 15. Significantly the office of the *escribanía de sacas* ("por cuyas manos pasaba todo el comercio de Sevilla") was bought by the duque de Lerma. Domínguez Ortiz, *Las clases privilegiadas*, 127

19. In pricing exports, foreign commercial houses included the presumptive profit on sales at Sevilla as well as presumptive profit on colonial sales. When realized, Michel Morineau argues, profits on the American trade were "super-bénéfices." *Incroyables gazettes*, 290–91.

20. Everaert, *Handel*, 898–99, 903–4.

21. The mark-up between prices listed on manifests at Sevilla and those current at colonial fairs (Portobelo, Cartagena) averaged 58 percent (1650–72), although varying from 100 (1650) to 30 percent (1667). The practice of pricing in vellon at Sevilla and converting to silver pesos at sales probably pushed the average mark-up to 70 percent at minimum. García Fuentes, *Comercio español*, 81–83.

22. Veitía Linaje's otherwise comprehensive manual does not discuss the colonial fair *(feria)* exchange mechanism. Haring's study covers only Castilian fairs; he refers briefly to a Jalapa fair, omitting sources *(Trade and Navigation*, 204 note 1). On Castilian fairs, see Sarabia de la Calle, *Instrucción de mercaderes*. On the *feria* at Portobelo drawing the appetite and imagination of Europeans, see Vila Vilar, "Las ferias de Portobelo," 275–337, especially 279–85. For late medieval European fairs with which the Spanish colonial fairs may be contrasted, see Verlinden, "Markets and Fairs," in Postan and Rich, eds., *Economic History of Europe*, vol. 4, chap. 3, and Bautier, *Sur l'histoire économique de la France médiévale*, chap. 7.

23. Schurz, *The Manila Galleon* (New York, 1939); Alvarez de Abreu, ed., *Extracto historial del comercio entre Filipinas y Nueva España.*

24. Morineau, *Incroyables gazettes*, 301, note 179. Textiles constituted by far the bulk of French exports in the 1690s (and probably earlier) to Spain, with better qualities reexported to the Spanish colonies. In fact, colonial prices help set French domestic levels (García Fuentes, *Comercio español*, 294 and Morineau, *Incroyables gazettes*, 263). In the seventeenth century it was reported that at Lima on "la esquina principal de la plaça que llaman de los mercaderes, salen dos calles, las mas ricas que ay en las Yndias, porque en ellas están las tiendas de los mercaderes, donde se benden todas las cosas preciosas y de estima, que Ynglaterra, Frandez, Alemania, Ytalia y España produzen, labran y tejen, porque todas las embian y van a parar a esta ciudad, de donde se distrybuyen por todo el Reino, de suerte que . . . thelas, brocados, terciopelos, panos finos, rajas, damascos, sedas, pasamanos, franjones, todo lo hallarán aqui y a medida de su boluntad, como se estubiera en las mas ricas y frequentadísimas ferias de Amberes, Londres, Leon en Francia, Medina del Campo, Sevilla y Lisboa . . . ." Murua quoted in Assadourian, *El sistema de la economía colonial*, 130, n. 4.

25. Even in the sixteenth century, imports of French and Flemish linens and Florentine, Genoese, and Flemish silks were notable. As early as 1516, Burgos's wool exporters preferred payment in Flemish, rather than Spanish, woolens. Basas Fernández, *Consulado de Burgos*, 132–33, 234–35.

26. Morineau, *Incroyables gazettes*, 298.

27. A case in point is the *derecho de Balbas* collected by the Consulado de Sevilla

(and its successor, Cádiz) after 1624. Penalized for grossly undervaluing cargo to Portobelo, the consulado had the fine transformed into a mock or pseudo-loan on which the government proceeded to pay interest to the "lenders" from the *derecho* over the next two centuries. Smith, *Guild Merchant*, 108, n. 82.

28. Morineau, *Incroyables gazettes*, 268.

29. Vicens Vives, *Economic History*, 67–69, 89, 112 offers scattered references to mining in premodern Spain, which is supplemented by Bilbao and Fernández de Pinedo's summary and bibliography, "Artesanía e industria," 105–90. Particularly stimulating are references to Spanish silver mining in Patterson, "Silver Stocks and Losses," 224–25, 227.

30. Hamilton, *American Treasure*, 95; Sauer, *The Early Spanish Main*, chap. 10; Crosby, *The Colombian Exchange*; and the graphic Bartolomé de Las Casas, *Brevíssima relación de la destrucción de las Indias* (Mexico, 1945).

31. The overview of silver mining in Spanish America is based on West, *Mining Community*; Bakewell, *Silver Mining and Society*; Brading and Cross, "Colonial Silver Mining," 545–79; Bakewell, "Mining in Colonial Spanish America"; and Bakewell, ed., *Mines of Silver and Gold*.

32. Schäfer, *El consejo real y supremo de las Indias*, vol. 2, 356, n. 83. In 1554, according to colonial officials in New Spain, Bartolomé de Medina claimed he knew a German mining expert whom peninsular officials had refused a license to leave for the colony, and who "sabe beneficiar los metales de plata con azogue a gran ventaja de lo que aca se haze y sabe." Ocharán Posadas, "Prólogo," xi. See also Probert, "Bartolomé de Medina," esp. 96–109.

33. The Fuggers claimed the contract as part payment of the large outstanding debt of Castile (3 million *ducados*). Matilla Tascón, *Minas de Almadén*, 1:87.

34. Bakewell, *Silver Mining*, 157–63. See also Matilla Tascon, *Minas de Almadén*, vol. 1, chap. 5 and 2:15; Lohmann Villena, *Las minas de Huancavelica*.

35. Miners in America initially relied upon manuals such as Pérez de Vargas, *De re metalica* (1569), which utilized the manuals of George Bauer and Vannoccio Berenguccio. Spanish miners were in contact with German miners employed by the Fuggers at Almaden and Guadalcanal mines. Apparently German technicians introduced the water-powered stamp-mill. West, *Mining Community*, 15–16.

36. Patterson, "Silver Stocks and Losses," 225, 271. In America's first peak period, 1590–1620, annual production totaled 7 million ounces; in 1630 all western Europe's mines produced 7 percent of that (500,000 ounces). Davis, *The Rise of the Atlantic Economies*, 96.

37. Brading and Cross, "Colonial Silver Mining," 556–57. For linkages between mining centers and supply zones in the Central Andes, see Assadourian, *El sistema de la economía colonial*.

38. Cf. "On extrayait de l'argent autant que l'on pouvait . . . Les efforts n'étaient pas dosés en fonction du marché. La mine produisait pour ainsi dire pour produire." Morineau, *Incroyables gazettes*, 253.

39. Morineau has lyrically caught investors' insatiable obsession with profit from silver mining: "On extrayait de l'argent autant que l'on pouvait, jusqu'au bout du filon, comme poussé par un démon et peu entravé par des considérations humaines. Les efforts n'étaient pas dosés en fonction du marché." *Incroyables gazettes*, 253.

40. The duque de Medina Sidonia (1615) quoted in Michele Moret, *Aspects de la société marchande*, 21, n. 43.

41. Matilla Tascón, *Minas de Almadén*, vol. 1, chaps. 2–10; Lohmann Villena, *Las minas de Huancavelica*, 101 ff.

42. A good introduction to the origin and investment of ecclesiastical funds (although dealing with eighteenth-century phenomena) is Wobeser, *El crédito eclesiástico*.

43. Cf. the observation of Viceroy Toledo about 1570: "Todo esto viene a parar cada año a España, e ninguna cosa, o muy poca, queda en este Reino . . . pues de cincuenta millones [de pesos] que se han sacado del cerro de Potosí y Porco . . . de veinte y dos anos que se descubrieron, no parece que haya en todo el Reino [del Peru] cuatro millones." Juan de Matienzo quoted in Assadourian, *El sistema de la economía colonial*, 149.

44. Postan and Rich, eds., *Economic History of Europe*, 4:386–87, 445, 447. According to the Brading and Cross estimate of Spanish American silver production, 1571/75–1696/1700, total output shows a slight upward bias because of rounding off. Still, total output was probably higher since Zacatecas's percentage of smelted silver, 1670–1700, was greater than the 15 percent employed to produce the estimates in column two. Bakewell notes the possibility of refining high grade ores by smelting—an operation financed by Mexico City merchants. Bakewell, *Silver Mining and Society*, 209–13, 243–44, 248.

The difference between Sevilla's receipts and colonial output, 1671–1700, may reflect, first, the use of unregistered mercury along with refining by smelting and, second, foreign reports of Sevilla's receipts—reports more accurate than officially revealed tallies as Everaert has observed.

45. Cross has calculated that the gap between registered and estimated real silver production at Charcas (Upper Peru) climbed from 8.8 percent (1621–30) to 36 percent (1641–50). "South American Bullion," 408.

46. Michel Morineau, *Incroyables gazettes*, 238, 267, table 44. As Harry Cross has concluded, "Hamilton's imports [at Sevilla] do not accurately reflect the levels of American production [of precious metals] and they far understate the amounts of bullion flowing to Europe." "South American Bullion," 418.

Reviewing the problem of silver receipts at Lower Andalusian ports, 1666–1700, Kamen has concluded that "the late seventeenth century was far from being a period of decline in bullion imports. *Spain in the Later Seventeenth Century*, 135–37. See also the data in his contribution to Jover Zamora, ed., *Historia de España*, 28:254.

47. The volume of unaccounted silver, mostly—but not entirely—exported to Europe, is not extraordinary when compared with hidden items in contemporary income data. In Colombia, for example, unrecorded drug sales totaled more than one billion dollars annually in the 1970s, equal to Colombian coffee sales. *New York Times*, 5 January and 25 October 1976.

48. Carande (based on Haring) has suggested that Sevilla's official receipts represented at least 50 percent of colonial precious metals' production. *Carlos V*, 1:234. Driving the "fraud factor" was sheer profitability. Again, to cite contemporary illicit Colombian drug exports: In Colombia one kilo of 80 percent pure cocaine costs roughly $2,000; abroad the wholesale price varies from $20,000 (New York) to $45,000 (London). The mark-up "pays for the corruption of police, of customs

agents, of airport authorities." If the trade remains illicit, dealers "will continue to receive these immense profits that allow them to corrupt everyone." *New York Times,* 8 July 1994.

49. Cf. Acarete du Biscay, *Account of a Voyage;* Arsans de Orsua y Vela, *Potosí,* 1:cxxi, 2:364; Cross, "South American Bullion," 411.

50. For example, roughly 24 million pesos were exchanged for smuggled goods along the Caracas coast, 1697–1703. Morineau, *Incroyables gazettes,* 254.

51. Were Indians relieved of working the Huancavelica mercury mines, the "crown" confessed that it "'would appear to be neglecting the universal well-being and the maintenance not only of my Kingdoms but of the Catholic religion.'" Bakewell, *Silver Mining and Society,* 160–61.

Patterson estimated 10 million deaths resulting from New World mining between 1550 and 1750. "Silver Stocks and Losses," 231. This averages 50,000 deaths per annum, probably exaggerated. Still, in the 1670s it was estimated that 9 of 10 miners could expect to die as a result of mine work.

52. West, *Mining Community* 47-48 and, especially, 48–51; Bakewell, *Silver Mining and Society,* 124, 127–29.

53. Bakewell, *Silver Mining and Society,*121–25; Brading, *Miners and Merchants,* 257–60.

54. On the spread of commercialization in the countryside, see Morin,*Michoacán;* Pastor, *Campesinos y reformas;* Danièle Dehouve, *Banquiers.*

55. Dobyns, "Estimating American Population," 395–460, and the comprehensive Cook, *Demographic Collapse.*

56. Spalding, "Social Climbers," 657–63; Bakewell, *Miners of the Red Mountain,* chap. 4; Cole, *The Potosí Mita,* 17 and passim.

57. Spalding, *Huarochirí;* Larson, *Colonialism;* Assadourian, *Economía colonial;* Stern, *Peru's Indian Peoples.*

58. The interest of Chinese exporters in New Spain is evident in Alvarez de Abreu, *Extracto historial.*

59. Ringrose, "Carting in the Hispanic World," 37–40.

60. West, *Mining Community,* chaps. 4–5; Bakewell, *Silver Mining and Society,* chap. 4 and 212–15. Note the comparable role of Hapsburg merchant financiers (the Fuggers) in developing Tyrol's mines. Postan and Rich, eds., *Economic History of Europe,* 4:402.

61. Le Riverend, *Historia económica de Cuba,* 87–94, 149–50; Guerra y Sánchez et al., eds., *Historia de la nación cubana,* 1:304–13.

62. Arellano Moreno, *Economía venezolana,* 75–101; Arcila Farías, *Economía colonial de Venezuela,* 63–98, 141 ff.; Brito Figueroa, *Historia económica y social,* 102–6.

63. Sempat Assadourian et al., *Historia argentina,* 63–112, 117–81; Braudel, "Du Potosí à Buenos Aires," 546–50; Levene, *Investigaciones,* vol. 1, chaps. 6–7.

64. In the early eighteenth century, Dutch traders exported two-thirds of Venezuela's annual cocoa production of 65,000 quintals. Malamud Rikles, *Cádiz y Saint Malo,* 42.

65. De Vries, *Economy of Europe,* 246; Hobsbawm, "Crisis of the Seventeenth Century," 40–41, 44.

66. After 1648 Dutch trade with Spain expanded, access to silver turned Amsterdam into the main international exchange for precious metals. Every autumn

thirty to fifty escorted vessels (*flotte d'argent*) entered Amsterdam from Spain. Perhaps 50 percent of American silver was ultimately unloaded there. Van Dillen, "Amsterdam, marché mondial," 196.

67. For example, Hollanders abandoning Brazil were responsible for the shift to large-scale sugar plantations on Barbados, bringing "Negroes, Coppers, Stills and all other Things Appertaining to the Ingenios for making of Sugar." Quoted in Sheridan, "Plantation Revolution," 11.

68. Boxer, *Dutch in Brazil*, and "The Portuguese in the East," in Livermore, ed., *Portugal and Brazil*, chap. 9; Wilson, *The Dutch Republic* and *Profit and Power*.

69. Actually English commercial exchanges with Spain and Portugal began decades earlier with "the enormous expansion of the unregulated Iberian trades after 1604." Davis, *Atlantic Economies*, 208. Cf. "Great are the advantages accruing to Britain from the trade between Jamaica and the Spaniards of Mexico . . . ." MacPherson, *Annals of Commerce*, 2:162.

70. Taylor, "Trade Neutrality" 236–60; Kepler, "English Carrying Trade," 261–81; Coleman, "An Innovation and its Diffusion," 417–29; Davis, *English Overseas Trade*, 11–40; Parry et al., *A Short History of the West Indies*, 45–80; McCusker, "The Business of Distilling," 3, 9, 11, 13; Mintz in Guerra y Sánchez, *Sugar and Society*, xiv.

71. Van Dillen, "Economic Fluctuations," 204.

72. Barbour, "Dutch and English Merchant Shipping," 1:239.

73. Lapeyre, *Une famille de marchands*, 503.

74. Braudel and Labrousse, eds., *Histoire économique*, 2:504; Rothkrug, *Opposition to Louis XIV*, chap. 4; Girard, *Le commerce français*; Dahlgren, *Les relations commerciales*; and Malamud Rikles, *Cádiz y San Malo*.

75. Rothkrug, *Opposition to Louis XIV*, 183–84, 188–89, 221, note 65; Dahlgren, *Relations commerciales*, 83 and note 2.

76. AAEPar, Mémoires et Documents, Espagne, 79, ff. 2–2v; Instructions to French ambassador, Madrid, Duc de Gramont, 12 April 1704 cited in Dahlgren, *Relations commerciales*, 323.

77. "Memorial que dio al Sr. Luis XIV un ministro de sus mayores tribunales proponiendo las maximas . . . para el mejor acierto de sus designios . . . 1666." BMus, Egerton, 367, f. 225.

78. "Memoire concernant le commerce et les colonies . . . au Sr. Marquis d'Harcourt . . . ." January, 1698. AAEPar, Mémoires et Documents, Espagne, 808, f. 6. Cf. " . . . les plus grandes resources pour la monarchie d'Espagne seront celles que le Roi Catholique peut retirer des Indes." Instructions to the Comte de Marais, cited in Dahlgren, *Relations commerciales*, 244.

79. Lüthey, *La banque protestante*, 1:8–9.

2. Financing Empire: The European Diaspora of Silver by War

1. Ruíz Martín, *Lettres marchandes*, xlviii–xlix. The fine introduction to *Lettres marchandes* has been published in Spanish translation: *Pequeño capitalismo, gran capitalismo*. See also Ruíz Martín's *Los destinos de la plata americana*. Cf. Spooner, *L'économie mondiale*, 19: "La difficulté, c'est de préciser quand et comment cet argent américain s'est inflitré en Europe en provenance de la péninsule."

2. Ruíz Martín, *Lettres marchandes*, lxxxvii; Braudel, 447–48. Cf. "En la bolsa de

Amberes, en Besançon, Augusta y Génova, determinar la fecha incierta de la llegada a Sevilla de una flota, tuvo mas resonancia en la especulación y en la actitud propícia o recelosa del mercado de dinero que los mismos acontecimientos políticos o militares." Carande, *Carlos V,* 1:247.

3. Carande, *Carlos V,* 2:101.

4. Rodríguez-Salgado, *Changing Face of Empire,* 24.

5. Domínguez Ortiz, *Política fiscal y cambio social,* 20.

6. Behind the *comuneros* Rodríguez-Salgado discerns protonationalist demands for "retrenchment, a return to sound finance, and an end to the use of Spanish money for foreign ventures." *Changing Face of Empire,* 22.

7. Carande, *Carlos V,* 3:371. Geoffrey Parker estimates that Charles V in 1552 was fielding in Germany, the Netherlands, Lombardy, Sicily, Naples, and Spain perhaps 150,000 soldiers, the majority of them non-Spaniards. *The Army of Flanders,* 13.

8. Ruíz Martín, *Lettres marchandes,* lxxxviii. For a masterful overview of the diaspora, see Braudel, *The Mediterranean,* 462–542.

9. Castillo Pintado, "El mercado del dinero," 102.

10. Cf. Spooner, *Economie mondiale,* 25: " La brutalité et . . . l'ampleur de cette révolution de l'argent. Cet argent arraché à l'Amérique, mal gardé par l'Espagne — économie et politique obligent — court le vaste monde."

11. Torres López, and Pérez-Prendes y Muñoz de Arraco, *Los juros,* 47.

12. Rodriguez-Salgado, *Changing Face of Empire,* 24.

13. Ruíz Martín, *Lettres marchandes,* xxxvii.

14. Felipe Ruíz Martín, "La Banca de España," 15–16. After 1450, Augsburg and Nuremberg merchant houses entered into silver and copper mining ventures. Earnings from such enterprises helped finance Maximilian's propensity for dynastic expansionism. Richard Ehrenbourg, *Le siècle des Fugger* (Paris, 1955), 184–85.

15. Speculation in Castile's public debt led Genoese merchant bankers to abandon "le véritable et honnête commerce . . . pour ne s'occupe que de la 'negoziazione e dei cambi.'" Braudel, *La Méditerranee,* 1:462.

16. Ruíz Martín, *Lettres marchandes,* xxix, xxxvii–xxxviii; Carande, *Carlos V,* 3:399, 469; Parker, *Army of Flanders,* 60; Spooner, *Economie mondiale,* 308–9.

17. Carande, *Carlos V,* 1:240 (based on Carande's conversion of Hamilton's data to *ducados*). European bankers' expectations were fueled by the rapid publication at Sevilla of Francisco de Xerez's *Verdadera relación de la conquista del Perú* (1534). Carande, 3:312.

18. Ibid., 2:34–35; Thompson, *War and Government,* 81. In three years (1551–55) ecclesiastical contributions to Castilian finance were significant, totaling 1.2 million *ducados,* virtually one year's income to the Castilian treasury. Rodriguez-Salgado, *Changing Face of Empire,* 227. For his part, Carande views the dependence of Castile upon church financial support as another "rastro de la Edad media." *Carlos V,* 2:36.

19. Carande, *Carlos V,* 1:140.

20. Ibid., 3:417. Cf. Rodriguez-Salgado, *Changing Face of Empire,* 63: "Bullion shipments soon became the most coveted form of repayment." Dependence upon foreign creditors, Braudel has proposed, ultimately led to a Spanish fiscal system "organized by the money-lenders to suit themselves." Braudel, *The Mediterranean,* 695.

21. Modesto Ulloa, *La hacienda real de Castilla,* 151–52. At least four *secuestros*

were carried out at Sevilla (1523–45). They netted the government 1.5 million *ducados*. Over a longer period, 1523–1664, 17 *secuestros* were reported. Haring, *Trade and Navigation*, 170; Céspedes del Castillo, *La avería*, 132; Carande, *Carlos V,* 3:414; and his *El crédito de Castilla*, 30–31; Thompson, *War and Government*, 83, 85.

22. Carande, *Carlos V,* 3:319.

23. Ibid., 3:313. In 1551 La Gasca returned with 1.9 million *ducados* of which the government promptly assigned 1.3 million to major creditors, the merchant banking houses of Welser, Schetz, Palavicino, Gamarry, Affaitadi, Spínola, Grillo, Dueños, and others.

24. Castillo Pintado, "Los juros," 52–53.

25. Carande, *El crédito de Castilla*, 15. Overnight *juros* became an "inversión segura . . . denotando . . . una predilección arraigada." Ibid., *Carlos V,* 2:90; Castillo Pintado, "Los juros de Castilla," 44–45; Vilar, *A History of Gold and Money*, 145. *Juros* had the added advantage that interest earned required no religious approval. Ibid., 47.

26. The Fuggers, for instance, complied with a request in 1557 from the Castilian government to send to the Netherlands 430,000 *ducados* on condition of reimbursement "sur les premiers arrivages d'or et d'argent des Indes." Ehrenbourg, *Le siècle des Fugger,* 73.

27. Rodriguez-Salgado, *Changing Face of Empire,* 61; Carande, *Carlos V.,* 2:93; Torres López and Pérez-Prendes, *Los juros,* 27–36, 58, 66; Parker, *Army of Flanders,* 150–52. Initially *juros* were a *privilegio* awarded for service to the crown. Later they became an interest-bearing investment, for one life or inheritable (*de por vida* or *perpétuo*), redeemable under certain conditions (*al quitar*), *juros de resguardo* or *caución*, a back-up guarantee if specific revenues assigned proved inadequate, were issued below par to make them more attractive to speculny cators. Castillo Pintado, "El mercado del dinero," 94. *Juros al quitar* were much sought after since they were negotiable; their price fluctuated with nominal value, type of guaranteed repayment, and current worth.

28. *Licencias de saca* were purchased from Castile's Hacienda at rates varying with demand. Ruíz Martín, *Pequeño capitalismo, gran capitalismo,* 36–37. Cf. Roberts, Lewes, *The Merchants' Mappe of Commerce,* quoted in Haring, *Trade and Navigation,* 178 note 1: "No Genoa merchant resident in Spain . . . but has a particular licence to transport the rials and plate . . . to a certain round sum annually."

29. Ruíz Martín, *Lettres marchandes,* xxxviii–xxxix; Carande, *Carlos V,* 1:235; Rodriguez-Salgado, *Changing Face of Empire,* 63. By the late 1530s Castile was involved in "vast indebtedness in a financial market unfettered by national or ideological restrictions," a structure favored by the Hapsburg patrimonial concept of empire. Tracy, *Financial Revolution,* 41.

30. Carande, *Carlos V,* 2:105. From 1519 to 1551 annual borrowing averaged only 500,000 *ducados*; it was already at the level of about 2 million in 1552. But between 1553 and 1555 it soared from 2.5 to 4.2 million (121).

31. Rodriguez-Salgado, *Changing Face of Empire,* 347. Cf. Carande, *Carlos V,* 1:140: "Causas múltiples . . . dejaron a Castilla empobrecida mientras llegaban y pasaban fugitivos, los tesoros mas cuantiosos de la economía moderna."

32. Rodriguez-Salgado, *Changing Face of Empire,* 343 table 12.

33. Ruíz Martín, "La Banca," 19–21 and *Lettres marchandes,* xxx–xxxi; Pulido

Bueno, *El real giro de España,* 14. Ruíz Martín blames the failure of this attempt at state enterprise on officers of *Contratación* who "solo tenian vocación de burócratas y de administradores." "La Banca," 21.

34. Maravall, *Estado moderno,* 2:294. The bankruptcies of Philip II and his successors (there were five of them between 1557 and 1647) have been likened to conversion of short- into long-term debt, a consolidated debt, and "une forme nouvelle de *juros.*" Ehrenbourg, *Le siècle des Fugger,* 331.

35. Rodríguez-Salgado, *Changing Face of Empire,* 224–25 table 10 and 248–49 table 11–2, 344; Thompson, *War and Government,* 41. With reason Philip II viewed the American colonies as the "manantial mas caudaloso." Carande, *Carlos V,* 3:380, 396.

36. Rodríguez-Salgado, *Changing Face of Empire,* 344; Thompson, *War and Government,* 275. Disbursements by Philip II's Hacienda were made from "whatever funds happened to be available "whether from general funds, colonial receipts, or local sources." Ibid., 71, 80.

37. Rodríguez-Salgado, *Changing Face of Empire,* 224–25, table 10.

38. Thompson, *War and Government,* 71–72.

39. Torres López and Pérez-Prendes, *Los juros,* 32, table 1, 33. In 1609 colonial income (3 million *ducados,* much understated) constituted 20 per cent of total revenues (15.6 million). Castile's aggregate revenues were more than double those of France (7.7 million) although its populaton was half that of France. Based on data given by Michel Morineau in Leon and Jacquart, eds., *Histoire économique,* 2:151–53.

40. Carande, *Carlos V,* 3:468; Thompson, *War and Government,* 71, 87–88, 100; Torres López and Pérez-Prendes, *Los juros,* 31; Ruíz Martín, *Pequeño capitalismo,* 152, note 10, and his *Las finanzas,* 171. In 1597 sale of the office of general overseer of Castile's foreign monetary transfers was a "measure of . . . alienation" of state authority. Thompson, *War and Government,* 88.

41. Morineau, *Incroyables gazettes,* 78.

42. Ruíz Martín, *Lettres marchandes,* xlviii; Domínguez Ortiz, "Los caudales," 330, 319, n. 6.

43. In 1663 Philip IV's Hacienda converted its outstanding debts to *juros,* which by 1667 amounted to 9 million *ducados.* Lynch, *Spain under the Hapsburgs,* 2:274.

44. Domínguez Ortiz, "Los caudales," 335–36, 339.

45. Ibid., 360; Castillo Pintado, "Los juros," 60–61.

46. Parker, *Spain and the Netherlands,* 189.

47. Domínguez Ortiz, "Guerra económica," 97.

48. Domínguez Ortiz, "Los caudales," 360.

49. Cf. Haring, *Trade and Navigation,* 51: "The steady flow of silver from the rents of Mexico and Upper Peru became essential to the maintenance of a bankrupt government."

50. Domínguez Ortiz, "Los caudales," 315, 317, n. 12.

51. Ibid., "Guerra económica," 92–93.

52. Ibid., "Los caudales," 342.

53. Ibid., "Guerra económica," 97 and "Los caudales," 328 and note 34.

54. Ibid., "Los caudales," 371.

55. For example, to continue the siege of Metz, Charles approved the sequestra-

tion at Sevilla of incoming silver on private account to satisfy creditors "si se quiere seguir contando con ellos." Carande, *Carlos V,* 3:401.

56. Domínguez Ortiz, "Los caudales," 339–40, 345. Without the American funds, Domínguez Ortiz has noted tongue-in-cheek, Velazquez might not have had the occasion to paint the surrender of Breda, commonly called "Las Lanzas."

57. Ibid., 361–62.

58. Haring, *Trade and Navigation,* 65, 214; Domínguez Ortiz, "Los caudales," 328.

59. Torres López and Pérez-Prendes, *Los juros,* 42.

60. Ibid., 46; Domínguez Ortiz, *Política fiscal,* 36. The large portfolio of foreign-held *juros* induced the early *arbitrista* Sancho de Moncada (1619) to record with bitterness that "Extrangeros tienen en España (según se dice) mas de un millón de juros, sin infinitos censos, toda la Cruzada, gran número de prebendas, encomiendas, beneficios y pensiones." Moncada, *Restauración política,* 102.

61. Ruíz Martín, *Las finanzas,* 121–23. Cf. Parker, *Army of Flanders,* 152–53: "The Spanish credit system . . . depended absolutely on specie and principally on the treasure of the Indies loaded at Sevilla for the King."

62. Torres López and Pérez-Prendes, *Los juros,* 47.

63. Ibid. 47, 51; Castillo Pintado, "Los juros," 60.

64. Castillo Pintado, "Los juros," 29–30, 47–51, 58–59, 65–70; Domínguez Ortiz, *Política fiscal,* 66, 75–76, 90–92 and "Los caudales," 349; Torres López and Pérez-Prendes, *Los juros,* 71; Garzón Pareja, *La hacienda de Carlos II,* 335–36; Kamen in Jover Zamora, ed., *Historia de España,* 28:277.

65. Melchor Macanaz, regalist and pro-Bourbon nationalist in the first half of the eighteenth century, complained that "es público y notorio que muchos juros se han comprado . . . aviendo sido las ventas a muy cortos prezios . . . han llegado a perzibir excesivos réditos" and "el abuso de los crecidos intereses y el fraude con que se han adquirido y reservado muchos juros." "Proyecto," 78, 81.

66. Torres López and Pérez-Prendes, *Los juros,* 52; Castillo Pintado, "Los juros," (1963), 52–55, 68–69.

67. Ruíz Martín, *Los destinos de la plata,* 32; Broens, *Monarquía y capital mercantil,* 34. Cf. Kristof Glamann in Cipolla, ed., *Economic History of Europe,* 2:510: the "Sound [entry to the Baltic] became a terminal point for part of the contents of the Spanish silver fleets."

68. Gascon, "La France du mouvement," in Braudel et al., *Histoire économique,* 1:2, 280.

69. Spooner, *Economie mondiale,* 24–25, 136–37 and plates iii and iv; Ruíz Martín, *Pequeño capitalismo,* 97–99, 152–53.

70. Chaudhuri, *Trade and Civilization,* 218; Hazan, "En Inde," 835–39; Wakeman, "Voyages," 15; Panuk, "Money in the Ottoman Empire," 965; Richards, ed., *Precious Metals,* 16–18, 269–92.

71. Parker, *Army of Flanders,* 60; Spooner, *Economie mondiale,* 144–45, 308–9.

72. Domínguez Ortiz, *Política fiscal,* 55, 127.

73. Broens, *Monarquía y capital mercantil,* 34. Broens notes two main routes via the western Pyrenees: Jaca to Puerto Sompart and on to Oloron Sainte-Marie, and Pamplona to Biarritz and Bayonne.

74. Spooner, *Economie mondiale,* 137–38, 163–64, 175, 277, 315.

75. Ibid., 356–62, 407–11, 532–34, graph 32. Based on French consular reporting and related materials collected by Albert Girard, Ruíz Martín's table of receipts of precious metals and their reexport, 1665–98, shows France as by far the principal destination of legal precious metals exports (13 percent) followed by the United Provinces (4.8 percent). Ruíz Martín, *Los destinos*, 42.

76. As early as 1578 Castilians perceived that suppressing revolt in the Netherlands "consumed the money and substance which has come from the Indies . . . ." Over the century after 1556 about 55 per cent of Castile's outlay on warfare in the Netherlands came from public (that is, royal) income from colonial treasuries. Parker, *Spain and the Netherlands*, 186–88.

77. Parker, *Army of Flanders*, 137, 272, appendix A. In 1640 when the Spanish contingent was also at a peak, it represented only about 20 percent of all Spanish-subsidized forces.

78. Ibid. 48, 51. Financing troop movements on the Spanish Road transferred Castilian funds to Milan where "the arms industry and the manufacture of quality textiles responded . . . to the demands of the market." Yun in Thompson and Yun Casalilla, eds., *The Castilian Crisis*, 315.

79. Magalhães Godinho, *L'économie de l'empire portugais*, 472–95; Parker, *Army of Flanders*, 155.

80. Parker, *Army of Flanders*, 50, 88–90, 92, 94. In Parker's summary on page 94: "The contract system was . . . in the best interests of everyone. The government ensured that the troops were properly fed; the soldiers . . . received their rations . . . the peasants were paid immediately by the contractors for the food they provided." Glamann in Cipolla, ed., *Economic History of Europe*, 2:512.

81. In 1687, for example, at least half of state revenues were assigned to service the public debt. Kamen, *Spain in the Later Seventeenth Century*, 367, 369.

82. Gelabert, in Thompson and Yun Casalilla, eds., *The Castilian Crisis*, 204; Thompson, *War and Government*, 42.

83. Carande, *Carlos V*, 3:396; Domínguez Ortiz, *Política fiscal*, 49 and "Los caudales," 335; Renate Pieper, *La real hacienda bajo Fernando VI*, 104; Thompson, *War and Government*, 65.

84. Domínguez Ortiz, *Política fiscal*, 64 and "Los caudales," 322.

85. It is plausible that Castilians under the later Hapsburgs were taxed "more heavily than any other people in Europe." Parker, *Spain and the Netherlands*, 188. And the burden on the peoples of Spain's American colonies?

86. Thompson, *Crown and Cortes*, chap. 5 and p. 91, and *War and Government*, 63. Yun has seen in the propensity for purchasing government office and entitlement a "retreat of business capital from the investments which could have set in motion the qualitative developments which were beginning to take place in northern Europe." Thompson and Yun Casililla, *The Castilian Crisis*, 315.

87. Cf. "No es aventurado afirmar que el monopolio estatal sobre el tráfico es hipotecado en favor de los propios comerciantes." Vila Vilar, "Las ferias de Portobelo," 311.

88. Torres López and Pérez-Prendes, *Los juros*, 37–38.

89. For example, Madrid sold (1634) the post of *escribano de flotas y galeones*, applying 5,000 *ducados* to pay the operators of Lierganés's cannon foundry. Domínguez Ortiz, *España de los Austria*, 161–62.

90. In addition, Olivares earned in one year alone 254,000 *ducados,* as *canciller de las Indias, alguacil mayor* in the Casa de Contratación, and by sales of cargo shipped to America—the equivalent of 56 per cent of his estimated income of that year. Quevedo, "Caída de su privanza y muerte del conde-duque de Olivares," 59.

91. Domínguez Ortiz, "Los caudales," 323–24.

92. Domínguez Ortiz, "Guerra económica," 102–3; Haring, *Trade and Navigation,* 65.

93. Domínguez Ortiz, "Los caudales," 324. As a result, in 1762 the office (alienated) of treasurer in the Mexico City mint "no rendía cuentas a nadie, mirandose como negociación particular todo el giro de la Casa." Fausto de Elhuyar, *Indagaciones sobre la amonedación en la Nueva España,* 7, 35.

94. Braudel, *The Mediterranean,* 2:688.

95. Yun in Thompson and Yun Casalilla, eds., *The Castilian Crisis,* 311.

96. Thompson, *Crown and Cortes,* chap. 5 and pp. 90, 96. Elsewhere Thompson has noted that office-holding as an honor constrained "the possibilities of discipline and reform" of the state apparatus. *War and Government,* 58.

3. Westphalia: The Legacy of Unequal Treaties

1. Morineau, *Incroyables gazettes,* 268, 298–99.

2. Barbour, "Dutch and English Merchant Shipping," 1:238.

3. West European nations insisted on treaties with Spain to insure "le principe de base des privilèges," namely "l'aspiration à une liberté de commerce aussi grande que possible." Everaert, *Handel,* 929. Everaert's extraordinary monograph has a summary in French ("Le commerce international et colonial des firmes flamandes à Cadix"). Albert Girard concluded that the treaties effectively blocked Spanish authorities from curbing smuggling. *Commerce français,* 594.

4. As Domínguez Ortiz phrased it, "Exagerados privilegios de ciertos grupos comerciales . . . un regimen no muy distinto del que las capitulaciones aseguraron a los europeos en Asia antes de la explosión de los nacionalismos orientales." "Los extrangeros," 392–93.

5. Beliardi, "Reflexiones" BNPar., Mss. Fonds Français 10766, f. 71.

6. Bourgoing, *Tableau de l'Espagne moderne,* 3:140.

7. Girard, *Commerce français,* 95–104.

8. Jenkinson, *Treaties,* 1:17–18.

9. Bourgoing, *Tableau,* 3:140.

10. Jenkinson, *Treaties,* 1:14–15.

11. Girard, *Commerce français,* 109. In its treaty with Holland, the Spanish government allowed the Dutch to act as neutral carriers during the ensuing Franco-Spanish conflict, so that "the entrepôt for Spanish silver shifted [from Dover, 1638–47] to Amsterdam." Kepler, "Carrying Trade," 277.

12. Probably Spain's concessions to England were more than substantial, in light of the recent conclusion that in 1638 "the English as masters of the Channel were also masters of Spanish trade" between Spanish ports and northwest Europe. Taylor, "Trade," 236–60.

13. Girard, *Commerce français,* 65, 96. In his chapter on the "Mercantile System," Adam Smith recognized that "By advantageous treaties of a commerce, particular

privileges were procured in some foreign state for the goods and merchants of the country, beyond what were granted to those of other countries." *Wealth of Nations,* 419.

14. Jenkinson, *Treaties,* 2:111. In 1682 the secretary of the Consejo de Estado, marqués de Mancera, argued that the cedulas were private contracts (not international treaties) between England's consul in Andalusia and the Consejo. Girard, *Commerce français,* 160–61.

Roger Coke—hardly disinterested observer of English overseas trade—concluded that Hispano-Dutch warfare permitted English interests to "become proprietors of the Trade with Spain, and by consequence great sharers in the Wealth of the West Indies." *Discourse,* intro.

15. Jenkinson, *Treaties,* 2:113–14.

16. Ibid., 116–17, 122–23. The cedula mentions "dispatches"—probably *despachos.* These were the lists presented by merchants to the Sevilla customs. Usually there were marked discrepancies between captains' bills of lading and merchants' "dispatches."

17. Ibid., 116–17, 122–23.

18. Sánchez de Sopranis, "Las naciones extrangeras en Cádiz," 810. At the end of the seventeenth century it was the practice of English merchants resident at Cádiz to employ the *gobernador* of Cádiz as unofficial judge-conservator, offering him "annually presents of greater value than the salary given to that officer; that for the sake of those presents, that governor protected them in the enjoyment of all their privileges and immunities as much as if he had been chosen into that office." King, *The British Merchant,* 3:176.

19. Jenkinson, *Treaties,* 2:124–25.

20. Taylor, "Trade," 239.

21. Quoted in Kepler, "Fiscal Aspects of the English Carrying Trade," 262, 277.

22. Taylor, "Trade," 246, 253 app. F.

23. Ibid., 255.

24. Violet Barbour distinguishes two English theaters of trade at this time: one covering southern Europe from the Bay of Biscay to east Mediterranean ports and another stretching to the Canaries, Madeira, Guinea and east India. "Dutch and English Merchant Shipping," 231.

25. Taylor, "Trade," 249, 251, 253. The abrupt rise in value of exports to "Italian" ports in 1638 and 1643 may indicate they were in fact destined for Spanish ports.

26. Ibid., 278.

27. Brenner, *Merchants and Revolution,* chap. 12.

28. Between 1660 and 1690 England's foreign trade (and that of France, too) doubled. Davis, *Atlantic Economies,* 193.

29. Girard, *Commerce français,* 84; Davis, *Atlantic Economies,* 82.

30. When Madrid considered allying with England against France in 1667, London insisted Spain cede the channel ports of Ostend and Nieuport, a request Spain rejected. "Voto del Inquisidor General [Padre Nithard], confesor de la Reyna . . . ." Madrid, 5 December 1667, Collection of the Duque de Montemar Papers, *Dolphin Catalogue,* n. 50. In the first Anglo-Dutch conflict (1652–54), one English goal was supplanting the Dutch in Spanish colonial markets. De Vries, *Economy of Europe,* 100–103.

31. Jenkinson, *Treaties,* 2:94.

32. Ibid., 95.

33. BMus, Additional Manuscripts 33030 (Newcastle Papers), f. 298.

34. Jenkinson, *Treaties,* 1:197. Re article ix: "Each of the parties stipulates *for himself* that his subjects shall not exercise any commerce in the ports of the others; but it is not stipulated that either of the powers shall exclude the subjects of the other from a commerce in his own ports, each party engaging only for the restraint of *his own* subjects . . . . But Great Britain does not at all engage, that the Spanish subjects shall not trade in the colonies of England." BMus, Additional Manuscripts 33030, ff. 298–99.

35. Girard, *Commerce français,* 115–20, 126, n. 20. Mazarin is reported to have asked Rouen's and Saint-Malo's merchants to delegate representatives to assist in treaty negotiations.

36. The treaty is in Vast, *Les grands traités,* 1:93–167.

37. Girard, *Commerce français,* 129, 149–50.

38. P. Catalan to Colbert, Cádiz, 15 October 1672. ANPar, Affaires Etrangères, B I, 211, f. 138; Catalan to Colbert, Cádiz, 9 October 1679, Ibid., f. 259; Girard, *Commerce français,* 215.

39. Kamen in Jover Zamora, ed., *Historia de España,* 28:248–49.

40. Domínguez Ortiz, "Los extrangeros," 328, 350, 353.

41. Ibid., 318.

42. Girard, *Commerce français,* 150–52.

43. Ibid., *La rivalité commerciale,* 43–45.

44. Sánchez de Sopranis, "Las naciones extrangeras," 785–87

45. Domínguez Ortiz, *Orto y ocaso de Sevilla,* 47. Báez Eminente administered the Aduanas of Cádiz, Andalucía (as far as Cartagena) and Castilla; under his tax farm were the administration of Cádiz's customs, *alcabalas reales,* the *bolsillo, nuevas alcabalas y viejas,* the *dos por ciento, uno y quarto en plata.* He was the *receptor del almojarifazgo,* supervisor of Cádiz's warehouses, and controller of *sellos.* Lantéry, *Un comerciante saboyano,* 18.

The sequence of Andalusia's Sephardic/*marrano* tax farmers is: 1642–47—Simón Rodríguez (Ruíz ?) Bueno; 1663–82—Francisco Báez Eminente, who shared it (1677–82) with his son, Tomás Antonio Eminente; 1681–82—Gaspar Ruíz (Rodríguez ?) Díaz, cousin of Simon Ruíz (Rodríguez ?) Díaz Pessoa; 1686–98—Francisco Báez Eminente; 1698–1711—Juan Eminente. Girard, *Rivalité commerciale,* 114–15. Henry Kamen has observed that "over forty years" Báez Eminente's group served Hapsburgs and then Bourbons "with credit, industry and zeal that were well known." *The Spanish Inquisition,* 224

46. Israel, *Race, Class and Politics,* 204, 215; Hoberman, *Mexico's Merchant Elite,* 21, 43, 126, 252, 268; Elliott, *The Count-Duke of Olivares,* 300–304, 449–50; and Boyajian, *Portuguese Bankers.*

47. Broens, *Monarquía y capital mercantil,* esp. chap. 3. In 1689, when a resident of Madrid, Báez Eminente was ranked among the wealthiest financiers of his time. Kamen, *Spain,* 116, 154, 305.

48. Céspedes del Castillo, *La avería,* 89–90. Cf. ". . . estaba dispensado por cedula de 1660 el registro de venida de Indias." Antonio Arnuero to José de Gálvez, Cádiz, 3 mayo 1782, AGI, Indiferente General 2312.

49. Note article xiii of the Anglo-Spanish treaty of 1667: "Ships belonging to the subjects . . . [may] anchor in the roads or bays . . . without being constrained to enter into port." Jenkinson, *Treaties,* 2:97. As a result, ". . . los perjuicios que se havian ocasionado desde el Congreso de Munster con las franquezas . . . en especial en la Bahia de Cádiz . . . ay en aquel puerto, Navios que sirven de almacenes, para ocultar los derechos de Almojarifazgo . . . ." Varinas to Crown, 1695, cited in Artiñano y de Galdácano, *Historia del comercio* 124.

50. Girard, *Rivalité commerciale,* 56; Arnuero to Gálvez, 3 May 1782, AGI, Indiferente General 2312.

51. "Observations sur . . . colonies en général." AAEPar, Mémoires et Documents, Espagne, 81, n. 17.

52. Girard, *Rivalité commerciale,* 51, n. 26, 59–60, 60 n. 41; *SEV* ii (1788), 38; Everaert, *Handel,* 887. Everaert claims the *gracia de pie de fardo* effectively reduced the quantity of dutiable textile imports by 33.3–40 percent.

53. There are many references to Eminente in Lantéry, *Memorias* 19, 188.

54. Girard, *Rivalité commerciale,* 71, 74. Presumably Báez Eminente's appointee in 1673 as administrator of the Customs of Cádiz, Andalusia and Castile, José Ladrón de Guevara, was related to Diego Ladrón de Guevara, bishop of Quito (Ecuador) and later viceroy of Peru (1710–16).

55. ANPar, AB xix, t. 382.

56. Girard, *Rivalité commerciale,* 60 and n. 41, 67–72; ANPar, Affaires Etrangères, B III, t. 342.

57. ANPar, K 907 n. 13; "Suplement . . . ," AAE, Mémoires et Documents, Espagne, 209, f.37. The *convenios* remained the basis of "la richesse réelle de deux plus grandes provinces . . . Bretagne et la Normandie" as late as 1764. "Extrait" of letter, Bertellet (Cartagena), 3 July 1764. BNPar., Mss. Fonds Français 10768, f. 551v. On the same point, see Bourgoing, *Tableau,* 3:193–94.

58. ANPar, B 7, t. 455; Boyetet to Sartine, Madrid, 22 February 1780. ANPar, Affaires Etrangères, B I, t. 795, 24v ff. José Gentil da Silva has concluded the *convenios* provided a virtual monopoly at Cádiz for European manufactures. *Desarrollo económico, subsistencia y decadencia en España* (Madrid, 1967), 177–78.

59. Cf. Girard, *Commerce français,* 170 and n. 73; Everaert, *Handel,* 887, 894.

60. Girard, *Rivalité commerciale,* 77–78; Kamen, "Confiscations," 519.

61. ANPar, Affaires Etrangères, B III, 342, n. 13 (1782).

62. Morineau, *Incroyables gazettes,* 267, table 44. Most were textiles (87 percent in linens, cottons, woolens, silks and mercery)—of which 43 percent consisted of French goods. The Spanish share was 3.1 percent.

63. Ibid., 263.

64. Gentil da Silva, *Desarrollo económico,* 73. Cf. "Les retours des flottes et des galions continuaient d'animer la vie économique en Europe." Léon and Jacquart, eds., *Histoire économique et sociale du monde,* 2:97

65. Girard, *Commerce français,* 558, 591; Everaert, *Handel,* 940.

66. For example, between 1605 and 1662 the number of French and Genoese merchants resident at Cádiz jumped from 10 to 43. García Fuentes, *El comercio español,* 46

67. Vilar, Pierre, *La Catalogne dans l'Espagne moderne,* 1:536–37.

68. In this light there was no defection of the Spanish bourgeoisie of the time—

structural factors inhibited and shaped its development. Cf. Braudel, *The Mediterranean,* 1:725–26.

69. Levin, *The Export Economies,* 10.

70. Domínguez Ortiz, "Los extrangeros," 314–15.

71. Ibid., 414.

72. In 1636 Lewes Roberts commented that one factor in Spaniards' minimal role in foreign trade was "the residence of many Genoa merchants . . . in good numbers . . . in every good city, especially on the sea coasts, whose skill and acuteness in trade far surpassing the native Spaniard and Portuguese . . . and by reason that the King of Spain . . . is ever engaged to their commonwealth for great and vast sums at interest. . . ." *The Merchants' Mappe,* 165, cited by Haring, *Trade and Navigation,* 178, n. 1.

73. Vayrac, *L'état présent de l'Espagne,* cited in Carrera Pujal, *Historia de la economía española,* 3:103; Veitia Linaje, *Norte,* bk. 1, chap. 18, para. 2

74. García-Baquero Gonzalez, *Cádiz y el Atlántico,* 1:195. Domínguez Ortiz has suggested that by lowering duty levels at Cádiz below those of Sevilla, Báez Eminente favored foreign businessmen who preferred to operate at Cádiz whose large bay facilitated smuggling. *Orto y ocaso de Sevilla,* 97.

75. Domínguez Ortiz, *Orto y ocaso de Sevilla,* 89–96; ANPar, AB XIX, 582; Girard, *Commerce français,* 87; Congreso Luso-Español para el Progreso de las Ciencias, 3lst, "La burguesía gaditana," *La burguesía gaditana,* 4–5.

76. García Fuentes, *El comercio español,* 58.

77. A further topographical element isolating Cádiz was the bay's hinterland of lagoons and inlets utilized as salt pans—and for smuggling.

78. The description of Cádiz is based on: Girard, *Commerce français,* 540–45, who consulted Bertaut, *Journal du voyage d'Espagne;* Vayrac, *Etat présent de l'Espagne,* and Laborde, *Itinéraire descriptif,* 3:275–78.

79. Taylor, "Trade," 242–43; Stols, "La colonia flamenca de Sevilla," 373; Girard, *Commerce français,* 58–59; Carrera Pujal, *Historia de la economía española,* 2:75–7; Pulido Bueno, *Almojarifazgos y comercio exterior,* 26–82.

80. Girard, *Commerce français,* 61, 136, n. 1. Between 1605 and 1662 the number of resident French merchants more than quadrupled (from 7 to 33). García Fuentes, *El comercio español,* 46.

81. *Wealth of French Residents, Spain (by province), 1680*

	mrs., plata	%
All Spain	160,031,403	100.0
Sevilla	137,771,980	86.0
San Lúcar	2,389,078	1.5
Cádiz	1,699,388	1.0

Adapted from Girard, *Commerce français,* 567–71.

82. Savary, cited in Girard, *Commerce français,* 463, 552–53.

83. Girard, *Commerce français,* 551–53.

84. Everaert, *Handel,* 875–76.

85. Ibid., 881; Girard, *Commerce français,* 551.

86. French producers for Spanish and Spanish colonial markets also relied on the commercial reporting of a wide network of consular agents assigned to 18 ports at the middle of the seventeenth century. Kamen in Jover Zamora, ed., *Historia de España,* 28:248–49.

87. Morineau, *Incroyables gazettes,* 263.

88. Girard, *Commerce français,* 338–48 Everaert. *Handel,* 890–91; Stols, "La colonia flamenca," 373.

89. Everaert, *Handel,* 878–79, 893, 896; Girard, *Commerce français,* 467, n. 122.

90. Everaert, *Handel,* 894–96.

91. At least one-third of incoming "French" cargo at Cádiz in 1691 consisted of non-French products. AAEPar, Mémoires et Documents, Espagne 79, f. 22.

92. *National Origin of Cádiz Imports (by value) 1685/86, 1691*
(%)

France	38.4
England	18.5
Genoa	16.5
Holland	9.9
Flanders	6.0
Hamburg	6.0
Spain	4.7

Everaert, *Handel,* 278, 292

93. AAEPar, Correspondence Politique, Espagne, 70, ff. 256v–257. This contains the detailed reports of France's *commissaire de la marine* in Spain, Patoulet.

94. Cf. the comment of an English exporter to his Cádiz correspondent: "I ordered so much to be put short of the contents of the short bays, because I am informed they pass them at the Custom house . . . without measuring." Gravil, "Trading to Spain and Portugal," 75.

95. AAEPar, Correspondence Politique, Espagne 70, ff. 257–58.

96. Ibid., ff. 258–258v.

97. "Mémoire touchant le commerce des Indes occidentales par Cadiz." 12 Oct. 1691. AAEPar, Mémoires et Documents, Espagne, 79, f. 12.

98. AAEPar, Correspondence Politique, Espagne 70, ff. 253v–254v.

99. García Fuentes, *El comercio español,* 181, 184 table 14.

100. In the late seventeenth century an *écu* or *escudo* was virtually the equivalent of the *ducado* of 11 *reales.* At 8 *reales* per peso, 3,000–4,000 *écus* represented about 4,125–5,500 *pesos* of 8 *reales* each. Kamen, *Spain in the Later Seventeenth Century,* xii–xiii.

101. AAEPar, Correspondence Politique, Espagne 70, ff. 259–259v, 263–267v.

102. AAEPar, Correspondence Politique, Espagne 70, ff. 211–12.

103. Ibid., f. 216v.

104. Everaert, *Handel,* 913–14. Note the observation made in 1705: "Les étrangers . . . ont trouvé un . . . moyen . . . de faire venir leurs vaisseaux chargés de marchandises dans les rades [Cádiz] lors du départ des flottes et des galions, sur lesquels ils embarquent leurs marchandises pendant la nuit, de concert avec les capitaines . . . ." "Mémoire . . . concernant le commerce . . . pour servir . . . au . . . Amelot." 29 April 1705, cited in Dahlgren, *Relations commerciales,* 332.

105. Stols, "La colonia flamenca," 374–75.

106. Savary, cited by Carrera Pujal, *Historia,* 2:29–30 and Girard, *Commerce français,* 464. *Prestanombres* seem to parallel the device of U.S. bankers to "street-name accounts" whereby banks create a "name that allows a bank to hide its investments." *Prestanombres* were, on the other hand, real persons.

107. Cf. "La confianza que los extrangeros, especialmente los franceses, se toman

con sus comisionistas españoles no constituye ningun secreto . . . es conocida en detalle en todos los países y en las Indias, aunque de ella nunca se habla para fundamentar un derecho . . . Los de la Contratación y del Consulado de Cádiz, y generalmente todos los que se enriquecen con ello, ayudan a cubrirla . . . un hombre expondría su honor y su vida si hubiese revelado en justicia este pretendido secreto." Quoted in Carrera Pujal, *Historia de la economía española*, 2:85.

108. AAEPar, Correspondence Politique, Espagne 70, ff. 205v–207; Everaert, *Handel,* 599. A sample *connoissement* is in Everaert, *Handel,* 769–770 app. x.

109. Everaert, *Handel,* 885–86.

110. French merchants considered the Dutch better prepared for Caribbean commercial operations because as holders of the slave *asiento* "sous ce pretexte ils y portent et y vendent toutes les autres marchandises." "Mémoire touchant le commerce des Indes occidentales par Cadix," 9 October 1691, AAEPar, Mémoires et Documents, Espagne 79, f. 28.

111. Ibid. Cf. Sée, "Documents sur le commerce de Cadix, 1691–1752," 465–520.

112. Everaert, *Handel,* 893–99, 903.

113. AAEPar, Correspondence Politique, Espagne 70, ff. 209–209v, 214v; Ibid., Mémoires et Documents, Espagne 79, f. 19.

114. Flemish business records suggest that anywhere from 20–90 percent of silver receipts at Cádiz were reexported clandestinely, although the average was about 20 percent. Everaert, *Handel,* 902, 908 and AAEPar, Correspondence Politique, Espagne 70, f. 215.

115. Note that with protection of local authorities, the sons of Breton noble families participated in smuggling with the nearby islands of Guernsey and Jersey. Meyer, *La noblesse bretonne,* 1:148–49.

116. AAEPar, Correspondence Politique, Espagne 70, ff. 214–214v.

117. AAEPar, Mémoires et Documents, Espagne 79, f. 20.

118. *Estimated Returns By Flotas From New Spain, 1670–97 in millions of pesos*

	(1)	(2)		(1)	(2)
1670	8.5*	22	1688	24	20
1679	12.0	16	1690	10	12
1681	10.0	11	1697	30†	23
1685	15.0	14			

*In patacones   †In écus.

(1) Everaert, *Handel,* 391, n. 2, 395, 902; (2) Morineau, *Incroyables gazettes,* 233–236, table 39.

119. AAEPar, Correspondence Politique, Espagne 70, ff. 215–215v. In 1670 and 1686 French ports received the largest percentage (30 and 26 percent respectively) of Cadiz exports by value to European ports. Everaert, *Handel,* 453.

120. AAEPar, Correspondence Politique, Espagne 70, ff. 254v.–255. Resort to the *indulto* which achieved almost formal status after 1660 seems to be the government's recognition of its inability to prevent illegal silver handling: on 31 March 1660 Madrid abandoned registry required of silver imports at Sevilla, which was followed by the adoption of formal quotas on Sevilla businessmen. Haring, *Trade and Navigation,* 80–81 and Hamilton, *American Treasure,* 11 refer to the cedula of 1660 detailed in Veitia Linaje, *Norte,* bk. 1, chap. 20, para. 48.

The *indulto* technique of distributing a tax burden has continued into twentieth-century Spain. In the 1970s social security taxes were collected by the Hacienda ministry, which first "decides the totals the companies will pay on a sector-by-sector basis." Businessmen then "decide how much individual companies in a given sector will pay." *New York Times,* 27 February 1977.

121. Estimated percentages of underregistry of Spain's precious metals imports vary from 22 percent (1620–30) to 67 percent (1632–42) to 55 percent (1643–59). Morineau, *Incroyables gazettes,* 240–42, table 41.

122. Everaert, *Handel,* 916–17. In *indultos generales* alone, García Fuentes calculates a total paid by Sevilla of 5.6 million pesos, exclusive of another 830,000 levied on illegal shipments of French textiles *(ropa). El comercio español,* 133–36.

123. AAEPar, Mémoires et Documents, Espagne 79, f. 22; Kamen in Jover Zamora, ed., *Historia de España* 27:248–49.

124. AAEPar, Correspondence Politique, Espagne 70, ff. 255–255v.

125. Ibid., ff. 256–256v.

126. On mercantilism as developmental policy, see the remarkable synthesis of Pierre Deyon, *Mercantilisme,* 13, 82–83, 88 and Klaveren, "Fiscalism, Mercantilism and Corruption," 142. Mercantilism in this context is discussed in chapter 5.

127. A notable exception to this generalization is Luíz Ortiz, who urged encouragement of domestic workshops and suspension of exports of raw materials but avoided solutions for handling the disrupting inflows of colonial silver. *Memorial,* 29–41.

128. Carey, *Essay on the State of England,* from the dedication.

129. Recently "official corruption" in the colonial trade has been viewed in the broad context of political economy. See Vila Vilar, "Las ferias de Portobelo," 302–11, 315–17. Vila sees such corruption as a relationship between Sevilla's merchants and the central government: the official accounts were "la punta del iceberg cuyo volumen es imprevisible." (311). See also: Pietschmann, "Burocracia y corrupción," 11–37; Saguier, "La corrupción administrativa," 269–303.

130. Klaveren, "Fiscalism, Mercantilism and Corruption," 149–50.

131. Solano, "Norte," in Veitia Linaje, *Norte,* xiv–xviii.

132. Ibid., lv, app. 2.

133. Ribot García, in Jover Zamora, ed., *Historia de España* 28:17–18, 119, 173.

134. Solano, "Norte," x–xiv.

135. This was reported by investigators checking his antecedents when he applied for membership in the Orden de Santiago.

136. Solano, "Norte," xx.

137. Ibid., xvii.

138. An official synthesis of the *Norte* reads: " . . . es un tratado de materias peculiares tocantes al buen govierno de ese [Contratación] tribunal, administración de la Real Hacienda, despacho y apresto de galeones y flotas, y cumplimento de las diligencias de los ministros políticos y militares que en esa Casa y en la Carrera sirven . . . ." Ibid. lv, app. 2.

139. Veitia had handled deposits of 3,000 pesos (in escudos of 10 reales de plata each) from Juan Alonso González de Guzmán of the town of Poza; and he had been overseeing *juros* of the conde de Villariego of Burgos. Overseas in New Spain were 6,000 escudos de plata in the hands of two Spaniards who had returned 4,000, the balance to be forwarded by Veitía's nephew, Juan José de Veitia Linaje, on the earliest flota returning, payable to Diego de Villatoro of Sevilla. Ibid. lxi–lxii, appendix 5. There are references to charges leveled against Juan José at Mexico City for mis-

use of office. Solano, "Norte," and Gómez Gómez, *Las visitas de la Real Hacienda,* 253–55.

140. This argument—originally advanced in Woodrow Borah's *New Spain's Century of Depression* and taken up in Pierre and Huguette Chaunu's *Séville et l'Atlantique.* vol. 8, pt. 2, 2:1557–61—is admirably synthesized by Peter Bakewell who offers as well a reasoned critique in *Silver Mining and Society,* 226–33. See also Hamilton, *American Treasure and the Price Revolution* and Chevalier, *La formation des grands domaines au Mexique.*

Contrary to these authors, Phillips sees demographic fluctuations and resource availabilities, not a colonial silver factor, as major determinants of stagnation in early- and mid-seventeenth-century Spain, and of signs of recovery at the century's end. Phillips, "Time and Duration," 531–62.

141. Tepaske and Klein, "The Seventeenth-Century Crisis in New Spain," 116–135, esp. 135.

142. Veitia Linaje, *Norte,* book 1, chap. 20, para. 48.

143. Everaert, *Handel,* 397, 935. The volume of illegal silver flows in the last half of the seventeenth century was reflected in the stability of prices in silver at a low level. *Handel,* 396.

144. Girard, *Commerce français,* 82.

145. Domínguez Ortiz, "Les extrangeros," 305.

146. Ibid., "La venta de cargos," 125–26.

147. Stols, "La colonia flamenca," 370.

148. Weiss, *L'Espagne depuis le règne de Philippe II,* 2:216–19.

149. AAEPar, Correspondence Politique, Espagne 70, f. 255v.

150. "Memorial sobre la perdida de Espana y su comercio dirigida a la reyna viuda de Felipe IV, 1668," reproduced in Gervasio Artiñano y de Galdácano's *Historia del comercio con las Indias durante el dominio de los Austria,* appendix. In 1662 he had recently returned from the American colonies. A Dominican ("padre regente") of the Orden de Predicadores, Castro represented Genoese financiers who were also tax-farmers and treasurers of the Santa Cruzada (Domingo Grillo, Ambrosio Lomelin) who had also held the slave *asiento.* To enhance their bid for the contract, they offered to finance naval construction—a bid that never materialized. Scelle, *La traite négrière,* 1:495–96, 522–23, 537, 560.

151. As he acknowledged the spread between registered value of imports from the colonies and their real value, "siendo incomparablemente mayor la cantidad que se oculta, que la que se registra, o indulta. . . ."

152. Foreign-born agents gathered valuable trade information on arrival at Lima, Castro reported, where they "examinan que calidad ha de tener el genero para su mayor abanco y mejor salida. Vuelven a España y mandan fabricar en su tierra los generos . . . como lo ha hecho Génova. . . ."

153. Martinez de Mata, *Memoriales y discursos,* 149–50. Gonzalo Anes, in a perceptive introduction to the thought and times of Mata, concludes that in editing Mata's manuscripts in the *Apéndice a la educación popular,* Pedro Rodríguez Campomanes suppressed paragraphs, among other of his editorial interventions, 35.

154. Ibid., 98, 109, 111.

155. Ibid., 583 n. 336. Campomanes interpreted Mata's *erario* as both *banco* and *banco nacional.*

156. Osorio y Redín, "Discurso I. Extensión política y económica," 11 October, 1686, 169. About 70 percent of the "Discurso" is devoted to Spain's colonial trades.

157. Ibid., 71–72.

158. Ibid., 75 ff.

159. Ibid., 73.

160. Ibid., 106–7, 109–12.

161. The fraud factor in undercounting *flota* tonnage was about 3; in cargo value, slightly over 5. Ibid., 126–27.

162. Each male, Osorio estimated, required per annum 26 *varas* of cloth for 3 shirts, 2 pairs of trousers, plus bed linen; each woman, 34 *varas* for petticoats (*enaguas*) and blouses. Multiplying each gender's textile requirements by 16,000 yields 960,000 *varas*; each *nao* carried, he calculated, 1,069,000 *varas* of linen. Again, multiplying the *naos* (25) by people clothed per *nao* (320,000 of both genders) gives 800,000 potentially clothed, of an aggregate demand of 3,200,000 colonial consumers. He allocated 200 pesos per capita expenditure by colonial consumers buying imported cloth, a sum, as Campomanes noted "sumamente excesivo." Ibid., 131 and n. 87.

163. Ibid., 126–28.

164. Ibid., 139. Here is his estimated state revenue if his recommendations were carried out:

	in millions of pesos
Frutos de medio-diezmo *(labradores)*	65
Crown land under cultivation	40
Inland customs *puertos secos*	6
Customs *(rentas de la mar)*	20
American colonies	50
Total	120

Ibid., 134–36.

Assuming that half of *rentas de la mar* represent customs on imports to be reexported to the colonies, then 50 percent of public revenue would derive from colonial sources.

165. Ibid., 168, 171.

166. Jover Zamora, ed., *Historia de Espana*, 28:122.

167. Ordered to Cadiz in 1687 to investigate illegal incoming silver shipments, Mancera recommended that the Cadiz merchant community be fined a 500,000-peso *indulto*. Does this explain why that same year Lira (as a *consejero de estado*) was consulted when French merchants (the largest bloc of foreign resident merchants) at Cadiz petitioned Madrid for an independent judge *(juez conservador)* to adjudicate cases between French merchants and Spanish authorities? Girard, *Commerce francais*, 160, 189.

168. *Mémoires et considérations sur le commerce et les finances d'Espagne. . .*, 2:3–9.

169. Ibid., 2:23–24.

170. Ibid., 2:44–45, 58–59, 61, 67–69; Muñéz Pérez, "reglamento de comercio libre," 16–17.

171. Ibid., 2:76–77, 89.

172. Deyon, *Le mercantilisme*, 48–49.

173. Ringrose, *Madrid*, 1–16, 143–92, 312–16.

174. Defined by Mauro Hernández Benítez as "la realidad del despotismo ilus-

trado es las de un intento de afianzar el poder de una monarquía cuya naturaleza está divorciada del cambio social. Una monarquía cuya 'propia legitimidad le obligaba a legitimar tambien todo aquello que, heredado del pasado, suponía un conjunto de privilegios disfrutados con el apoyo de los monarcas a quienes habia sucedido.'" Hernández Benítez, "Carlos III: Un mito progresista," 22.

4. Conjunctural Crisis: War and the Utrecht Settlement

1. Amphibious operations by European forces were still unable to seize and hold Spanish or Portuguese continental colonies in America. Holland had to withdraw from northeastern Brazil (1654) while England had to trade with Brazil indirectly through the Lisbon entrepôt.

2. *Essay on the State of England,* 125–26; Armytage, *The Free Port System,* 15–16. Another English observer phrased it pithily: "We exchange our goods with 'em for nothing but Gold and Silver, & the Goods we traffick with are only wearing apparel and negroes for their mines." Quoted in Nettels, "England and the Spanish American Trade," 20.

3. Armytage, *The Free Port System,* 16–18.

4. Curtin, *The Atlantic Slave Trade,* 119, table 34; Davis, *The Atlantic Economies,* 135.

5. ". . . sous pretexte de nous faire passer des marchandises aux Indes, et en avoir des retours en argent et en marchandises." Abbé d'Estrées (1692) in Scelle, *La traite négrière,* 2:107; ANPar, Affaires Etrangères, B I, 767.

6. Between 1660 and 1685 English exports expanded from an annual average of £4.1 (1660) to £6.5 million (1680). In roughly the same period, shipping to and from Spanish Caribbean ports (Portobelo, Cartagena) and also Jamaica rose. Minchinton, ed., *The Growth of English Overseas Trade,* 12; Nettels, "England and Spanish American Trade," 15–16.

7. Rodríguez de Campomanes, "Apuntaciones relativas al comercio," AHN, Estado 3208[1]; there is another copy, BRPal, Mss. Ayala, 2867.

8. Grillo was a prominent court banker; a Grillo (Domingo or Francisco) purchased the title of *grande* in 1691. Kamen, *Spain in the Late Seventeenth Century,* 250, 259, n. 140.

9. Scelle, *Traite négrière,* 1:509 ff., 523–24. Cary enthused over the African and "West India" trade by the Royal African Company in moving slaves and manufactures to Jamaica and Barbados for reexport to the Spanish colonies. *Essay,* 65, 67, 74–77.

10. Scelle, *Traite négrière,* 1:575–76.

11. Ibid., 578–87, 602–3, 620.

12. Ibid., 560 ff., 619.

13. This is clear in the fine monograph of Malamud Rikles, *Cádiz y Saint Malo,* esp. chaps. 2–3.

14. Girard, *Commerce français,* 334.

15. On the perception of France's commercial and financial backwardness especially vis-à-vis Holland, see the summary in Goubert, *Louis XIV,* 53–57, 62.

16. Savary, it was reputed, also had a hand in drafting Colbert's *Ordonnance de*

commerce (1673), which merchants of Paris had requested to regulate trade practices throughout France. Sée, *Histoire économique,* 1:226.

17. Rothkrug, *Opposition to Louis XIV,* 183–84.

18. Ibid., 162, n. 45, 184, 207, n. 44.

19. Ibid., 187–88.

20. Alcedo y Herrera, *Piraterías y agresiones,* 5–6.

21. "Memorial que dió al Sr. Luis XIV . . . proponiendo las máximas . . . para el mejor acierto de sus designios según el estado que tenía su monarquía y la de España . . . 1666." Madrid, 18 Dec. 1759. BMus, Egerton 367, ff. 219v, 221–223v, 225. On the large contingent of French migrants in Aragon, see Domínguez Ortiz, "Los extrangeros," 353–54. French agents at Madrid reported that Spanish officials openly declared that Spain "ne concourroit jamais avec la France, c'estoit assez dire que'Elle luy céderoit en tout et par tout." AAEPar, Correspondance Politique, Espagne 63, f. 178.

22. Archbishop of Toulouse to Colbert, 29 August 1690. ANPar, Affaires Etrangères, B I, 766. Evidence abounds of diplomatic reports on France's trade with Spain's colonies in America, 1648–98. See: "Mémoire des affaires concernant le commerce . . . jusqu'à . . . 1689," AAEPar, Correspondance Politique, 63, and "Mémoire concernant le commerce et les colonies. Janvier 1698." AAEPar, Mémoires et Documents, Espagne, 80.

23. Penetration of the Caribbean and Pacific coast by French commercial interests is treated with a wealth of detail in Dahlgren, *Relations commerciales* and Malamud Rikles, *Cádiz y Saint Malo.*

24. Lévy, *Capitalistes,* 122–23.

25. Kamen, *War of Succession,* 45, 127.

26. Debien, Gabriel, *Une plantation de Saint-Domingue,* 34.

27. Dahlgren, *Relations commerciales,* 116; Debien, *Une plantation de Saint-Domingue,* 35.

28. Danycan's commercial enterprises with Spain's American colonies had produced by 1710 an extraordinary fortune of between 25 and 30 million *livres tournois.* Malamud Rikles, *Cádiz y Saint Malo,* 58. Danycan was the son of a Norman merchant shipper who had migrated to Saint-Malo circa 1640. Dahlgren, *Relations commerciales,* 116.

29. Debien, *Une plantation de Saint-Domingue,* 26–35; Lévy, *Capitalistes,* 138–40, 157, 166–67.

30. Klaveren, "Fiscalism, Mercantilism and Corruption," 158.

31. AAEPar, Mémoires et Documents, Espagne 199, ff. 163–163v; Smith, *Wealth of Nations,* 434.

32. Through the contacts of Malouin merchants like Guillaume Eon with Marseille and other merchants, European cities—Geneva, Genoa, Leghorn, and Hamburg—were drawn into trade with Spain's Pacific coast colonies. Malamud Rikles, *Cádiz y Saint Malo,* 60–61, 80.

33. A careful estimate of returns from Spanish America in this period indicates that the French treasury probably received more than that of Spain. Kamen, in Jover Zamora, ed., *Historia de España,* 28:291.

34. Girard, *Commerce français,* 84–85, 363.

35. Rothkrug, *Opposition to Louis XIV,* 218–19; Lévy, *Capitalistes et pouvoir,* 130; ANPar, Affaires Etrangères, B I, 221, f. 39; Girard, *Commerce français,* 143–45.

36. García Fuente, *El comercio español con América,* 46; "Liste des négocians" (1714), ANPar, Affaires Etrangères, B I, 221.

37. Vilar, *Oro y moneda,* 292; Meyer, *La noblesse de Bretagne,* 1:337.

38. A Guillaume Eon (sieur de Villegille) had been France's consul at Cádiz, 1662–67. Malamud Rikles, *Cádiz y Saint Malo,* 59–60

39. Lévy, *Capitalistes,* 130.

40. In a memoire to Pontchartrain, Danycan and Jourdan de Grouée (4 March 1698) declared their intention to penetrate the Spanish overseas commercial system in both the Caribbean and along the Pacific coast. Lévy, *Capitalistes,* 125. See also Scelle, *Traite négrière,* 2:112–13.

41. Cf. Palmer, *Slaves of the White God.*

42. Lévy, *Capitalistes,* 131–32.

43. Scelle, *Traite négrière,* 2:109–10.

44. Lévy, *Capitalistes,* 139.

45. Ibid., 132.

46. Scelle, *Traite négrière,* 2:459, n. 2.

47. The following overview is based on Kamen, *War of Succession,* chap. 2, his *Spain in the Later Seventeenth Century,* chaps. 14–15, his contributions to Domínguez Ortiz, ed., *Historia de España,* 6:64–70, and Jover Zamora, ed., *Historia de España,* 28:207–98; Domínguez Ortiz, *El antiguo régimen,* 401–16.

48. In 1701, four of twelve *grandes de primera clase,* rejecting a Bourbon monarchy in Spain, contacted Anglo-Dutch groups. Two years later among *grandes* of dubious loyalty to Philip V were Medina Celi, Montalto, Infantado, Condestable, Carpio, Frigiliana, and Leganés. Leganés, for example, was dismissed as gobernador-general of Cádiz. Kamen, *War of Succession,* 88, n. 15, 96–97, 99. Also, Francis, *The Methuens and Portugal,* 140

49. For example, Oropesa's administration in 1691 attempted to downsize the excessive number of employees in the bureaucracy of the Casa de Contratación, and to lower the volume of salary arrears; both efforts failed. Schäfer, *Consejo real,* 1:334–39.

50. Kamen has noted that many among the Castilian nobility "were, or pretended to be, in a precarious economic position." *War of Succession,* 101.

51. Working with Oropesa were two prominent bureaucrats (Francisco Manuel de Lyra and Manuel García de Bustamente) who hoped to revitalize colonial navigation and trade by following the model of Holland's East India Company to encourage the export of colonial dyestuffs and shipbuilding facilities. Jover Zamora, ed., *Historia de España,* 28:190–91, 220.

52. Vast, *Les grands traités,* 3:5

53. Ibid., 2:19. Bolingbroke referrred to a "furious memorial" by Spanish critics of the proposed partition in *Defence of the Treaty of Utrecht,* 95.

54. In 1698 English representatives sought French agreement for seizing some Spanish colonies on the death of Charles II. The French insisted on the integrity of the Spanish empire in America—their motivation was hardly altruistic. This position may have reinforced pro-Bourbon sentiments among some Spanish elites. Scelle, *Traite négrière,* 2:456.

55. García-Baquero, *Cádiz y el Atlántico*, 1:232–33.

56. Among many of Spain's political class French military and naval power were now considered "la única garantía de la supervivencia de la monarquía como una unidad." Domínguez Ortiz, ed., *Historia de España*, 6:166.

57. Parry, *The Spanish Seaborne Empire*, 270; Kessell and Hendricks, eds., *By Force of Arms*, 11–35.

58. MacLeod, *Spanish Central America*, 345–46; Guthrie, "Riots in Seventeenth-Century Mexico City," 243–58.

59. Bakewell, *Zacatecas*, 232–33.

60. Much the same could be said for the other major mining colony, Peru. Lynch, *Spain under the Hapsburgs*, 2:199, 223–24.

61. Dahlgren, *Relations commerciales*, 650.

62. The testament was more significant than commonly recognized. It settled what had been at the center of European diplomatic interest for decades and was the "punto de partida de un nuevo equilibrio mundial de fuerzas e indirectamente también de una nueva estructuración del Estado español. "Introducción," *Testamento de Carlos II*, 1.

63. Scelle, *Traite négrière*, 2:458.

64. Ibid., 124, 459; Ségur-Dupeyron, *Histoire des négotiations*, 2:268; AAEPar, Mémoires et Documents, Espagne, 208, n. 19, f. 173.

65. Bartolomé de Flon y Morales and Hubert Hubrecht (both originally from Zeeland) were heavily involved in peninsular finance and colonial trade. When Cardinal Portocarrero's nephew was a high official in Galicia, they held the salt tax farm there. In 1710 and 1711 Flon lent Madrid 56 million reales—presumably funds invested by French groups. To compensate Flon for financial assistance at critical moments during the war, Philip enobled him with a *título de Castilla* in perpetuity, conde de la Cadena. (A descendant, Manuel de Flon, was intendant of Puebla [New Spain] in 1808). Kamen, *War of Succession*, 71–73; Lévy, *Capitalistes*, 146; Domínguez Ortiz, *Sociedad y estado*, 350.

Together they fashioned a network of contacts with Spanish colonial officials. They were correspondents of José de Santiago Concha (an *alcalde* at Lima), advanced travel costs to Castell dos Rius (viceroy of Peru), and bought the *presidencia* of Panama for the marqués de Villaroca. Scelle, *Traite négrière*, 2:216, 218, n. 2; Lévy, *Capitalistes*, 146. Hubrecht was the Compagnie de Guinée's Madrid agent, and collaborated with Parisian banker Bernard Crozat, an investor in the Compagnie de Guinée; on his way to the viceroyalty of New Spain, the conde de Linares visited Crozat. Crozat aimed to "établir un commerce reglé avec les Espagnols du Mexique." Scelle, *Traite négrière*, 2:417, n. 1; Lévy, *Capitalistes*, 409, 448.

66. Scelle, *Traite négrière*, 2:335; Cantillo, *Tratados*, 32, 36–40, 42.

67. Arias was considered one of the pro-Bourbon group or faction. Later archbishop of Sevilla, at his death in 1718 he was a cardinal. Lévy, *Capitalistes*, 150 and n. 83. Sevilla's consulado, let it be noted, rejected the offer of the *asiento*. Scelle, *Traite négrière* 2:132, n. 4.

68. Bergeyck to Philip V (1712) in Scelle, *Traite négrière*, 2:426, 459 n. 2; Nettels, "England and the Spanish American Trade," 19.

69. Jenkinson, *Treaties*, 1:326–29; Ségur-Dupeyron, *Histoire des relations commerciales*, 2:282–83; Clarke, "War Trade," 262. Cf. "The main object of the present war is

the Indies trade and the wealth it produces." quoted in Kamen, *War of Succession*, 135. Spanish naval historian Zeferino Ferret later concluded that the Anglo-Dutch treaty (1701) was intended to "apoderarse de nuestras Américas, y hacer cada una perpetuamente suya la parte que ocupase con sus armas." "Exposición historica" (1813). MN, ms. 444, f. 204v. In 1702 it was calculated that 20 percent of England's aggregate foreign trade earnings or about £400,000 were generated by trade with Spain. Carrera Pujal, *Economía española*, 3:76–79.

70. On Bristol's sixteenth-century trade with Andalusia, see Sacks, *Trade, Society and Politics*, 574–76, 613–25. For broader treatment, see the very substantial article of Pauline Croft, "English Commerce," 236–63.

71. Cary, *Essay*, 65, 74–75, 77, 115–16.

72. For example, the 1670 *flota* from Veracruz brought 8.5 million pesos mainly in silver. In one month alone, 4.1 million was reexported, more than 1.1 million to France (to Saint-Malo, 1.08). Kamen in Jover Zamora, ed., *Historia de España*, 28:255.

73. Lévy, *Capitalistes et pouvoir*, 130–31; Dahlgren, *Relations commerciales*, 101–2. In 1670 perhaps one-quarter of Cádiz's reexports of silver from New Spain were shipped to Saint-Malo. ANPar, Affaires Etrangères, B I, 211, f.39.

74. Dahlgren, *Relations commerciales*, 247 and n. 1.

75. Ibid., 250–51. French ambassador d'Estrées managed to have the Consejo de Castilla block the Consejo de Indias from investigating this incident.

76. Walker, *Spanish Politics*, 48.

77. Dahlgren, *Relations commerciales*, 152, 186–209 and especially 321–57; Malamud Rikles, *Cádiz y Saint Malo*, 48. (There is a list of shipping between Spain and America, 1701–15 in Kamen, *War of Succession*, 178, table 3). On page 400, Kamen has opined that the "movement of the port of Saint-Malo could well shed more light on the Atlantic trade than the movement of the ports of Sevilla and Cádiz."

78. Lévy, *Capitalistes*, 402.

79. Dahlgren, *Relations commerciales*, 336.

80. Ibid., 242–43.

81. On Pontchartrain's interest in French expansion into the western Atlantic, see: Frostin, "Les Pontchartrain," 307–36.

82. Born at Gisors in the south of France, Mesnager had been a merchant at Rouen, then traveled on business in western Europe and the Spanish colonies in America, retiring in 1692 to practice law at Rouen. Lévy, *Capitalistes*, 256–57. As a specialist knowledgeable in colonial trade, he sat on the Conseil de Commerce (created in 1700) beside Saint-Malo's mayor, La Motte Gaillard. Scoville, "The French Economy," 231–32.

83. Dahlgren, *Relations commerciales*, 322–24. Mesnager and Daubenton had participated in formulating French policy toward Spain in the late 1690s. Once in Spain they were subordinate to French representatives Amelot de Gournay and then Jean Orry, meanwhile corresponding with key ministers at Paris, Pontchartrain, Chamillart, and Desmaretz, who also relied on advice of a Malouin extended merchant family, the Magon. Pontchartrain and the others consulted with merchant bankers Crozat and Bernard (both involved in chartered companies in the African slave trade and trade with East Asia). In 1712 Antoine Crozat was the "proprietor" (governor) of Louisiana. Bannon, *The Spanish Borderlands*, 109.

84. Dahlgren, *Relations commerciales,* 255. Daubenton concluded (1702) that the Consejo de Indias jointly with its Casa de Contratación at Sevilla blocked innovation in colonial trade structures because they "reçoivent des pensions des officiers des Indes et font des profits sur l'armadille"—a reasonable conclusion.

85. Ibid., 259. Daubenton collaborated with Spanish personnel of pronounced pro-Bourbon leanings, e.g., Bernardo Tinagero de la Escalera, Baltasar Pando de Figueroa, Manuel de Aperreguy, and Miguel de Errasquin, Ibid., 88, 267, n. 3, 483, 499.

86. Ibid., 259–61.

87. Cf. "Los franceses se inmiscuian en todo e intentaban explotar las limitadas posibilidades económicas de España." In many ways, Kamen claims, Spain was "una colonia económica de Francia." Kamen in Jover Zamora, ed., *Historia de España,* 28:289.

88. Dahlgren, *Relations commerciales,* 268–70. One year earlier (1704) Malouin merchant Grandville-Locquet had proposed a remarkably similar project, to send secretly galleons under French escort vessels around the Horn to the Peruvian coast. Daubenton rejected it. Ibid., 257.

89. Ibid., 325.

90. Ibid., 327, n. 1

91. The Junta was charged with reorganizing trade and navigation with the American colonies; it reviewed the formation of a chartered company (open to Spanish and non-Spanish investors) and individual sailings (*registros sueltos*) from more than one peninsular port. García-Baquero, *Cádiz y el Atlántico,* 1:152.

92. Dahlgren, *Relations commerciales,* 336, 339–40.

93. Kamen, *War of Succession,* 155.

94. Dahlgren, *Relations commerciales,* 343 and n. 1. Orry, Amelot, Mesnager and Daubenton were advised in turn by resident French merchant houses in Lower Andalusia, e.g., Jolif, Eon, Gilly, Magon de la Lande. Kamen, *War of Succession,* 77.

95. Walker, *Spanish Politics,* 31.

96. Dahlgren, *Relations commerciales,* 349; "Rémonstrance par laquelle le commerce de Seville demande qu'on empêche le commerce que les étrangers font en fraude dans les ports des Indes tant du nord comme du sud" (1707). ANPar, B 7, 246. See also "Respuesta fiscal (1706)." AHN, Estado, 2312. Twenty-one representatives of Lower Andalusia and other affected areas lodged complaints at Madrid along with one from the merchants of Lima. Legarra, Juan de, "Comercios de España e Indias. Estado actual de ellos: causa de que demana su decadencia y medios por restablecerlos. Madrid, 1719." BRAHM, ms. 4666; Moreyra y Paz Soldan, *El tribunal,* 1:xliv.

97. Dahlgren, *Relations commerciales,* 481–83. Anxious to receive colonial silver on government account, Madrid agreed to cover the expenses of French convoys to Callao and Veracruz. Ducasse commanded the *flota* returning from Veracruz. Walker, *Spanish Politics,* 32–33.

98. Dahlgren, *Relations commerciales,* 485. The Andalusian merchants' protest was sent not only to Philip, but also to the Consejo de Indias and the Junta de Comercio.

99. BNPar, Mss. Fonds Espagnol, 152.

100. Monségur, "Nouveaux mémoires touchant le Mexique ou la Nouvelle

Espagne. Recueillis sur les lieux . . . par . . . depuis corrigés et augmentés en 1713 et en 1714." (Madrid, 15 Juin 1709). BNPar, Mss. Fonds Français, 24, 228. I am indebted to Jean-Pierre Berthe for directing me to this manuscript, the one cited henceforth. He has located other copies in the Biblioteca Nacional (Madrid), and the Bibliothèque de l'Arsenal (Paris). Harvard University's Houghton Library also has a version. There is a recent Mexican edition: *Las nuevas memorias del capitán Juan de Monségur*, edited by J.-P. Berthe.

101. Dahlgren, *Relations commerciales*, 350–51, 402–3. At the same time English colonial authorities at Jamaica contacted Havana, Portobelo, and Cartagena seeking recognition of the Austrian Archduke Charles. Nettels, "England and the Spanish Trade," 44. See also Borges, "Los aliados," 321–70.

102. It is presumptive that Monségur had letters of introduction to those wholesale merchants who bought directly from Cádiz suppliers using their own funds, as well as to those who accepted capital sent from Cádiz for local investment.

103. Monségur, "Mémoires," f. 296.

104. Using minimum figures (300,000 and 100,000 respectively), just the top nineteen incomes concentrated over 4 million silver pesos—these were truly merchant princes. The incomes listed exclude capital invested in their mercantile operations by colonial religious corporations and individuals.

105. Monségur, "Mémoires," ff. 88–89, 92–94, 97, 100. Among the largest capitalized merchants was Luís Sainz de Tagle (marqués de Altamira) with 2 million pesos borrowed from religious corporations. (He also listed among the wealthiest a Beytia, perhaps a Veitia Linaje?).

106. Ibid., ff. 84–85.

107. His opposition to the Manila-Acapulco trade was based on the flow of silver to the Far East which provided merchandise that Europe proceeded to reexport to America. Ibid., ff. 84–85, 331–32, 372–73.

108. Ibid., ff. 294–95, 297.

109. Ibid., f. 287.

110. Unambiguously he defended restoring the Hapsburg system of managed trade "par la voye de Cádiz comme il devoit estre pour le bien général de l'Espagne et de l'Europe." Ibid., ff. 296–98.

111. Dahlgren, *Relations commerciales*, 489, 491.

112. Maxwell, *Pombal*, 41–42 and n. 9.

113. Francis, *The Methuens and Portugal*, 208, 214.

114. Scelle, *Traite négrière*, 2:461–63 and passim. Catalan interests were represented in the English negotiations by a confirmed supporter of the Archduke, José Folch de Cardona, supported by the conde de Oropesa, Manuel Garcia Alvarez de Toledo y Portugal. Kamen, *War of Succession*, 307. For a Catalan enterprise designed to enter the "Castilian" colonial trade circuits to which Catalan entry had been blocked, see Vilar, *Le 'Manual de la Companya nova de Gibraltar.'*

115. Cantillo, *Tratados*, 48–52.

116. Clarke, "War Trade," 278.

117. Copies of the treaty were discovered aboard a vessel seized by French corsairs. Dahlgren, *Relations commerciales*, 571, n. 1.

118. Scelle, *Traite négrière*, 2:417, n. 1.

119. Lévy, *Capitalistes*, 393.

120. Scelle, *Traite négrière*, 2:243, 272, 282 ff.

121. Ibid., 2:426–33.

122. Ibid., 2:477, 480.

123. Bergeyck tried to protect Flander's textile manufactures from growing English and Dutch competition imports; local Flemish opposition led to his resignation and subsequent move to Spain. Deyon, *Mercantilism*, 42. As an example of Franco-Spanish collaboration, Madrid authorities advised a penurious Castell dos Rius about to depart for Peru (1703) as viceroy, to borrow travel expense money from members of the Compagnie de Guinée, e.g., Bernard and Crozat. Scelle, *Traite négrière* 2:428.

124. Lévy, *Capitalistes*, 432; Kamen, *War of Succession*, 140–66, 176–93, 381–82, 392–93.

125. King, *The British Merchant* 3:198.

126. Coxe, *Memoires*, 1:126–27. One of the major stockholders of the South Sea Company was William Paterson, a founder of the Bank of England and a mover behind the South Sea Company (1698), whose original intention was to establish a commercial entrepôt on the Isthmus of Panama. Lévy, *Capitalistes*, 153–54.

The impressive increase in the value of Jamaica's imports indicated potential sales to Spain's Caribbean colonies:

Average Annual Jamaican Imports from England, 1694/1705–1715

	(£)
1699–1705	136,500
1706–12	176,100
[?] 1715	196,000

Nettels, "England and the Spanish Trade," 28–29

127. Dahlgren, *Relations commerciales*, 638.

128. Baudrillart, *Philip V*, 1:451–53.

129. Sperling, *The South Sea Company*, 9–14.

130. Levene, ed., *Documentos*, 5:xxvi.

131. Scelle, *Traite négrière* 2:528–530 and n. 1.

132. Jenkinson, *Treaties*, 1:375–97.

133. Between 1680 and 1700 Jamaica's merchants sold slaves to Genoese merchants Porcio and Borroso [sic], who exercised the *asiento* awarded nominally to Sevilla's merchants. Nettels, "England and the Spanish Trade," 2, 19.

134. Scelle, *Traite négrière* 2:463.

135. Tinagero participated in the Junta formed by the Spanish government to review carefully the terms of the *asiento*. Other Junta members: conde de Bergeyck, conde de Frigiliana, Alonso de Araziel, José de los Rios and Antonio de la Vega Calo. Ibid., 540, n. 4.

136. Jenkinson, *Treaties*, 1:397–99.

137. Ibid., 179–84.

138. Monteleone, Spain's ambassador at London and a descendant of Hernan Cortes, was advised that Madrid had accepted Gilligan's proposed articles and was ordered to "régler l'Assiente à la satisfaction du Sieur Gilligan." Scelle, *Traite négrière*, 2:541–42. By granting English merchants special arrangements for direct access to Spain's colonies—which could not be extended to other nations as part of most-favored-nation agreements—Madrid substantiated Dahlgren's conclusion that

"Toute la politique espagnole de cette époque est caracterisée par la plus grande complaisance à l'égard des Anglais." *Relations commerciales,* 723.

139. As Curtis Nettels summed up the situation, "Jamaica remained the center of coin in British America." "England and Spanish American Trade," 30, 32.

140. Jenkinson, *Treaties* 2:88–144, 173–75.

141. Ibid., 69.

142. "Démostration géometrique. . . ." ANPar, F 12, ff. 647–48.

143. Penetrating the commercial circuits of Spain (and Portugal) at the end of the seventeenth century stimulated the growth of English manufactures and overseas trade, a foundation for England's later industrialization. Cf. Hobsbawm, "The Crisis of the Seventeenth Century," 50–52.

144. AAEPar, Mémoires et Documents, Espagne 129, f.315. Brittany, Normandy, Champagne and Paris were France's major areas producing for Spanish colonial consumers. Girard, *Commerce français,* 596–97.

145. Sée, "Documents," 466; Malamud Rikles, *Cádiz y Saint Malo,* 150.

146. Antonio de Ulloa traced the decline of Saint-Malo in the eighteenth century to the preoccupation of newly wealthy merchant households with "procurar un lustre a la familia mas recomendable que él que tenían por sí; con este fin solicitaron casamientos vantajosos fuera del propio paíz, compraron empleos de nobleza, y de esta suerte se deposeyeron de las mismas riquezas que avían adquirido . . . ." "Memoria" to Ensenada. Marina 712, AGSim, f. 573. Poor roads between Saint-Malo and its hinterland were a further factor leading to a contraction in the port's maritime activity. Sée, *Histoire économique,* 1:331.

147. Arnould, *De la balance du commerce,* vol. 3, tables 1a–d, 2a–b. Cf. Fetter, "'Favorable Balance of Trade,'" chap. 5.

148. Muñóz Pérez, "La publicación del reglamento de comercio libre," 20.

5. Conditions of Growth, 1700–1759

1. For an excellent summary of recent scholarship, see Jover Zamora, ed., *Historia de España,* vols. 28 and 29, bks. 1 and 2.

2. There is a growing literature on the early phase of the global trading system linking America, west Europe, and Asia. The older literature is found in Braudel, *The Wheels of Commerce.* For a succinct overview of the role of American precious metals in the development of the economy of the Indian Ocean: Chaudhuri, *Trade and Civilization,* 215–19 and especially his "World Silver Flows." Chaudhuri argues that the high value of silver in Asia lowered the cost of Asian products in Europe and sustained demand there. "World Silver Flows," 76–77. For more of the recent literature, see the essays in Tracy, ed., *The Political Economy of Merchant Empires.*

3. Gándara, *Apuntes,* 52. Cf. Gándara's observation with that of Campillo y Cosío: "En tanto que España dormía, las otras naciones la devoraban . . . ." Campillo y Cosío, "España despierta," 119.

4. In the case of the port of London, see Zehediah, "London and the Colonial Consumer in the Late Seventeenth Century," 239–61.

5. North, "Institutions," 24, 26–29. See also North's earlier version, "Transaction Costs in History," 557–76.

6. Manuscript of the Minute Book of "Committee concerning Trade, 1669," quoted in Letwin, *Origins of Scientific Economics,* 44.

7. Sombart, *Le bourgeois,* 382–83.

8. H. R. Trevor-Roper's phrase in his "The General Crisis of the Seventeenth Century," 72.

9. This is the formulation of Jacob Viner, "Power versus Plenty," 81.

10. Savary appeared in five editions between 1675 and 1715, followed by many more. As for Huet, his publication had at least six editions under varying titles between 1712 and 1717: Rouen (1712), two at Paris (1713, 1714), two at Amsterdam (1717) and one at London (1717). There were subsequent editions at Brussels and Lyon.

11. Wilson, *Profit and Power,* 152; Heckscher, *Mercantilism,* 2:337; Viner, "Power versus Plenty," 71.

12. Heckscher, "Mercantilism," 22.

13. This conspectus reflects: Deyon, *Le mercantilisme,* an extraordinary synthesis; Coleman, ed., *Revisions in Mercantilism;* Cole, *Colbert;* Heckscher, *Mercantilism.*

14. Quoted in Viner, "Power versus Plenty," 77.

15. Muñóz Pérez, "Los proyectos sobre España e Indias," 169–85.

16. James Whiston quoted in Viner, "Power versus Plenty," 77, n. 1. As a Spaniard phrased it, "quiere la Inglaterra estancar en su Reino los comercios de todos los otros." Alsedo y Herrera, *Piraterías,* 267–68.

17. Chaudhuri, "Reflections," 429.

18. Ertman, "Britain and War"; Uztáriz, "Prologo," in Huet, *Comercio de Holanda* (There is a second edition, Madrid, 1746).

19. Cf. "The aim of mercantilist interventionism was . . . to catch up with the leading economic powers of Northwestern Europe." Kriedte, *Peasants, Landlords and Merchant Capitalists,* 116.

20. In Colbert's time the Dutch "seemed masters of French commerce, far outdistancing the English." Butel, "France, the Antilles and Europe," 158–59. That conclusion has been substantiated in recent analyses. See the contributions of Pierre and Huguette Chaunu and especially Robert Gascon in Braudel et al., *Histoire économique,* vol. 1, p. 1, 247, 321–22, 335, 342–49. In Gascon's view, "Les faiblesses des structures commerciales et bancaires, les survivances des mentalités archaïques, les occasions manquées, la dépendance vis-à-vis des marchands étrangers dans la plupart des secteurs essentiels du commerce extérieur sont autant de traits qui constituent et expliquent le retard français" (357).

21. Michel-Jean Amelot (marquis de Gournay) had served in diplomatic posts (Venice, Portugal, and Switzerland) after 1682. Between 1699 and 1700 he was a director of French commercial policy, becoming president of the Conseil de Commerce. Kamen, *War of Succession,* 45, 48, 114–15, 201–3; Dahlgren, *Relations commerciales,* 329. The Franco-Spanish treaties of the last half of the seventeenth century (Pyrenees, Nimègue, and Ryswick) eased the entry into Spain of merchants from Saint-Malo, Nantes, La Rochelle, Bayonne, and Marseille. In 1711 there may have been 20,000–30,000 semi-permanent French residents. Kamen, *War of Succession,* 121.

22. Uztáriz, *Theórica,* 97.

23. The following paragraphs are based primarily upon Deyon, *Le mercantilisme,* especially chapter 2 and Cole, *Colbert,* 1:301, 333, 338, 344, 346, 351; 2:34, 54–55. Recent studies have underscored Colbert's skill in achieving his goals by reconciling conflicting interests. (We have profited from Michael Mahoney, "Organizing Expertise.")

24. Chaunu in Braudel et al., eds., *Histoire économique,* vol. 1, pt. 1, 191.

25. At Richelieu's death, roughly 7,000 French (mainly Bretons and Normans) inhabited St. Christophe, Martinique, Guadeloupe, Sainte Lucie, and Tortue in the Caribbean and were responsible for developing the slave trade at Senegal and Gambia. Braudel et al., eds., *Histoire économique,* vol. 1, pt. 1, 356–57.

26. While Deyon recognizes the shortcomings of Colbert's dynamism, he grants that at his death his interventionism left "una marine reconstituée, une législation commerciale moins archaïque, une draperie à nouveau prospère et une manufacture des toiles de lin et de chanvre qui est devenue la première d'Europe." *Le mercantilisme,* 28. For Domínguez Ortiz, Colbert's policies among other factors required "el mantenimiento del río de la plata" from Spanish sources, legal and smuggled. "Guerra económica," 72.

27. "Mémoire du Roy," in Kamen, *War of Succession,* 125–26. Kamen provides a detailed analysis of French policy toward potential Spanish manufacturers (125–38, 378).

28. Dahlgren, *Relations commerciales*; Legarra, "Comercios de España y Yndias. Estado actual de ellos: causas de que dimana su decadencia; y medios por restablecerlos." BRAHMad, ms. 4666.

29. MacLachlan, *Trade and Peace,* 26, 85–86; Walker, *Spanish Politics,* 131.

30. Uztáriz recorded that the French government actively intervened to expand sales of textiles to Spain and through Spain to its American colonies. In 1701, for example, French export duties were lowered on linens, gold and silver cloths, satins, velvets, and damasks destined for Spain. In 1703, they were lowered on bays, perpets, and serges. *Theórica,* 101. Even earlier, at the end of the sixteenth century, a significant volume of Breton and Norman linens were reexported from Sevilla to the colonies. Sanz, *Comercio de España,* 1:445.

31. "The negligence which the Spanish have hitherto shown in founding manufactures obliges them always to take from foreign countries the goods they need for the lands they possess in the Indies . . . ." "Mémoire du Roy," in Kamen, *War of Succession,* 125–26.

32. Few historians have laid out more clearly than Ramon Carande the early and lasting effects of colonial silver on sixteenth-century Castile's economy: its finance, trade, and industry. The following chapters refer to themes discussed in his *Carlos V y sus banqueros* vol. 1, chaps. 7, 10, 11, and vol. 3, chap. 1. See also Rodríguez-Salgado, *The Changing Face of Empire,* 63, 68–70, 334. Equally illuminating is the incisive essay of José Larraz López, *La época del mercantilismo en Castilla,* especially chap. 6.

33. Fayard, *Les membres du Conseil de Castille,* 170.

34. Under Charles II, Spain "continued to be governed," Henry Kamen has concluded, "by a kind of consensus between various local interests. . . . Habsburg Spain was stable because it was largely self-governing, not because it was governed by an absolute monarchy." *Spain in the Later Seventeenth Century,* 17.

35. Fayard, *Conseil de Castille,* 7, 170–72; Bernard, *Conseil espagnol des Indes,* 30–31; Kamen, *War of Succession,* 108–17; Anes Alvarez, *El antiguo régimen,* 300, 304–6.

36. Alvarez de Abreu, ed., *Extracto historial.*

37. Bernard, *Conseil espagnol des Indes,* 6–8, and "Consulta del Consejo de Indias al Rey sobre el comercio, 24 December 1713," BRAHM, Colección Sempere y Guarinos.

38. Note the infatuation with the past: "Pues haviendo conserbado las Indias por el transcurso de dos siglos, bajo la mano de los gloriosos progenitores de VM que las conquistaron, aumentaron y conservaron, esto se a devido mediante la justísima máxima, tener cerrados las puertas de aquellos Bastos Dominios para que no entrase a comerziar en ellos ningun extrangero sobre que se ha promulagado infinitas Leyes," "Consulta del Consejo de Indias," BRAHM, Colección Sempere y Guarinos.

39. This refers to the "uso y práctica del contrato de haverías." The contract (1661) stipulated total payment for convoy costs would be 790,000 *ducados de plata* annually. Of this, 150,000 were payable by the Treasury; the balance was payable, on convoy arrival in colonial ports and cargo sales, by Sevilla merchants and their counterparts in the colonies. Céspedes del Castillo, *La avería,* 89–92.

40. On the organs of censorship and their role, see: Enciso Recio and Almuna, "La prensa española"; Egido, *Opinión pública.* These are summarized in Enciso Recio's contribution to Jover Zamora, ed., *Historia de España,* 29(1):222–32.

41. There is a wealth of detail about the penetration of Chinese textiles via Manila into New Spain at the end of the seventeenth and the early decades of the eighteenth century in *Extracto historial,* edited by Alvarez de Abreu. Alvarez de Abreu brought to his editorial work colonial experience, as an investigator of smuggling and fraudulent operations in colonial treasuries, later as governor of Venezuela. Walker, *Spanish Politics,* 100.

42. James Fallows, *New York Times,* 1 August 1993.

43. Huet, *Comercio de Holanda.* The second edition (1742) is the one cited here.

44. Caro Baroja, *Hora navarra.* Supplementing this rich and richly illustrated source is Alfonso de Otazu y Llanas, *Hacendistas navarros en Indias.* See also Pio Sagues Azcona, *Congregación de San Fermín de los Navarros* and Rodrigo Rodrigues Garraza, *Tensiones de Navarra.*

45. For biographical details of Juan de Goyeneche, see Caro Baroja, *Hora navarra,* chaps. 3–6. See also Kamen, *War of Succession,* 139, n. 77.

46. Kamen, *Spain in the Later Seventeenth Century,* 373.

47. Goyeneche also teamed with Melchor Macanaz to propose replacing a consumption tax *(millones)* and its redundant bureaucracy with—remarkable for its time—a single tax on income, a *contribución única.* The project was pigeon-holed, only to be revived four decades later under the administration of the marqués de la Ensenada.

48. Caro Baroja, *Hora navarra,* 200–201.

49. Goyeneche married the daughter of a finance expert in the *millones* tax bureau. As was customary. he favored extended family members, in his case those of his mother (Gastón de Iriarte). Miguel Gastón spent his youth in the American colonies, returned to Madrid and became a *dependiente* of Goyeneche.

50. Caro Baroja, *Hora navarra,* 193.

51. Feyjóo dedicated one volume of his *Teatro crítico universal* to Juan de

Goyeneche, another to Goyeneche's son, Francisco Xavier. Steffoni, in Jover Zamora, ed., *Historia de España*, 29(2):61.

52. Goyeneche made "Nuevo Baztán" into a mini-factory town by calling upon the distinguished architect José Benito de Churriguera to design the factory, a sumptuous private residence, and a church. See the comments of María Jesús Quesada Martín in Jover Zamora, ed., *Historia de España*, 29(2):373. The censor of Francisco Xavier de Goyeneche's translation of Huet, who was also chaplain to the Consejo de Indias, lauded the industrial entrepreneurship of Juan de Goyeneche, his *fábricas* and *manufacturas*. The remarks are in *Comercio de Holanda*.

53. Huet, *Comercio de Holanda*, introduction.

54. By 1717 there were at least three French editions, two at Paris (1713, 1714). Goyeneche noted that his Amsterdam copy was anonymous (to which he added, *por obviar quexas*); in fact the 1718 Amsterdam edition (not that of 1717) bears only the title.

55. After the Restoration, English political economists found a model in "Dutch society, whose organization seemed to them . . . intelligent and dynamic" while as late as the 1750s the Dutch model "remained in the minds of theorists and writers on trade as the greatest example of the fusion of statesmanship, economic policy, and commercial success." Dickson, *Financial Revolution*, 4. See also Van Dillen, "Amsterdam," 196–97; Chaudhuri, "Reflections," 428.

56. Savary was read by Spain's commercial and political elite. As we will see, Uztáriz noted its popularity and its many foreign editions, even quoted it at length. *Theórica*, 243.

57. Sources for the biography of Uztáriz include: Mounier, *Les faits et les doctrines;* Uztáriz, *Theórica*, ix–xx; Caro Baroja, *Hora navarra*, 289–95; and two contributions by Ruíz Rivera, "La Casa Uztáriz," 183–99 and "Rasgos de modernidad," 12–17.

58. Apparently he ordered publications on political economy from London. *Theórica*, 64.

59. Kamen, "Melchor de Macanaz," 699–716. For biographical details: Kamen, *War of Succession*, 386; Vilar, *La Catalogne dans l'Espagne moderne*, 1:164 n.; Fayard, *Les membres du Conseil de Castille*, 57–58; "Précis historique" ANPar, K 907, n. 12, f. 10; Macanaz, *Regalías,* which contains a brief autobiography as of 1739; Lafuente, *Historia general de España*, vol. 13 ; Martín Gaite, *El proceso de Macanaz*. For Macanaz's writings, see Kamen, *War of Successsion*, appendix 7, which reviews the contents of some manuscripts. *Regalías,* lxxi–lxxx describes eight volumes of manuscripts on the Spanish colonies in America. Also: Macanaz, "Auxilios," 215–303.

60. Kamen, *War of Succession*, 55.

61. Uztáriz, *Theórica*, 60.

62. The chaplain of the Consejo de Indias (young Goyeneche was a member of the Consejo—his father had bought him the office) set the tone for Uztáriz's *aprobación*. In evaluating Huet's publication he noted that Goyeneche undertook the translation to stimulate Spanish entrepreneurs to enter manufacture like his father, with the purpose of reducing the level of Spain's raw materials exports.

63. The following paragraphs are based on the main section of Uztáriz's *aprobación* to Goyeneche's 1717 Spanish edition of Huet, reproduced in the facsimile edition of Uztáriz's *Theórica*, 60–63.

64. Ibid., 60.

65. Ibid., 64.

66. Ibid., 60.

67. *Comercio de Holanda* cited in Uztáriz, *Theórica*, 93; Gómez Gómez, *Visitas*, chaps. 1–5.

68. A reading of the anonymous "F.X.B." article in the *Espíritu de los mejores diários literarios*, n. 142 (18 October 1788), 278 suggests that just before 1720 there was pressure to form one or more *compañías generales* for the colonial trade. This is a recommendation advanced in Legarra, "Comercios de España y Yndias."

69. Huet, *Comercio de Holanda*, cited in Uztáriz, *Theórica*, 93.

70. We have utilized the facsimile second edition of 1742 with introduction by Gabriel Franco, part of his series, *Clásicos españoles de la economía*.

71. In the introduction, Uztáriz lists as part of his background, service (*dependencias*) in the ministries of Guerra y Marina, and Treasury. In discussing the tobacco monopoly later, he cited as an informant, Francisco Varas y Valdés ("práctico en los negocios de Indias") of the Casa de Contratación, as of 1725 its president. *Theórica*, 366.

72. For analyses of Uztáriz as mercantilist rather than economic model-seeker, see (among others) Mounier, *Les faits et la doctrine économiques* and Hamilton, "The Mercantilism of Gerónimo de Uztáriz."

73. Uztáriz, *Theórica*, 412.

74. Ibid., 46.

75. Ibid., 1–2. The Jesuit who censored the second edition of the *Theórica* concurred with Uztáriz on the need to "imitarlas [other nations] en las máximas del gobierno."

76. Ibid., 70.

77. Ibid., 89.

78. Ibid., 46–47. The initial chapter of this section devoted to France is titled in part "Motivos que obligan a referir los Exemplares de Estado bien governados . . . dando el primer lugar a . . . Francia."

79. Ibid., 52.

80. Ibid., 74.

81. He reminded his readers of the *Parfait négociant*'s "gran aprobación que ha merecida dentro y fuera" France; it was then in its seventh edition. Ibid., 242–43.

82. Ibid., 54–56.

83. Ibid., 60–63.

84. Uztáriz's discomfort with the tariff schedule at Cádiz inspired an outburst of indignation: "mas parecen disposiciones de nuestros émulos, executadas con absoluta libertad, y como quien impone duras leyes a sus esclavos." Ibid., 242.

85. Ibid., 242–43. These details were already publicly known, for Veitia Linaje's guide to the mechanisms of Spain's colonial trade system, *Norte de la contratación* (1672) had revealed them, at least to careful readers.

86. While Spain's customs receipts (a major category of *rentas generales*) averaged about 14 per cent of total state income (1753–65), in some years they could reach as much as 35–50 percent. Andalusia alone (basically Cádiz) frequently produced more than 40 percent of Spain's customs receipts. Pieper, *Real Hacienda*, 109–10.

87. Uztáriz, *Theórica*, 241.

88. Ibid., 244.

89. Ibid., 242, 244.

90. Ibid., 249–50.

91. Ibid., 391.

92. Ibid., 70–73.

93. Braudel et al., eds., *Histoire économique*, 2:351–59; Sée "Que faut-il penser," 181–94. Sée viewed Colbert's policy as driven less by developmental concerns than fiscal imperatives, concluding he failed at "des reformes profondes, parce qu'il ne pouvait détruire le régime des privilèges, qui tenait à toute la constitution sociale de l'époque." Ibid., 182, 193–94. For recent reservations about Colbert's performance, see Goubert, *Louis XIV.*

94. Cf. "By . . . giving Credit to Traders out of the Royal Treasury, . . . the celebrated Monsieur Colbert first enabled France to rival England in the Woollen manufactury" and once France met its domestic needs, "they turned their Thoughts upon supplanting us at foreign Markets." Postlethwayt, *Considerations*, 18.

95. Uztáriz, *Theórica*, 242, 413.

96. Uztáriz, *Theory and Practice*. There were two French translations in 1753, by François Veron de Forbonnais and Plumart de Dangeul.

97. Joachim de Villareal, "Aprobación," in Uztáriz, *Theórica.*

6. Changing Patterns in the Transatlantic System: *Flotas* and *Registros*, 1720–1759

1. "Observations concernant le projet de traité de commerce à concluire avec l'Espagne," ANPar, M 785, no. 8.

2. In 1716 London, eager to obtain silver for its expanding trade with the Far East, obliged Madrid to concede that if no *feria* were held within four months of the scheduled arrival of Spanish convoys, the "permission ship" could commence sales. Walker, *Spanish Politics*, 69, 74, 85–86.

3. Levene, ed., *Documentos*, 5:21–45; García-Baquero, *Cádiz y el Atlántico*, 2:152–56; Walker, *Spanish Politics*, 108–12.

4. Southwell, "Proyecto. . . ." 4 June 1788, Estado 3188, AHN.

5. Carrera Pujal, *Historia*, 3:84, 86, 89; González Enciso, *Estado e industria*, 269–71 279–81. Naranjo's "Antorcha . . . para empezar la restauración económica de España . . . por medio de . . . fábricas. . . ." was addressed to the Consejo de Castilla in 1703, coincident with the petition of Guadalajara's clergy for a start-up grant from Madrid to provide local employment and discourage the outmigration of workers. González Enciso, *Guadalajara*, 269.

6. Carrera Pujal, *Historia*, 3:125–32.

7. Ibid., 132.

8. Carrera Pujal, *Historia*, 3:129–30. Woolen goods of the Guadalajara manufactury were consigned by Patiño to the Consulado de Cádiz for export aboard the 1725 *flota* to Veracruz. The Consulado's three *diputados* aboard the *flota* were made responsible for the sale and remission of earnings. "Instrucción que el Consulado de Cádiz otorga. . . ." Cádiz, 12 July 1725, AGN, Consulado 269, exp. 2, ff. 17–25. Also quoted in Yuste, ed., *Comerciantes mexicanos*, 61–62.

9. Gonzalez Enciso, *Guadalajara*, 626, 674–75.

10. Ibid., 672.

11. In 1720 the Junta de Comercio proposed to the Consejo de Indias that Madrid subsidize textile mills designed to supply colonial demand. The *consejo* concurred, agreeing on the importance of demand in both Peru and New Spain. Real Orden, 29 December 1720, AHN, Estado 2941.

12. González Enciso, *Guadalajara*, 639, 642, 676–79.

13. Ibid., 272.

14. Ibid., 311–12. Teodoro Ventura de Argumosa published an account of his European survey, *Erudición política, despertador sobre el comercio, agricultura y manufacturas, con avisos de buena política y aumento del Real Erario* in Madrid in 1743. Carrera Pujal, *Historia* 3:174.

15. González Enciso, *Guadalajara*, 22–23, 311.

16. Ibid., 639, 642.

17. Ibid., 689.

18. Carrera Pujal, *Historia*, 3:84. Or is Eric Hobsbawm's formulation more apt: the structure of society may constrain the "scope of capitalist expansion?" "The Crisis of the Seventeenth Century," 15–16.

19. González Enciso, *Guadalajara*, 693–94; Carrera Pujal, *Historia*, 3:130. On his second tour of inspection (1727) Uztáriz found only 50 of 100 installed looms in operation. Note that the trajectory of another comparable state-sponsored enterprise, Sevilla's Compañía de Comercio y Fábricas operating over forty years, was a "fracaso." González Sánchez, *La Real Compañía*, 126.

20. Macanaz, in Torres López and Pérez-Prendes y Muñóz de Arraco, *Los juros*, 74.

21. Cf. the observation of Antonio Elorza: "Los dos primeros Borbones constituyen un simple trasfondo. . . ." Campillo y Cosío, *Lo que hay de mas y de menos*, 5.

22. For example, the "Royal Princess" of the South Sea Company arrived at Veracruz *before* the 1717 *flota*. Worse, merchants aboard introduced a marketing innovation in the form of printed lists of goods and prices distributed to potential buyers at the port. Walker, *Spanish Policy*, 91.

23. From the rest of western Europe came "ruanas, bretañas, morleses y demás lencerías, encajes, paños de Inglaterra y de Holanda, tejidos de seda de Francia. . . ." Alvarez de Abreu, *Extracto historial*, 2:103.

24. Mesa, 3 October 1787, AGI, Mexico 2505.

25. Borchart de Moreno, *Los mercaderes*, 66–95.

26. For excellent introduction to pre-1750 Mexico City merchants, see: Hoberman, *Mexico's Merchant Elite* and Borchart de Moreno, *Los mercaderes*.

27. Consulado de Mexico, "Instrucción," AGN, Archivo Historico de Hacienda, 635–38.

28. Real Díaz, *Las ferias de Jalapa*, 53–57.

29. Morineau, *Incroyables gazettes*, 368 fig. 55. In García-Baquero's view, Madrid resolved to "sacar aquel fabuloso imperio del estado de abandono en que habia quedado sumido bajo los últimos Austrias." *Cádiz y el Atlántico*, 1:90.

30. Walker, *Spanish Politics*, 228–29; Morineau, *Incroyables gazettes*, 356–57.

31. Morineau, *Incroyables gazettes*, 362–66 fig. 24.

32. Parry et al., *Short History*, 86–87. The South Sea Company insisted that its barrels of flour and bolts of coarse linens were required to feed and clothe slaves awaiting sale in the barracoons in Spanish Caribbean ports. Spanish authorities, on

the other hand, accused the company's agents of concealing goods in the flour barrels. Junta, "Consulta" (1765), AHN, Estado 2314, f. 42v.

33. "Mémoire sur les expediens . . . " AAEPar, Mémoires et Documents, Angleterre 40, f. 216.

34. AAEPar, Mémoires et Documents, Espagne 80, f. 111v.

35. Robertson, *The History of America,* 3:329.

36. "La suspension en 1739 de la flotte qui étoit déjà chargée pour la Nouvelle Espagne a causé une préjudice considerable au commerce et principalement à celui de la France qui y étoit le plus interessé; les frais d'embarquement et de débarquement qui étoient très considerables ont été de pure perte pour lui." "Mémoires sur le commerce d'Espagne," ANParis, M 785, no. 8.

37. Garamendia Arruebarrena, *Tomás Ruíz de Apodaca,* 142; Heredia Herrera, "Apuntes para la historia del consulado de la universidad de cargadores a Indias, en Sevilla y en Cádiz," *AEA,* 27 (1970), 247, no. 86.

38. The registro system permitted closer monitoring, allowing the government to "suivre de plus près les opérations jornalières, de se menager des moyens pour la réforme des abus en changeant l'ordre des choses, d'encourager les naturels à ce commerce. . . ." "Extrait . . . ," in "Observations," AAEPar, Mémoires et Documents, Espagne, 81, f. 181v.

39. "Mémoire sur le commerce d'Espagne." ANPar. M 785, no. 8. Before 1739 a merchant lost much time in soliciting a permiso and arranging cargo. "Hasta tenerlo [permiso] no puede pedir géneros de fuera, y después de pedidos necesita muchos meses antes que puedan llegar a Cádiz, y salir de aquel puerto para su destino." Campillo y Cosío, *Nuevo sistema,* 160.

40. *Mercurio peruano,* 32 marzo 1791, p. 242.

41. García-Baquero, *Cádiz y el Atlántico,* 2:66, serie c; "Observations sur . . . colonies en general." AAEPar, Mémoires et Documents, Espagne, 81, no. 17, ff. 118–118v.

42. Tomás Ruíz de Apodaca obtained a license for a *registro* to Veracruz of 200–250 tons in return for carrying government mercury. To conceal Spanish ownership, he arranged with the French firm of Casaubon, Béhic et Cie at Cádiz to furnish the ship's papers and a French crew. Garamendia Arruebarrena, *Apodaca,* 147–48.

43. ANPar, M 785, no. 17; BRAHM, Mata Linares, 6, f. 356v; Levene, ed., *Documentos,* 5:118–19.

44. Boyetet, "L'idée générale du commerce" BNPar, Fonds Français, 10769, f.6v.

45. Postlethwayt, *Dictionary,* vol. 2, "Mexico,"; Robertson, *History of America,* 3:329.

46. "Memoria de instituto . . . 1804." Mexico 2996, AGI, ff. 11–12. In 1741, Madrid even offered Agustín Ramírez Ortuño a ten-year monopoly for supplying New Spain "todos los frutos de regular consumo." This was rescinded under pressure from the Cádiz consulado. Consulado de Cádiz to Madrid, 27 mayo 1778. AGI, Consulados, Libro de correspondencia 87, ff. 7–14v.

47. Cf. the anonymous French observer who reported in the 1750s that "les permissions pour les vaisseaux de registre sont accordées à des personnes favorisées qui

agissent trop arbitrairement dans l'exécution." "Mémoire sur le commerce d'Espagne," ANPar M 785, no. 8.

48. Ibid.

49. "Apuntes sobre comercio de Europa con Nueva España," Mexico, 31 December 1797, BNMex, Mss. Reales Ordenes 1396.

50. Cf. ". . . quando por el arqueo de Cádiz se han avaluado algunos buques malouinos que pasan con registros a las Indias por de menos toneladas que las que estiman en el mismo S. Malo. . . ." Antonio de Ulloa to Ensenada, "Memoria," AGSim, Marina 712, f. 572. Postlethwayt reported in the same vein that registros licensed for 300 tons actually were of 600. *Dictionary,* vol. 2, "Mexico." (It was estimated that a 500–ton merchant vessel could carry textiles to clothe 32,000 consumers for a whole year. Miguel de Cervera, "Discurso," 26 February 1761, AHN, Estado, 2851 no. 112).

51. "Testamento político de España," BRAHM, Mata Linares, 6, f. 132v.

52. Between 1739 and 1744 alone, 69 of 120 vessels departing Cádiz for the Spanish colonies failed to return to that port. Walker, *Spanish Politics,* 211–12. See also: Rambert, "La France et la politique," 278–79.

53. Miguel de Cervera, "Discurso" 26 February 1761, AHN, Estado 2851, no. 112.

54. The last registro arrived at Veracruz in March 1756. "Lista general de las flotas y azogues," NYPub, Mss. Rich 5, f.107. Of 43 registros to Veracruz, 1739–1743, 39 were French. "Observations sur l'utilité des colonies en général," AAEPar, Espagne 81, no. 17.

55. At Bordeaux, the years 1749–55 saw record growth in foreign trade. Crouset, "La conjuncture bordelaise," 300, 302.

56. The rate of 50 pesos per ton is based upon a minimum license fee of 30,000 pesos for an effective tonnage of 500. Cf. Postlethwayt, *Dictionary,* vol. 2, "Mexico." With some exaggeration Francisco Montes, versed in the colonial trade to New Spain, asserted that the state earned in license fees and a variety of customs duties and other charges on a 500–ton registro about 280,000 pesos or about 560 pesos per ton. Francisco Montes to Múzquiz, San Ildefonso, 2l August 1782, AGI, Indiferente General, 2311.

57. Morineau, *Incroyables gazettes,* 368, fig. 55, 377, fig. 57, and 393, fig. 59; Gálvez, "Discurso y reflexiones de un vasallo," Estado 86, AGI. For García-Baquero, the 1740s marked an upward inflection when "se aceleró el ritmo del casi estancamiento en que ha venido debatiendose el comercio colonial desde el final de la crisis del XVII." *Cádiz y el Atlántico,* 1:543.

58. "Mémoire sur le commerce d'Espagne." ANPar, M 785, no. 8. Imposition of more effective exchange controls formed part of the nationalistic policy of the minister of Hacienda, Ensenada. Rodríguez Villa, *Don Cenón de Somodevila, Marqués de la Ensenada,* 117.

59. Macanaz, "Discursos," Mss.(9-26-7/4998), BRAHM. Cf. the representation of Mateo Bernal, who claimed to have accumulated much capital by trading with Veracruz and Lima, 1746–57. AGI, Indiferente General 2314.

60. Adapted from García-Baquero, *Cádiz y el Atlántico,* 2:167–68.

61. Rodríguez Villa, ed., *Ensenada,* 117.

62. There is wide discrepancy in estimates of wartime profit-taking. García-Baquero quotes a Cádiz pamphlet indicating 16 percent on sea loans. One French

firm obtained 200 percent, although such rates may have averaged only 120 percent. *Cádiz y el Atlántico,* 1:522–23.

63. "Apuntes sobre comercio de Europa en Nueva España, 31 December 1792," BNMex, Mss. Reales Ordenes 1396, f. 92.

64. Data on illegal silver transfers from America to Europe are slippery. Morineau's data show far more pesos (264 million) arriving elsewhere than received in Spain (213.7) in the period 1740–55. Morineau, *Incroyables gazettes,* 475, fig. 70.

65. Andrés de Hay to Ensenada, Madrid, 26 September 1750, BMus, Additional Manuscripts 13,796, f. 268.

66. "Extrait d'un mémoire intitulé 'Mémoire sur l'état et le système de l'Espagne,'" 22 May 1752, AAEPar, Mémoires et Documents, Espagne 81, f. 174v.

67. Muñóz Pérez, "La publicación del reglamento," 24; Consulado de Cádiz to Madrid, 17 January 1778, AGI, Consulados, Correspondencia, libro 87, ff. 7–14. See also Ward, *Proyecto económico,* 335.

68. Real Díaz, *Ferias,* 92 note 2.

69. Pérez Herrero, "Actitudes," 151. Eusebio Ventura Beleña later recalled that over the period 1736–57 there were "crecidas quiebras atribuyendose a no haber venido flotas. . . ." "Informe reservado," BNMex, Reales Ordenes, Mss. 1334, f. 125.

70. Real Díaz, *Ferias,* 93 note 3; Pérez Herrero, "Actitudes," 151–52; Sarrablo, *Fuenclara,* 2:321.

71. AGI, Consulados, libro 84, ff. 174–174v.

72. In the early 1750s, perhaps at Ensenada's initiative, *Contratación* prepared a report on exports to the colonies for the period 1749–51. García-Baquero, *Cádiz y el Atlántico,* 1:326.

73. BMus, Additional Manuscripts 13, 976, f. 268v; Walker, *Spanish Politics,* 216.

74. The French saw in some Madrid bureaucrats "le plus grand obstacle au rétablissement des flottes et galions, qui peut remettre ce commerce sur un pied convenable à l'interet général." "Extrait d'un mémoire intitulé 'Mémoire sur l'état et le système de l'Espagne,'" AAEPar, Mémoires et Documents, Espagne, 81.

75. The junta consisted of Ricardo Wall, Sebastián de Eslava, the Conde de Valparaíso, Esteban de Abaría, and Francisco Fernández Molinillo, the latter recently back from Mexico City where he had been Viceroy Fuenclara's secretary. Real Díaz, *Ferias,* 95. Wall's junta consulted Cádiz merchants Alonso García, Andrés del Hoyo, Manuel Clemente Rodríguez, Nicolás del Vasto, Nicolas Mace and Jacinto José de Barrios. García-Baquero, *Cádiz y el Atlántico,* 1:161. Ensenada, it appears, had been reluctant to follow Cádiz's recommendation for convoy resumption. "Impugnación," BRAHM, Mata Linares, 6, f. 217.

76. The consulado impressed upon its agents that delaying the *flota's* departure was their most important task. "Instrucciones," 1755, AGN, Archivo Historico de Hacienda, 635–38.

77. Sée, "Le commerce français," 24.

78. Arriaga in 1758 received 32,000 pesos (presumably a gift) from the Consulado de Mexico, a payment ordered off-the-record and without the usual signed receipt. AGN, Archivo Historico de Hacienda, 129–31.

79. For example, in 1761 Jamaican trade in smuggled goods with the Caribbean mainland was estimated at 6 million pesos annually. Salvucci, *Textiles and Capitalism,* 157.

80. *Spain: Imports from America, 1748–1752 (Livres tournois)*

	Primary Products	Precious Metals	Total
All colonies	19,871,712	89,095,049	108,966,761
Mexico	12,020,486	44,196,047	56,216,533

Raynal, *Histoire philosophique*, vol. 3, "Tableau des productions. . . ."

81. Morineau, *Incroyables gazettes*, 393, fig. 59.

82. Whitaker, "Antonio de Ulloa," 175; Carrasco, Francisco, "Memoria," AHN, Estado 3211, 2a pte. See also Rodríguez Villa, ed., *Ensenada*, 109–43.

7. Critical Voices, 1720–1759

1. Campillo y Cosío, *Lo que hay de más y de menos*, 88. Perhaps Campillo was responding to foreign publications reporting on the devices of European merchants for circumventing Spain's efforts to exclude them from its colonial trade preserve.

2. Prakash, "Precious Metals," 89–91.

3. Sarrablo Aguareles, *El conde de Fuenclara*, vol. 1, chap. 8; Fonseca and Urrutia, eds, *Historia de Real Hacienda*, 2:30–31.

4. Castillo Pintado, "Los juros de Castilla," 43–70.

5. Uztáriz, *Theórica*, 389. It is hardly surprising that in 1714 the Lower Andalusian zone including Sevilla and Cádiz held 16 per cent of total *juro* indebtedness, more than that of Toledo-La Mancha or even Madrid.

6. Patiño knew Antonio de Ulloa's father, Bernardo, both having served jointly on the Casa de Contratación at Cádiz.

7. Whitaker, "Antonio de Ulloa," 159–60. Ramos Gómez, on the contrary, denies that the formal *instrucción* to Juan and Ulloa went beyond their purely scientific work. The thrust of his critique of the *Noticias secretas* is that the manuscript reflected in part their recollections and materials that "proceden de otras manos." Ramos Gómez, *Epoca, Génesis y texto*, 1:22–31, 373–77.

8. Morachimu, *Manifiesto*.

9. Ramos Gómez, *Epoca, Génesis y texto*, 2:653.

10. See the conclusion of Elorza in his edition of José del Campillo y Cosío, *Lo que hay de más y de menos*, 16.

11. The censor (marqués de la Regalía) who approved publication of the *Relación histórica* noted that "ocultabamos a los Extrangeros nuestra situación [colonial], govierno y presidios; el tiempo la ha hecha vana y rídicula en las Yndias." Whitaker, "Antonio de Ulloa," 168.

12. Rodríguez Villa claims it was Ensenada's policy to seek out "reservadamente de personas imparciales acerca del estado político de nuestras posesiones ultramarinas . . . de la conducta de sus jefes y empleados, . . . justicia." *Ensenada*, 149. On returning from Peru, Ulloa's ship was taken by English warships. Ulloa tossed overboard a "description of the civil and political government" of the South America he knew, retaining other papers. His preserved notes ("original memoranda scattered through rough drafts and loose notes") were probably the basis of his "confidential report" (Whitaker later rephrased it as a "pathological secret report"), the "Discurso" or *Noticias secretas* published by David Barry in London in 1826. Whitaker, "Antonio de Ulloa," 167, n. 30 and "Antonio de Ulloa, the *Délivrance* and the Royal Society," 369. On Barry's edition, see Merino, *Estudio crítico*, chap. 1.

The manuscript of the "Discurso" (dated 1749) bears the warning annotation, "Para el uso privado de la Secretaria del Despacho de Indias."

13. Campillo y Cosío, *Lo que hay de mas y de menos,* 120.

14. According to a critical anonymous *representación,* it was alleged that Campillo "empezó su carrera en Cádiz de comprador de Lasqueti, uno de los muchos comerciantes de aquella ciudad." "Representación a Phelipe 5 sobre la vida y costumbres de Dn. Joseph Campillo," ANPar, AB XIX, 596.

15. For biographical details, see Astraudi, "Memoria curiosa y contestación del comisario ordenador, Coruña, 22 December 1776" and Campillo to Antonio Gerónimo de Mier, Guarnizo, 28 July 1726, in Rodríguez Villa, *Patiño y Campillo,* 130–44, 153–60; Tiryakian, "Campillo's Pragmatic New System," 233–57; Martínez Cardós, "Don José del Campillo y Cosío," 503–42. Also, Artola, "Campillo y las reformas de Carlos III," 685–714.

16. Earlier (1712) Manuel López Pintado (sometime *flota* commander) had contracted with Madrid to construct ten 800–ton vessels at Havana. The contract was rescinded two years later. Walker, *Spanish Politics,* 75–76.

17. Calderón Quijano, ed., *Los virreyes de Nueva España,* 1:621; Gándara, *Apuntes,* 139, n. 483.

Alvarez de Abreu (1688–175?), a Canary Islander and graduate of Salamanca with multiple family connections in America, was returning to Spain from a post as interim governor of Caracas. A protégé of both Macanaz and Patiño, he was subsequently a prominent member of the Consejo de Indias and editor of treatises on colonial policy cited elsewhere, notably his *Extracto historial del comercio entre Philipinas y Nueva España.* On his early career, see Borges Jacinto del Castillo, *Alvarez de Abreu;* for his role in the establishment of the Caracas Company, see Hussey, *The Caracas Company.*

18. Campillo to Inquisidor Antonio Gerónimo de Mier, Guarnizo, 28 July 1726, in Rodríguez Villa, *Patiño y Campillo,* 159.

19. Cavo, *Los tres siglos de Méjico,* 124; Gómez Gómez, *Visitas,* 112–20, 123, 175–76.

20. Herrán's report may explain why Patiño ordered young Campillo to proceed from Havana to Mexico City. Herrán claimed the real value of *alcabala* receipts was 500,000 pesos per annum, almost double the claim of consulado officials. Diego Joseph González de la Herrán to Madrid, 6 May 1726, AGN, Archivo Historico De Hacienda, 217–1, and the consulado's defense, "Apresentación del memorial . . . al Rey y al Consejo de Indias . . . cabezón de alcabalas," in Yuste, ed., *Comerciantes mexicanos,* 95.

21. AGN, Archivo Historico de Hacienda, 217–1; Fonseca and Urrutia, eds., *Historia general de Real Hacienda,* 2:30–31. Among Campillo's other informants in the colonial bureaucracy were the brother of Campillo's secretary (Astraudi), a bureaucrat in the colonial service at Mexico City; a nephew (José Huergo, also in Mexico City) on the staff of the conde de Fuenclara, viceroy of New Spain; and Campillo's brother-in-law, conde de Castelblanco, president of the Audiencia de Guatemala. Rodríguez Villa, *Patiño y Campillo,* 132; Sarrablo Aguareles, *Fuenclara,* 2:29.

22. On the general problems of New Spain at this time, see Navarro García, *Hispanoamérica en el siglo XVIII,* and his "La administración virreinal en México," 359–69—the report of Viceroy Duque de Alburquerque transported to Veracruz aboard

a French *flota;* Calderón, *Historia económica,* and García Martinez, et al., eds., *Historia general,* vol. 3.

23. Cavo, *Los tres siglos,* 125.

24. Ibid., 125.

25. Ibid., 124.

26. Ibid., 124; Villaseñor y Sánchez, *Theatro americano,* 2:268–271.

27. See "Zúñiga, Baltasar" in *Catálogo alfabético* 3:691. See also Bugarin, *Visita de las misiones del Nayarit* and Meyer, ed., *El Gran Nayar.*

28. Cavo, *Los tres siglos,* 127.

29. Gómez Gómez, *Visitas,* 95; Linares, "Relación," 786–87. Moreno Cebrián, *El corregidor de indios,* chap. 3. On the general theme, see Noonan, *Bribes,* 392 ff.

30. Consulado de Mexico, 6 August 1722, to its agent at Cádiz/Puerto Santa María, AGN, Archivo Historico de Hacienda, 225.

31. Gómez Gómez, *Visitas,* 115.

32. See the *informe* of Captain Diego Joseph González de la Herrán y Mier, Mexico, 6 May 1726 to Madrid concerning his father's participation in mismanagement of the alcabala tax farm held by the Consulado de Mexico since 1696. His father had been *contador mayor* of the Mexico City customs office and left a secret account of his role in the fraud. AGN, Archivo Historico de Hacienda, 217-1. On mismanagement in the Mexico City mint and its repercussions, see *Memorial ajustado*; Chaudhuri, "World Silver Flows," 69, 72.

33. Rodríguez Villa, ed., *Patiño y Campillo,* 150.

34. Linares, "Relación," 776.

35. Ibid., 773–74.

36. Ibid., 785–86. After investigating the presidios, Garzarón tried to control the rapacity of garrison commanders and their aviadores by formulating a price schedule covering goods sold to garrison soldiers. Cavo, *Los tres siglos de Méjico,* 128.

37. Linares, "Relación," 784.

38. Gómez Gómez, *Visitas,* 112, 134. The resort to "skimming" resulted from the colonial treasury's constant illiquidity since its funds were drained away to the metropole particularly during the War of Succession. Creditors who could not cash their *libranzas* (bills of exchange) on presentation had to adopt one of two procedures: pay a premium (*regalía* or bribe) deductible from the *libranza* in order to be placed high on the list of potential payees, or obtain funds from the office of the collector of *Tributos y Alcabalas,* handing over their IOUs to the treasury. This practice, of course, deepened the short-term illiquidity of the Cajas Reales. Ibid., 152.

39. Linares, "Relación," 784.

40. Ramos Gomez, *Epoca, Génesis y texto,* 2:151 ff. Assuming (what is now contested) Campillo's authorship of the *Nuevo sistema de gobierno económico para la América,* his remark about sources of information is credible: "o lo sabemos por haberlo tocado por la experiencia, o por auténticas noticias." *Nuevo sistema,* 62

41. Rodríguez Villa, *Patiño y Campillo,* 130–44.

42. Cf. "hombre lleno de fuego y de imaginación . . . más irritable que firme, más capaz que ningun otro por su vigor de destruir los abusos." Cabarrús, *Elogio del conde de Gauza,* 13. Also cited in Campillo y Cosío, *Lo que hay de más y de menos,* 11.

43. "Representación a Phelipe V," ANPar, AB XIX, 596.

44. Ulloa's "Discurso y reflexiones políticas" (when published, *Noticías secretas*) labeled the open collusion in smuggling between colonial civil servants and businessmen as the practice of "comer y dejar comer." Ramos Gómez, *Epoca, Génesis y texto,* 2:126.

45. "Representación a Phelipe V," ANPar, AB XIX, 596.

46. This referred to European gazettes which alerted merchants of returns in silver on goods sold in the Spanish colonies. For the role of the gazettes, see Morineau, *Incroyables gazettes,* chap. 1.

47. Campillo y Cosío, *Lo que hay de más y de menos,* 88.

48. Ibid., 114.

49. Ibid., 120.

50. Ibid., 124; "Representación a Phelipe V," ANPar, AB XIX, 596.

51. Campillo y Cosío, *Lo que hay de más y de menos,* 126.

52. Ibid., 151–53.

53. Rodríguez Villa, *Patiño y Campillo,* 131–44.

54. Probably Campillo authorized the second edition of Uztáriz's *Theórica* (1742).

55. Recent work questions the authorship of the *Nuevo sistema,* long credited perhaps erroneously to Campillo. In fact, the *Nuevo sistema* (1789) may have borrowed from Ward's earlier *Proyecto económico en que se proponen providencias dirigidas a promover los intereses de España . . . para su plantificación* (1779). Did Pedro Rodríguez de Campomanes edit both? See the carefully argued critique by Luís Navarro García, "Campillo y el *Nuevo sistema,*" 22–29. Evidently Campillo inspired the preparation of a "descripción general" of New Spain which led to José Antonio Villaseñor y Sánchez's classic *Theatro americano. Descripción general de los reynos y provincias de la Nueva España.* On this point, see Solano, ed., *Relaciones geográficas* 1:11.

56. Whitaker, "Antonio de Ulloa," 359–60.

57. "Representación a Phelipe V," ANPar, AB XIX, 596.

58. Molinillo came from an old bureaucratic family; he was also a member of the prestigious Order of Santiago. In 1739 a Gabriel Fernández de Molinillo was posted to Mexico City as the mint's superintendant.

59. Sarrablo Aguareles, *Fuenclara,* 2:16–27, 235, 252. Did Molinillo's supervision of *libranzas* submitted for payment reflect Campillo's earlier exposure to New Spain?

60. Yuste, ed., *Comerciantes mexicanos,* 97–98.

61. Campillo to Inquisitor Antonio Gerónimo de Mier, 28 July 1726. Rodríguez Villa, ed., *Patiño y Campillo,* 151–55.

62. Astraudi, "Memoria curiosa," 139–40; Eizalde Itta y Parra, *La sombre imagen de . . . Campillo y Cosío.*

63. Ulloa, *Restablecimiento.* Thirteen years later an Amsterdam edition appeared, translated by Plumard de Dangeul, *Rétablissement des manufactures et du commerce d'Espagne.*

64. Ulloa, *Restablecimiento.* xiii, xix.

65. Gonzalo Anes has concluded with reason that Ulloa lacked a "critical spirit" (*Restablecimiento,* xlii). His edition includes a hitherto unpublished section, the third, of 1746 on "daños que reciben las fábricas, la población y el erario."

66. Campomanes, *Reflexiones sobre el comercio español a Indias,* 8.

67. Carrera Pujal, *Historia,* 3:264–65, citing Ulloa, *Restablecimiento,* 53.

68. Such was the mutual trust of merchants at the Portobelo fairs, Ulloa wrote admiringly, that "ni los caxones abrían, como ni los fardos se reconocían" while often "se encontró entre los talegos de plata alguno de oro . . . que no entró en la quenta." *Restablecimiento,* 109.

69. Ibid., 18, 24.

70. Ibid., 72–73.

71. Ibid., 104–37.

72. Ibid., 115.

73. Ibid., 162.

74. Ibid., 79–81. This was the position of Sevilla and Cádiz interests in their running controversy with Manila exporters of Chinese silks to New Spain. Alvarez de Abreu, *Extracto historial,* passim.

75. Astraudi in Rodríguez Villa, *Patiño y Campillo,* 144. It is noteworthy that Astraudi did not mention the *Nuevo sistema de gobierno económico,* later attributed to Campillo, and finally published with the apparatus of official approval in 1789.

76. Luis M. Enciso Recio in Jover Zamora, ed., *Historia de España,* 29(2):252, n. 19.

77. "Representación a SM sobre el estado de los Comercios de España e Indias, con expresión de las causas de que proviene su decadencia, y medios para restablecerlo, reintegrando en el uso de ellos a los Españoles," included in "Comercios de España e Indias," Colección Sempere y Guarinos, BRAHM, Ms. 4666.

78. Rodríguez Villa, *Patiño y Campillo,* 128; Muñóz Pérez, "Los proyectos," 169–85; Alcedo y Herrera, Dionisio, *Piraterías y agresiones,* 478–79.

79. For instance, he noted that imports of mainly Dutch shipments of cocoa at Cádiz had benefited in 1718 from a 90 percent reduction in duties; meanwhile, Dutch operations off the "Caracas" coast involved annually 3.5–4 million pounds of cocao and 24–30 vessels.

80. A Cádiz merchant, Ysidro de Heraso, who offered an *informe* responding to Legarra's representation, reported that in 1696 Cádiz had received only 10 percent of the 7 million pesos presumably produced in Upper Peru's mines. "Ynforme," in "Comercios de España e Indias," BRAHM, Ms. 4666.

81. The mentality of the "pobres hombres" was captured by Ysidro de Heraso in rebutting Legarra. Wrote Heraso (extolled by a former *intendente de Marina* at Cádiz as the merchant "más práctico y experimentado en . . . Sevilla y Cádiz"): "haviendo Dios dado a los Reyes Católicos los Reynos incógnitos de las Yndias, deven conservarlos a su limitación con dos puntos contrarios, el primero es, que de este Reyno, y principalmente deste Puerto se remitan a las Yndias, todos los efectos de Mercanzias que necesitan; y el segundo, a que vengan de ellas todos los que produzen de plata, oro y frutos, sin que se extravie cosa alguna." Heraso claimed 35 years' experience in "las tierras firmes, y del Perú y Nueva España, sin dejar Provincia que no ubiese andado, desde la de Caracas hasta Lima." "Informe," in "Comercios de España e Indias," BRAHM, Ms. 4666.

82. Legarra also criticized Madrid merchants (he meant the Cinco Gremios Mayores) for refusing to handle domestic textiles "quizá porque les tiene maior cuenta la venta de los extrangeros."

83. Acevedo y Hermosa (conde de Torre-Hermosa) reacted predictably. He was

a consistent backer of Cádiz commercial interests: an early supporter of Philip V who appointed him to the Junta de Comercio (he became its president, 1720), Acevedo rejected a proposed general trading company for colonial commerce advanced by a member of the Consejo de Indias (Manuel García de Bustamente). In the same vein he approved shifting the consulado from Sevilla to Cádiz. Dahlgren, *Relations commerciales,* 343, n. 1.

84. Macanaz's support of French influence in the new Bourbon dynasty was not unqualified. He remained suspicious of the way French groups used the alliance after 1701 to "acabar con España y irla despojando de lo que es lo suyo." "Varias notas," 229.

85. Valladares, "Explicación jurídica," 3. Macanaz was prepared to curb the political intervention of the Inquisition and of the graduates of *colegios mayores* who dominated the Consejo de Castilla, forming a "grupo social privilegiado," a bulwark of the Hapsburg era. Antonio Mestre Sanchis in Jover Zamora, ed., *Historia de España,* 29(1):295–98.

86. For a biography, see Martín Gaite, *El proceso de Macanaz.* Also: Lafuente, *Historia general de España,* 8:59, n. 3, 71–72, 159, 163; Kamen, "Melchor de Macanaz," 699–716.

87. Macanaz's library contained at least eight manuscript volumes with colonial content: "Memorias para la historia de España y Nuevo Mundo" (2 vols.); "Cartas y memorias, 1729–1730" (with notes on America); "Crítica a varias obras del Nuevo Mundo Meridional, 1639–1733"; "Memoria sobre la historia de España y Nuevo Mundo" with comments on *abusos* in the colonies; "Miscelanea" on the Spanish empire in America and "Males del Peru y su Remedio." Maldonado Macanaz, *Regalías,* lx, lxxi–lxxx.

Antonio Valladares, Macanaz's publisher who boasted he was the first to print some of his manuscripts, referred to ten volumes of his unpublished works (some on "comercio, fraude, y la forma de remediarlos") and hoped that "la superioridad permitiese su impresión." Valladares also admired the extraordinary range of Macanaz's interests: "En una palabra, nuestro autor no ha dexado piedra, rincón, ríos, fuentes, bosques, montes, llanos, mares, ni otra cosa de España y de todo el universo nuevo mundo, que no haya examinado y revuelto de dos mil modos." Valladares, "Nota del editor," 6–11.

88. Madrid maintained contact with Macanaz for reports on French government figures and policy. Ensenada instructed the duque de Huéscar, ambassador extraordinary posted to Paris (1747) to prepare for the 1748 settlement, to consult Macanaz for "muy útiles noticias" but always to use an intermediary as contact. Rodríguez Villa, *Ensenada,* 70.

89. Macanaz, "Discurso sobre la America Española," BRAHMad, 9-26-7/4998. (This was called to our attention by Professor Navarro de la Torre).

90. Navarro García, "Campillo y el *Nuevo sistema,*" 22–29; Llombart Rosa in Campomanes, *Reflexiones sobre el comercio español a Indias,* xxx, n. 83. Further clouding the manuscript's paternity is the fact that the second part of Bernardo Ward's *Proyecto económico* (completed in 1762 and edited later by Campomanes for publication in 1779) duplicates closely the edition of Benito Cano in 1789 attributed to Campillo. Oddly, when the *Nuevo sistema* apppeared, neither Jovellanos (a censor acting for the Real Academia de la Historia) nor Campomanes responded to Cano's

doubts of Campillo's authorship. Elorza in Campillo y Cosío, *Lo que hay de más y de menos*, 12–13.

91. Macanaz, "Auxilios," 215–303.
92. Macanaz, "Discurso," f. 2.
93. He reported that before the "presente guerra" (1739–48?) France exported annually 16 million pesos in goods to its American colonies and imported 38 million from them. England exported more than 5 million and received 15.5 million. In a Voltarean mode he intimated that such profitability could hardly be attributed to the "benignidad del trato que se dan a los naturales, no queriendo cargarlos demasiados de tributos." Macanaz, "Discurso," ff. 2v, 27v.
94. Ibid., ff. 14v–15.
95. Macanaz, "Auxilios," 235.
96. Ibid., "Discurso," ff. 2v–3, 7v–8, 59v–60.
97. Ibid., "Auxilios," 243.
98. Ibid., "Discurso," ff. 13v, 15v, 55.
99. Ibid., f. 16v.
100. Ibid., ff. 8v, 16v, 96v.
101. Ibid., f. 18.
102. Ibid., ff. 37v, 39, 55.
103. Ibid., ff. 86–87v.
104. Ibid., ff. 16, 37v, 87.
105. Ibid., ff. 94v–95.
106. Ibid., f. 87.
107. Ibid., f. 100v. To allay fears at the Hacienda ministry of immediate revenue loss in ending collection of the traditional *toneladas* and *palmeo*, Macanaz would begin with just one geographical sector of the American colonies. Next, to establish a revenue baseline to measure his predicted revenue increase, Madrid would ascertain "por la Aduana de Cádiz lo que importaron los derechos, que adeudaron los productos de España que se embarcaron en las dos últimas flotas, con los azogues intermedidos, y en todos los registros que salieron en tiempo que corresponde a dichas flotas." "Discurso," f. 100v. This implies the government's striking ignorance of the proximate returns from a basic source of its *rentas generales*, Andalusia's customs.
108. Ibid., f. 88.
109. The Spanish transatlantic system based on exchanges of foreign merchandize for colonial silver troubled him. Although every year, he complained, *flotas* returned to Cádiz with silver, "apenas estas [flotas] desembarcan, nos las [platas] quitan de las manos, dexandonos por ellas los géneros que labran de nuestras propias cosechas." Macanaz, "Representación . . . desde Lieja," 179.
110. Macanaz, "Discurso," ff. 90, 93v, 95.
111. Ibid., f. 89v.
112. Hancock, *Citizens of the World*, 14.
113. "Discurso," ff. 92–93.
114. Ibid., ff. 95–96.
115. Ferrer del Rio, *Historia del reinado de Carlos III*, 1:165–66.
116. Gándara, *Apuntes*.
117. Ibid., xxiv–xxv.

118. Mateos Dorado, "La actitud de Carlos III," 1:299–321.
119. Barbier, "Towards a New Chronology," 335–53.
120. Gándara, *Apuntes*, 7.
121. Ibid., 224, 234.
122. Ibid., 224–225.
123. Ibid., 95–96.
124. Ibid., 31–32.
125. Ibid., 243.
126. Ibid., 243.
127. Ibid., 245.
128. Ibid., 15.
129. Ibid., 249.
130. Ibid., 234.
131. Ibid., 132–33.
132. Ibid., 130, 133.
133. Ibid., 130, 202–3.
134. Ibid., 131.
135. Following the coup d'etat of 1766 that forced Charles III to accept Esquilache's resignation, the Consejo de Castilla initiated a judicial process against those fingered as responsible for the *motín*, namely the Jesuit order and its supporters. Among those involved were Gándara and Ensenada because of their known friendship for the Jesuit order.

8. Toward the Mid-Century Crisis: Ensenada, 1743–1754

1. So concluded Gaspar Jovellanos in rejecting Campillo's two manuscripts of the early 1740s, in his role as a government censor in 1788. Campillo y Cosío, *Lo que hay de más y de menos*, 12–13.
2. Postlethwayt, *Considerations*, 4.
3. Perhaps Klaveren's explanation of underperforming economies fits the Spanish case: "Mercantilism becomes meaningful only in a community which has obtained the necessary maturity to react positively when stimulated by economic policy." "Fiscalism, Mercantilism and Corruption," 150. Or is it relevant to consider an explanation of the structural rigidity in the United States at the end of the twentieth century? "Past declining economic powers all lacked the capacity to negotiate policies of shared sacrifice and national revitalization." Kevin Phillips, *New York Times*, 10 January 1993.
4. Artola, *La hacienda del antiguo régimen*, 253, 257, 261; García-Cuenca Ariati, in Artola, ed., *Estudios de hacienda de Ensenada a Mon*, 250 and graphs, 268–70.
5. Gándara, *Apuntes*, 53, 86.
6. Parry, *The Spanish Seaborne Empire*, 298–99.
7. MacPherson, *Annals of Commerce*, 2:162. Postlethwayt with characteristic hyperbole claimed that over the life of the English-held asiento, the asientists outsold the English merchants trading to the Spanish colonies through Cádiz by a factor of ten. *Considerations*, 8.
Between 1741 and 1745 western Europe received 41.4 million silver pesos from America, of which England alone received 31 percent (12.8 million) (Table 3).

8. *Registros Sueltos, Arrivals, Veracruz, June 1740—March 1756*

	Number	%
Spanish	119	72.6
Neutral		
French	40	
Dutch	3	
Imperial	1	
Total	164 [?]	100

Morineau, *Incroyables gazettes*, 372, n. 33.

9. Sée, "Notas," 183–90. Symptomatic of France's capacity to earn Spanish American silver pesos is the fact that its annual average of silver coined, 1740–62 (3.8 million pesos), was up by 35.7 percent over the previous period, 1726–39. Morineau, *Incroyables gazettes*, 465, table 68.

French Exports to Spain, 1730–1765
(in millions of *livres tournois*)

Year	Total Exports	To Spain	% Spain
1730	130.9	44.7	34.1
1740	243.8	64.1	26.3
1765	346.2	76.4	22.1

Adapted from Butel, "France, the Antilles and Europe," 163, table 4.2.

10. The *Nouvelles d'Amsterdam* (2 August 1748) reported the arrival of two vessels from Jamaica at Portsmouth with 205 tons of silver and 5 tons of gold, roughly 9 million pesos. Morineau, *Incroyables gazettes* 395. Some of these funds may have been remittances by French merchants in the Caribbean. Beliardi, "Mémoire à la cour de France," BNPar, Mss. Fonds Français, 10764. See also Tarrade, *Le commerce colonial* 1:95, 97–98.

11. *Exports, Spain to American Colonies, 1748–1753*
(in pesos)

Total	71,550,896
To New Spain	35,698,395 (49.8%)

Raynal, *Histoire philosophique*, vol. 3, "Tableau des marchandises. . . ."

12. *Exports Of Precious Metals by the East India Company, 1660–1760*
(kgs)

1681–85	240,952
1716–20	250,851
1751–55	398,041

Adapted from Chaudhuri, *Trading World*, 177, table A.7.

13. *Restablecimiento*, 111.

14. Recent estimates indicate that New Spain's silver production, 1725–1810, grew at the rate of 1.2 percent annually. Garner and Stefanou, *Economic Growth*, 109. There are other estimates of silver receipts from America, 1748–53. Magens claimed 76,197,598 pesos with 77.3 percent (58,906,083) from Veracruz. If one includes Havana shipments (1,098,551) this percentage rises to 78.7. Morineau's figures total 115,793,541, of which Veracruz (including Havana, Cartagena shipments) sent 68.9 per cent. Magens, *Further Explanations*, 15–16 and Morineau, *Incroyables gazettes*, 385–89, table 18.

15. Villaseñor y Sánchez, *Theatro americano*, vol. 1, bk. 1, p. 44; Campomanes, *Reflexiones*, 445; Ossun to Choiseul, Madrid, 10 February 1766. AAEPar, Correspondance Politique, Espagne 345.

16. Rodríguez Villa, ed., *Ensenada,* 20.

17. Ibid., 85. Ensenada was particularly critical of the Hacienda bureaucracy "pues, por mantenernos los Ministros, unos por solas las personas, otros por adelantar sus familias, otros por saciar la codicia, y otros por todos tres motivos, no hemos hecho presente en las urgencias el verdadero estado de la Hacienda." *Ibid.,* 139.

18. Ibid., 47. In 1753–54 royal household expenditures absorbed 5.4 percent of the state budget. Pieper, *La real hacienda,* 160–61 and table 26. Three decades later government outlays in the Madrid area on the royal household consumed roughly 16–17 percent of net state (crown) revenues. Ringrose, *Madrid,* 318.

Commented Ensenada on clientelism and patronage practiced in Hacienda and Marina e Indias: "se han dado plazas con el título de doctales, a los que han casado con criadas y con hijas de criadas, y a creados por premio, así como a algunos arrendadores o sus hijos por el distinguido mérito de haber prestado caudales." Rodríguez Villa, ed., *Ensenada,* 47–48.

19. Ensenada's Italian exposure had convinced him that Rome's curia scorned Spaniards as "pródigos de sus caudales y supersticiosos en la religión." Ensenada to Fernando VI, 15 December 1747, in Rodríguez Villa, ed., *Ensenada,* 168

20. See Ruíz Martín, "La Banca," 159–60; Anes Alvarez, *Antiguo régimen,* 125, 261–62, 287–88. See also the monograph of Pulido Bueno, *El real giro de España.*

21. Rodríguez Villa, ed., *Ensenada,* 134–35. In such matters he claimed the high ground of impartiality since "Yo no he sido colegial mayor, manteístas, ni abogado." Kagan, *Students and Society,* 190–95, discusses social origins of *manteístas* at the universities.

22. Rodríguez Villa, ed., *Ensenada,* 3, 19.

23. Ibid., 5–7.

24. José Antonio Escudero in Jover Zamora, ed., *Historia de España,* 29(1):131. Rather than exaggerated modesty, it was probably recognition of the responsibility he would have to bear that led Ensenada to write Scoti candidly of his own shortcomings: "Yo no entiendo una palabra de Hacienda; de Guerra, lo mismo . . . y la Marina en que me he criado es lo menos que hay que saber." Colonial affairs were reduced to "el comercio de Indias no ha sido mi genio . . . ." Rodríguez Villa, ed., *Ensenada,* 20–21. Incidentally, Ensenada amassed a library of some 3,000 volumes by 1754.

25. Real Decreto 21 June 1737 countersigned by Sebastián de la Cuadra. Rodríguez Villa, ed., *Ensenada,* app. 8.

26. Ibid., 261; Egido López, *Opinión pública,* 211; "Extrait d'un mémoire particulier à M. le duc de Duras," AAEPar, Mémoires et Documents, Espagne 81, ff. 202–203v; Ramos Gómez, *Epoca, Génesis y texto,* 1:367, n. 60. Ensenada seems to have favored the Basque faction at Madrid. Ordeñana y Goyenechea, a dependable colleague, first served under Ensenada as his *oficial mayor* at Parma and at one time was prefect of the Basque Congregación de San Ignacio. One of Ensenada's patrons, Sebastián de la Cuadra y Llanera (marqués de Villarias), a Basque, was also exprefect of the Congregación de San Ignacio, reputed "jefe de los Vizcaínos" in the capital and a channel for placing fellow vizcaínos in the civil service. Rodríguez Villa, ed., *Ensenada,* 25, 27; Ozanam, *La diplomacia de Fernando VI,* 99 and passim; *Noticias,* 75, 77.

27. Of five political "movers" in court circles, three were close to Ensenada: Ordeñana, Sebastián de la Cuadra, and Nicolás Mollinedo y la Cuadra (marqués de los Llanos). "Mémoire particulier," AAEPar, Mémoires et Documents, Espagne 81, f. 202. Cuadra and Mollinedo came from the town of Balmaceda.

28. The following paragraphs are based upon Ozanam, "Estudio preliminar" in his *Diplomacia de Fernando VI;* Mozas Mesa, D. *José de Carvajal y Lancaster,* which contains Carvajal's *Pensamientos;* Rodríguez Villa, *Ensenada,* 25; and Ruíz de Vergara y Alava, *Historia del colegio.* vol. 2.

29. Philip V and his senior officials probably shared a distancing from the Spanish aristocracy reminiscent of Louis XIV's recommendation to agent Amelot at Madrid: "Preserve all the natural prerogatives of their rank and exclude them from all matters which might give them a part in the government." Kamen, *Spain, 1469–1714,* 270.

30. Carbajal y Lancaster, "Pensamientos," 7 Junio 1753, BRPal, Mss. 2852, f. 154.

31. Fonseca y Urrutia, *Historia de Real Hacienda,* 1:334

32. Carvajal found in Philip one who had "restaurado el honor de la Nacional Española" rendering "respetable y temida una Nación que haviendo sido en otro tiempo el terror de Europa y de la mayor parte de la America, havia llegado a ser muy poco considerada aun de los Potencias de menos clase." Ruíz de Vergara y Alava, *Colegio viejo de San Bartolomé,* 2:677.

33. "la America . . . es el alma de nuestra grandeza." Carvajal, "Testamento político," BNMad, Mss. 11065, f. 200v. His foreign policy is summarized in Ozanam's *Diplomacia de Fernando VI,* 75. There can be little doubt of Carvajal's reservations about French policy toward Spain: "[Francia] nos ha de asesinar siempre, y que nos hará mucho daño, siendo amigo que siendo enemigo." Carvajal y Lancaster, "Testamento político," BNMad, Mss. 11065, ff. 15–16.

34. France, Carvajal reasoned, drew "un río de oro y plata" from trade with Spain and the colonies, a realization that led him to turn against "union" with France. With England, on the other hand, he saw no conflict of interest since it was a "Nación bizarra y de buena fee." Carvajal y Lancaster, "Testamento político" BNMad, Mss. 11065, ff. 19–20.

35. Carbajal, "Pensamientos," 7 Junio 1753. BRPal. Mss. 2857, f. 160.

36. González Enciso, *Guadalajara,* 314–15. There is a also the succinct yet comprehensive monograph on San Fernando by González Sánchez, *La Real Compañía.*

37. The major reports: "Representación . . . sobre el estado del Real Erario" (1747) and the most famous, "Representación." (1751) are in Rodríguez Villa, ed., *Ensenada,* 43–65 and 113–42; Ozanam, *Diplomacia,* 67–124.

38. Rodríguez Villa, ed., *Ensenada,* 133.

39. Carrera Pujal, *Historia,* 3:394.

40. *Mémoires et considérations sur les finances d'Espagne,* 2:31.

41. Rodríguez Villa, ed., *Ensenada,* 115.

42. From data collected by the *catastro de Ensenada,* Spain's ecclesiastical establishment received 73 percent of all "censo" and "rentas hipotecarias" income. Vilar, "Structure de la société espagnole," 428–30.

43. Rodríguez Villa, ed., *Ensenada,* 52, 90, 138–39. Ensenada commissioned an official who worked closely with him, Bartolomé de Valencia, to investigate the possible yield of the proposed *única contribución* were it applied to the province of

Guadalajara. Valencia calculated it would equal all the revenues of the multiple *rentas provinciales.* Pieper, *La Real Hacienda,* 62.

44. Yun Casalilla, *Sobre la transición,* 456, n. 1–3. Yun Casalilla refers to Artola, *La hacienda del antiguo régimen,* 267–69 and Vilar, "Estructuras," 63–92. Predictably, the Sevilla-Cádiz jurisdiction ranked among the highest in regional income.

45. Fonseca and Urrutia, eds, *Historia de la real hacienda,* 1:184–185. Under Horcasitas' viceregal stewardship (1748–54) New Spain's tax revenues grew by 123 percent (from 318,560 to 712,488 pesos). *Ibid.,* 2:57. The consulado's request (1753) for renewal of its contract for the alcabala farm is in Yuste, ed., *Comerciantes mexicanos,* 91–101.

46. Moreno Cebrián, *El corregidor de indios,* esp. chaps 2–4.

47. For Ensenada's interest in a tobacco monopoly in New Spain, see Deans-Smith, *Bureaucrats, Planters and Workers,* 8–9.

48. Barbier, "'Depositaria de Indias,'" 337.

49. Rodríguez Villa, ed., *Ensenada,* 41.

50. Pieper, *La Real Hacienda,* 131–32.

51. Cf. Improved distribution of grains via the Canal could lower imports during subsistence crises, possibly avoiding the outflow of "millones de pesos" in silver "que se llevan los ingleses y otros con los granos que traen a vender." Rodríguez Villa, ed., *Ensenada,* 97 and 142–43; Pere Molas, in Jover Zamora, ed., *Historia de España* 28:628.

52. Rodríguez Villa, ed., *Ensenada,* 273; Gárate Ojanguren, *Comercio ultramarino,* 69.

53. Rodríguez Villa, ed., *Ensenada,* 120, 275.

54. Alejo Gutiérrez de Rubalcava, president of the Casa de Contratación at Cádiz (1747), rejected the petition of the Consulado de Mexico to restore *flotas* to Veracruz, and Gabriel Gutiérrez de Rubalcava was alcalde mayor in the valuable, cochineal-rich Nexapa jurisdiction of New Spain. Sarrablo, *Fuenclara,* 2:324.

55. Rodríguez Villa, ed., *Ensenada,* 144–49, 274.

56. Ibid., 109.

57. Hence the marginal notation of Fernando VI on Ensenada's recommendation in 1748 for building up the navy: you will make the necessary arrangements "con el disímulo posible." Ibid., 111.

58. Ibid., 160.

59. Among the company's shareholders was Ensenada's close collaborator, José Banfi y Parrilla, as well as prime minister Carvajal y Lancaster and Juan Francisco Güemes y Horcasitas (captain-general and governor of Cuba and shortly viceroy of New Spain). Ensenada's correspondence shows his close watch of the performance of Havana's shipyards. He appointed Lorenzo Calvo *comisario de los reales astilleros* of Havana; Calvo and one of the directors of the Compañía de la Havana (Martin de Aróstegui) kept both Ensenada and Alonso Pérez Delgado abreast of the process of naval construction there. Gárate Ojanguren, *Comercio ultramarino,* 37, 70, 72–73, 82, 89.

60. Rodríguez Villa, ed., *Ensenada,* 145, 149–50. Ensenada was responsible for limiting circulation of the candid manuscript of Ulloa and Juan to secretaries of state and a few other high officials. Whitaker, "Documents," 512.

61. Between 1716 and 1754 Madrid had received no viceregal *instrucciones* (or *memorias*) from New Spain. Horcasitas, "Instruccion," 2:795.

62. His *instrucción* is supplemented by reports on New Spain's silver mines at Bolaños. Ibid., 847–52, 861–64.

63. Ibid., 807, 811, 824.

64. Horcasitas was simply voicing the argument of the Consulado de Mexico in a petition to Viceroy Conde de Fuenclara in 1745. See "Cédula real . . . atendiendo a las denuncias del . . . Consulado de Mexico." Yuste, ed., *Comerciantes mexicanos,* 85–88, and 119.

65. Ibid., 99–100.

66. Horcasitas, "Instrucción," 811–12.

67. Horcasitas commented in a communication to Ensenada a propos Mexico City's poor: "los vicios que les eran propios se echaban a ver . . . en toda su extensión." Cited in Alaman, *Historia de Mexico,* 1:35.

68. Horcasitas, "Instrucción," 796, 798, 800, 804. In July 1741 Campillo had ordered New Spain's alcaldes mayores to respond to a questionnaire on their practices. Dehouve, *Quand les banquiers étaient des saints,* 189, n. 1.

69. Horcasitas, "Instrucción," 798, 804–5.

70. Ibid., 819.

71. Banfi to Wall, 6 August 1754, Rodríguez Villa, ed., *Ensenada,* 390; "Mémoire particulier donné a M. le Duc de Duras avant son départ en octobre 1752 concernant l'Espagne." AAEPar, Mémoires et Documents, Espagne 81, ff. 202–03v.

72. Banfi to Wall, 6 August 1754. Rodríguez Villa, ed., *Ensenada,* 388–89.

73. Rodríguez Villa, ed., *Ensenada,* 120. Patiño had once remarked drily to Ensenada that the most effective Spanish diplomat at London might well be "un basto marinero que supiese . . . el . . . modo de hacer el comercio ilícito." Ibid., 62.

74. Ibid., *Ensenada,* 115.

75. Gándara, *Apuntes.*

76. Rodríguez Villa, ed., *Ensenada,* 62.

77. García Herreros to Revillagigedo, "Sobre . . . decadencia en el comercio," 8 julio 1791. AGNMex, Consulado 123, exp. 1; Ozanam, *Diplomacia,* 264, n. 3.

78. González Sánchez, *La real compañía,* 20–21, 25–26. Among the company directors were three large Flemish shareholders; other shareholders later included Los Heros and Arriaga (Ibid., 36–37).

79. Rodríguez Villa, ed., *Ensenada,* 63, 79.

80. Viaña, "Memoria," 27 July 1814, AGI, Indiferente General 2463.

81. Walker, *Spanish Politics,* 216–17. Ensenada's criticism of the Cádiz commercial community aside, he felt that peninsular businessmen merited respectful status.

82. Garmendia Arruebarrena, *Tomás Ruíz de Apodaca,* 73.

83. Antúñez y Acevedo, *Memorias históricas,* 300–301.

84. On the principle that Spaniards (*prestanombres*) fronting for foreign resident merchants at Cádiz had no national interest at heart, Ensenada authorized an investigation of the financial resources of merchants in colonial trade to ascertain the real sources of their capital and, most important, their creditors. Carrera Pujal, *Historia,* 3:396.

85. Bringas, "Papel." BRPal, Mss. Ayala 2872, f. 340.

86. AHN, Estado 3211, 2a pte. A consistent supporter of basic reform before and

during the era of Charles III, Carrasco collaborated with the marqués de Esquilache (1759–66). Moxó, "Un medievalista en el Consejo de Hacienda," 627.

87. BNPar, Mss. Fonds Français 10769, ff. 5–5v; Matilla Tascón and Capella, *Los Cinco Gremios,* 110 ff. In 1757 the drapers' guild (one of the Cinco Gremios) leased the state-owned Guadalajara woolen mill. Anes, *Antiguo régimen,* 261–62.

88. Tedde de Lorca, *El Banco de San Carlos,* 24–25.

89. Ensenada to Fernando VI, 15 December 1747. Rodríguez Villa, ed., *Ensenada,* 168. See also: Barbier, "'Depositária de Indias,'" 335–353.

90. Rodríguez Villa, ed., *Ensenada,* 64. See also Pulido Bueno, *El real giro de España,* 25–27, 63.

91. Pieper, *La Real Hacienda,* 131.

92. Rodríguez Villa, ed., *Ensenada,* 101–2, 114–15; Anes, *Antiguo régimen,* 262.

93. Rodríguez Villa, ed., *Ensenada,* 118–19.

94. Ibid., 31–32, 37. These measures were recommended by a commission that included veteran colonial officers Sebastián de Eslava (exviceroy of New Granada) and Francisco Fernández Molinillo (former secretary to New Spain's Viceroy Fuenclara).

95. Rodríguez Villa, *Ensenada,* 263–64.

96. Egido López, *Opinión pública,* 191; Giovanni Steffoni in Jover Zamora, ed., *Historia de España* 29(2):12.

97. Rodríguez Villa, *Ensenada,*; Pieper, *La Real Hacienda,* 131–32.

98. The receipts rose from 65.3 to 106.6 million reales de vellon. Calculated from Barbier, "'Depositaria de Indias,'" 342, table 1.

99. Mogrevejo to duque de Losada, 20 July 1751. Rodríguez Villa, ed., *Ensenada,* 396.

100. Ibid., 182; Egido López, *Opinión pública,* 199. Madrid's foreign embassies had apparently learned of so-called secret orders issued by Madrid's ministries. French ambassador duc de Duras was informed early of the effort to expel English logwood cutters/smugglers from the Campeche and Yucatan coasts. "Extrait d'un mémoire," October 1752. AAEPar, Mémoires et Documents, Espagne, 81, f. 203.

101. Egido López, *Opinión pública,* 217.

102. Rodríguez Villa, ed., *Ensenada,* 281.

103. Ensenada's seemingly Francophile policy drift troubled England's ambassador, Keene. He viewed Ensenada as partial to the French East India Company (then loading silver at Cádiz for its China trade) and supportive of Jesuit missions in Paraguay, which resisted their transfer to Portuguese control and the consequent penetration by English personnel and goods. Ensenada's attitude was considered an expression of friendship with Fernando VI's confessor, the Jesuit Padre Rávago. Escudero in Jover Zamora, ed., *Historia de España,* 29(2):139.

104. Rodríguez Villa, ed., *Ensenada,* 192–94, 396–97. Ensenada lacked confidence in Spain's diplomatic representation at London. Ibid., 187.

105. Rodríguez Villa, ed., *Ensenada,* 270, 279; Bernard, *Conseil espagnol des Indes,* 49.

106. Rodríguez Villa, ed., *Ensenada,* 115. This policy was probably the target of a pasquinade charging Ensenada with emptying the treasury, having "vendido grandísimas cantidades de dinero de la America." "Cargos que se hicieron al . . . Ensenada," cited in Egido López, *Opinión pública,* 205.

107. Rodríguez Villa, ed., *Ensenada*, 85.

108. González Sánchez, *La real compañía de comercio*, 42.

109. Sarrablo, *Fuenclara*, 2:258; AGN, Archivo Historico de Hacienda, 129–31; Smith, "Sales Taxes in New Spain," 2.

110. Rodríguez Casado, *La política y los políticos del reinado de Carlos III*, cited in Egido López, *Opinión pública*, 199; José Antonio Escudero in Jover Zamora, ed., *Historia de España*, 29(1):137, 139.

111. To quote Ensenada: "Yo mas infiriendo por no ignorar el caracter de algunas gentes, que oyendo, pude meses há, ver o adivinar el nublado que se fraguaba y venía sobre mí . . . ." Ensenada to Farinelli, 1754. Rodríguez Villa, ed., *Ensenada*, 209.

112. For Ensenada's dismissal, see Rodríguez Villa, ed., *Ensenada*, 194–97; for its aftermath, see Escudero in Jover Zamora, ed., *Historia de España*, 29(1):138–41.

113. Naval officers Jorge Juan and Antonio de Ulloa very pointedly visited Ensenada (in exile at Granada) in late 1754 and early 1755. Rodríguez Villa, ed., *Ensenada*, 204. In June 1761 Beliardi reported the rehabilitation of Ensenada's associates Pérez Delgado and Banfi by Charles III and the marqués de Esquilache, ANPar, Mss. Fonds Français, 10764, f. 221v.

114. "Ynforme . . . intendencias," para. 348, NYPub, Mss. Rich Collection; Moreno Cebrián, *El corregidor de indios*, 307–10; Navarro García, *Intendencias en Indias*, 109.

115. Hussey, *The Caracas Company*, 129–53.

116. Cf. Ensenada's remark in a letter years later: "Yo solo deseo vivir y morir en donde el Rey mande." Rodríguez Villa, ed., *Ensenada*, 206.

117. Egido López, *Opinión pública*, 194–96. "Solían hablar de [Ensenada]," Banfi once commented, "poco ventajosamente, como harán de cualquiera que se halle en su lugar, porque en lo general estas gentes creen unos estafadores a todos los empleados en la Corte." Rodríguez Villa, ed., *Ensenada*, 279.

118. This is the observation of Giovanni Stiffoni in Jover Zamora, ed., *Historia de España*, vol. 29(2):141.

119. González Enciso, *Guadalajara*, 310, 315.

120. Egido López, *Opinión pública*, 218.

121. Ossun to Choiseul, Madrid, 10 February 1766, AAEPar, Correspondance Politique, Espagne 345.

122. Enciso Recio in González Enciso, *Guadálajara*, 11.

123. The Spanish defense establishment must have suspected English naval plans to attack Havana in a war with Spain. By preventing "Spain's bringing home any Treasure during the War, their commerce from Caracas down to Veracruz will be totally at an end, as no ship can return . . . without passing by the Havana or between Porto Rico and the East end of Hispaniola." BMus, Additional Manuscripts 33030, ff. 388–90.

124. Gándara, *Apuntes*, 229.

Bibliography

Books

Acarete du Biscay. *An Account of a Voyage up the River de la Plata and Thence Overland to Peru.* London, 1698.

Alamán, Lucas. *Historia de México.* 5 vols. Mexico City, 1942.

Alcedo y Herrera, Dionísio de. *Piraterías y agresiones de los ingleses.* Edited by Justo Zaragoza. Madrid, 1883.

Altman, Ida. *Emigrants and Society. Extremadura and America in the Sixteenth Century.* Berkeley, 1989.

Alvarez de Abreu, Antonio, compiler. *Extracto historial del comercio entre Filipinas y Nueva España.* Edited by Carmen Yuste. 2 vols. Mexico City, 1977.

Anes Alvarez, Gonzalo. *El antiguo régimen: Los Borbones.* Madrid, 1975.

Antúnez y Acevedo, Rafael. *Memorias históricas sobre la legislación y gobierno del comercio de los españoles con sus colonias en las Indias.* Madrid, 1981.

Archivo Histórico Nacional, *Títulos del reino y grandezas de España.* 3 vols. Madrid, 1951–54.

Arcila Farías, Eduardo. *Economía colonial de Venezuela.* Caracas, 1960.

Arellano Moreno, A. *Orígenes de la economía venezolana.* 2d ed. Caracas, 1960.

Arnould, Amboise Marie. *De la balance du commerce et des relations commerciales extérieures de la France dans toutes les parties du globe.* 3 vols. Paris, 1791,

Arsans de Orsúa y Vela, B. *Historia de la villa imperial de Potosí.* Edited by Lewis Hanke and Gunnar Mendoza. 3 vols. Providence, 1965.

Artiñano y Galdácano, Gervasio. *Historia del comercio con las Indias durante el dominio de los Austria.* Barcelona, 1917.

Artola, Miguel. *La hacienda del antiguo régimen.* Madrid, 1982.

—— ed. *Enciclopedia de historia de España.* 7 vols. Madrid, 1988–1993.

Artola, Miguel, et al. *Estudios de hacienda de Ensenada a Mon.* Madrid, 1984.

Assadourian, Carlos Sempat. *El sistema de la economía colonial.* Mexico City, 1983.

Aston, T., ed. *Crisis in Europe, 1560–1660.* London, 1965.

Bakewell, Peter J. *Silver Mining and Society in Colonial Mexico: Zacatecas, 1540–1700.* Cambridge, 1971.

———. *Miners of the Red Mountain: Indian Labor in Potosí, 1545–1650*. Albuquerque, 1984.

———. ed. *Mines of Silver and Gold in the Americas*. Brookfield, Vt., 1997.

Bannon, John F. *The Spanish Borderlands Frontier, 1513–1821*. Albuquerque, 1993.

Basas Fernández, Manuel. *El consulado de Burgos en el siglo XVI*. Madrid, 1963.

Baudrillart, Alfred. *Philip V et la cour de France d'après des documents inédits*. 5 vols. Paris, 1890–1901.

Bautier, Robert Henri. *Sur l'histoire économique de la France médiévale. La route, le fleuve, le foire*. Norfolk, Eng., 1991.

Bernard, Gildas. *Le secretariat d'état et le conseil espagnol des Indes (1700–1808)*. Paris, 1972.

Bethell, Leslie, ed. *Cambridge History of Latin America*. 11 vols. New York, 1984–.

Blaug, Mark, ed. *The Later Mercantilists*. Cambridge, 1992.

Bolingbroke, Henry Saint-John. *Defence of the Treaty of Utrecht (letters VI-VII of the Study of History)*. Cambridge, 1932.

Borah, Woodrow W. *New Spain's Century of Depression*. Iberoamericana, 35. Berkeley, 1951.

Borchart de Moreno, Christina R. *Los mercaderes y el capitalismo en la ciudad de México, 1759–1778*. Mexico City, 1984.

Borges, Analola. *Alvarez de Abreu y su extraordinaria misión en Indias*. Tenerife, 1963.

Bourgoing, Jean F. *Tableau de l'Espagne moderne*. 3rd ed. 3 vols. Paris, 1803.

Boxer, Charles R. *The Dutch in Brazil, 1624–1654*. Oxford, 1957.

Boyajian, James C. *Portuguese Bankers at the Court of Spain, 1626–1650*. New Brunswick, N.J., 1983.

Brading, David. *Miners and Merchants in Bourbon Mexico, 1763–1810*. Cambridge, 1971.

Braudel, Fernand. *La Méditerranée et le monde méditerranéen à l'époque de Philippe II*. 2d ed. 2 vols. Paris, 1966.

———. *The Mediterranean and the Mediterranean World in the Age of Philip V*. Translated by Sian Reynolds. 2 vols. New York, 1973.

———. *The Wheels of Commerce. Civilization and Capitalism, 15th-18th Centuries*. New York, 1982.

Braudel, Fernand, et al. *Histoire économique et sociale de la France*. 4 vols. Paris, 1977–82.

Brenner, Robert. *Merchants and Revolution. Commercial Exchange, Political Conflict and London's Overseas Traders, 1551–1653*. Princeton, 1993.

Brito Figueroa, Federico. *Historia económica y social de Venezuela*. 2d ed. Caracas, 1973.

Broeno, Nicolas. *Monarquía y capital mercantil: Felipe IV y las redes comerciales portuguesas (1627–1635)*. Madrid, 1989.

Bugarín, José A. *Visita de las misiones del Nayarit*. Mexico City, 1993.

Burkholder, Mark A., and D. S. Chandler. *From Impotence to Authority: The Spanish Crown and the American Audiencias, 1687–1828*. Columbia, Md., 1977.

Bustos Rodríguez, Manuel, ed. *Un comerciante saboyano en el Cádiz de Carlos II (Las memorias de Raimundo de Lantéry, 1673–1700)*. Cadiz, 1983.

Cabarrús, Francisco. *Elogio del conde de Gauza*. Madrid, 1786.

Calderón, Francisco. *Historia económica de la Nueva España en tiempo de los Austria.* Mexico City, 1988.

Calderón Quijano, José Antonio, ed. *Los virreyes de Nueva España en el reinado de Carlos III (1759–1787).* 2 vols. Sevilla, 1967.

Campillo y Cosío, José del. *Lo que hay de más y de menos en España para que sea lo que debe ser y no lo es.* Elorza, Antonio, ed. Madrid, 1969.

Campomanes, Pedro Rodríguez. *Reflexiones sobre el comercio español a Indias.* Edited by Vicente Llombart Rosa. Madrid, 1988.

———, ed. *Apéndice a la educación popular.* 4 ptes. Madrid, 1775–77.

Canny, Nicholas, and Anthony Pagden, eds. *Colonial Identity in the Atlantic World, 1500–1800.* Princeton, 1982.

Cantillo, Alejandro del. *Tratados, convenios y declaraciones de paz y de comercio que han hecho con las potencias extranjeras los monarcas españoles de la casa de Borbon.* Madrid, 1843.

Carande, Ramon. *El crédito de Castilla en el precio de la política imperial. Discurso leído ante la Real Academia de la Historia.* Madrid, 1949.

———. *Carlos V y sus banqueros.* 2d ed. 3 vols. Madrid, 1965–69.

Caro Baroja, Julio. *La hora navarra del XVIII. Personas, familias, negocios e ideas.* Pamplona, 1969.

Carrera Pujal, Jaime. *Historia de la economía española.* 5 vols. Barcelona, 1943–47.

Carus-Wilson, Eleanor M., ed. *Essays in Economic History.* 3 vols. London, 1954–62.

Cary, John. *Essay on the State of England in relation to its Trade, its Poor, and its Taxes, for carrying on the present War against France.* Bristol, England, 1695.

Catálogo alfabético de los . . . títulos del reino y grandezas de España. 3 vols. Madrid, 1951–54.

Cavo, Andres. *Los tres siglos de Méjico.* Edited by Carlos María de Bustamante. Mexico City, 1851.

Céspedes del Castillo, Guillermo. *La avería en el comercio de Indias.* Sevilla, 1945.

Chaudhuri, K. N. *Trade and Civilization in the Indian Ocean.* Cambridge, 1985.

———. *The Trading World of Asia and the English East India Company, 1660–1760.* Cambridge, 1978.

Chaunu, Huguette, and Pierre Chaunu. *Séville et l'Atlantique (1504–1650).* 8 vols. Paris, 1955–60.

Cipolla, C. M., ed. *The Fontana Economic History of Europe.* 6 vols. Glasgow, 1974.

Cohn, Henry J., ed. *Government in Reformation Europe, 1520–1560.* New York, 1970.

Coke, Roger. *A Discourse of Trade . . . The Reason of the Decay of the Strength, Wealth and Trade of England.* London, 1670.

Cole, Charles W. *Colbert and a Century of French Mercantilism.* 2 vols. New York, 1939.

Cole, Jeffrey A. *The Potosí Mita, 1573–1700. Compulsory Indian Labor in the Andes.* Stanford, 1985.

Coleman, D. C., ed. *Revisions in Mercantilism.* London, 1969.

Congreso luso-español para el progreso de las ciencias, 31st. Cadiz, 1974, *La burguesía mercantil gaditana (1650–1868).* Cadiz, 1976.

Consulado de Lima. *Cuaderno de Juntas.* Lima, 1956.

Cook, Noble David. *Demographic Collapse, Indian Peru, 1520–1620.* Cambridge, 1981.

Cortés Conde, Roberto, and Stanley J. Stein, eds. *Latin America. A Guide to Economic History, 1830–1930.* Berkeley, 1977.

Coxe, William. *Memoires of the Life and Administration of Sir Robert Walpole.* 3 vols. London, 1798.

Crosby, Alfred W. *The Colombian Exchange: Biological and Cultural Consequences of 1492.* Westport, Conn., 1972.

Curtin, Philip. *The Atlantic Slave Trade. A Census.* Madison, 1969.

Dahlgren, Erik. *Les relations commerciales et maritimes entre la France et les côtes de l'océan pacifique.* Paris, 1909.

Davis, Ralph. *The Rise of the Atlantic Economies.* Ithaca, 1975.

———. *English Overseas Trade, 1500–1700.* London, 1973.

Deans-Smith, Susan. *Bureaucrats, Planters and Workers. The Making of the Tobacco Monopoly in Bourbon Mexico.* Austin, 1992.

Debien, Gabriel. *Une plantation de Saint-Domingue: La sucrerie Galbaud du Fort, 1690–1802.* Cairo, 1941.

Dehouve, Danièle. *Quand les banquiers étaient des saints.* Paris, 1990.

De Vries, Jan. *The Economy of Europe in an Era of Crisis (1600–1750).* New York, 1976.

Deyon, Pierre. *Mercantilisme.* Paris, 1969.

Dickson, Peter G. M. *The Financial Revolution in England. A Study in the Development of Public Credit, 1686–1756.* London, 1967.

Dios, Salustiano de. *El consejo real de Castilla (1385–1522).* Madrid, 1982.

Domínguez Ortiz, Antonio. *Orto y ocaso de Sevilla.* Sevilla, 1946.

———. *La sociedad española en el siglo XVII.* Madrid, 1955.

———. *Las clases privilegiadas en la España del antiguo régimen.* Madrid, 1979.

———. *Política fiscal y cambio social en la España del siglo XVII.* Madrid, 1984.

———. *Instituciones y sociedad en la España de los Austrias.* Barcelona, 1988.

———. *El antiguo régimen: Los reyes católicos y los Austrias.* Madrid, 1988.

———, ed. *Historia de España.* 12 vols. Madrid, 1980–88.

Earle, Peter, ed. *Essays in European Economic History.* Oxford, 1974.

Egido López, T. *Opinión pública y oposición al poder en la España del siglo XVIII (1713–1759).* Valladolid, 1971.

Ehrenbourg, Richard. *Le siècle des Fugger.* Paris, 1955.

Eizalde Itta y Parra, José Mariano Gregorio de. *La sombra imagen de la grandeza de D. Joseph del Campillo y Cosío.* Mexico City, 1744.

Elhuyar, Fausto de. *Indagaciones sobre la amonedación de la Nueva España* [1818]. Mexico City, 1964.

Elliott, John H. *The Old World and the New.* Cambridge, 1970.

———. *The Count-Duke of Olivares. The Statesman in an Age of Decline.* New Haven, 1986.

Everaert, J. *De internationale en Koloniale handel der vlaamse ferma's te Cadiz, 1670–1700.* Brugge, 1973.

Fayard, Janine. *Les membres du Conseil de Castille à l'époque moderne (1621–1746).* Geneva, 1979.

Ferrer del Rio, Antonio. *Historia del reinado de Carlos III.* 4 vols. Madrid, 1856.

Fichtner, Paula Sutter. *Ferdinand I of Austria: The Politics of Dynasticism in the Age of the Reformation.* New York, 1982.

Fischer, W., et al. *The Emergence of a World Eonomy, 1500–1914. Part I. 1500–1850.* International Congress on Economic History, IX, Wiesbaden, 1986.

Fonseca, Carlos de, and Fabián de Urrutia. *Historia de Real Hacienda.* 6 vols. Mexico City, 1845–63.

Francis, Alan D. *The Methuens and Portugal, 1691–1708.* Cambridge, 1966.

Gamboa, Francisco Xavier. *Comentarios a las ordenanzas de minas dedicados al . . . Carlos III.* Madrid, 1761.

Gándara, Miguel Antonio de la. *Apuntes sobre el bien y el mal de España* [1811]. Edited by Jacinta Macías Delgado. Madrid, 1988.

Gárate Ojanguren, Montserrat. *Comercio ultramarino e ilustración. La Real Compañía de la Habana.* San Sebastian, 1989.

García-Baquero González, Antonio. *Cádiz y el Atlántico (1717–1778).* 2 vols. Sevilla, 1976.

———. *Andalucía y la carrera de Indias (1492–1824).* Sevilla, 1986.

García Fuentes, Lutgardo. *El comercio español en América, 1650–1700.* Sevilla, 1980.

García Marín, José María. *La burocracia castellana bajo los Austria.* 2d ed. Madrid, 1986.

García Martínez, Bernardo, et al. *Historia general de México.* 4 vols. Mexico City, 1976–77.

Garmendia Arruebarrena, J. *Tomás Ruíz de Apodaca, un comerciante alavés con Indias (1709–1767).* Victoria, Spain, 1990.

Garner, Richard, and Spiro E. Stefanou. *Economic Growth and Change in Bourbon Mexico.* Gainesville, 1993.

Garzón Pareja, Manuel. *La hacienda de Carlos II.* Madrid, 1980.

Gentil da Silva, José. *Desarrollo económico, subsistencia y decadencia en España.* Madrid, 1967.

Girard, Albert. *Le commerce français à Seville et à Cadix aux temps des Habsbourgs. Contribution à l'étude du commerce étranger en Espagne aux XVIe et XVIIe siècles.* Paris, 1932.

———. *La rivalité commerciale et maritime entre Séville et Cadix jusqu'à la fin du XVIIe siècle.* Paris, 1932.

Gómez Gómez, Amalia. *Las visitas de la Real Hacienda novohispana en el reinado de Felipe V (1710–1733).* Sevilla, 1979.

Góngora, Mario. *Studies in the Colonial History of Spanish America.* Translated by R. Southern. Cambridge, 1975.

González Enciso, Agustín. *Estado e industria en el siglo XVIII. La fábrica de Guadalajara.* Madrid, 1980.

González Sánchez, Carlos Alberto. *La real compañía de comercio y fábricas de San Fernando de Sevilla (1747–1787).* Sevilla, 1994.

Goubert, Pierre. *Louis XIV et vingt millions de français.* 2d ed. Paris, 1991.

Grupo Madrid de Estudios Históricos. *Carlos III, Madrid y la ilustración. Contradicciones de un proyecto reformista.* Madrid, 1988.

Guerra y Sánchez, Ramiro. *Sugar and Society in the Caribbean. An Economic History of Agriculture.* Mintz, Sidney, ed. New Haven, 1964.

Guerra y Sánchez, Ramiro, et al. *Historia de la nación cubana.* 10 vols. Havana, 1952–.

Guiard-Larrauri, Teófilo. *Historia del consulado y casa de contratación de Bilbao y del comercio de la villa.* Bilbao, 1913.

Hamilton, Earl J. *American Treasure and the Price Revolution in Spain, 1501–1650.* Cambridge, Mass., 1934.

Hancock, David. *Citizens of the World: London Merchants and the Integration of the Atlantic Community, 1735–1785.* New York, 1995.

Haring, Clarence H. *Trade and Navigation between Spain and the Indies in the Time of the Hapsburgs.* Cambridge, Mass., 1918.

Hauterive, Alexandre Maurice Blanc. *De l'état de la France à la fin de l'an VIII.* Paris, 1800.

Heckscher, Eli F. *Mercantilism.* 2 vols. London, 1935.

Heredia Herrera, Antonia. *Inventario de los fondos de consulados (sección XII) del Archivo General de Indias.* Archivo General de Indias. Madrid, 1979.

Himes, Norman E., ed. *Economics, Sociology and the Modern World.* Cambridge, Mass., 1935.

Hoberman, Louise. *Mexico's Merchant Elite, 1590–1660. Silver, State and Society.* Durham, N.C., 1991.

Huet, Pierre-Daniel. *Comercio de Holanda, o el gran thesoro historial, y político del floreciente comercio . . . su órigen, sus grandes progresos . . . obra necesaria para todos los comerciantes.* Translated by Francisco Xavier de Goyeneche, 2d ed. Madrid, 1746.

Hussey, Roland D. *The Caracas Company, 1728–1784. A Study in the History of Spanish Monopolistic Trade.* Cambridge, Mass., 1934.

Inalcik, H., ed. *An Economic and Social History of the Ottoman Empire, 1300–1914.* New York, 1994.

Israel, Jonathan I. *Race, Class and Politics in Colonial Mexico, 1610–1670.* Oxford, 1975.

Jenkinson, Charles. *A Collection of all the Treaties of Peace, Alliance and Commerce between Great Britain and other Powers from the Treaty signed at Munster in 1648 to the Treaties signed at Paris in 1783.* 3 vols. London, 1968.

Jover Zamora, José María, ed. *Historia de España (Menéndez Pidal).* Vols. 19, 25, 28, and 29 (pts. 1 and 2). Madrid, 1982–89.

Kagan, Richard. *Students and Society in Early Modern Spain.* Baltimore, 1974.

——. *Lawsuits and Litigants in Castile, 1500–1700.* Chapel Hill, 1981.

Kamen, Henry. *The Spanish Inquisition.* London, 1965.

——. *The War of Succession in Spain, 1700–1715.* London, 1969.

——. *Spain in the Later Seventeenth Century, 1665–1700.* London, 1980.

——. *Spain, 1469–1714. A Society of Conflict.* London, 1983.

Kann, Robert A. *A History of the Hapsburg Empire, 1526–1918.* Berkeley, 1974.

Kessell, J. L., and Rick Hendricks, eds. *By Force of Arms. The Journals of Don Diego de Vargas, New Mexico 1691–1693.* Albuquerque, 1992.

King, Charles. *The British Merchant.* 3 vols. 2d ed. London, 1743.

Kriedte, Peter. *Peasants, Landlords and Merchant Capitalists. Europe and the World Economy, 1500–1800.* Cambridge, 1983.

Laborde, Alexandre. *Itinéraire descriptif de l'Espagne.* 6 vols. 3d ed. Paris, 1828–34.

Lafuente, Modesto. *Historia general de España.* 25 vols. Barcelona, 1887–90.

Lanterey, Raimundo. *Memorias de Raimundo de Lantery, mercader de Indias en Cadiz, 1673–1700.* Cadiz, 1949.

Lapeyre, Henri. *Une famille de marchands: Les Ruíz. Contribution a l'étude du commerce entre la France et l'Espagne au temps de Philippe II.* Paris, 1945.

Larraz López, José. *La época del mercantilismo en Castilla, 1500–1700.* Madrid, 1963.

Larson, Brooke. *Colonialism and Agrarian Transformation in Bolivia: Cochabamba, 1550–1900.* Princeton, 1988.

Léon, Pierre, and J. Jacquart. *Histoire économique et sociale du monde.* 6 vols. Paris, 1977–78.

Le Riverend, Julio. *Historia económica de Cuba.* Havana, 1967.

Letwin, William. *Origins of Scientific Economics. English Economic Thought, 1660–1778.* London, 1963.

Levene, Ricardo, ed. *Documentos para la historia argentina. V. Comercio de Indias. Antecedentes legales (1715–1778).* Buenos Aires, 1915.

———. *Investigaciones acerca de la historia económica del virreinato del Plata.* 2d ed. Buenos Aires, 1952.

Levin, Jonathan. *The Export Economies: Their Pattern of Development in Historical Perspective.* Cambridge, Mass., 1960.

Lévy, Claude-Frédéric. *Capitalistes et pouvoir au siècle des lumières. Des origines à 1715.* Paris, 1969.

Livermore, H. V., ed. *Portugal and Brazil. An Introduction.* Oxford, 1953.

Lohmann-Villena, Guillermo. *Las minas de Huancavelica en los siglos XVI y XVII.* Sevilla, 1949.

Lüthey, H. *La banque protestante en France de la révocation de l'édit de Nantes à la révolution.* 2 vols. Paris, 1959.

Lynch, John. *Spain under the Hapsburgs.* 2 vols. New York, 1984, 1969.

———. *The Spanish American Revolutions, 1808–1826.* London, 1973.

Macanaz, Melchor. *Regalías de los señores reyes de Aragón.* Edited by Joaquín Maldonado Macanaz. Madrid, 1879.

MacLachlan, J. O. *Trade and Peace with Old Spain, 1667–1750: A Study of the Influence of Commerce on Anglo-Spanish Diplomacy.* Cambridge, 1940.

MacLeod, Murdo. *Spanish Central America: A Socio-economic History.* Berkeley, 1973.

MacPherson, David. *Annals of Commerce.* 4 vols. London, 1805.

Magalhães Godinho, Victorino. *L'économie de l'empire portugais aux XV et XVI siècles.* Paris, 1969.

Magens, Nicolas. *Further Explanations of Some Particular Subjects Relating to Trade, Coin and Exchanges.* London, 1756.

Malamud Rikles, Carlos Daniel. *Cadiz y Saint Malo en el comercio colonial peruano (1698–1725).* Cadiz, 1986.

Maravall, José Antonio. *Estado moderno y mentalidad social (siglos XV a XVII).* 2 vols. Madrid, 1972.

Martínez de Mata, Francisco de. *Memoriales y discursos.* Edited by Gonzalo Anes. Madrid, 1971.

Martínez Shaw, Carlos, ed. *Sevilla en el Siglo XVII. El corazón de las riquezas del mundo.* Madrid, 1993.

Martín Gaite, Carmen. *El proceso de Macanaz. Historia de un empapelamiento.* Madrid, 1970.

Matilla Tascón, Antonio. *Historia de las minas de Almadén.* 2 vols. Madrid, 1958.

Matilla Tascón, Antonio, and Miguel Capella. *Los Cinco Gremios Mayores de Madrid. Estudio crítico-histórico.* Madrid, 1957.

Maxwell, Kenneth. *Pombal, Paradox of the Enlightenment.* Cambridge, 1995.

Mélanges à la mémoire de Jean Sarrailh. 2 vols. Paris, 1966.

Mémoires et considérations sur le commerce et les finances d'Espagne avec des réflexiones sur la nécessité de comprendre l'étude du commerce. 2 vols. Amsterdam, 1761.

Memorial ajustado . . . sobre el defecto de la lay y peso de las monedas de plata. Madrid, 1734.

Merino, Luís. *Estudio crítico sobre las 'Noticias secretas de América' y el clero colonial (1720–1765).* Madrid, 1956.

Meyer, Jean. *La noblesse bretonne au XVIIIe siècle.* 2 vols. Paris, 1966.

—— ed. *El Gran Nayar.* Mexico City, 1989.

Minchinton, W. E., ed. *The Growth of English Overseas Trade in the Seventeenth and Eigthteenth Centuries.* London, 1969.

Moncada, Sancho de. *Restauración política de España y deseos públicos.* Edited by Jean Vilar. Madrid, 1974.

Monségur, Jean de. *Las nuevas memorias del capitán Juan de Monsegur.* Edited by J. P. Berthe. Mexico City, 1994.

Morachimu, Vicente. *Manifiesto de los agravios, bexaciones y molestias que padecen los Indios del . . . Peru.* Madrid, 1732.

Moreno Cebrián, Alfredo. *El corregidor de indios y la economía peruana del siglo XVIII (Los repartos forzosos de mercancías).* Madrid, 1977.

Moret, Michèle. *Aspects de la société marchande de Séville au début du XVIIe siècle.* Paris, 1967.

Moreyra y Paz Soldán, Manuel. *El tribunal del consulado de Lima. Cuaderno de juntas.* Lima, 1956.

Morin, Claude. *Michoacán en la Nueva España del siglo XVIII.* Mexico City, 1979.

Morineau, Michel. *Incroyables gazettes et trésors merveilleux. Les retours des trésors américains d'après les gazettes hollandaises (XVIe-XVIIIe siècles).* London, 1985.

Mounier, André. *Les faits et les doctrines économiques en Espagne sous Philippe V: Gerónimo de Uztáriz, 1670–1732.* Bordeaux, 1919.

Mozas Mesa, Manuel. *D. José de Carvajal y Lancaster, ministro de Fernando VI.* Jaen, 1924.

Nadal Oller, Jorge. *La población española (siglos XVI a XX).* Barcelona, 1966.

Navarro García, Luís. *Intendencias en Indias.* Sevilla, 1959.

——. *Hispanoamérica en el siglo XVIII.* Sevilla, 1975.

Noonan, John T. *Bribes.* New York, 1984.

Notcias del origen . . . de la Congregación de San Ignacio. Madrid, 1896.

Nuevo sistema de gobierno económico para la América. Arcila Farías, Eduardo, ed. Mérida, Venezuela, 1971.

Núñez de Salcedo, Pedro. *Relación verdadera de todos los títulos . . . sus rentas, solares, linages . . . manuscrito del siglo que se custodia en la Biblioteca de el Escorial.* Madrid, 1918.

Ogden, Adele, and Engel Sluiter, eds. *Greater America. Essays in Honor of Herbert Eugene Bolton.* Berkeley, 1941.

Ortiz, Luís. *Memorial del contador Luís Ortiz a Felipe II.* Edited by José Larraz López. Valencia, 1970.

Otazu y Llanes, Alfonso. *Hacendistas navarros en Indias.* Bilbão, 1970.

Otte, Enrique. *Sevilla y sus mercaderes a fines de la edad media.* Bernal, Antonio-Miguel and Antonio Collantes de Teran, eds. Sevilla, 1996.

Ozanam, Didier. *La diplomacia de Fernando VI: Correspondencia reservada entre Carvajal y el duque de Huéscar, 1744–1749.* Madrid, 1975.

Palmer, Colin. *Slaves of the White God: Blacks in Mexico, 1550–1650.* Cambridge, Mass., 1976.

Pariset, François Georges, et al., eds. *Histoire de Bordeaux au XVIIIe siècle.* Bordeaux, 1968.

Parker, Geoffrey. *The Army of Flanders and the Spanish Road, 1569–1659: The Logistics of Spanish Victory and Defeat in the Low Countries' Wars.* Cambridge, 1972.

———. *Spain and the Netherlands: Ten Essays.* London, 1979.

Parry, John H., *The Sale of Public Office in the Spanish Indies under the Hapsburgs.* Berkeley, 1953.

———. *The Spanish Seaborne Empire.* New York, 1966.

Parry, John H., et al. *A Short History of the West Indies.* 4th ed. New York, 1987.

Pastor, Rodolfo. *Campesinos y reformas. La Mixteca, 1700–1756.* Mexico City, 1987.

Phelan, John L. *The Kingdom of Quito in the Seventeenth Century: Bureaucratic Politics in the Spanish Empire.* Madison, 1967.

Pieper, Renate. *La Real Hacienda bajo Fernando VI y Carlos III: Repercusiones económicas y sociales.* Madrid, 1992.

Pike, Ruth. *Enterprise and Adventure: The Genoese in Seville and the Opening of the New World.* Ithaca, 1966.

———. *Aristocrats and Traders: Sevillan Society in the Sixteenth Century.* Ithaca, 1972.

Postan, M. M., and E. E. Rich, eds., *Cambridge Economic History of Europe.* 4 vols. 1941–.

Postlethwayt, Malachy. *Considerations on the Revival of the Royal-British Assiento.* London, 1749.

Pulido Bueno, Ildefonso. *Almojarifazgos y comercio exterior en Andalucía durante la época mercantilista, 1526–1740.* Huelva, 1993.

———. *El Real Giro de España, primer proyecto de banco nacional.* Huelva, 1994.

Quevedo y Concillon, Eloy García de. *Ordenanzas del consulado de Burgos de 1536.* Burgos, 1905.

Ramos Gómez, Luís J. *Epoca, génesis y texto de las 'Notícias secretas de América' de Jorge Juan y Antonio de Ulloa.* 2 vols. Madrid, 1985.

Raynal, Guillaume Thomas François. *Histoire philosophique et politique des établissemens européens dans les deux Indes.* 10 vols. Paris, 1783–1784.

Real Diaz, José Joaquin. *Las ferias de Jalapa.* Sevilla, 1959.

Richards, J. F., ed. *Precious Metals in the Later Medieval and Early Modern Worlds.* Durham, N.C., 1983.

Ringrose, David. *Madrid and the Spanish Economy 1560–1850.* Berkeley, 1983.

Robertson, William. *The History of America.* 3 vols. 4th ed. London, 1783.

Rodríguez Garraza, Rodrigo. *Tensiones de Navarra con la administración central, 1778–1808.* Pamplona, 1974.

Rodriguez-Salgado, M. J., *The Changing Face of Empire: Charles V, Philip II and Habsburg Authority, 1551–1559.* Cambridge, 1988.

Rodriguez-Salgado, M. J., and Simon Adams, eds. *England, Spain and the 'Gran Armada,' 1585–1604.* Edinburgh, 1991.

Rodríguez Villa, Antonio. *Don Cenon de Somodevila, marqués de la Ensenada. Ensayo biográfico.* Madrid, 1878.

——. *Patiño y Campillo. Reseña histórica-biográfica de estos dos ministros de Felipe V.* Madrid, 1882.

Rothkrug, Lionel. *Opposition to Louis XIV: The Political and Social Origins of the French Enlightenment.* Princeton, 1965.

Ruiz de Vergara y Alava, Francisco. *Historia del colegio viejo de San Bartolomé, mayor de . . . Salamanca.* Edited by Joseph Roxas y Contreras. 2d ed. 2 vols. Madrid, 1766–70.

Ruiz Martín, Felipe. *Lettres marchandes entre Florence et Medina del Campo.* Paris, 1965.

——. *Los destinos de la plata americana (siglos XVI y XVII).* Madrid, 1990.

——. *Pequeño capitalismo, gran capitalismo: Simón Ruiz y sus negocios en Florencia.* Barcelona, 1990.

——. *Las finanzas de la monarquía española en tiempos de Felipe IV, 1621–1625.* Madrid, 1990.

Sacks, David H. *Trade, Society and Politics in Bristol, 1500–1640.* New York, 1985.

Sagues Ancona, Pio. *Congregación de San Fermín de los Navarros en Madrid, 1613–1961.* Madrid, 1967.

Salvucci, Richard J. *Textiles and Capitalism in Mexico: An Economic History of the Obrajes, 1539–1840.* Princeton, 1987.

Sanz, Eufemio Lorenzo. *Comercio de España con América en la época de Felipe II.* 2 vols. Valladolid, 1979.

Sarabia de la Calle. *Instrucción de mercaderes.* Medina del Campo, 1544.

Sarrablo Aguareles, E. *El conde de Fuenclara, embajador y virrey de Nueva España (1687–1752).* 2 vols. Sevilla, 1955.

Sauer, Carl O. *The Early Spanish Main.* Berkeley, 1969.

Scelle, Georges. *La traite négrière aux Indes de Castille, contrats et traites d'assiento.* 2 vols. Paris, 1906.

Schäfer, Ernesto. *El consejo real y supremo de las Indias: su historia, organización y labor administrativa hasta la terminación de la casa de Austria.* 2 vols. Sevilla, 1935–47.

Schurz, William L. *The Manila Galleon.* New York, 1939.

Sée, Henri. *Histoire économique de la France.* 2 vols. Paris, 1939–42.

Smith, Adam. *An Inquiry into the Nature and Causes of the Wealth of Nations.* Edited by E. Cannan. New York, 1937.

Smith, Robert C. *The Spanish Guild Merchant: A History of the Consulado, 1250–1700.* Durham, N.C., 1940.

Solano, Francisco, ed. *Relaciones geográficas del arzobispado de México, 1743.* 2 vols. Madrid, 1988.

Sombart, Werner. *Le bourgeois. Contribution à l'histoire de l'homme économique moderne.* Paris, 1926.

Spalding, Karen. *Huarochirí, An Andean Society under Inca and Spanish Rule.* Stanford, 1980.

Sperling, John G. *The South Sea Company: An Historical Essay.* Harvard University, Kress Library of Business and Economics, publication no. 17. Cambridge, Mass., 1962.

Spooner, Frank G. *L'économie mondiale et les frappes monétaires en France, 1493–1680.* Paris, 1956.

Stern, Steve J. *Peru's Indian Peoples and the Challenge of Spanish Conquest: Huamanga to 1640.* Madison, 1982.

Steward, Julian H., ed. *Handbook of South American Indians.* Vol. 2. Washington, D.C., 1946.

Suarez Fernández, Luís. *Navegación y comercio en el golfo de Vizcaya. Un estudio sobre la política marinera de la casa de Trastámara.* Madrid, 1959.

Tarrade, Jean. *Le commerce colonial de la France à la fin de l'ancien régime: L'évolution du régime de l'exclusif.* 2 vols. Paris, 1972.

Tedde de Lorca, Pedro. *El banco de San Carlos (1782–1829).* Madrid, 1988.

Testamento de Carlos II. Madrid, 1982.

Thompson, I. A. A. *War and Government in Habsburg Spain, 1560–1620.* London, 1976.

———. *Crown and Cortes. Government Institutions and Representation in Early-Modern Castile.* Brookfield, Vt., 1993.

Thompson, I. A. A., and B. Yun Casalilla, eds. *The Castilian Crisis of the Seventeenth Century: New Perspectives on the Economic and Social History of Seventeenth-Century Spain.* Cambridge, 1994.

Torres López, M., and J. M. Pérez-Prendes y Muñóz de Arraco. *Los juros. Aportación documental para la historia de la deuda pública de España.* Madrid, 1967.

Torre Villar, Ernesto de la, ed. *Instrucciones y memorias de los virreyes novohispanos.* 2 vols. Mexico City, 1991.

Tracy, James D. *A Financial Revolution in the Habsburg Netherlands: Renten and Renteniers in the County of Holland, 1515–1565.* Berkeley, 1985.

———, ed. *The Rise of Merchant Empires. Long Distance Trade in the Early Modern World, 1350–1750.* New York, 1990.

———, ed. *The Political Economy of Merchant Empires. State Power and World Trade, 1350–1750.* New York, 1991.

Ubieto, Antonio, et al. *Introducción a la historia de España.* 9th ed. Baracelona, 1972.

Ulloa, Bernardo. *Restablecimiento de las fábricas, tráfico, y comercio marítimo de España. Segunda parte: Que trata del comercio y tráfico marítimo que tiene España con las naciones, y en la América: causas de su decadencia.* Edited by Gonzalo Anes. Madrid, 1992.

Ulloa, Modesto. *La hacienda real de Castilla en el reinado de Felipe II.* Madrid, 1977.

Uztáriz, Gerónymo de. *Theórica y práctica de comercio y de marina.* Edited by Gabrial Franco. Madrid, 1968.

———. *Theory and Practice of Commerce and Maritime Affairs.* Translated by John Kippax. London, 1751.

Vast, Henri. *Les grands traités du règne de Louis XIV.* 3 vols. Paris, 1893.

Vayrac, Jean de. *Etat présent de l'Espagne où l'on voit une géographie historique du pays.* Paris, 1718.

Veitia Linaje, José de. *Norte de la contratación de las Indias occidentales.* Edited by Francisco Solano. Madrid, 1981.

Vicens Vives, J. *An Economic History of Spain.* Princeton, 1969.

———. *Aproximación a la historia de España.* Barcelona, 1960.

Vilar, Pierre. *La Catalogue dans l'Espagne moderne. Recherches sur les fondements économiques des structures nationales.* 3 vols. Paris, 1962.

———. *Le 'Manual de la Companya nova de Gibraltar,' 1709–1723.* Paris, 1962.

———. *Oro y moneda en la historia, 1450–1920.* Barcelona, 1964.

———. *Hidalgos, amotinados y guerrilleros: Pueblos y poderes en la historia de España.* Translated by F. Gallego. Barcelona, 1982.

———. *A History of Gold and Money, 1450–1920.* London, 1991.

Villaseñor y Sánchez, J. A. *Theatro americano. Descripción general de los reynos y provincias de la Nueva España.* 2 vols. Mexico City, 1746–48.

Walker, Geoffrey. *Spanish Politics and Imperial Trade, 1700–1789.* Bloomington, Ind., 1979.

Ward, Bernardo. *Proyecto económico en que se proponen providencias dirigidas a promover los intereses de España . . . para su plantificación.* Edited by José Luís Castellano. Madrid, 1982.

Weiss, Charles. *L'Espagne depuis le règne de Philippe II.* 2 vols. Paris, 1844.

West, Robert C. *The Mining Community in Northern New Spain: The Parral Mining District.* Ibero-americana, 30. Berkeley, 1949.

Whitaker, Arthur P. *The Huancavelica Mercury Mine. A Contribution to the History of the Bourbon Renaissance in the Spanish Empire.* Cambridge, Mass., 1941.

Wilson, Charles. *Profit and Power. A Study of England and the Dutch Wars.* London, 1957.

———. *The Dutch Republic and the Civilization of the Seventeenth Century.* New York, 1968.

Wobeser, Gisela von. *El crédito eclesiástico en la Nueva España, Siglo XVIII.* Mexico City, 1994.

Yun Casalilla, Bartolomé. *Sobre la transición al capitalismo en Castilla.* Salamanca, 19787.

Yuste, Carmen, ed. *Comerciantes mexicanos en el siglo XVIII.* Mexico City, 1991.

Articles

The following is a list of abbreviations used in this section of the bibliography:

AEA   *Anuario de Estudios Americanos*
AESC   *Annales: Economies, Sociétés, Civilisations*
AHDE   *Anuario de Historia del Derecho Español*
AHES   *Anuario de historia económica y social*
AHR   *American Historical Review*
BA   *Boletín Americanista*
EHR   *Economic History Review*
EHSE   *Estudios de Historia Social de España*
EMDL   *Espíritu de los mejores diários literarios*
EngHR *English Historical Review*
HAHR   *Hispanic American Historical Review*
IAA   *Ibero-amerikanisches archiv*
JEEH   *Journal of European Economic History*
JEH   *Journal of Economic History*
JMA   *Journal of Modern History*
NA   *Nova america*
PP   *Past and Present*

RI   *Revista de Indias*
REP   *Revista de Estudios Políticos*
RH   *Revue Historique*
SEV   *Semanario Erudito de Valladares*

Artola, Miguel. "Campillo y las reformas de Carlos III." *RI* 12 (1952): 685–714.
Astraudi, Jorge. "Memoria curiosa." In *Patiño y Campillo,* edited by Rodríguez Villa, 131–44.
Atienza Hernandez, Ignacio. "'Refeudalisation' in Castile During the Seventeeth Century: A Cliche?" In *The Castilian Crisis,* edited by Thompson and Yun Casalilla, 249–370.
Bakewell, Peter J. "Mining in Colonial Spanish America." In *Cambridge History of Latin America,* edited by Bethel, vol. 2, chap. 4.
Barbier, Jacques. "Towards a New Chronology for Bourbon Colonialism: the 'Depositaria de Indias' of Cadiz, 1722–1789. *IAA* 6 (1980): 335–53.
Barbour, Violet. "Dutch and English Merchant Shipping in the Seventeenth Century." In *Essays in Economic History,* edited by Carus-Wilson, 1:227–53.
Bilbao, Luís Mario, and Emiliano Fernández de Pinedo. "Artesanía y industria." In *Enciclopedia de historia de España,* edited by Artola 1:105–90.
Borges, Analola. "Los aliados del Archiduque Carlos en la América virreinal." *AEA* 22 (1970): 321–70.
Boxer, C. R. "The Portuguese in the East (1500–1800)." In *Portugal and Brazil. An Introduction,* edited by Livermore, 185–247.
Brading, David A., and Harry E. Cross. "Colonial Silver Mining: Mexico and Peru." *HAHR* 52 (1972): 545–79.
Braudel, F. "Du Potosí à Buenos Aires. Une route clandestine de l'argent (fin du XVI, début du XVII siècles)." *AESC* 3 (1948): 546–50.
Butel, Paul. "France, the Antilles and Europe in the Seventeenth and Eighteenth Centuries: Renewals of Foreign Trade." In *The Rise of Merchant Empires,* edited by Tracy, 153–73.
Castillo Pintado, Alvaro. "Los juros de Castilla: apogeo y fin de un instrumento de crédito," *Hispania* 23 (1963): 43–70.
———. "El mercado del dinero en Castilla a finales del siglo XVI. Valor nominal y curso de los juros castellanos en 1594." *AHES* 3 (1970): 91–104.
Cavillac, Michel. "El patio del monopodio: la Sevilla marginal." In *Sevilla en el siglo XVII,* edited by Martínez Shaw, 139–56.
Chaudhuri, K.N. "World Silver Flows and Monetary Factors as a Force of International Integration, 1650–1750 (America, Europe, Asia)." In *The Emergence of a World Economy, 1500–1914,* edited by Fischer et al., 83–96.
———. "Reflections on the Organizing Principle of Premodern Trade." In *The Political Economy of Merchant Empires,* edited by Tracy, 421–42.
Chevalier, François. "En lisant les 'novelas': La vie en Séville au siècle d'or." *AESC* 2 (1947): 105–30.
Christelow, Allen. "Contraband Trade between Jamaica and the Spanish Main, and the Freeport Act of 1766." *HAHR* 22 (1942): 309–43.
Clarke, G. N. "War Trade and Trade War, 1701–1713." *EHR* 1 (1927–1928): 262–80.

Coleman, D. C. "An Innovation and its Diffusion in the 'New Draperies.'" *EHR* 22 (1969): 417–29.

Croft, Pauline. "English Commerce with Spain and the Armada Way, 1558–1603." In *England, Spain and the 'Gran Armada,'* edited by Rodríguez-Salgado and Adams, 236–63.

Cross, Harry E. "South American Bullion Production and Export, 1550–1750." In *Precious Metals*, edited by Richards, 397–423.

Crouset, François. "Economie et société (1715–1789)." In *Histoire de Bordeaux au XVIIIe siècle*, edited by Pariset et al., 191–323.

Dobyns, H. F. "Estimating American Population." *Current Anthropology* 7 (1966): 395–416.

Domínguez Ortiz, Antonio. "Los caudales de Indias y la política exterior de Felipe IV." *AEA* 13 (1956): 311–83.

———. "Los extranjeros en la vida española durante el siglo XVII." *EHSE* 4, pt. 2 (1960): 291–426.

———. "La burgesía gaditana y el comercio de Indias desde mediados del siglo XVII hasta el traslado de la Casa de Contratación." In Congreso luso-español para el progreso de las ciencias, 31, *La burguesía mercantil gaditana, 1650–1868*, 3–41.

———. "La venta de cargos y oficios públicos en Castilla, y sus consecuencias económicas y sociales." *AHES* 3 (1970): 105–37.

———. "Guerra económica y comercio extranjero en el reinado de Felipe IV." *Hispania* 23 (1963): 71–110.

Fetter, F. W. "The Term 'Favorable Balance of Trade.'" In *The Later Mercantilists*, edited by Blaug, chap. 2.

Frostin, Charles. "Les Pontchartrain et la pénétration commerciale française en Amérique Espagnole." *RH* no. 498 (1971): 307–06.

García-Cuenca Ariati, T. "Los ingresos procedentes de las rentas generales de aduanas, 1740–1744." In *Estudios de hacienda de Ensenada a Mon*, edited by Artola et al.

García Sanz, Angel and Sanz Fernandez, J. "Agricultura y ganadería." In Artola, Miguel, ed. *Enciclopedia de historia de España*, edited by Artola, vol. 2.

Gravil, R. "Trading to Spain and Portugal, 1670–1700." *Business History* 10 (1968): 71–88.

Guthrie, C. L. "Riots in Seventeenth-Century Mexico City." In *Greater America. Essays in Honor of Herbert Eugene Bolton*, 243–58.

Hamilton, Earl J. "The Mercantilism of Geronimo de Uztariz: A Re-examination." In *Economics, Sociology and the Modern World*, edited by Himes, 111–29.

Hazan, A. "En Inde aux XVIe et XVIIe siècles: Trésors américains, monnaie d'argent et prix dans l'empire mogul." *AESC* (1969): 835–59.

Heckscher, Eli. "Mercantilism." In *Revisions in Mercantilism*, edited by Coleman, 19–34.

Heredia Herrera, Antonia. "Apuntes para la historia del consulado de la universidad de cargadores a Indias, en Sevilla y en Cadiz." *AEA* 27 (1970): 219–79.

Hernández Benítez, Mauro. "Carlos III: Un mito progresista," in *Carlos III, proyecto reformista*. Equipo Madrid de Estudios Historicos. Madrid, 1988, 1–23.

Hobsbawm, Eric. "The Crisis of the Seventeenth Century." In *Crisis in Europe*, edited by Aston, 5–58.

Horcasitas, "Instrucción." In *Instrucciones,* edited by Torre Villar, 2: 795–837.

Hoppit, J. "Political Arithmetic in Eighteenth-Century England." *AHR* 49 (1996): 516–40.

Israel, Jonathan L. "The Decline of Spain: A Historical Myth?" *PP* no. 91 (1981): 170–80.

Kamen, Henry. "Melchor de Macanaz and the Foundation of Bourbon Power in Spain." *EngHR* 80 (1965): 699–716.

———. "The Decline of Spain: An Historical Myth?" *PP* no. 81 (1978): 24–50.

———. "Confiscations in the Economy of the Spanish Inquisition." *EHR* 18 (1965): 511–25.

Kepler, J. S. "Fiscal Aspects of the English Carrying Trade during the Thirty Years War." *EHR* 25 (1972): 261–81.

Klaveren, J. van. "Fiscalism, Mercantilism and Corruption." In *Revisions in Mercantilism,* edited by Coleman, 140–61.

Kubler, George. "The Quechua in the Colonial World." In *Handbook of South American Indians,* edited by Steward, 2:231–410.

Linares, duque de. "Relación." In *Instrucciones,* edited by Torre Villar 2: 771–792.

Looseley, Allyn C. "Puerto Belo Fairs." *HAHR* 13 (1933): 314–55.

Macanaz, Melchor de. "Auxilios para bien gobernar una monarquía católica." *SEV* 5 (1787): 215–303.

———. "Avisos políticos, máximas prudentes, y remedios universales," *SEV* 8 (1788): 217–37.

———. "Proyecto." In *Los juros,* by Torres López and Pérez-Prendes.

———. "Representación . . . desde Lieja." *SEV* 7 (1788): 158–204.

———. "Varias notas al Teatro Crítico . . . Feyjoo." *SEV* 7 (1988): 205–80.

Macera, Pablo, and Shane J. Hunt. "Peru." In *Latin America. A Guide to Economic History,* edited by Cortes Conde and Stein, 571–649.

Mahoney, Michael. "Organizing Expertise: Engineering and Public Works under Colbert, 1662–1683." Davis Center Seminar Paper, Princeton University, 1980.

Martínez Cardós, José. "Don José del Campillo y Cosío." *RI* 30 (1970): 503–42.

Martínez Shaw, Carlos. "Cataluña y el comercio con América: el fin de un debate," *BA* 25 (1980): 223–36.

——— "Un microcosmos de oro y barro." In *Sevilla en el siglo XVII,* edited by Martínez Shaw, 15–235.

Mateos Dorado, Dolores. "La actitud de Carlos III durante el año 'sin rey' (1758–1759)," Congreso Internacional sobre "Carlos III y la ilustración." *Actas* 1 (1989): 299–321

McCusker, John. "The Business of Distilling in the Old World and the New World." Davis Center Seminar Paper. Princeton University, 1996.

Mintz, Sidney. "Foreword." In *Sugar and Society in the Caribbean,* by Guerra y Sánchez, xi-xliv.

Moreyra y Paz Soldán, Manuel. "La toma de Portobelo por . . . Vernon, y sus consecuencias económicas." *Mercurio peruano* 23 (1948): 298–329.

Moxó, Salvador de. "Un medievalista en el Consejo de Hacienda: Don Francisco Carrasco, marqués de la Corona (1715–1791)." *AHDE* 29 (1959): 609–88.

Muñóz Pérez, José. "La publicación del reglamento de comercio libre de Indias de 1778." *AEA* 4 (1947): 615–44.

———. "Los proyectos sobre España e Indias en el siglo XVIII: el proyectismo como género." *REP* no. 81 (1955): 169–85.

Navarro García, Luís. "Campillo y el *Nuevo sistema:* una atribución dudosa." *Temas americanistas* 2 (1983): 22–29.

———. "La administración virreinal en México en 1703." *RI* 29 (1969): 359–69.

Nettels, Curtis. "England and Spanish American Trade, 1680–1715." *JMH* 3 (1931): 1–32.

North, Douglas C. "Institutions, Transaction Costs and the Rise of Merchant Empires." In *The Rise of Merchant Empires,* edited by Tracy, 22–40.

———. "Transaction Costs in History." *JEEH* 14 (1985): 557–76.

Ocharán Posadas, M. "Prólogo." In *Historia de las minas de Almadén,* by Matilla Tascón, 1:vii–xii.

Osorio y Redín, Miguel. "Extensión política y económica. Discurso I." In *Apéndice a la educación popular,* edited by Campomanes, 1:7–206.

Ozanam, Didier. "Representación del marqués de la Ensenada a Fernando VI (1751)." *Cuadernos de investigación histórica* 4 (1980): 67–124.

Panuk, S. "Money in the Ottoman Empire." In *Ottoman Empire,* by Inalcik, 947–80.

Patterson, C. C. "Silver Stocks and Losses in Ancient and Medieval Times." *EHR* 25 (1972): 205–33.

Pérez Herrero, Pedro. "Actitudes del consulado de México ante las reformas comerciales borbónicas (1718–1765)." *RI* no. 171 (1983): 97–182.

Phillips, Carla Rahn. "Time and Direction: A Model for the Economy of Early Modern Spain." *AHR* 92 (1988): 531–62.

Pietschmann, Horst. "Burocracia y corrupción de Hispanoamérica colonial: Una aproximación tentativa." *NA* 5 (1982): 11–37.

Prakash, Om. "Precious Metals Flows in Asia and World Economic Integration in the Seventeenth and Eighteenth Centuries." In *The Emergence of a World Economy,* edited by Fischer et al., 61–82.

Probert, Alan. "Bartolomé de Medina, the Patio Process and the Sixteenth-Century Silver Crisis." In *Mines of Silver and Gold,* edited by Bakewell, 96–109.

Quevedo, Francisco de. "Caída de su privanza y muerte del conde-duque de Olivares." *SEV* 3 (1787): 1–70.

Rambert, Gaston. "La France et la politique commerciale de l'Espagne au XVIIIe siècle." *Revue d'histoire moderne et contemporaine* 6 (1959): 369–88.

Ringrose, David A. "Carting in the Hispanic World: An Example of Divergent Development." *HAHR* 50 (1970): 30–51.

Rowe, John. "The Incas under Spanish Institutions." *HAHR* 37 (1957): 155–99.

Ruíz Martín, Felipe. "La banca de España hasta 1782." In *El Banco de España, una historia económica,* 1–196.

Ruíz Rivera, Julián B. "La casa Uztáriz, San Ginés y Compañía." In *La burguesía mercantil gaditano,* published by Congreso luso-español para las ciencias, 183–99.

———. "Rasgos de modernidad en la estrategia comercial de los Uztáriz, 1766–1793." *Temas americanistas* 3 (1983): 12–17.

Saguier, Eduardo R. "La corrupción administrativa como mecanismo de acumulación y engendrador de una burguesía comercial local." *AEA* 46 (1989): 269–303.

Sánchez de Sopranís, Hipólito. "Las naciones extranjeras en Cadiz durante el siglo XVII." *EHSE* 4 (1960): 639–77.

Scoville, W. "The French Economy in 1700–1701: An Appraisal by the Deputies of Trade." *JEH* 22 (1962): 231–52.

Sée, Henri. "Le commerce français à Cadix et dans l'Amérique espagnole au XVIIIe siècle." *Revue d'histoire moderne* 3 (1928): 13–31.

———. "Notas sobre el comercio français en Cadiz y particularmente sobre el comercio de las telas bretañas en el siglo XVIII." *AHDE* 2 (1925): 182–90.

———. "Que faut-il penser de l'oeuvre économique de Colbert?" *RI* no. 152 (1926): 181–94.

———. "Documents sur le commerce de Cadix, 1691–1752." *Revue de l'histoire des colonies françaises* 14 (1926): 465–520.

Sheridan, Richard B. "The Plantation Revolution and the Industrial Revolution, 1625–1775." *Caribbean Studies* 9 (1969): 5–25.

Smith, Robert S. "Sales Taxes in New Spain, 1575–1770." *HAHR* 28 (1948): 2–37.

Solano, Francisco De. "Nota sobre la vida y obra del autor del 'Norte de la Contratación de las Indias Occidentales.'" In *Norte de la contratación de las Indias occidentales*, by Veitia Linaje, ix–xxxv.

Spalding, Karen. "Social Climbers:Changing Patterns of Mobility among the Indians of Colonial Peru." *HAHR* 50 (1970): 645–64.

Stols, Eddy. "La colonia flamenca de Sevilla y el comercio de los Países Bajos españoles en la primera mitad del siglo XVII." *AHES* 2 (1969): 363–81.

Tandeter, Enrique. "Forced and Free Labour in Colonial Potosí." In *Mines of Silver and Gold*, edited by Bakewell, 131–69.

Taylor, Harland. "Trade, Neutrality and the English Road, 1630–1648." *EHR* 25 (1972): 236–60.

Tepaske, John, and Herbert Klein. "The Seventeenth-Century Crisis in New Spain: Myth or Reality?" *PP* no. 90 (1981): 116–35.

Thompson, I. A. A. "The Appointment of the Duke of Medina Sidonia to the Command of the Spanish Armada." In *War and Society*, chap. 5.

Tiryakian, Josefina. "Campillo's Pragmatic New System. A Mercantile and Utilitarian Approach to Indian Reform in Spanish Colonies of the Eighteenth Century." *History of Political Economy* 10 (1978): 233–57.

Trevor-Roper, H. R. "The General Crisis of the Seventeenth Century." In *Crisis in Europe*, edited by Aston, 59–95.

Uztáriz, Gerónimo de. "Prólogo." In *Comercio de Holanda*, by Huet, 1746.

Valladares, Antonio. "Nota del autor." In Macanaz, Melchor de. "Explicación jurídica e histórica de la consulta. . . ." *SEV* 9 (1788): 3–4.

———. "Nota del editor." *SEV* 7 (1788): 1–11.

van Dillen, J. G. "Economic Fluctuations in the Netherlands, 1650–1750." In *Essays in European Economic History*, edited by Earle, 199–211.

———. "Amsterdam, marché mondial des métaux précieux aux XVIIe et XVIIIe siècles," *RH*, no. 152 (1926), 194–201.

Verlinden, Charles. "Markets and Fairs." In *Cambridge Economic History of Europe*, edited by Postan and Rich, vol. 4, chap. 3.

Vilar, Pierre. "Structure de la société espagnole vers 1750." In *Mélanges à la mémoire de Jean Sarrailh*, 2:425–47.

———. "Estructuras: Algunas lecciones del catastro de Ensenada." In *Hidalgos, amotinados y guerrilleros*, 63–92.

Vila Vilar, Enriqueta. "Las ferias de Portobelo: Apariencia y realidad del comercio de Indias." *AEA* 39 (1984): 275–337.

Viner, Jacob. "Power versus Plenty as Objectives of Foreign Policy in the Seventeenth and Eighteenth Centuries." In *Revisions in Mercantilism,* edited by Coleman, 61–91.

Wakeman, F., Jr. "Voyages." *AHR* 98 (1993): 1–17.

Whitaker, Arthur P. "Antonio de Ulloa." *HAHR* 15 (1935): 155–94.

———. "Documents. Jorge Juan and Antonio de Ulloa's Prologue to Their Secret Report of 1749 on Peru." *HAHR* 18 (1938): 507–13.

———. "Antonio de Ulloa, the *Délivrance* and the Royal Society." *HAHR* 46 (1966): 357–70.

Yun Casalilla, Bartolomé. "Spain and the Seventeenth-Century Crisis in Europe: Some Considerations." In *The Castilian Crisis,* edited by Thompson and Yun Casalilla, 301–20.

Zehedia, Nuala. "London and the Consumer in the Late Seventeenth Century." *EHR* 47 (1994): 239–61.

Index

Library of Congress Cataloging-in-Publication Data

Stein, Stanley J.
  Silver, trade, and war : Spain and America in the making of early modern Europe / Stanley
J. Stein and Barbara H. Stein.
   p.   cm.
Includes bilbiographical references (p.   ) and index.
ISBN 0-8018-6135-7 (alk. paper)
    1. Spain—Colonies—America—Commerce—History.   2. Spain—Commerce—
America—History.   3. America—Commerce—Spain—History.   4. Silver industry—
America—History.   5. Spain—Commercial policy.   6. Spain—Economic conditions.
I. Stein Barbara H.   II. Title
HF3685.S74   2000
382'.0946'07—dc21   99-38574   CIP